*the cinema of* THE COEN BROTHERS

**DIRECTORS' CUTS**

*the cinema of*
# THE COEN BROTHERS

*hard-boiled entertainments*

Jeffrey Adams

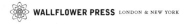 **WALLFLOWER PRESS** LONDON & NEW YORK

A Wallflower Press Book
Published by
Columbia University Press
Publishers Since 1893
New York • Chichester, West Sussex
cup.columbia.edu

A complete CIP record is available from the Library of Congress

ISBN 978-0-231-17460-2 (cloth : alk. paper)
ISBN 978-0-231-17461-9 (pbk. : alk. paper)
ISBN 978-0-231-85081-0 (e-book)

Series design by Rob Bowden Design

Cover image of the Coen Brothers courtesy of the Kobal Collection

Columbia University Press books are printed on permanent
and durable acid-free paper.
This book is printed on paper with recycled content.
Printed in the United States of America

# CONTENTS

ACKNOWLEDGEMENTS

I would like to thank the College of Arts and Sciences of the University of North Carolina, Greensboro for granting me a research leave in the spring semester of 2013, during which I was able to research and write large portions of this book.

I would also like to express copious thanks to Yoram Allon, Commissioning Editor of Wallflower Press, whose patient and cheerful support made the publication of this book an unusually pleasant process. Thanks go also to the editorial staff at Wallflower Press, whose comments and suggestions for revisions were invaluable and contributed greatly to the final shape of this book.

Many, many thanks are owed to Dr. Will Dodson for his generous assistance and insightful commentary during the final preparation of the manuscript, and for his always upbeat collegiality and friendly encouragement. I would also like to thank all the students who over the years have taken my courses on the Coen brothers and on film noir, most notably, Budd Wilkins, Clayton Dillard, Steve Carter, Riannon Clarke, Wil Davis, Melissa Willenborg, Katie Campbell, Will Sharpe, Robert 'Ren' Brugger, Kevin Harrison, and Tom Barker, for stimulating, challenging, and deepening my knowledge and understanding of the texts that inform this book.

I would like especially to thank my wife, Anita Campitelli, for her loving support of my work, for her patience during my frequent scholarly hermitages, and for sharing with me not only the life of the mind, but a life of family and friendship all these years – still my fantasy girl.

Finally, I would like to dedicate this book to my sons – Jason, Dennis, Matthew, and Joseph. Our little achievers, and proud we are of all of them.

# INTRODUCTION

By now, after three decades of critically acclaimed filmmaking, the Coen brothers, Ethan and Joel, hardly need an introduction. Since their debut in 1984, the Coens have risen from unknown independent filmmakers to the elite ranks of contemporary American film directors, producing a substantial body of work largely on the periphery of the mainstream movie industry. In this sense, the Coens have become a model for the triumph of the 'indie' auteur over Hollywood. Working in tandem, the Coens write, direct and edit all their films, maintaining complete control over the finished product without interference from the movie studios with whom they partner to finance their productions. 'We're mercifully free of the Hollywood committee development process,' says Joel. 'The studios understand that if they are going to do a movie with us, they'll let us do it our way' (Allen 2006: 169). Freed from external pressures of the movie industry – demands of studio producers and expectations for commercial profit – the Coens have enjoyed an unsurpassed degree of creative autonomy and can lay legitimate claim to being independent auteurs. Yet, for all their freedom and creative control, the Coens would not define themselves as auteurs, understood as film directors who imprint their work with a unique vision articulated in a recognisable stylistic 'signature'. Nor would the Coen brothers subscribe to the latest definition of the auteur as 'star director', the new role for the prominent filmmaker whose auteur identity, according to Timothy Corrigan, functions commercially as marketing strategy that exploits for profit the 'cult status of the auteur' (1991: 103). In the eyes of many, the Coen brothers have attained a cult-like status, but in truth they could not be less interested in cultivating an iconic media persona as a promotion and marketing tool. In the blunt words of Barry Sonnenfeld, the Coens' director of photography for the early films, 'that's the great thing about Joel and Ethan. They don't want to be on the *Today* show. They don't want to be in *People*. They don't give a shit' (Allen 2006: 23).

Indeed, the Coen brothers are indifferent to media attention and unaffected by popular cultural trends. As filmmakers, they are mavericks among mavericks. Unlike other contemporary independent filmmakers, whose films tend to be autobiographical showcases for what R. Barton Palmer calls 'the idiosyncrasies of individual authorship' (2004: 28), the Coens prefer to work in impersonal generic forms, changing styles with each new film. One of the few consistent patterns in their development as film-makers has been a desire to do something different in each film. When interviewer Andrew Pulver noted that each Coen film 'seems independent of the others and of the people who made them', Joel responded: 'I just see it as moving from story to story. There's no development, except that you try to do something a little different each time' (Allen 2006: 156). When asked if they cultivate a personal style, he replied: 'I don't think there's a thread, at least a conscious thread, anyway, between the stories we're telling.' Ethan finished the thought: 'It's what you call style in retrospect only. At the point of actually making the movie, it's just about making individual choices. [...] If there's some consistency to it, they say, "Well, that's their style"' (Bergen 2000: 29). If there is any quality that lends their oeuvre unity and consistency, it is, paradoxi-cally, the plurality of generic styles and cultural sources they utilise to tell their stories. Although, as Palmer points out, some critics may discern a 'consistent authorial tone' in the Coens' films, in particular, 'an unsympathetic, cynical, and derisive attitude toward [their] characters', such consistency is offset by the intentional discontinuity of their body of work, which Palmer attributes to the Coens' postmodern 'anti-authorial' attitude (2004: 54, 55).

If any label can be usefully applied to the Coens, it might be Palmer's term, the 'commercial/independent'. Along with such contemporaries as Jim Jarmusch, Steven Soderbergh and David Lynch, the Coens have managed to achieve commercial success *and* continue making independent films. To maintain this balance, the Coens acknowledge the necessity of pleasing their audiences and stress their commitment to the entertainment value of their films. In response to criticism that their films are more entertainment than serious art, the brothers quote Raymond Chandler, who said, 'All good art is entertainment and anyone who says differently is a stuffed shirt and juvenile at the art of living' (Allen 2006: 11). This refusal to take themselves and their films too seriously suggests the posture of the aesthete who, like Chandler, views life as an art and living as a matter of style, the only authentic choice in a world of diminishing meaning and substance. When asked by Barry Sonnenfeld about their vision for *Miller's Crossing* (1990), the Coens would only say, 'It should be a handsome movie about men in hats.' As for the significance of the recurring image of the hat, the brothers insist that 'it's not a symbol, it doesn't have any particular meaning'. As Joel explains, 'It's an image that came to us that we liked. It's a kind of practical guiding thread, but there is no need to look for deep meanings' (Allen 2006: 44).

Because they find the past exotic and thus more interesting than the present, the Coens prefer period pieces – *Miller's Crossing* and *O Brother, Where Art Thou?* (2000) are set in the 1930s, *Barton Fink* (1991) and *The Man Who Wasn't There* (2001) in the 1940s and *A Serious Man* (2009) in the 'Summer of Love' of 1967. This frequent retreat into fictionalised past eras has prompted commentators like Emanuel Levy to complain that Coen movies are detached from contemporary concerns and lack social relevance which is, he writes, 'a result of their creating sealed universes that have few references outside the world of cinema' (1999: 223). Mark Bould supports this view, noting that the Coens' films, especially noir-influenced movies like *Miller's Crossing*, exhibit a pronounced a-historical tendency. 'Like the many film noirs that yearned for an earlier stage of capitalism and older versions of masculinity,' Bould writes, 'the Coens register a profound dissatisfaction with the present,' and thus their hermetic and historically disconnected films, 'become exquisitely-crafted comedies of this self-knowledge' (2005: 96). To these charges the Coens reply: 'Setting a story in the past is a way of further fictionalizing it. It's not about reminiscence because our movies are about a past that we have never experienced. It's more about imagination' (Allen 2006: 182). Because their films seem disconnected from topical concerns, detractors see them as lifeless artifacts that recycle an imaginary past devoid of contemporary relevance, creating what J. Hoberman considers 'a form of Trivial Pursuit, used to connote the past or provide a sense of pseudo-historical depth' (1991: 7). The Coens do little to discourage this view. As Joel puts it, 'I don't feel I have a burning desire to make an important statement. I'm not an Oliver Stone' (Mottram 2000: 15). To paraphrase the prophetic blind handcar driver in *O Brother, Where Art Thou?*, we seek a treasure in each Coen brothers film, but the treasure we find may not be the one we were looking for. The viewer seeking meaningful relevance in their movies should take heed; if we believe what the brothers say, their sole ambition as filmmakers is to provide entertainment. But we should also keep in mind that the Coens make no distinction between art and entertainment. This too identifies their films as 'postmodern'.

Despite the filmmakers' disclaimers, Coen brothers movies invite, indeed, mischievously encourage hermeneutic treasure hunting, challenging audiences to engage actively with the film text, often tempting viewers to decipher what appears to be a hidden code. The interpretive effort is seldom rewarded. The brothers refer to this intentional ambiguity as 'teasing the animals in the zoo' (Allen 2006: 181). Their teasing takes many forms and infuses their entire body of work, often as a kind of practical joking. In the early films, for instance, the mischievous idea of listing 'Roderick Jaynes' as their editor was a prank that eventually caused trouble when Jaynes was awarded an Academy Award nomination for his work on *Fargo* (1996), forcing the Coens to reveal themselves as 'Roderick Jaynes'. The brothers ascribe this particular prank to their sense of modesty and good taste, saying 'it would be bad taste to have our names on our movies that many times' (Allen 2006: 185). 'Jaynes' is also the author of the prefaces to several of the Coens' published screenplays, where, in a smug and self-aggrandising tone, the stuffy old-schooler makes snide comments about the brothers' 'inept' scriptwriting and 'silly' camera work. Such identity pranks and others like them are quite obviously intended as self-ironic gestures announcing the filmmakers' refusal to take themselves too seriously, but at the same time meant to spoof reviewers and film critics whose commentaries constantly mystify and amuse the Coens. 'It's a weird impulse,' says Joel, 'when people feel the need to read things as code – and very specific code, at that' (Allen 2006: 94). In an interview with *Playboy* magazine, they were asked if critics read too much into their movies. Joel replied, 'That's how they're trained to watch movies. Several critics interpreted *Barton Fink* as a parable for the Holocaust. They said the same thing about *Miller's Crossing*.' In

*Barton Fink*, they admit, 'we may have encouraged it. The movie is intentionally ambiguous' (Allen 2006: 181).

Their teasing extends to every level of the filmic text, articulated in the nearly constant and always self-conscious use of parody and pastiche, and in the ambiguity and lack of interpretive closure that characterises their narratives. These textual and intertextual functions are in accord with the aesthetic practices of postmodernism designed to destabilise assertions of epistemological certainty and univocal textual meaning, short-circuiting 'serious' discourse with artistic playfulness and ironic, often crude humour. Such are the aesthetic strategies shaping the Coen brothers' films, where the only certainty is uncertainty and the best means of expressing uncertainty are the ironic forms of parody. Critics refer frequently to their films as empty *tours de force* signifying nothing more than the pleasure the filmmakers derive from being mischievously obscure and inscrutable. John Harkness condemns the Coens as crypto-nihilists who 'don't believe in much of anything', writing that 'they have enormous abilities, but are sphinxes without riddles' (Woods 2000: 127). Is it any wonder that in the preface to the *Blood Simple* (1984) screenplay the Coens take pleasure in describing critics as 'ugly, bitter people, fat and acned for the most part, often afflicted with gout, dropsy, and diseases of the inner ear' (1988: ix)?

Although the Coens' films are considered by many as definitively postmodern, the brothers pretend not to understand what postmodernism means. Occasionally, however, they shed their pretense of ignorance, as they did when asked by an interviewer which film genres they would like to try in the future. Jokingly, the Coens imagined making a 'Ma and Pa' farm comedy or remaking *Guess Who's Coming to Dinner?* (1967). Asked if the latter might be untimely, Ethan responded, 'Well, it'd be an interesting exercise in postmodern aesthetics' (Allen 2006: 141). This comment identifies a central feature of postmodern art: the remaking or rewriting of antecedent texts, which is, perhaps not coincidentally, one of the most prominent aspects of the Coen brothers' *oeuvre*. The practice of parodic pastiche that informs every Coen brothers movie is the formal expression of their prankish teasing, manifested in their densely allusive reinventions of past styles and ancestral sources, a technique which allows them to mock received notions of artistic ownership and hegemonic discourses of textual criticism, and, in a larger sense, to subvert philosophical claims to epistemic meaning. Although parody and pastiche are generally considered central to postmodern artistic practice, in certain theories of postmodernism, parody has been declared dead and replaced by 'blank' pastiche. According to influential theorist Fredric Jameson, postmodern pastiche is, like parody, an 'imitation of a peculiar or unique style, the wearing of a stylistic mask, speech in a dead language' (1998: 5). But unlike traditional forms of parody capable of meaningful social commentary, Jameson sees postmodern pastiche as 'a neutral practice of such mimicry, without parody's ulterior motive, without the satirical impulse, without laughter' (ibid.). Postmodernism is recognisable as 'the moment at which pastiche appears and parody becomes impossible'; this is so, thinks Jameson, because in the postmodern era 'cultural production has been driven back inside the mind' (1998: 10). If there is in any connection with historical reality in postmodern pastiche, it is founded on the realisation that we are 'condemned to seek the historical past through our own pop images and stereotypes about the past, which itself remains forever out of reach' (ibid.). In Jameson's narrow denotation, postmodern pastiche has become a derogatory term signifying a loose network of intertextual references brought together for no reason other than to gratify the intellectual narcissism of viewers sufficiently film-literate to participate in the trivial game of identifying citations and sources.

Considering the variety of meanings attached to the term 'pastiche', one could easily ignore Jameson's dismissive view, were it not for the fact that his understanding of pastiche has become a critical commonplace. When not used in its derogatory sense, however, pastiche might also refer to art works that playfully imitate or rework precursor texts as a form of tribute, without the satirical sub-commentary of parody. Indeed, some theorists have defined pastiche as a basic operational feature of all cultural texts. One of the first to propose such an understanding of pastiche was Russian linguistics theorist Mikhail Bakhtin who argued that every text is a pastiche of pre-existing texts, a gathering of citations pluralised within the diverse cultural and aesthetic discourses, which constantly engage each other in 'dialogue'. Although his writings on dialogism first became popular in the 1960s and 1970s along with the emergence of post-structuralist thinkers such as Roland Barthes, Jacques Derrida and Michel Foucault, Bakhtin's 'dialogical' models of intertextuality and authorship were published as early as the 1930s, far in advance of what is now called postmodernism. In his foundational essay 'The Problem of Speech Genres', Bakhtin advances the proposition that linguistic 'utterances' – whether simple everyday speech acts or complex artistic texts – do not exist or function in isolation. In Bakhtin's words, 'utterances are not indifferent to one another, and are not self-sufficient; they are aware of and mutually reflect one another' (1986: 91). As a result, writes Bakhtin, 'each utterance is filled with echoes and reverberations of other utterances to which it is related by the communality of the sphere of speech communication' (ibid.), which is to say that all linguistic acts exist in dialogue with other speech acts, and by extension, all texts (as organised utterances) resonate within the diverse cultural discourses of any given epoch. Bakhtin is concerned with the diffusion and dissemination of texts as they intersect, interact and engage in mutual dialogue to produce pluralised rather than singular, determinant meaning. According to Bakhtin's dialogical model of intertextuality, cultural texts, especially works of art, are in constant dialogue with pre-existing traditions and conventions, communicating with a multiplicity of prior texts, assuming various stances toward anterior models, responding to or elaborating a parent text, often revising or correcting it. Both present and past texts are thus mutually interdependent; they exist and produce their meanings in a continuous and inescapable dialogical exchange. In this view, the true aim of textual analysis should not be the search for the singular, unified meaning of a work inscribed by an originating subjectivity – the author/auteur – but rather, the discovery of the processes by which each text recomposes prior texts. This does not mean the author/auteur is reduced to an archivist of others' writings. Rather, the author is still sensitive to the dialogic resonance of the voices and texts which he not only reproduces, but responds to, questions or inflects. The space of the text is not inscribed by the singular, originating voice of the author, but rather by a gathering of quotations of other texts and other voices, which, assembled as an intertextual composition, redefine the author/auteur as the 'orchestrator' of pre-existing texts. Understood in this theoretical framework, Coen brothers films cannot be said to repeat the past in a regressive, nostalgic mode of recollection. Rather, their mimetic repetition of prior texts and discourses has as its result a progressive renewal, reinterpretation and reinvigoration of the past.

Another key Bakhtinian concept useful in understanding the Coens' *oeuvre* is the 'carnivalesque', a theory that analyses the socially disruptive forces operative in popular art forms. Bakhtin develops his theory of the carnivalesque in *Rabelais and His World*, a study of the satiric fiction of François Rabelais. There, Bakhtin traces the history of the carnivalesque back to medieval ritual festivals that sanctioned and celebrated the abandonment of order and authority, permitting otherwise socially unacceptable behaviours, especially crude breaches of propriety and sacrilegious satire. In its historical sense, carnival generally denotes a holiday period when festive celebration supersedes daily work routines and inhibitions are loosened to allow public displays (satire, farce, masquerade) mocking social conventions and strictures enforced by the established cultural institutions of religion and government. The humour of the carnivalesque is intended to inspire laughter that is linked to 'the lower stratum of the body, the life of the belly and reproductive organs'; thus, bodily functions otherwise repressed by social taboo are put on display in a style Bakhtin calls 'grotesque realism' (1984: 21, 20). The grotesque realist like Rabelais creates a ribald, earthy humour intended to bring the body and the material world into the abstract realm of art, enacting a symbolic degradation of 'high' art by bringing it 'down to earth'. The 'low' or bodily humour of the carnivalesque also has an important ideological function, working to defeat hierarchies of power, class differences and all forces of social oppression. Indeed, for Bakhtin the laughter evoked by carnivalesque humour has 'a deep philosophical meaning, it is one of the essential forms of truth concerning the world as a whole' (1984: 66).

The Bakhtinian carnivalesque is particularly applicable to Coen comedies like *Raising Arizona* (1987), where slapstick pratfalls and cartoon violence contribute to a lower, more 'bodily' humour, or *The Big Lebowski* (1998), where the Coens' irreverent spoof of Raymond Chandler constitutes an attempt, as J. M. Tyree and Ben Walters suggest, 'to deface the work of the greatest of the "old masters" of the American detective story' (2007: 43). The carnivalesque is an integral element of the Coens' films, particularly evident in their trans-generic fusions of film noir and comedy, where instances of grotesque realism proliferate. Another hybridisation that contributes to the Coens' grotesquery is the fusion of film noir and horror found in films like *Barton Fink,* a noir comedy influenced by the psychological horror of Roman Polanski's early films, *Repulsion* (1965) and *The Tenant* (1976) and Stanley Kubrick's *The Shining* (1980). Carnivalesque hybridity of this sort is on display throughout their film work, in scenes like the 'Thompson jitterbug' in *Miller's Crossing*, where we witness the ultra-violent death of a mob hit-man choreographed as a gory music-and-dance number to the tune of the Irish ballad 'Danny Boy'; and in gruesome burlesques like Julian Marty's protracted roadside interment in *Blood Simple* or Carl Showalter's gory burial-by-wood-chipper in *Fargo*. Humour mixes with creeping horror in *Barton Fink*, where a serial killer who decapitates his victims salts his dialogue with constant references to 'heads'.

In Coen films darkness and levity meet at the threshold of what Pauline Kael (in reference to *Blood Simple*) called 'gross-out humour', the kind of crude physical comedy found in the horror movies of director Sam Raimi, for whom Joel worked as an assistant editor on the low-budget horror classic *The Evil Dead* (1981). Later, both brothers would collaborate with Raimi on the script of *Crimewave* (1985), a noir-inflected comedy that finds black humour in depicting the homicidal antics of two crazed exterminators who expand their purview to include the elimination of human pests. Under Raimi's influence, the Coens can be said to collude with contemporary horror auteurs like Wes Craven, Peter Jackson and many others who have embraced the hybridisation of horror and comedy. Interestingly, when the Coens began their collaborations with Raimi in the late 1970s and the 'gross-out' taste in comedy was coming into vogue in the youth culture, Bakhtin's concept of the carnivalesque was exerting its strongest influence on academic as well as public discourse. It was at this juncture that Raimi introduced what actor Bruce Campbell (star of *The Evil Dead*) has called 'splatstick' – a hybridisation of two 'low' movie genres: splatter-gore horror and slapstick comedy, fueling the emergence of an aesthetic of bad taste that grew out of an increasingly profane public discourse and the demands of movie audiences for graphic depictions of grotesque violence. Responding to these trends, violations of good taste and social decorum abound in Coen movies. Consider the grotesquery of *Blood Simple*'s ending, where Abby impales the hand of sleazy private eye Visser with his own knife; then, believing he is her husband, Marty, shoots him, yet, at the moment of his grisly and ironic death, he goes out laughing. Bad taste itself is parodied in the pervasive use of crude expletives and jokes about paedophilia in *The Big Lebowski* which, despite the obvious comedic irony, some audiences found offensive. 'It's easy to offend people,' says Ethan. 'We blew up a rabbit in *Raising Arizona* and people were upset about that, too,' adds Joel. 'Shooting people was fine, but they didn't like seeing a rabbit get hurt' (Allen 2006: 177). The Coens' fondness for gross-out humour may also explain the recurring motif of vomiting in Coen movies, the repeated acts of regurgitation serving perhaps as a self-reflexive in-joke on the filmmakers them-

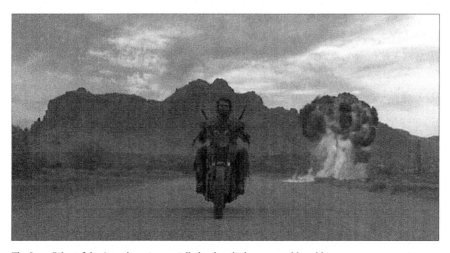

The Lone Biker of the Apocalypse is especially hard on little creatures like rabbits.

selves, mocking their creative practice of feeding on and 'regurgitating' prior texts and styles.

In *The Dialogic Imagination* Bakhtin examines what he terms the 'intentional dialogized hybrid', a pastiche within which a mixture of 'languages and styles actively and mutually illuminate one another' (1981: 361). A preeminent aspect of Coen brothers films, the practice of dialogical hybridisation can be observed in the merging of literary and cinematic noir that characterises much of their film work. Often their films display the dual influences of film noir and pulp fiction, fusing classic literary and filmic sources to create generic innovations such as their debut, *Blood Simple*, a transposition of James M. Cain's fiction to 1980s Texas that subsequently spawned the sub-generic form of 'desert noir'. *Miller's Crossing* blends the gangster movie with film noir to adapt the fiction of Dashiell Hammett. *Barton Fink* conjoins film noir with horror to undergird an adaptive rewriting of Nathanael West and Clifford Odets. *The Big Lebowski* is a comedic send-up of Raymond Chandler's pulp novel *The Big Sleep* (1939), parodying Chandler's famously incoherent plot and populating it with latter-day Chandlerian oddballs. In their adaptation of Cormac McCarthy's 2005 novel *No Country for Old Men* (2007) the Coens return to the desert noir of *Blood Simple* to create their special brand of hard-boiled entertainment.

Given their attraction to film noir, it is not surprising that when they cite cinematic influences, the Coens mention most often the European directors who emigrated to Hollywood in the 1930s and 1940s and directed some of the best classical film noir: German director Edgar Ulmer, whose *Detour* (1945) they cite as an important influence on *Blood Simple*; Austrian Billy Wilder, whose adaptation of James M. Cain's *Double Indemnity* (1944) the Coens greatly admire; and Robert Siodmak, whose influence is particularly noticeable in *The Man Who Wasn't There*. The Coens make it clear that they revere these filmmakers as much for their independence as for their cinematic achievements. These were filmmakers who, despite the limitations of the old studio system, managed to make artistically ambitious films that would later qualify them, in the eyes of French film critics, as 'auteurs' of cinema.

Despite their admiration for selected classic filmmakers and their otherwise extensive knowledge of film history, the Coens tend to give first priority to their literary sources. As creative artists, they consider themselves storytellers first and filmmakers second. 'We're fond of stories,' says Ethan, 'and movies are a way of telling stories. [...] It's not as if we have some mystical attachment to film' (Allen 2006: 183). When the Coens make a movie in the film noir tradition, they emphasise that their ambition is 'to emulate the literary source that those movies came from rather than the movies themselves' (Allen 2006: 14). Asked why they privilege the novels of classic pulp fiction over the movies based on them, Joel responds: 'Most of the [film noir] movies aren't as good as the books, although there are exceptions. John Huston's film noirs like *The Maltese Falcon* [1941] and *The Asphalt Jungle* [1950] are great, but many film noirs are crummy. Everyone loves *Out of the Past*, for instance, but it's a little overcooked' (Allen 2006: 181). As storytellers, the Coens consider themselves the heirs to the literary tradition of pulp fiction represented by Cain, Hammett and Chandler, with whom at times they engage in a dialogical exchange bordering on plagiarism. *Miller's Crossing*, for instance, which Ethan refers to jokingly as 'a shameless rip-off' of Hammett's *The Glass Key* (1931), is in fact an intricate and highly creative rewriting of the novel. Nathanael West's novel *Day of the Locust* (1939) and the plays and writings of Clifford Odets are the principal sources for *Barton Fink*, as is the Southern fiction of William Faulkner, while the stories of Flannery O'Connor provide colourful models for characters in *Raising Arizona*. That the Coens identify themselves primarily as writers is also demonstrated by the fact that many of their screenplays have been published in printed book format (the title of their *Blood Simple* script is revealing: '*Blood Simple: An Original Screenplay* by Joel Coen & Ethan Coen'). Meanwhile, Ethan has gradually established himself as a *bona fide* man of letters. In addition to his screenplays with Joel, Ethan has published several volumes of original literary fiction and poetry including *The Gates of Eden* (1999), *The Drunken Driver Has the Right of Way* (2009) and *The Day the World Ends* (2012).

Because nearly everything the Coen brothers write is influenced in one way or another by literary sources, most of their films can be categorised as variations of adaptation. Their approach to the adaptation of these sources, however, departs significantly from conventional notions of adaptation as the attempt to render 'faithful' translations of the originals. Instead, the Coens seek to rework their literary sources in a process of 'free adaptation', not merely preserving and reproducing them, but inhabiting the style and fictional world of the precursor to create something quite like the original yet new. According to Robert Stam, film adaptations can either strive for fidelity to the original or they can take an 'activist stance' toward their sources. Freed of the limitations of fidelity, an activist adaptation is, in Stam's Bakhtinian analysis, 'less an attempted resuscitation of an original than a turn in an ongoing dialogical process' which, generally speaking, informs the creation of all cultural texts (2000: 64). Rather than copying and preserving the literary original, an activist adaptation offers a new reading. So understood, film adaptation, traditionally conceived as the translation of literary discourse into the language of cinema, receives a different meaning, making possible an alternative understanding of adaptation as intertextual dialogism. To accommodate the Coens' unique approach, R. Barton Palmer suggests an expansion of the usual definition of adaptation, arguing that, in this expanded sense, adaptation is 'fundamental' to the Coens' creative process, so much so, that in his view 'all of their films can be considered adaptations of one kind or another' (2004: 57).

Because the Coen brothers identify primarily as writers or storytellers rather than filmmakers, they generally take an ambivalent stance *vis-à-vis* filmic influences. A notable exception is Preston Sturges, whose classic screwball comedies they hold in highest esteem. Sturges' influence is especially visible in *O Brother, Where Art Thou?*, a film that borrows much, including its title, from Sturges' comedy *Sullivan's Travels* (1942). The brothers' fondness for Sturges extends beyond his artistic achievements to include his remarkable career in the movie industry, which, one can assume, provides an inspiration for the Coens as independent filmmakers. Sturges was a gifted writer who started his career as a New York playwright, then moved to Hollywood to become one of the first directors of the studio era to write, direct, and produce his own screenplays. In 1941 he wrote and directed *The Great McGinty*, which received an Academy Award for Best Original Screenplay, the first time an award was given in that category. In the early 1940s Sturges enjoyed a meteoric rise to prominence as writer-director of some of classic Hollywood's finest comedies, including *The Lady Eve* (1941), *The Palm Beach Story* (1942) and *The Miracle of Morgan's Creek* (1944). The Coens' respect for Sturges has no doubt something to do with the unheard-of creative autonomy and control he achieved within the old studio system as writer, director and producer of his films – the kind of creative freedom and control the Coen brothers have always demanded and received in a contemporary movie industry still dominated by big studios.

As already noted, the Coens' affection for older directors and their movies, which they often recreate in meticulously constructed genre and period pieces, has caused critics to see their movies as vacant virtuosity without meaningful relation to social and historical reality. But there is an alternative view, in which the Coens' recreations of ancestral literary sources and classic movie genres are seen not as a shallow recycling of the past, but as a sincere exploration of antecedent texts that excavates and critiques the cultural myths and ideologies layered beneath previous representations of the past to create, in the words of Palmer, an 'engaged reinvention' of American history and national myth (2004: 158). Indeed, if we look beyond the irony and play of ambivalence in their movies it is possible to find elements of socio-critical commentary, albeit in the most unlikely places. The sharper eye will see in their body of work sly commentaries, cleverly disguised, but nevertheless trenchant critiques of American society. *The Big Lebowski*, for instance, a Coen brothers film where one would think last to look for socio-political subtext, establishes the connection between present US military policy and the folly of past military involvement in the Vietnam War with a running joke about President George H. W. Bush's justification for the Gulf War, expressed in his declaration, 'This aggression will not stand.' This is comically reiterated by Walter and the Dude to justify their animus toward the millionaire ('Big') Jeffrey Lebowski, a figure clearly intended to parody the right-wing, war-hawking conservatives who emerged in the Vietnam era and were succeeded by the neo-cons of the Reagan and

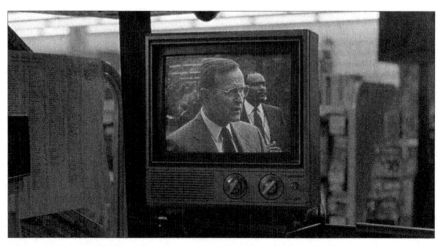

'This aggression will not stand.'

Bush administrations. At the same time, *The Big Lebowski* reminds us of the upsurge in radical left-wing politics with repeated references to the emergent New Left of the 1960s: the SDS (Students for a Democratic Society), the Port Huron Statement and the Seattle Seven, of which the Dude claims he was a founding member. A reference to the communist revolution in Russia is suggested in the Dude's preference for White Russians, his favorite beverage but historically also the name of a political faction in Russia whose adherents supported the Tsar and vied with the Bolsheviks for power in the 1917 Revolution. In fact, references to Communist Russia are a recurring motif in Coen brothers films. The very first words spoken by any Coen character concern Russia and the relative virtues of communism vs. capitalism. 'In Russia,' says private investigator Loren Visser in the prologue of *Blood Simple*, 'they got it mapped out so that everyone pulls for everyone else … that's the theory, anyway. But what I know is Texas, and down here, you're on your own.' With its connotations of the Wild West and pioneer individualism, 'Texas' serves here as a metaphor for modern American society, where capitalist competition creates widespread social alienation and personal isolation. Later, meditating on the profitability of murder-for-hire, Visser observes, 'In Russia they make only fifty cent a day.' Even in the goofy comedy *Raising Arizona*, the merits of socialism versus capitalism are weighed in Hi's observation that 'it seems unfair that some should have so many when others have so few'. The soundtrack music by Pete Seeger, a well-known American socialist, surreptitiously underscores Hi's folksy revolutionary philosophy.

The Coens, of course, deny making intended statements of ideology in their films, but there is nonetheless often a hidden polemic beneath the dark comedy. Here we should recall the epiphany of film director John L. Sullivan in Sturges' *Sullivan's Travels* that comedy is just as impossible as politics, and thus, any art form committed exclusively to one or the other is bound to fail. As the Coens' films suggest, it may be that socio-political commentary is communicated more effectively when staged as comedy. This artistic ethos seems to be reflected in the tastes of many contemporary Americans, millions of whom prefer to get their TV news and political commentary from shows like Comedy Central's *The Daily Show* and *The Colbert Report*. Clearly, at least for these viewers, the funny 'fake' news is more palatable, and reliable, than the ostensible 'reality' reported by mainstream television and media outlets. This is the audience to which the Coens make their greatest appeal.

Following the commonsense logic that a book on the Coen brothers' films should not be tedious, there has been no attempt in this study to mount a unified and comprehensive treatment of their entire body of work. The chapters that follow address what I propose as a core corpus of Coen brothers films – movies that best represent the Coens' artistic achievement and offer themselves as the richest and most rewarding objects of study. In keeping with Andrew Pulver's previously cited thought that each film by the Coen brothers is 'independent of the others and of the people who made them', the ensuing chapters are conceived as more or less self-contained essays. Genres, common themes and repeated motifs provide binding threads from film to film, but there has been no attempt to unify these elements and thereby impose unnecessary interpretive limits on a body of film texts designed to generate a multiplicity of meanings, none of which make a claim for superior or final validity. For reasons of economy, but also because they constitute what are considered to be the minor or less successful works of the Coens' *oeuvre*, the following films have been omitted: *Intolerable Cruelty* (2003), *The Ladykillers* (2004), *Burn After Reading* (2008), *True Grit* (2010) and their most recent release *Inside Llewyn Davis* (2013). These omissions warrant justification.

Generally, with the exception of *Inside Llewyn Davis*, these movies have been judged for various reasons to be disappointments. Roger Ebert, for instance, said he liked *True Grit* well enough but, as he puts it, 'this isn't a Coen Brothers film in the sense that we usually use those words'. He goes on to explain that the usual expectation for a Coen brothers movie is that it be 'eccentric, quirky, wry, or flaky'. It seemed to Ebert that in 2010, after twenty-five years of maverick independent filmmaking, the Coens had reached a point in their career where they decided, in his words, 'to coast on the sheer pleasure of good old straightforward artistry', meaning presumably, that the Coens had finally conceded to make a mainstream commercial movie. Ebert praised *True Grit* as a 'splendid western', but was nevertheless 'surprised the Coens [had] made this film, so unlike their other work, except in quality'. The trend toward commercial filmmaking Ebert describes actually had its beginning much earlier in the Coens' career. In this regard it is important to note that all of the films thought to be disappointments and therefore excluded from this study were produced in the years between 2002 and 2010 when the Coens began to test the waters of mainstream cinema. In the reviews of *True Grit* there was a general sense, expressed by J. Hoberman of the *Village Voice*, that the western genre, once so popular, has become moribund and somehow inaccessible to contemporary filmmakers. For years, thinks Hoberman, nearly every 'credible' western (citing such films as Clint Eastwood's *Unforgiven* [1992], Jim Jarmusch's *Dead Man* [1995] and Andrew Dominik's *The Assassination of Jesse James by the Coward Robert Ford* [2007]) has been an 'oddity, if not a walking corpse', and in Hoberman's estimation the Coens' *True Grit* belongs to these 'ghost stories' of a dying genre.

As a genre in decline, the western has suffered a fate similar to the screwball comedy, an outdated mode of representation that cannot be reinvented in the age of postmodern irony. This may account for the mixed reception of *Intolerable Cruelty*, which, like *The Hudsucker Proxy* (1994) before it, struggled to resuscitate the comedic sensibility of a bygone era and fell short. In general, critics gave *Intolerable Cruelty* good marks for its sophisticated and witty dialogue (one of the Coens' great strengths), but there lingered for many a sense that it didn't quite 'feel' like a Coen brothers movie, which, in at least one important sense, it was not. Some background from the film's production history helps clarify this point. Significantly, this was the only time in their filmmaking career the Coens consented to direct a screenplay they themselves had not originally conceived and written. The screenplay's original authors – Robert Ramsey, Matthew Stone and John Romano – had pitched it to Universal Studios in the early 1990s. The Coens were hired by Universal in 1993 to do rewrites and punch up the dialogue. Pleased with their efforts, the studio then asked the Coens to direct the movie. They declined, saying the material was too commercial for them. Thus orphaned, the script was passed around in Hollywood for nearly a decade before the Coens were finally persuaded. The film's glamorous setting in Beverly Hills and its lavish production values, including the casting of attractive Hollywood stars George Clooney and Catherine Zeta-Jones, pleased some critics, like Peter Bradshaw of *The Guardian* who praised it as 'sophisticated Blue-chip entertainment'. The general critical consensus was somewhat less enthusiastic. Assessments of the film have not improved with time. In a recent retrospective review Jacob Hall called it a 'trifle' and 'the worst' of all the Coen brothers movies to date. The Coens seem to have trouble writing stories set in the present day. As an updated screwball farce, *Intolerable Cruelty* fails to rekindle the flame of the classic exemplars by Preston Sturges and Frank Capra and, for all its glitz, does not compare well with the Coens' more assured and affectionate reinvention of classic screwball comedy in *The Hudsucker Proxy*.

The brothers followed *Intolerable Cruelty* with *The Ladykillers*, a remake of the 1955 British comedy starring Alec Guinness and Peter Sellers, the one and only time the Coens have undertaken a direct remake of a prior film. Again, like *Intolerable Cruelty*, *The Ladykillers* did not originate as a Coen brothers project. It was another orphan, which this time they took over from Barry Sonnenfeld, who had worked as the Coens' director of photography on their early films and moved on to direct his own movies. Sonnenfeld had closed a deal with Disney Studios to direct a remake of the original *Ladykillers* (produced by Ealing Studios and directed by Alexander MacKendrick) and hired the Coens to write the screenplay. When Sonnenfeld left the project for other work, the Coens agreed to take over as directors. Like *Intolerable Cruelty*, *The Ladykillers* is set in the present, transporting the original story from dingy post-war London to contemporary rural Mississippi. But it doesn't travel well. In place of the subtler, more refined sense of black humour and reserved acting of the original, *The Ladykillers* substitutes a pack of contemporary vulgarians and a constant barrage of profanity and crude sexual and scatological jokes. In a retrospective ranking of the Coens' films, Christopher Orr wrote in *The Atlantic* that *The Ladykillers* was 'by a substantial margin, the worst movie the Coen brothers have ever made', damning it as 'a complete failure' – 'a broad, slack, grating farce that bears little resemblance to the understated original'. As if in some way apologizing for their misstep, the Coens penned a satirical auto-critic of *The Ladykillers* (under the pseudonym of Roderick Jaynes) and included it as the preface to the published screenplay. There, in his typical pompous manner, Jaynes describes to the reader his efforts 'to prevail upon [the Coens] to forgo this particular outrage', his pleadings only to end with Ethan rudely telling the incensed editor to 'get *stuffed*', which, notes Jaynes with mock British reserve, 'while not Ethan's exact word, does share some of its letters, notably "f" and "u"' (2004: vi).

After the highly acclaimed and profitable *No Country for Old Men*, the Coens released *Burn After Reading*, a social satire spoofing the disconnected themes of international espionage and Americans' narcissistic obsession with youth and physical beauty. Ethan called it their version of a Tony Scott action movie, 'only without the explosions' (Nathan 2012: 79). But in fact *Burn After Reading* is more about the fear of terrorism after 9/11 and the national paranoia that fed a rapid expansion of the US 'intelligence' community. However, as was the case with *The Ladykillers*, the Coens' real interest in *Burn After Reading* is not in topical satire so much as vulgar farce. As much as anything, the film serves as a vehicle for Hollywood A-list actors like George Clooney,

Tilda Swinton, John Malkovich and Brad Pitt to take part in a comedic farce that allows them to break away from the constraints of their celebrity personas by playing self-mocking roles in an off-Hollywood production. But all the familiar super-star faces ruin the illusion, and the story goes nowhere, at least nowhere of much interest. The principal characters lead lives without much meaning or purpose. Nothing they do makes much sense and that seems to be the movie's only point, prompting David Denby to dismiss *Burn After Reading* as 'a case of terminal misanthropy' because, he argues, the movie's characters are universally treated by their creators as stupid, foolish and completely devoid of sympathetic qualities. The underlying purpose for the movie seems to be an opportunity for the filmmakers to lampoon the Hollywood cult of celebrity that adores mega-star actors like Clooney and Pitt – a cult to which the Coens emphatically do not belong.

*Inside Llewyn Davis*, at the time of writing the brothers' most recent release, signals a return to the kind of film audiences have come to expect of the Coens. In some ways, comments Catherine Shoard, it 'feels like nothing so much as a Coen brothers film', citing *A Serious Man* as its 'closest cousin' in the Coens' *oeuvre*. Indeed, both are small, unpretentious films focused on anti-heroic characters experiencing professional and emotional crises. For Llewyn Davis, the crisis is that of the struggling artist. His is the story of a young folk musician (played by Oscar Isaac) trying to make it in the music business, but at the same time it is a subtle psychological study of a man with great talent, but little wisdom. *Inside Llewyn Davis* also returns to one of the Coens' most character-istic preoccupations: the restoration and exploration of forgotten cultural history. As such, the film resurrects an interesting but nearly forgotten period of American cultural history in its reconstruction of a little-known and neglected time and place – the late 1950s and early 1960s of New York's Greenwich Village, before the arrival of Bob Dylan and the commercialisation of folk music, when the Village was a mecca for sincere young musicians dedicated to preserving ethnic musical traditions. The songs are performed live (many of them by actor Isaac) in front of the camera with careful attention to preserving the authenticity of the musical style. Music, it seems, is one of the few things the Coens do not subvert or trivialise in their films.

Undoubtedly, *Inside Llewyn Davis*, as well as the other Coen films omitted, offers much of interest and merits further study. I will leave that good work to future commentators. There is still much to do. In the past three decades the Coens have written prodigiously, so much in fact that most of their screenplays will likely never be produced. This was already apparent in 1999 when the BBC aired a fifty-minute documentary about the brothers. There, in one brief shot, the camera pans over a large bookcase in the Coens' office stuffed with dozens of unproduced scripts. The titles are intriguing: 'Meet Bobby Buttman', 'The Concierge', 'Cult Cop', 'A Man in Shades', 'Red Harvest' (presumably an adaptation of Dashiell Hammett's novel), 'Respect Your Godfather' and many more. At some point in the future scholars will no doubt gain access to these archives and these neglected gems from the Coens' imagination will provide film historians abundant work for generations to come.

# CHAPTER ONE

# Blood Simple: 'It's the same old song'

Released in 1984, *Blood Simple* was the Coen brothers' debut feature film. An independently produced neo-noir, financed with money the Coens had raised themselves, it was well-received at film festivals including the Toronto Film Festival, the New York Film Festival and the US Film Festival (later renamed Sundance), where it won the Jury Prize. The story is a tale of deceit, betrayal and bloody revenge, written in the pulp fiction style of James M. Cain. Its plot hinges on a romantic triangle, recounting the illicit doings of a naive young man led astray by an unfaithful wife to become the rival of an older, possessive husband who jealously plots the adulterers' murder.

The setting is a small town in West Texas, where bartender Ray (John Getz) indulges in an extra-marital affair with Abby (Frances McDormand), the wife of Ray's saloon-owner boss Julian Marty (Dan Hedaya). Abby would like to exit her unhappy marriage to Marty, who has hired sleazy private investigator Loren Visser (M. Emmet Walsh) to keep tabs on his wayward wife. Seeking revenge for his wife's infidelity, Marty hires Visser to murder the adulterous couple. Trusting Visser to honour their contract for murder proves to be a crucial mistake and ultimately Marty's undoing.

This first effort by unknown independent filmmakers drew an unusual amount of critical attention. Critics from coast to coast praised the film upon its initial theatrical run. Writing for the *New York Times*, Janet Maslin called *Blood Simple* 'a directorial debut of extraordinary promise', while *Los Angeles Times* reviewer Kevin Thomas thought the Coens' debut was 'a dazzling *comedie noire*'. *Time* magazine's Richard Corliss applauded *Blood Simple* for its 'elegant variations on a theme as old as the fall' and praised the Coens' dark thriller for its simultaneous subversion and revitalization of the film noir genre. The movie's signature song – 'It's the Same Old Song (But with a Different Meaning)' – signals the filmmakers' ironic self-awareness that they are telling an archetypal story, but also revising and updating it for contemporary audiences. For these critics *Blood Simple* was a movie with vitality and wit, an unexpected surprise and a welcome change-of-pace in American independent cinema.

As the initial reviews show, one reason for the positive reception of *Blood Simple* was its appeal to a venerable cinematic genre, film noir, which had experienced a recent revival in the decade that preceded the release of *Blood Simple*. By 1984, so-called 'neo-noir' was on the verge of becoming the most popular and influential generic style of contemporary American cinema. But *Blood Simple* is more than a neo-noir thriller that embroiders a well-worn narrative with flashy visual stylisations. Its mixture of sex and violence may exploit the genre of film noir somewhat shamelessly for its appeal to the lower instincts, but at the same time it inventively renovates aging generic conventions to deliver something more than a film-school exercise in genre deconstruction.

The overwhelming majority of these early reviews were laudatory, but there were some who criticised *Blood Simple* as too derivative. In her review for the *New Yorker*, Pauline Kael considered *Blood Simple* so generically predictable that it hardly qualified as a 'thriller'. Kael questioned the Coens' motives as 'independent' filmmakers, asking, 'What's the glory of making films outside the industry, if they're Hollywood films at heart?' What seems to be missing in this assessment and others like it is the possibility of making genre films independently, outside the Hollywood mainstream. The assumption is simply that genre and big-budget commercial filmmaking are synonymous, and therefore that 'genre' and 'independent' are mutually exclusive terms.

For these reasons *Blood Simple* represents, in Kael's view, what was wrong with so many young filmmakers at the time, namely, that their films were becoming too self-consciously referential and lacked substantive, interesting plots, credible characters and meaningful thematic content. In Kael's view, the new generation of filmmakers had sold out their values and integrity to make self-indulgent genre entertainment. From the mid-1960s through the mid-1970s, Kael had witnessed the flourishing of the so-called 'Hollywood Renaissance' as exemplified by the films of auteurs like Stanley Kubrick, Francis Ford Coppola, Robert Altman and Martin Scorsese, films she considered more relevant and original than what post-Renaissance cinema was producing. Ironically, the very auteurs Kael admired and championed constituted the first wave of the neo-noir revival and are also among the filmmakers whom the Coens most revere and to whom they are often compared. Nevertheless, what she considered the shallow and derivative films that emerged in the immediate post-Renaissance years signified to Kael a general decline in American film art. Elliot Stein shared Kael's view, describing *Blood Simple* as a pastiche of genre conventions gleaned from 'Prof. Lawrence Kasdan's Film Noir 101', an allusion to Kasdan's *Body Heat* (1981), a commercially successful neo-noir that had a few years earlier boosted the resurgence of film noir. For these reviewers *Blood Simple* seemed to exemplify the kind of movie made by a younger generation of auteurs who, born into an era of creative exhaustion, could now only assemble vacuous compilations of movie allusions mounted on flimsy generic frameworks, calculated to satisfy a growing audience appetite for pseudo-highbrow content delivered in lowbrow forms.

But R. Barton Palmer offers a different perspective, arguing that the Coens' noir-influenced films in particular, with their pronounced emphasis on existentialist themes, 'engage deeply' with serious social problems, thus 'offering a riposte to those critics who think [the Coens'] films to be much ado about nothing' (2004: 31). Elsewhere, Palmer concludes that in *Blood Simple* we can discern the Coens' attempt to 'extend through complex gestures of restructuring and updating Cain's analysis of the socio-psychological malaise affecting Depression-era America' (2009: 268). By this reading *Blood Simple* reinscribes Cain's stories of American greed and self-interest, resituating them in the contemporary wasteland of the Reagan years, but representing its characters as no less tawdry or misguided than their models in Cain's pulp fiction.

*Reinventing Film Noir*

When asked why they chose the noir genre for their first film, the Coens responded: 'We've liked that type of story for a long while: James M. Cain, Dashiell Hammett and Raymond Chandler. It's a genre that really gives us pleasure.' At the same time they admit that they chose film noir for practical reasons: 'We knew we weren't going to have much money. Financing wouldn't permit other things. We could depend on that type of genre, on that kind of basic force' (Allen 2006: 33). Generally, the Coens do not make genre movies simply because they are more reliably bankable, and they don't make genre movies merely because they love old-fashioned films and hope to recreate the forgotten magic of classic Hollywood cinema. In fact, they contend that they did not approach *Blood Simple* as generic film noir at all. According to Ethan: 'When people call *Blood Simple* a film noir, they're correct to the extent that we like the same kind of stories that the people who made those movies liked.' But, he hastens to add, 'We tried to emulate the [literary] source that those movies came from rather than the movies themselves' (Allen 2006: 14). A more common practice among contemporary filmmakers is to take classic film noirs as source texts, remaking them with varying degrees of fidelity. Prominent examples would be *The Postman Always Rings Twice* (Bob Rafelson, 1981), a faithful remake of the 1946 Garnett adaptation, Steven Soderbergh's *The Underneath* (1995), a remake of Robert Siodmak's *Criss Cross* (1949), or Kasdan's *Body Heat*, an update of Billy Wilder's *Double Indemnity*.

Unlike these filmmakers, the Coens have little interest in remaking prior adaptations of Cain. Instead, their aim was to 'write a story in Cain's style', a hybrid re-adaptation of his two best-known novels, *The Postman Always Ring Twice* (1934) and *Double Indemnity* (1936). As defined by Thomas Leitch, re-adaptations ignore previous cinematic adaptations (like Garnett's and Rafelson's filmings of *The Postman Always Ring Twice*) and strive for a fresh adaptation of the literary source (2002: 45). By comparison, Kasdan's *Body Heat*, a film to which *Blood Simple* is often disparagingly likened, is more directly indebted to its cinematic model. In contrast to the Cain homage of *Blood Simple*, *Body Heat* is actually an unacknowledged remake of Billy Wilder's adaptation of *Double Indemnity*. Although in *Body Heat* the Cain story is updated to a contemporary setting, Kasdan otherwise appropriates Wilder's plot wholesale and at times mimics the precursor's dialogue, both of which depart significantly from the Cain novel. Despite its obvious borrowings, however, Kasdan, who also wrote the screenplay, presents *Body Heat* as his original story. The film credits read simply: 'Written and directed by Lawrence Kasdan.' There is no mention of Cain, much less Billy Wilder's adaptation, the true sources of Kasdan's film. The publicity slogan used to promote the movie, however, reveals quite clearly Kasdan's stance toward his sources: '*Body Heat* echoes the powerful impact of 40s film noir melodramas like *Double Indemnity* and *The Postman Always Rings Twice* – but with energy, irony, and passion that could only flare out of the 80s.' Thus, in a transparent act of disavowal, Kasdan performs what Leitch calls a 'dance of invocation and denial' *vis-á-vis* his precursor (2002: 52). His paradoxical stance toward antecedents in classic film noir entails both the explicit naming of sources and the implied promise of re-energising the originals and accommodating them to a contemporary audience by inventing a new and more relevant version of an archetypal story. In Leitch's view, *Body Heat* strives to be 'the definitive version that renders its model obsolete' (2002: 53). In an attempt to establish its priority Kasdan's film 'takes what is presented as a classic, time-less story and updates it – partly by the paradoxical attempt to remove all markers of any historical period whatever' (2002: 52).

Because it harks back to classic film noir, attempting to reawaken a sense of that historical period (the 1940s), Fredric Jameson considers *Body Heat* an example of the contemporary trend toward 'nostalgia films', which he thinks proliferate in postmodern cinema, 'invading and colonizing' even those movies with contemporary settings (1998: 9). Here Jameson is not referring to heritage cinema or period films that faith-fully recreate and thereby restore bygone eras. Rather, he has in mind contemporary films that make a sentimental appeal to the history of cinema, reproducing the stories and generic styles of an imaginary past. This is problematic for Jameson because, as he sees it, contemporary filmmakers have become incapable of producing authentic artistic representations of their own historical present. If this is so, writes Jameson, 'it is a terrible indictment of consumer capitalism itself – or at the very least, an alarming and pathological symptom of a society that has become incapable of dealing with time and history' (1998: 9–10). Thus, *Body Heat*, in its attempt to recycle Cain via Wilder and repackage it as contemporary noir, becomes a specimen of the 'blank' parody Jameson finds characteristic of postmodern art, which he understands as 'a neutral practice, without parody's ulterior motive' (1998: 5). Synonymous with postmodern pastiche, 'blank parody' is parody that has lost its sense of humour. But, more impor-tant for Jameson, it is also a brand of parody that has lost any sense of its ulterior motive, which Jameson would identify as its socio-critical or ideological function.

Upon its debut, critics attributed a similar logic of parody to *Blood Simple*, seeing little difference between the Coens' approach to film noir and Kasdan's. There are, however, fundamental differences. While Kasdan appropriates both Cain's novel and Wilder's adaptation as his own, disavowing any influence from original sources, the Coens pay tribute to Cain, eagerly acknowledging their debt to his fiction. They say they set out to write their story 'in the style' of Cain as a tribute to his literary accom-plishments, but the result is an inventive re-adaptation which, somewhat paradoxically, they can still claim as their own. Kasdan might also make such a claim for *Body Heat*, but closer scrutiny reveals direct borrowings from Wilder's movie, which in Jameson's view often border on plagiarism. Thus, in a film widely labeled 'postmodern', Kasdan's disavowal of ancestral precursors positions *Body Heat,* oddly, in the belated tradition described by Harold Bloom in *The Anxiety of Influence* (1973), a study of the aesthetic strategies used by authors to defeat the precursor's influence and thus preserve the originality of their writings. As authentically postmodern filmmakers, the Coens find value in honouring ancestral models whom they admire and whose style they hope to revive, not simply by means of conventional adaptation, but in an act of creative reinvention.

As an act of creative reinvention, *Blood Simple* is a text that in Palmer's view 'can hardly be understood properly apart from its literary source', of which it is essentially what he terms a 're-composition' (2009: 268). Developing this concept, Palmer proposes the Coens' neo-noirs (especially *Blood Simple* and *The Man Who Wasn't There*) as examples of what theorist Peter Brooker has called 'imaginative remaking', a postmodern artistic practice which, rather than striving for originality, undertakes a 're-functioning' of antecedent texts (2007: 114). Adopting this intertextual strategy, the contemporary writer/filmmaker attempts to renovate the source text, renewing its significance while simultaneously modifying its discursive features to accommodate changing cultural and artistic sensibilities. By freely reinventing pre-existing sources the postmodern film-auteur aims to re-configure anterior texts which, as is the case for *Blood Simple*, pay tribute to ancestral writers and simultaneously circumvent the conventions of fidelity, imaginatively recomposing the precursor text. Much more than what Jameson dismisses as postmodern pastiche, *Blood Simple* engages Cain's fiction in a creative negotiation, reconstituting the writer's fictional universe so completely that, in Palmer's view, *Blood Simple* ultimately constitutes a text that is 'more Cainian than the fiction upon which [it] draws' (2009: 268).

*In Dialogue with Pulp Fiction*

In an interview following *Blood Simple*'s release the brothers eagerly admitted their fascination with Cain's fiction: 'We read all of Cain six or seven years ago when they reissued his books in paperback. Chandler and Hammett too. We've also pored through a lot of Cain arcana' (Allen 2006: 13). Jokingly, Joel said, 'We've always thought that up at Low Library at Columbia University, where the names are chiseled up there above the columns in stone – Aristotle, Herodotus, Virgil – that the fourth one should be Cain' (ibid.). As a commemoration of Cain's literary *legerdemain*, *Blood Simple* inaugurates a practice repeated in subsequent films such as *Miller's Crossing* and *Barton Fink*, where the Coens rediscover undervalued ancestral authors like Dashiell Hammett, Nathanael West and Clifford Odets. Here it is important to recall that in the early 1980s when the Coens penned *Blood Simple*, Cain was still not held in high esteem. As late as 1989, literary scholar Paul Skenazy characterizes Cain as 'a creature of the paperback racks of bus stations and airports and the mystery shelves of used bookstores', still regarded 'more as a cultural phenomenon than as a writer of substance' (1989: ix).

Drawing on *The Postman Always Rings Twice* and to a lesser extent on *Double Indemnity*, *Blood Simple* relocates Cain in an early 1980s rural Texas to voice one of the writer's most prominent thematic concerns: the disintegration of community and the social alienation fostered by capitalist economic competition. In this regard, *Blood Simple* offers what Palmer describes as a 'penetrating reading of Cain', a reinscription which not only recreates the author's fictional world but also the Cainian themes of crime for profit and the inevitability of betrayal (2009: 269). In its essentials the story of *Blood Simple* follows the narrative pattern Frank Krutnik has called 'the Cain-text' (1982: 33), which in his understanding relies heavily on pop-Freudian notions of oedipal desire that attracted Cain as well as many other early twentieth-century American writers. In Krutnik's psychoanalytic reading, the Cain-text stages a Freudian 'testing of masculinity in relation to the law' (1991: 163). Typically, the Cain-text casts a virile younger man as the oedipal son who comes in conflict with an older father-figure (typically the cuckolded husband) representing patriarchal power. Father and son compete for possession of an eroticised mother-figure (the unfaithful wife). In *Blood Simple* this pattern is reproduced by pitting Ray, a younger man, against his older boss, Marty, whose younger and sexually attractive wife, Abby, is unhappy in their marriage and seeks escape. Andrew Spicer calls this Freudian triangulated scenario 'the paradigmatic master narrative' of classic film noir (2002: 25), but as Krutnik rightly contends, the true origins of this archetypal narrative are found in Cain's literary fiction.

In terms of narrative, the 'song' remains more or less the same, but the 'performers' undergo important changes that modify and reshape their Cainian counterparts. In *Blood Simple* the principal players (Ray, Abby and Marty) recall the central figures of *The Postman Always Rings Twice*: A young drifter, Frank Chambers, goes to work for a patriarchal elder, the Greek immigrant Nick Papadakis, whose attractive younger wife, Cora, presents Frank with an irresistible erotic temptation. An adulterous affair develops, as the younger man and the unhappily married wife are inevitably drawn to each other. Eventually, urged by Cora, Frank hatches a murder scheme to eliminate the naïve and unsuspecting husband and acquire his business, a roadside diner. Similarly, in Cain's *Double Indemnity* Phyllis Nirdlinger betrays her older, inattentive husband, plots his murder and manipulates her younger lover, insurance agent Walter Huff, to carry out her plan. Cain's stories are ignited by a chance encounter – an unwary man meets a dangerous woman and there is an immediate and mysterious attraction that quickly becomes a fatal obsession. Chance soon becomes fate, as the seductive power of the *femme fatale* draws the oedipal suitor ever closer to a destiny of self-destruction.

Compared with Cain's *femme fatales*, Abby represents a major departure from the archetype. The fatal woman in Cain's fiction is typically unfaithful and deadly, indeed, in some cases (like Phyllis Nirdlinger) explicitly psychopathic. In the many adaptations of Cain by noir filmmakers, the fatal woman is endowed with a physical beauty that intensifies her powers of seduction. Accordingly, the film noir *femme fatale* is portrayed by glamorous film stars like Lauren Bacall, Lana Turner and Barbara Stanwyck. This Hollywood image of the *femme fatale* as beautiful but dangerous has become the definitive representation of women in the classic film noir. Here *Blood Simple* departs from the generic film stereotype, hewing closer to its origins in Cain. Abby simply does not conform to the conventions of film noir. For one thing, as played by Frances McDormand, Abby is not a 'raving beauty'. In contrast to the film noir *femme*, Abby is rather plain, her feminine beauty more ordinary, much like Cain's Cora as described by Frank the first time he sees her: 'Except for the shape, she really wasn't any raving beauty, but she had a sulky look to her' (1982: 4). Cain had no interest in creating Hollywood images of feminine beauty. His eye was drawn to the common people whose ordinary, unglamorous crimes are the meat of tabloid journalism. Not surprisingly, Cain modeled his Cora on a real-life woman he had met at a gas station in southern California, whom he described as 'common, but sexy, the kind you have ideas about' (Skenazy 1989: 21). Later, when Cain saw in the newspaper that she had schemed to murder her husband, this ordinary woman from everyday life became the inspiration for Cora and her tabloid tale of betrayal and homicide became the impetus for *The Postman Always Rings Twice*. Thus, Abby's wholesome girl-next-door appeal corresponds more accurately to Cain's picture of Cora than to any of the glamorous *femme fatales* of classic Hollywood noir.

Abby also departs significantly from the stereotypical *femme fatale* in her lack of devious ulterior motives. She does not conspire with Ray in a plot to murder Marty. Apparently she just wants to escape her unhappy marriage. One could argue that her infidelity eventually causes the trouble that leads to the deaths of her husband, her lover and the private investigator, but she can hardly take the blame. She remains, in Joel's words, 'relatively innocent' throughout the movie (Allen 2006: 19). Lacking at least one cardinal virtue, she does commit adultery and that action does trigger the subsequent fatal events of the plot. In the end, though, she emerges as the survivor, and while the men around her all act stupidly, she is the only one to keep her head and not 'go simple'. Still, there are some unanswered questions. Why, for instance, does Abby make a point of retrieving her handgun? Is she afraid Marty will use it to harm her? Could she be planning to defend herself? Or perhaps she plans to have someone else use the gun on Marty? We never know her thoughts. We are left guessing, making assumptions, just as all the characters in this story are in the dark about others' intentions, forcing them to draw erroneous and fatal conclusions.

It is possible that the modifications of the *femme fatale* in *Blood Simple* are intended as a revisionary cleansing of the misogynistic image of women in film noir and that, in a larger sense, the Cainian archetypes of *Blood Simple* are reconfigured to accommodate the shift in the moral values of 1980s America. Marty, for instance, is clearly modeled on Nick the Greek, but as Joel puts it, 'a little less cheerful and fun-loving' than Nick Papadakis, whom the Coens describe as a 'greasy, guitar-strumming yahoo' (Allen 2006: 13). In *The Postman Always Rings Twice*, Nick the Greek disgusts Cora because she thinks he is 'greasy', a racist stereotype of Mediterranean immigrants. Her perception of Nick's 'greasiness', however, reveals itself as a projection of her own self-loathing: Her lover, Frank, works as a garage mechanic, a 'grease monkey', while Cora works in Nick's kitchen preparing greasy diner food. Marty is 'greasy' too, but in a different way. In addition to casting Dan Hedaya, whose dark features convey a Mediterranean ethnicity, the Coens intensify Marty's foreignness by depicting him as an East Coast city slicker, out of place in rural Texas. The most compelling sources of Marty's 'sleaziness', however, lie in his cowardly mendaciousness and lack of moral scruples. Portrayed as a greedy, tyrannical boss and a lecherous hustler, Marty is most despicable as the vindictive coward who buys the murder he cannot commit himself.

Unlike Nick the Greek, Marty's sleaze is a manifestation of his bankrupt morality rather than a signifier of his ethnic identity. In contrast to Nick, a harmless and trusting guitar-strummer, Marty is a brooding, ill-tempered sociopath who trusts no one and is far from harmless. Compared with the likeable Nick, Marty, mean-spirited and seemingly without redeeming qualities, arouses little sympathy. Even Mr. Nirdlinger, the grumpy, controlling husband in Cain's *Double Indemnity*, inspires more compassion than Julian Marty.

Cain's male protagonists consistently share qualities of physical and moral cowardice. They are men with disabling weaknesses, often profoundly impotent, a condition signified in a number of Cain's stories by wounds to the leg or groin, an allusion to the myth of Oedipus where, according to Freud, the wounded member symbolises a universal male fear of castration. This Freudian defect commonly associated with the younger oedipal suitor in Cain's fiction is transferred in *Blood Simple* to Marty, the oedipal patriarch, whose cowardly impotence is exposed and humorously punished by Abby's castrating kick to the groin – after she has already broken his 'pussy finger'. Ray, watching the drama from a distance, wields Abby's (phallic) gun, as Marty, in one final act of humiliation, is forced, vomiting, to retreat. Elsewhere, Marty himself makes allusions to ancient stories of castration, in particular by insulting Visser with a reference to the Greek custom of beheading the messenger who bore bad news. Marty's fishing trip to Corpus Christi (establishing an alibi for the murders committed by Visser) seems to allude to the Fisher King of the Grail legend who, like Oedipus, suffers from a debilitating ailment in need of a cure, as well as to Christ's death and resurrection, soon to become Marty's fate as well. The central motifs of degeneration, death and resurrection in these myths are played for laughs in *Blood Simple*, in particular by casting Marty as a small-time anti-Christ whose death and return from the dead are staged as grotesque farce. After he is buried alive by Ray, Marty is resurrected in Abby's dream, where his spectre returns to haunt the cheating wife, this time vomiting blood.

The one-dimensional patriarchs of Cain's stories function solely to supply the sacrificial third-party in the triangulated oedipal romance. More fully developed and integral to the plot, Marty refuses to play the passive victim. Instead, he actively seeks revenge, but as a coward would, by hiring a hit man to do his killing. Even after he is shot point blank Marty refuses to die, still trying to kill his murderer with his last breath. His malignance is finally transferred to Visser, who unwillingly enacts Marty's revenge, forced by his own stupidity to honour a contract for murder ordered by a dead man. In *The Postman Always Rings Twice*, Nick's murder is also a protracted affair requiring repeated attempts, finally culminating in a staged auto accident. Ironically, at the story's tragic end Frank accidentally kills Cora in a car wreck and is wrongfully sentenced to death. This ironic duplication of the death sentence (announced in the novel's title) reverberates in Visser's ominous warning that 'something can always go wrong'.

Like many film noirs of recent vintage, *Blood Simple* does not eschew vivid spectacles of physical violence. The movie's final scene depicting Visser's demise at the hands of Abby is an inventive staging of agonising death that owes more to the horror genre than to the *roman noir*. Another example is, of course, the wordless fifteen-minute sequence depicting Ray's agonising disposal of Marty in which elements of horror and comic burlesque mingle to recast the murder victim as a horror-movie monster who, refusing to die, keeps coming back from the dead. Although the Coens cite Cain as *Blood Simple*'s central precursor, downplaying the importance of cinematic influences, they have admitted that this sequence riffs on Hitchcock's *Torn Curtain* (1966), which at one point stages the murder of an East German secret police agent by an American spy (played by Paul Newman) as a series of gruesomely clumsy attacks, ending with a very messy but perversely entertaining death. As the brothers explain, Ray's repeated inept attempts to finish off Marty were intended not only as a Hitchcock homage but also as an attempt to outdo Hitchcock's black-comedic scene. In *Torn Curtain* the scene runs about five minutes; Marty's burial clocks in at three times that length, creating a mixture of humour and horror that knowingly recreates the signature dark humour identified with Hitchcock, prompting Hal Hinson to conclude that 'what the Coens have learned from Hitchcock, whose spirit hovers over [*Blood Simple*], is that murder can be simultaneously tragic and comic' (Allen 2006: 7). Asked how they were able to strike a generic balance between comedy and thriller, Joel replied, 'I think this gets back to Chandler and Hammett and Cain. The subject matter was grim but the tone was upbeat. They're funny … and that keeps the stories from being grim.' 'Humourless thrillers,' he adds, 'are dull, flat. They take themselves too seriously in a way that undercuts the fun of the movie' (Allen 2006: 14).

Edmund Wilson famously labeled the kind of crime fiction Cain specialised in 'tabloid murder', observing that Cain was 'particularly ingenious in tracing from their beginnings the tangles that gradually tighten around the necks of the people involved in those bizarre and brutal crimes that figure in the American newspapers' (Spicer 2002: 7). In the vein of Cain's tabloid fiction, *Blood Simple* tells the story of ordinary small-town people caught in a web of strange and violent crimes. But unlike Cain, who elevated the quotidian crimes of the proletariat to the level of operatic tragedy, the Coens find such ordinary crimes, plotted by simple minds, a particularly rich source of dark humour.

As a story of simple-minded crime, *Blood Simple* owes more to the fiction of Dashiell Hammett than to Cain. Acknowledging Hammett, the film's title quotes a phrase uttered in his *Red Harvest* (1927). In its original context, 'blood simple' describes the key symptom of an outbreak of criminal violence infecting the corrupt city of 'Poisonville', a contagion eventually poisoning the story's protagonist, the Continental Op (an 'operative' of the Continental Detective Agency). At one point the Op remarks: 'This damn burg's getting to me. If I don't get away soon, I'll be going blood-simple like the natives' (135). In *Blood Simple* it is easier to say who does *not* go 'blood simple'. The appellation certainly applies to the male characters; Abby remains the only one who does not lose her wits. Vamping on Hammett's hard-boiled idiom, the Coens coin the phrase 'money simple', used by Visser to express how the lure of easy money obtained by criminal activity often poisons sensible thinking and results in acts of outrageous stupidity. The Coens' subsequent neo-noirs are littered with 'blood simpletons' – ordinary people who in the commission of ill-conceived crimes make comically stupid mistakes. In *Blood Simple* this type is exemplified by Ray, a simple-minded Everyman (appropriately under-acted by John Getz), easily seduced by Abby and willing to risk becoming an accomplice to murder to protect her. Compared to his Cainian forebears, Ray enacts a counter-type, working against the grain of his literary models. In contrast to Frank Chambers, for instance, who is presented as the tough, streetwise commoner, Ray affects a gullible innocence, playing the part of the dupe, or what Frank Chambers calls a 'sap'. In every instance, he passively follows Abby's lead, constantly operating on false assumptions about Abby's guilt while casting himself romantically as her saviour.

The inclusion of private eye Loren Visser also marks a significant deviation from the Cain-text, where the protagonists are typically not private investigators or police detectives. Here Hammett rather than Cain appears to provide the inspiration for Visser's characterisation, following the model of the anonymous detective of Hammett's stories, the Continental Op. Often credited as the first private eye to appear in the pages of what came to be called 'pulp fiction', the Op has a place of prominence in the history of pulp fiction gumshoes, but as drawn by Hammett, the Op represents a different breed of noir detective. Unlike later pulp fiction heroes such as Raymond Chandler's Philip Marlowe, a tough guy who fights crime in the 'mean streets' but, in Chandler's famous words, 'is himself not mean', the Continental Op presents a much shadier, morally ambiguous figure operating on a porous boundary between crime and legality. Ruthless in his pursuit of criminals, he is not above certain kinds of misconduct, including illicit sexual affairs with clients, excessive alcohol consumption and, if necessary, occasional blunt, brutal violence, even murder – whatever it takes to crack the case. Visser (whose name is never mentioned in dialogue and so like the Op remains nameless) embodies an even more pathological version of Hammett's hardboiled operator. Although the Op can and does occasionally transgress legal and moral boundaries, if the situation requires it, his ethics ultimately define a line he will not cross. Visser, on the other hand, shows no hint of conscience. Driven solely by monetary incentives, he will do the job 'if the money's right'. Despite his ironically sunny demeanor, he can be malicious, apparently murdering Marty simply to spite him for his disrespectful insults. Without blinking, he murders his unsuspecting employer, after which he pronounces the epitaph: 'Who looks stupid now?' His clothing and physicality are also reminiscent of Hammett's Op. More cowboy than pulp fiction private eye, Visser's ten-gallon hat and Western boots fit in with the West Texas setting, but are a far cry from the snap-brim hats and tailored suits of stylish noir gumshoes like Philip Marlowe. Like the Op, who describes himself as 'short, middle-aged, and thick-waisted', Visser is overweight and slovenly (described in the screenplay as 'a large, unshaven man in a misshapen yellow leisure suit'). His sweaty corpulence is the outward sign of inner moral corruption, as are his tasteless canary yellow suit and the flies that buzz about and land on his face, suggesting a kinship with vermin (an image reinforced by the VW 'Bug' he drives). He also shares the Op's cynical wit, which manifests itself in Visser's darkly self-ironic wisecracks. After Marty mentions that the ancient Greeks decapitated messengers bearing bad news, Visser cracks: 'Well, gimme a call whenever you wanna cut off my head … I can crawl around without it.'

In Cain's fiction the illicit lovers' crimes often go undetected and eventually mistrust and greed drive them to betray and destroy each other. This is not the case with Ray and Abby, who may mistrust each other but are not bent on mutual destruction. Departing from the *femme fatale* stereotype, Abby does not calculate or contribute directly to Ray's death; false assumptions pave the path to his destruction. In the absence of a cunning *femme fatale* the Coens write in a sleazy private investigator as the agent of ill-fate. Visser is cast as the *homme fatal* (fatal man) ultimately responsible for the deaths of Marty and Ray, and finally his own. A further deviation from the Cain-text is the elimination of passionate heterosexual romance, one of Cain's trademarks. As Hal Hinson describes it, 'In *The Postman Always Rings Twice*, Frank and Cora were so hot for each other that sparks seemed to arc between them; their passion was so volatile that it almost had to erupt into violence' (Allen 2006: 7). Countering Cain's fiery passion with a bloodless extramarital encounter, Ray and Abby's affair is tepid at best, lacking the animal lust that so forcefully attracts Cora and Frank to each other. To compensate for the lack of heterosexual heat the Coens insinuate a homoerotic undercurrent in the relationship between 'Julian' Marty and 'Loren' Visser. Although their feminine-sounding first names are suppressed in the movie (Visser's first name is known only from the inscription seen on his cigarette lighter, which he forgetfully leaves behind at the scene of Marty's murder, thus implicating himself in the crime), Visser makes a point of addressing Marty on a first-name basis, arrogantly assuming an uninvited personal intimacy. Here again we sense the influence of Hammett's pulp fiction, where a whiff of homoeroticism hangs perpetually in the atmosphere. As James Naremore points out, Hammett's manly Sam Spade 'moves with ease through an underworld composed almost entirely of women and bohemian homosexuals, so that even his masculinity seems ambiguous' (1998: 53). In Hammett's *The Glass Key* (1931) themes of masculine friendship become increasingly important, resulting in a latently homoerotic narrative of male bonding set in the tough-guy culture of gangsters. Similarly, Julian and Loren's mutual antagonism belies an underlying homoerotic attraction slyly implied by Visser's mischievous flirtations.

One scene in particular illustrates this homoerotic undertow. Visser and Marty arrange a clandestine meeting to plan the murder of Ray and Abby at a romantic overlook or lovers' lane outside of town, where young people typically congregate to engage in illicit activities. As Marty approaches Visser's car, Visser turns to the teenage girl he's chatting up, saying 'sorry sweetheart, my date is here'. Visser then opens the back door of his VW for Marty, implying that the 'back seat' is the best place to conduct their business. Marty refuses the invitation and sits in the front seat, whereupon Visser draws Marty's attention to a small topless doll suspended from the rearview mirror. Visser gives it a tap and, as it swings back and forth, two small red lights, one behind each bare breast, blink on and off. With childish delight, Visser exclaims, 'Idnat wild?' Eyeing the splint on Marty's finger (the result of his humiliating 'castration' by Abby), Visser queries with crude geniality: 'Stick your finger up the wrong person's ass?' When Marty refuses to acknowledge this lewdly suggestive query, Visser launches into an anecdote concerning broken fingers and the anal region, concluding with the remark: 'That's the test, ain't it? The test of true love.' The homoerotic innuendo suffusing the

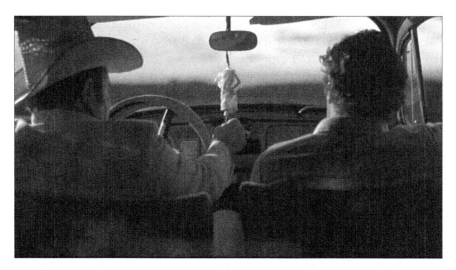

'Idnat wild?'

scene threatens to breach the barriers of repression, and at the same time creates an oddly humorous mood. Later, in their final meeting, Marty calls his relationship with Visser an 'illicit romance' and says, 'we've got to trust each other to be discreet'. Visser replies: 'For richer, for poorer' – a promise usually made in conventional marriage vows.

### In Dialogue with Classic Film Noir

As storytellers the Coens acknowledge their affiliation with literary antecedents, but in filming their Cain story the brothers were also aware of working in a classic movie genre. When asked about the influence of classic film noir, however, the Coens assume a guarded stance, deflecting questions of derivation. '*Blood Simple* utilizes movie conventions to tell the story,' Joel comments. 'In that sense, it's about other movies – but no more so than any other film that uses the medium in a way that's aware that there's a history of movies behind it' (Allen 2006: 14). Ethan adds, 'It's plain, mean, ordinary people doing bad things to each other in the dark, so I guess that qualifies it as film noir' (Allen 2006: 137). Despite their feigned ignorance, their knowledge of classic film noir appears to be extensive, and regardless of what they might say about their relationship with that tradition, the Coens have expressed great admiration for classic noir auteurs, Billy Wilder and Edgar Ulmer among them (Allen 2006: 189). In his landmark essay 'Notes on Film Noir', Paul Schrader observes that 'film noir was first of all a style' (1972: 91), by which he means that film noir emerged first – historically (in the 1940s) – as a set of cinematic techniques which would only later, in retrospect, become a recognisable genre. As Schrader points out, classic film noir is more interested in style than theme. In the world of film noir, he contends, 'style becomes paramount; it is all that separates one from meaninglessness' (1972: 86). 'Because film noir worked out its conflicts visually rather than thematically,' Schrader notes, 'it was able to create artistic solutions to sociological problems' (1972: 91). Thus, Schrader devotes a large part of his essay to the analysis of film noir's visual style, which he praises not only for its aesthetic value but equally for its power to reflect the cynical worldview of film while creating 'a new artistic world which went beyond a simple sociological reflection' (ibid.). Schrader's insights do not seem lost on the Coens, who embrace the visual aesthetic of classic film noir but also reinterpret its conventions to create a visual approach suited to *Blood Simple*'s noir melodrama. In addition to extreme, disorienting high- and low-angle camera angles and the accelerated ground-level 'shaky-cam' shot (a trademark of Sam Raimi), the Coens accentuate the 'darkness' of their story with the frequent use of low-key, so-called 'mystery' lighting, one of the most recognisable techniques of classic film noir. The Coens say they were decidedly opposed to making what they describe as 'a Venetian blind movie', meaning a film that merely apes the clichés of noir *mise-en-scène*. As Joel describes it, 'I wanted [*Blood Simple*] to have a pronounced visual look. Although it's made in colour, I wanted it to have the feeling of the old black and white movies' (Mottram 2000: 22).

Before shooting *Blood Simple,* the Coens took cinematographer Barry Sonnenfeld to see two films they thought exemplified the visual style they hoped to realise: Bertolucci's *The Conformist* (1971) and Carol Reed's classic film noir *The Third Man* (1949). Both of these exemplary black and white films are famous for their masterful use of chiaroscuro lighting, creating striking imagery by juxtaposing starkly contrasting visual fields of light and dark. The Coens were reticent to film entirely in black and white, fearing it would mark their movie as too 'independent' or as an art-house film. Thus, to achieve a chiaroscuro effect in colour they chose to incorporate neon into the set design wherever possible, exploiting the potential of neon lighting to intensify and draw attention to colours, creating added visual interest and offering a range of symbolic meanings not available to black and white. When set against a dark background, coloured neon tends to heighten the visual contrast and create what amounts to, in comparison to black and white films, a new kind of chiaroscuro. A striking example of such neon-chiaroscuro is found in Marty's roadhouse, appropriately named 'Neon Boots'. The barroom (itself a stock setting in classic film noir) is, as its name announces, a country and western joint bathed in neon light inside and out. The multi-coloured jukebox, the Budweiser signs, the magenta neon trim that frames the window separating Marty's office from the barroom – such imagery pays homage to classic noir but at the same time inflects noir style with neo-expressionist touches of neon. One particularly notable instance of the neon effect occurs when Ray returns to 'Neon Boots' to collect his back pay. As Ray finds Marty sitting on the back steps, contemplating two workers throwing trash into the orange flames of an incinerator, the monochromatic foreground of the shot is bathed in shades of blue light emanating from a neon electric bug-zapper which snaps and crackles during their brief conversation (an audio effect that underscores the anger seething just below the surface of Marty's stiffly repressed demeanor). Behind Marty, the bar's interior provides a dark background, dotted with contrasting accents of yellow and orange neon heightening the overall chiaroscuro effect and visually communicating the atmosphere of menace caused by their mutual antagonism.

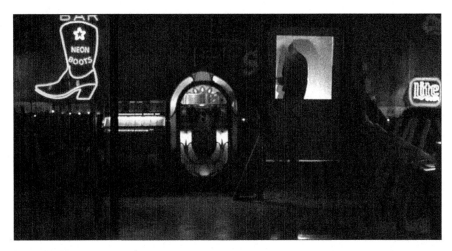

'Neon Boots'

The neon noir *mise-en-scène* is supplemented with resonances of old-style noir, particularly in the choice of iconography, illustrated in the movie's opening scene with the image of Ray and Abby speeding down a dark highway, oncoming headlights intermittently illuminating the rain-swept road before them. The calculated choice of imagery here evokes the venerable noir theme of illicit lovers on the run, exemplified by Nicholas Ray's *They Live by Night* (1949). The precise visual referent, however, seems to be Edgar Ulmer's *Detour* (1945), a low-budget classic noir featuring an ill-fated road trip through the desert southwest during a stormy night, exploited to full effect as the backdrop for a dazzling display of black and white chiaroscuro imagery. The influence of *Detour* on *Blood Simple* is most apparent in the dark desert highway as the setting for the lovers' getaway, evoking *Detour*'s most basic iconography as well as its existentialist symbolism, not only the image of lovers-on-the-run, but also the 'lost highway' motif, suggesting an escape route with 'no exit'. Accordingly, Abby's attempt to flee her oppressive marriage to Marty fails, and she ends up back in small-town Texas, entangled in a new relationship with Ray, which as the story progresses turns out to be just another emotional dead end. The opening shot of Ray and Abby driving through dark expanses of desert, trapped in a cramped car interior, conveys a sense of separation from their surroundings that prefigures their eventual alienation from each other. As the narrative unfolds, these lovers, like all the characters in *Blood Simple*, become painfully aware of a profound personal isolation, caused by persistent failures of communication and the resulting lack of trust. To reinforce the theme of existential isolation, the Coens frame many shots as restrictive close-ups and show a preference for shot/reverse-shot editing (avoiding medium two-shots) as a way of isolating the characters from each other visually. While the viewers are given knowledge of each character's actions and motives, the characters themselves remain isolated, each with their own perspective on the events that occur. In the diegetic world of *Blood Simple* they are, as Visser puts it, 'on their own'. By the 1990s the detour motif had become a favored trope of neo-noir, featured in a series of movies including Dennis Hopper's *The*

*Hot Spot* (1990), John Dahl's *Red Rock West* (1993) and Oliver Stone's *U-Turn* (1997). Such films, which relocate the Cain-text in the desert southwest, are now numerous enough to be considered a sub-genre of neo-noir and, in R. Barton Palmer's estimation, should be considered 'remakes' of *Blood Simple*, which he considers the original 'desert-noir' (2004: 23).

Although the symbolic setting and iconography of *Detour* make a strong impression on the visual style, prompting film critic J. Hoberman to call *Blood Simple* 'a *Detour* for the 1980s', these elements constitute only part of Ulmer's influence. The storylines and principal characters of both films also exhibit remarkable parallels. Martin Goldsmith's screenplay (adapted from his 1939 novel) follows the narrative pattern the Cain-text as it recounts the story of a passive, emotionally pliable Everyman who falls into the clutches of a dangerous woman who blackmailed him for the accidental death of a stranger whose identity he has stolen. The protagonist, Al Roberts, is not actually guilty of the murder, but must nevertheless, like *Blood Simple*'s Ray, deal with its consequences. In *Detour* as in *Blood Simple*, the deceased returns to haunt his accidental killer, not literally as Marty does when he refuses to die, but as a figment of Al's guilt-fueled imagination. Additionally, both films share a fascination with what James Mottram calls 'the mechanics of death' (2000: 27). In *Blood Simple* this fascination manifests itself in the horrific ordeal of Marty's burial, but also in the bizarre logistics of Visser's demise. In the final showdown with Visser, Abby first stabs then shoots her unknown assailant through a wall without ever knowing his true identity. A similar scene concludes the story of *Detour* where Al refuses to cooperate in a scheme of identity fraud. Threatening to turn him in for the unintentional death of a stranger, his nemesis, Vera, locks herself in an adjoining room and tries to call the police. In a desperate attempt to block the call, Al pulls vigorously on the telephone cord, now entangled around the neck of a drunken Vera, unwittingly strangling her to death and thus repeating the accidental murder that had already forced him into this predicament. Ironically, the difference between Al and Abby is that Al knows his unseen victim's identity all too well, while Abby is left completely in the dark.

Further affinities with *Detour* are evident in *Blood Simple*'s dialogue, which in places seems almost to quote Goldsmith's script. In wording and tonality, certain passages of Al's world-weary and cynical voiceover seem to reverberate in Visser's sardonic prologue. When, for instance, at the outset of *Detour*, Al protests that 'the world is full of sceptics. I know. I am one', the resemblance to Visser's opening line is unmistakable: 'The world is full of complainers. But the fact, is nothing comes with a guarantee.' The fundamental difference in their worldviews is that Al Roberts is not merely a sceptic, but a hardened pessimist. Weak, insecure and whiney, he blames his misfortunes on the absurd machinations of a higher power he cannot comprehend, summed up in his self-pitying nihilistic prophesy: 'Someday fate, or some mysterious force, can put the finger on you or me for no reason at all.' As self-defeating anti-hero, Al Roberts epitomises a common archetype of classic film noir: the perpetual loser who seeks but never achieves personal freedom because he imagines his fate is controlled by some mysterious force beyond his comprehension rendering all human endeavors inconsequential and pointless. Visser, however, offers an alternative to Ulmer's depressing vision of the human condition. Visser is not bemoaning the fate of mankind; rather, he is complaining about the complainers like Al Roberts, whose naïve expectation that life should be fair and humans should act with compassion toward their fellows annoys him:

> The world is full of complainers. But the fact is, nothing comes with a guarantee. And I don't care if you're the Pope of Rome, President of the United States or Man of the Year, something can always go wrong. Go ahead, complain. Tell your problems to your neighbor. Ask for help and watch him fly. In Russia they got it mapped out so that everyone pulls for everyone else. That's the theory, anyway. What I know is Texas, and down here, you're on your own.

Like Al Roberts, Visser espouses an essentially pessimistic view of humanity's lot. It doesn't matter who you are, 'something can always go wrong', even if you are 'Man of the Year' (an honour bestowed on Visser himself). Ironically, his opening prologue prophesises his own fate, for something *does* go terribly wrong. But unlike *Detour's* pathetic Al, Visser has transcended the pathos of pessimism to embrace life's absurdity without personal resentment. His Zen-like acceptance of life's unpredictable vicissitudes is on full display at the moment of his imminent death. As he bleeds to death beneath a sink, fatally wounded by Abby, she shouts (thinking he is Marty), 'I'm not afraid of you, Marty!' With mock cordiality Visser's replies, 'If I see him, I'll sure give him the message.' Then, as the camera shifts to Visser's point of view, we see a droplet of water forming on the underside of the sink, which Visser observes with mild interest as it is about to fall into his eye. Suddenly, in the face of death, he lets out a jovial laugh, his final utterance signaling a sense of self-irony completely absent in Al Roberts. He recognises the absurdity of his predicament and can, in his last moment, appreciate without self-pity the irony of his reversal of fortune.

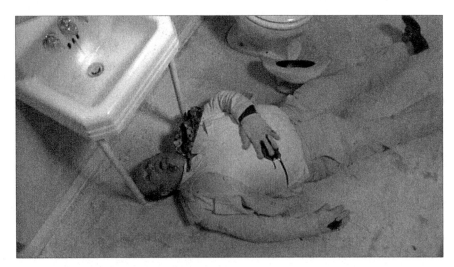

'If I see him, I'll sure give him the message.'

Unmistakably, this is a philosophical moment in the story, perhaps as close as the Coens come in *Blood Simple* to making a meaningful statement. As a philosophical stance, Visser's self-mockery might be understood as an expression of 'joyful wisdom' in the sense that German philosopher Friedrich Nietzsche gave it in his book *Die fröhliche Wissenschaft* (1882; translated as *Joyful Wisdom*). There Nietzsche extols a self-transcendent affirmation of human existence, however painful and tragic it might be, calling this affirmation '*amor fati*' – love of fate – which he understood as the 'pessimism of strength', in contradistinction to fellow German philosopher Arthur Schopenhauer's 'pessimism of weakness', In a discussion of Nietzsche, nihilism and neo-noir, philosopher Thomas S. Hibbs renames the weak pessimists 'passive nihilists'. Against the weak or passive nihilists, who represent a decadent decline in the human spirit, Nietzsche pits his 'pessimists of strength', whom Hibbs renames 'active nihilists' – those who view the decline of traditional values and beliefs as an occasion for the destruction of antiquated and corrupt social institutions and the creation of a new order of values. 'Beyond good and evil', active nihilists appear as amoral, often demonic figures in contemporary film noir, villains who escape the snares of noir fatalism by engaging in acts of 'exuberant amoral energy' (2007: 140). Thus, while both *Detour* and *Blood Simple* share the noir theme of fatalism, the defining difference lies in the contrast between Ulmer's passive vision of 'weak pessimism' and the Coens' revisionary activism. The figure of Loren Visser voices rejection of passive pessimists, 'the complainers', who capitulate to capricious powers beyond human comprehension. Shifting the spotlight to the comedy of human errors, *Blood Simple* negates the noir pessimist with the joyful wisdom of its actively nihilistic narrator.

CHAPTER TWO

# Raising Arizona: A State of Mind

After their dark and downbeat debut, the Coen brothers said they wanted to make a film 'as different from *Blood Simple* as possible – galloping instead of languorous, sunny instead of lurid, genial and upbeat instead of murderous and cynical' (Allen 2006: 17–18). The result was *Raising Arizona*, the story of H. I. McDunnough (Nicolas Cage), a loopy small-time criminal who specialises in convenience store hold-ups. During one of his frequent stays at the Maricopa County jail, Hi (as he likes to be called) conceives a desire for a better life as a free and law-abiding citizen. When he meets pretty prison photographer Edwina (Holly Hunter), who goes by Ed, Hi begins to see the path to a better future in which he will finally put his lawless years behind him, settle down with Ed, and live a 'normal' family life. The discovery that Ed is unable to conceive children makes this dream seem unattainable, until the widely-publicised birth of the 'Arizona Quints' to local businessman Nathan Arizona (Trey Wilson) and wife Florence (Lynne Dumin Kitei), an event that offers an alternative way of acquiring the baby that Ed insists she must have. Hi is dispatched to kidnap one of the Arizona quintuplets, the first in a series of kidnappings as the stolen quint quickly becomes a hot commodity, sought by a bounty hunter (Randell 'Tex' Cobb), the Lone Biker of the Apocalypse, as Hi calls him, who hopes to collect the reward put up by Nathan Arizona. When Hi's prison buddies, the Snopes brothers Gale (John Goodman) and Evelle (William Forsythe), get wind of the McDonnough's subterfuge, they join the chase, kidnapping the kidnapped baby. Hi's boss Glen (Sam McMurray) and his wife Dot (Frances McDormand), who already have more than they can handle, covet Nathan Jr. as well. Hi and Ed's struggles to possess, and re-possess, the stolen baby constitute the remainder of the narrative.

Upon its theatrical release, mainstream critics gave *Raising Arizona* mixed reviews, divided along critical lines established in earlier reviews of *Blood Simple*. Some reviewers raved. *Time* magazine film critic Richard Corliss, an ardent supporter of *Blood Simple*, hailed *Raising Arizona* as 'exuberantly original'. David Denby of *New York* admired the Coens' 'deranged fable of the New West', which, in his estimation, turns 'sarcasm into a rude yet affectionate mode of comedy'. Rita Kempley, writing for the *Washington Post*, had nothing but admiration for the Coens' new movie, labeling it 'a wacky, happy, daring, darkly comic tale'. Dissatisfied critics repeated criticisms leveled at *Blood Simple*, especially the movie's lamentable triumph of 'empty' style over 'human' substance. Pauline Kael thought *Raising Arizona* pure cinematic artifice, describing the movie as a 'contraption', well-built in a technical sense, but 'storyboarded like a comic strip', racing from one sight gag to the next. Writing for the *New York Times*, Vincent Canby complained similarly that like *Blood Simple*, the film is 'full of technical expertise but has no life of its own'. For critics like these, the Coens' latest effort was too mannered, too self-conscious and therefore 'lifeless', as if the weight of the film's stylisation had crushed the human spirit of its characters. In one of the most damning reviews, Roger Ebert of the *Chicago Sun-Times* complained that everyone in the movie talks in a 'funny' and 'distracting' way, which presumably means in an unnatural, affected idiom. 'I have a problem,' writes Ebert, 'with movies where everybody talks as if they were reading out of an old novel about a bunch of would-be colourful characters.' Adding to his distractions, it bothered Ebert that, as a cinematic narrative, the film failed to make a clear distinction between reality and fantasy, which, he believes, causes viewer confusion and disorientation. For Ebert, *Raising Arizona* is a movie that 'cannot decide if it exists in the real world of trailer parks and 7-Elevens and Pampers, or in a fantasy world of characters from another dimension'.

Ebert's complaint that *Raising Arizona* cannot decide whether it exists in the 'real world' or the realm of fantasy is symptomatic of those detractors who judged the movie by conventional standards of cinematic realism, with the expectation that unless presented explicitly as fantasy, a movie should depict a unified and credible reality.

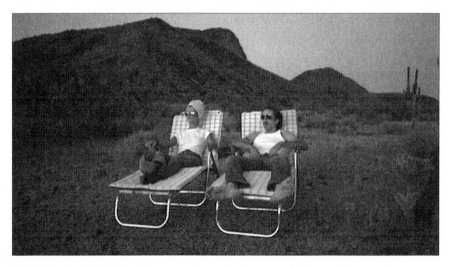

Hi and Ed enjoy 'the salad days'.

Movies can be either realistic or fantastic, but apparently not both simultaneously. What such assessments overlook, however, is the possibility that the entire narrative could be a product of Hi's imagination, an escapist fantasy dreamed up to pass the time in jail. The story's epilogue hints at this possibility, intimated in Hi's final speech: 'I don't know. You tell me. This whole dream ... was it wishful thinkin'? Was I just fleein' reality, like I know I'm liable to do?' As James Mottram points out, the film is designed to blur the boundary between fantasy and reality, not only with its contrived comic-book story and characters, but by formal means such as the avoidance of conventional continuity techniques (fades or dissolves) to signify transitions from dream to reality (2000: 38). What bothers Ebert and others is the Coens' refusal to make clear distinctions between the planes of reality and fantasy. Unlike *Blood Simple*, which was fashioned as a realistic 'slice of life', *Raising Arizona* asks to be read as a cartoonish fantasy that renders not a specific social reality but a peculiar state of mind.

## An Amalgam of Genres

Asked if they prefer to work in specific genres since their first two films were so clearly genre pieces (crime and comedy), Joel responded: 'We were more conscious of working in a genre with *Blood Simple* than with *Raising Arizona*. *Arizona* seems more absurd, an amalgam of genres.' Ethan adds that in writing the screenplay 'we didn't begin by thinking of diving into a genre. We wanted to broadly make a comedy with two main characters. We concentrated on them, more than the movie in a general sense' (Allen 2006: 25). Instead of a genre movie, the Coens conceived *Raising Arizona* as a character-based narrative, but despite the initial focus on character, the finished motion picture contrives much of its humour by blending standard movie genres with diverse styles of film comedy, orchestrating these forms to create an amalgamation of filmic discourses Jim Collins terms 'ironic hybridization' (1993: 243). Like *Blood Simple*, *Raising Arizona* exemplifies a broader category of postmodern cinema: reflexive films that explore the possibilities of genre by intertextual means, conducting referential dialogues with previous generic models. As one of the first theorists to establish the centrality of hybridisation in the literary text, what Mikhail Bakhtin writes about the novel can be applied equally to the filmic text: 'The novelistic hybrid is an artistically organized system for bringing different languages in contact with one another, a system having as its goal the illumination of one language by means of another' (1984b: 361). As Bakhtin continually reminds us, all texts are pastiches of citations, pluralised by the plethora of generic discourses. This is particularly true of the artistic text, which in Bakhtin's view is by definition a 'hybrid construction'.

In *Raising Arizona* this interplay of diverse generic models engenders a referential dialogue that is both resonant and dissonant, but always calculated to produce laughter. The introductory montage recounting Hi's frequent incarcerations in the Maricopa County jail and his courtship of Ed invokes the conventions of a prison movie. The desert setting, outlaw motif and frequent gunplay evoke Hollywood westerns. These are supplemented by elements of apocalyptic science fiction (with specific references to the *Mad Max* movies) and the gangster genre (a kidnapping committed by a Bonnie-and-Clyde outlaw couple). As generic hybrid, *Raising Arizona* relies on these standard forms, but the over-arching genre is comedy, and as such it depends heavily on the crude farce of slapstick that was an integral feature of early silent comedies. Thus many sequences in *Raising Arizona* are staged like the early silent comedies of Buster Keaton, Fatty Arbuckle and Harold Lloyd, getting laughs primarily from the idiotic and improbable pratfalls of foolish characters enacting harmless violence on each other. Many of these early comedies were produced by Mack Sennett, best known for the Keystone Kops, the motion picture precursor of animated cartoons. As critics rightly noted, *Raising Arizona* has a cartoonish quality, disconcerting for some, who scorned the movie for being written and performed like a manic comic strip. In *Raising Arizona* this 'animated' effect is created by highly stylised camera movements incorporated into elaborate sequence shots that mimic the visual mannerisms of animated comedy, particularly the antic kinesis of the Chuck Jones *Road Runner* TV series which, like the Coens' movie, takes place in an imaginary Arizona desert. Like the hapless *Roadrunner* antagonist, Wile E. Coyote, Hi endures endless physical abuse without ever suffering serious injury. He is punched in the face (by Ed), shot at (by police and town-folk), hurled against and through walls (by Gale Snopes) and dragged over highway asphalt behind a motorcycle (by Smalls) without suffering so much as a scratch. The Woody Woodpecker/Mr. Horsepower tattoo shared by Hi and the apocalyptic biker offers a visual clue to their shared identity within a cartoon-inspired dream world where the boundary between fantasy and reality is permeable and unstable.

Apparent in the visual conception and technique of *Raising Arizona's* cartoon-like stylisation is the influence of Sam Raimi, with whom the Coens had recently collaborated on the movie *Crimewave*. This Coen/Raimi collaboration, also known as *The XYZ Murders*, is an outrageous black comedy whose humour results in large measure from the slapstick violence of two exterminators who target human victims as well as rodents (their advertising slogan is 'We Kill All Sizes'). Raimi's influence on *Raising Arizona* is evident in applications of technical excess, especially in Raimi's trademark 'shakicam' shot, achieved by mounting a camera with wide-angle lens on a wooden board and pulling it manually close to ground level. One of the most notable examples occurs at the end of Hi's dream-vision of the Lone Biker of the Apocalypse. To convey the 'fury' that Hi imagines Florence Arizona will feel when she realises her baby is missing, the filmmakers construct a fast-motion sequence in which a wobbly camera rushes toward the exterior of the Arizona's mansion, leaps over a parked car, then quickly scales the rungs of a ladder leading to the open window of the quints' bedroom, halting abruptly on a close-up of Florence Arizona's gaping mouth as she screams. The sequence, divided into three segments, employs the ground-level shakicam shot plus footage from a remote-controlled camera as well as some tricky upside-down point-of-view shots, all of it over-cranked to create the desired zany intensity. To heighten the visual sense of animation, the Coens had cinematographer Barry Sonnenfeld use wide-angle lenses for the high-speed tracking shots to create an unnatural distortion of the images and intensify their cartoonish energy.

One of the most memorable illustrations of *Raising Arizona's* 'pinball animation' occurs in the Huggies hold-up sequence, a slapstick tour-de-force worthy of Sennett's

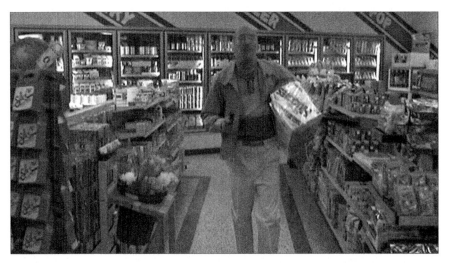

'I'll be takin' these Huggies and whatever cash you got.'

Keystone Kops. It begins innocently enough when Hi stops at a 7-Eleven to pick up Huggies for the baby. Once inside the store, however, Hi's outlaw nature takes control and he can't resist the urge to take what he needs at gunpoint. Hurriedly exiting the store with the stolen Huggies, he realises that Ed has abandoned him. As he freezes in terror and disbelief, the camera rushes toward him at ground level, visually capturing his sense of panic and initiating the frantic action that ensues. In seconds, the cops show up, guns blazing, joined by the store clerk wielding a Dirty Harry-sized hand cannon, all of them firing furiously at Hi as he gallops madly down the street, unharmed. Seeking refuge in a suburban backyard, Hi is attacked by a ferocious dog which appears suddenly from the darkness. Here the camera itself seems to attack Hi, assuming the dog's point-of-view as it rushes toward him in a high-speed, shakicam tracking shot. The attacks are now coming at Hi from every direction. Suddenly he is hit by a truck – but again, no harm done. Racing to his rescue, Ed finally returns to the store and as they speed away Hi casually scoops up the Huggies he had dropped while madly dodging gunfire. Tightly edited and optically intensified by hyper-kinetic camera movements, this remarkable piece of action filming reads simultaneously as homage to the Keystone Kops and as parody of the free-wheeling, high-octane violence-for-entertainment that fuels contemporary Hollywood action movies.

In addition to its cartoonish slapstick, *Raising Arizona* also borrows and reworks fundamental elements of classic 'screwball' comedies, drawing to a large extent on two directors widely considered masters of this kind of comedy: Howard Hawks and Preston Sturges. Hawks' comedies such as *Bringing Up Baby* and *His Girl Friday* (both released in 1940) find their humour in marital or romantic conflicts and the comic confusion caused by clashing gender roles, usually pitting an independent woman resisting traditional feminine roles against the more conventional expectations of her husband or lover. Romantic conflict is also at the heart of comedies by Preston Sturges. As noted in the Introduction, in movies like *The Lady Eve* and *The Palm Beach Story*, Sturges invented a witty and acerbic brand of screwball laced with cynical satire. One of the Coens' favorites by Sturges, *The Palm Beach Story*, takes a satirical look at sex and its uses in the acquisition of wealth, as Sturges lampoons the idle rich and the American obsession with money and social status. Its story concerns Tom and Gerry, a married couple in financial straits. Tom is an inventor who struggles to provide the good life for his wife Gerry, who like any good American woman wants to 'get ahead'. To do so, she uses her feminine wiles to manipulate a wealthy suitor for money, which she (virtuously) plans to use to subsidise Tom's commercial success. The romantic conflict engendered by her enterprising flirtations provides a rich context for a story that exploits the changing social definitions of masculinity and femininity for screwball laughs.

Initially conceived as a character-driven story, *Raising Arizona*'s narrative is grounded in the classic conflict of masculine vs. feminine. But while the comedies of Hawks and Sturges generally play out this conflict in a glamorised middle- or upper-class milieu, the McDonnoughs inhabit the lower socio-economic regions of American society. Yet despite cultural and class differences they are caught in the same comedic predicament as their upscale screwball predecessors. The incongruous marriage of Hi and Ed (whose names are only the most obvious manifestation of their confusion about gender roles) presents an improbable variation on the classic themes of conflicted romance and the reversal of gender roles. As a prison guard, Ed is an atypical variant of the classic independent woman. Hi plays the confused husband unsure of his masculine identity and trying to find his place amidst the progress of social changes. As her name suggests, 'Ed' has pronounced masculine characteristics, starting with her work in the male-dominated profession of law enforcement. Her job has taught her to be an authoritarian taskmaster, a habit she carries over into family life where she is clearly the one in charge. Her habit of laying down the law is well illustrated when she commands the Snopes brothers to leave their 'decent' family home, prompting Gale to express doubts about Hi's patriarchal status when he suggests that Ed seems to 'wear the pants' in the McDunnough household. Doubts about Hi's status as family breadwinner reach a zenith after Hi has assaulted his obnoxious boss and lost his job, as Ed asks: 'Where does that leave me and Nathan Jr.?' Hi can only think to reply: 'With a man for a husband.' Hi's insecurity about masculine identity is humorously underscored by implying his femininity. Such implications become a running joke. In contrast to the masculine formality of Ed's monochrome police uniform, Hi prefers the bright colours and floral patterns typically associated with female apparel. In contrast to the no-nonsense formality of Ed's police talk, Hi prefers a more affectionate, sometimes poetic, idiom adorned with floral metaphors (he calls Ed his 'sweet desert flower'). The joking about Hi's 'femininity' reaches a crescendo in a sight gag during the Huggies hold-up when he pulls a nylon stocking over his head as a mask. The baffled hayseed driver who later gives Hi a lift can only say, 'Son, you got a panty on your head!'

At the conclusion of Hi's story, as he narrates his dream vision of a brighter future, one senses again the influence of Sturges. After having decided to return Nathan Jr. to his real family, devastated by the surrender of the baby that had brought them so much joy, Hi and Ed contemplate dissolving their improbable union. Maybe it was, as Ed says, 'just a fool's paradise'; Nathan Arizona cautions prudence and deliberation, telling the couple they should at least 'sleep on it'. That night Hi has a dream of the future, one in which he and Ed stay married, raise a family (whose members are not too 'screwed up') and finally grow old together in peaceful harmony. But even in his dream of wish fulfillment Hi has doubts yet still harbours hope, saying 'But me'n Ed, we can be good too … And it *seemed* real. It *seemed* like us. And it seemed like … well … our home … If not Arizona, then a land, not *too* far away, where all parents are strong and wise and capable, and all children are happy and beloved … I dunno, maybe it was Utah.' His conclusion is as inconclusive as it is laughable. Realistically, it is doubtful that Utah, just as barren and uninhabitable as Arizona, could offer anything approaching the utopia of Hi's dream vision. In Sturges' *Palm Beach Story* the ultimate fate of Tom and Gerry's marriage is likewise put in doubt in the film's final frame which poses the question: 'And they lived happily ever after – or did they?' The ending of Hi and Ed's story is similarly ambiguous, leaving in question the outcome of a perhaps ill-fated marriage of two 'screwed up' Arizona hayseeds.

Sturges is well known for his use of comic stereotypes but, in a manner analogous to the Coens, he tended to exaggerate the characters to make them more, rather than less, sympathetic, slyly using stereotypes to insinuate biting social commentaries. The stereotyping in *Raising Arizona* follows a similar strategy. Critics objected to what they perceived as the film's mocking arrogance toward its characters, but the Coens do not see the condescension: 'If the characters talk in clichés,' says Joel, 'it's because we *like* clichés' (Allen 2006: 24). Nevertheless, the Coens were censured by a Tempe, Arizona reporter who read an unauthorised copy of the script during production and published a newspaper article scolding the brothers for their hayseed stereotyping of Arizonans. Ethan mounted a public defence of the movie, saying that their portrayal of Arizonans as backward hicks was not meant to be realistic: 'Of course it's not accurate,' said Ethan. 'It's not supposed to be. It's all made up. It's an Arizona of the mind' (Levine 2000: 56). The most extreme call for censure was, however, yet to come. After its national release Mike Zink, pastor of Family Life Centers in Seattle, Washington organised a demonstration against the movie because, in Zink's words, 'it encourages people to view children as objects and, in that way, encourages child abuse, child neglect, and kidnap' (Robson 2007: 71). The Coens did not dignify this accusation with a response, but they might have said, as Gale does when Ed accuses the Snopes brothers of being a bad influence, 'we sure didn't mean to influence anybody'.

As far as the Coen brothers are concerned, ethnicity is essential to character identity: 'If you want to make a character specific, his ethnicity is part of who he is.' In their view, if characters are to have validity, the filmmaker has to be 'specific about how they talk, and how they behave, how they do everything. And their ethnicity is naturally going to be part of that' (Allen 2006: 124–125). Thus to lend their characters the necessary specificity, the Coens give them an exaggerated drawl accentuating a (supposedly) Southwestern dialect. This regional idiom, at least in the Coens' imagination, is peppered with colourful expressions, many of which are voiced by Nathan Arizona Sr. Describing his employees, the unpainted furniture baron says, 'Without my say-so they wouldn't piss with their pants on fire.' Speaking to an employee on the phone, Nathan Sr. barks: 'Yeah, and if a frog had wings, he wouldn't bump his ass a-hoppin'.'

Cultural stereotyping is reinforced by costume and make-up. Criminal types like Hi and the Snopes brothers wear flamboyant floral-pattern shirts. Glen's attire reflects his personality: gaudy and tasteless. In his TV commercials wealthy businessman Nathan Arizona appears in a cheap polyester suit and cowboy hat. Hairstyles also comment on social class. After their jailbreak the Snopes brothers get spruced up by slicking their hair back with a thick layer of pomade, a practice only the 'greasers' of a past era would consider a cosmetic improvement. Meanwhile, Hi's disheveled hair seems to fly in all directions, at times sticking straight up like Woody Woodpecker's spiky head tuft. Ethan recalls that during the filming Nicolas Cage was 'obsessed by his hair, like Woody Woodpecker. The more depressed the character was, the more flamboyant the tuft became. There was a curious capillary rapport!' (Allen 2006: 29).

It should hardly be surprising that *Raising Arizona* relies on stereotyping for comedic effects. Stereotypes are common in many forms of comedy, especially situation comedy and stand-up routines. More to the point, in one form or another, stereotypes of gender, race and ethnicity have always been a staple of mainstream Hollywood comedies. Unlike the classic Hollywood comedies of Sturges and Hawks, whose stereotypes are drawn from the middle- and upper-classes, the Coens choose to focus on lower-class 'trailer trash'. Their residence is a tiny mobile home parked in an expanse of desert on the edge of town, which Hi politely refers to as 'suburban Tempe'. After his release from prison, Hi takes a job 'drilling holes in sheet metal' where his workmate Bud (M. Emmet Walsh) regales him with bizarre stories from his paramedic days about severed body parts found on the highway, stories that Bud finds hilarious. Hi is surrounded by such idiots. His company during stints in the county jail consists of moronic cell mates and dunces like the Snopes brothers who are quite happy to think of crime as their professional calling. 'Work,' says Evelle, 'is what's kept *us* happy.' The world outside of prison does not offer Hi much better. Hi's foreman Glen is a bigoted fool who thinks tasteless Polish jokes are hilarious. The real joke, however, is that Glen, who stereotypes 'Polacks' as stupid, is the one who looks stupid, so stupid in fact that he can't even tell his simple-minded Polack jokes right. Rather than mocking the local ethnicity, as some may have thought, Glen's lame attempts at joke-telling reveal ethnic stereotyping for what it really is: an expression of stupidity. The Coens' stereotyping operates on a much different level and serves very different purposes than Glen's mindless jokes.

*Theories of Laughter and Humour*

A major objection to the humour in *Raising Arizona* is that it assumes a posture of superiority toward its characters, a concern first voiced by Sheila Benson who thought that the film came 'swathed in a caul of superiority towards its characters'. Subsequent commentary reinforces Benson's critique. In R. Barton Palmer's view, the Coens' *oeuvre* generally manifests 'a consistent authorial tone, an unsympathetic, cynical, and derisive attitude toward the characters and their desires for success or release' (2004: 54). Historically, the idea that superiority is the basis of humour has its origins in ancient Greek philosophers like Plato and Aristotle. The superiority theory was promoted by the eighteenth-century English philosopher Thomas Hobbes, whose view of humour is based on the presupposition that all humans compete for social power or status. In this eternal struggle for advantage, when our competitors fail, we feel successful or superior. Humour, therefore, arises from the pleasurable recognition that we are better, or better off, than others who have failed and are thus inferior. To the charge of superiority the Coens plead innocent. If some viewers were offended by the characters, say the Coens, it was not their intention to be condescending. Says Joel, 'the characters were certainly supposed to be sympathetic. We got a lot of pleasure out of writing them' (Allen 2006: 32).

Another philosophy of humour better suited to account for Coen comedy was advanced by the eighteenth-century German philosopher Immanuel Kant, who proposed an aesthetic of humour and laughter based on the principle of incongruity. As Kant explains, when we encounter something that does not correspond with or violates our routine expectations, it causes laughter. Laughter arises when there is a discrepancy between abstract concepts of the normative and that which in everyday experience exceeds the bounds of normality. He also emphasises the physical aspect of amusement. The pleasure of humour, Kant theorises, is not the kind of 'high' pleasure we experience in the contemplation of aesthetic beauty or the sublime delight we take in moral goodness. For Kant, humour is a sensory experience based on feelings of physical, visceral well-being that come to expression in laughter.

In *Raising Arizona* the Coen brothers exploit the comic potential of incongruity fully, generating comedy by juxtaposing characters as opposites and forcing them into incongruous relationships and absurd situations. Actually, the entire narrative hinges on the central (laughable) incongruity of marrying Hi, a recidivist convict, with Ed, the straight-arrow cop, a disjunction visually highlighted in their wedding ceremony, where half of the celebrants gathered for the occasion consists of Hi's criminal friends dressed in Hi's fashion-signature floral shirts, while the other half, representing Ed, are policemen dressed in dark monochromatic uniforms. One of the most striking incongruities is certainly Hi's double-voiced speech – the humorous disjunction, that is, between the elevated, faux-literary diction of his voiceover narration and the generally dim-witted remarks of his spoken dialogue. In his voiceover monologues Hi often holds forth in a style that is oddly philosophical and sage. Lying in his jail bunk, he spouts lines of melancholy jail poetry: 'The joint is a lonely place after lock-up and lights out, when the last of the cons has been swept away by the sandman.' Speaking of Ed's obsessive need for a child to complete the McDunnough 'family unit', Hi waxes philosophical: 'Her point was that there was too much love and beauty for just the two of us and every day we kept a child out of the world was a day he might later regret having missed.' Describing Ed's infertility, Hi intones with biblical inflection: 'Her insides were a barren place where my seed could find no purchase.' Speaking of the Lone Biker of the Apocalypse, Hi's rhetoric assumes a folksy kind of literariness: 'I didn't know where he came from or why. I didn't know if he was dream or vision. But I feared that I myself had unleashed him for he was The Fury That Would Be, as soon as Florence Arizona found her little Nathan gone.' Indeed, even Hi's nightmare-vision of the Lone Biker is rendered with poetic flourish: 'He left a scorched earth in his wake, befouling even the sweet desert breeze that whipped across his brow.' At the end of his story the idiot-poet in Hi ascends to new heights of lyricism: 'That night I had a dream ... I dreamt I was as light as ether, a floating spirit visiting things to come ... The shades and shadows of the people in my life wrestled their way into my slumber.'

In comic contrast to the elevated style of his voiceover narration, Hi's spoken dialogue reveals a simpler mind. When, for instance, Hi asks for Ed's hand in marriage, he proudly announces, 'I'm walkin' in here on my knees, Ed, a free man proposing', completely oblivious to the hilariously mixed metaphor he has concocted. When Ed begins to worry about the moral implications of kidnapping Nathan Jr. Hi responds with absurd illogic: 'Well now, honey, we been over this and over this. There's what's right and there's what's right, and never the twain shall meet.' His crude, unenlightened dialogue is consistent with his 'bone-head' behaviour: locking himself out of his own car during a 7-Eleven stick-up or punching his boss in the face.

Another form of humorous incongruity in *Raising Arizona* is the paradox of adults acting like children. Needless to say, Hi is a man who still acts like a kid, the 'bad boy' who fails to mature into a productive, law-abiding man. Chronically incapable of assuming the adult responsibilities of husband and father Hi seems destined to return continually to jail, his repeated imprisonments a metaphor for his infantile return to the womb-like security of incarceration. The Snopes brothers, reminders of Hi's regressive tendencies, also act like spoiled children, loafing around in Hi's trailer home, eating junk food and generally causing a mess. Like defiant kids, they refuse to observe Ed's house rules. When something goes wrong they scream at the top of their lungs, as happens (several times) when they realise that they have sped off and left the kidnapped baby in the middle of the highway. Their lack of mature development is given symbolic shape during their escape from prison. Turning sight gag into a visual metaphor of childbirth, Gale crawls from a hole in the ground, amid mud and pouring rain, as if emerging from the womb. Reaching back into the mud hole, he assists Evelle's emergence in a kind of breach birth. Then, covered in muck and mire, they both begin to howl with infantile enthusiasm in celebration of their entry into the outside world of adults. Glen is not much farther along in his emotional development. The proverbial 'bad father', he imposes no limits on his children's behaviour and acts like one of the kids, encouraging their childish pranks and joining in. Aside from Ed, who also has some childish moments, the only characters who consistently act with adult restraint are, ironically, the babies. The Arizona quints are never seen to fuss like real-life babies. In the published screenplay the Coens compare them to 'a small but distinguished panel on *Meet the Press*' (2002: 139). Nathan Jr. is especially notable in this regard. Even when he is knocked off the roof of the Snopes' getaway car, baby Nathan is always seen peacefully observing the adults around him as they howl in fits of hysteria.

Another theory of laughter and humour applicable to *Raising Arizona* is found in Freud's study *Jokes and their Relation to the Unconscious* (1905), which proposes the idea that the function of jokes and laughter is to assist in the regulation of the psychic economy, releasing pent-up energy caused by repression, thus often referred to as the 'relief theory'. In Freud's psychoanalytic view, humour and laughter work to breech

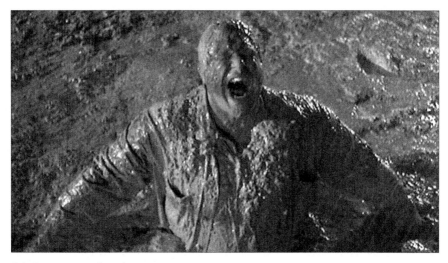
Gale Snopes emerges from the sewer.

the boundaries of repression, giving sublimated expression to forbidden feelings or thoughts, momentarily suspending social limits on propriety and transgressing cultural taboos, especially those relating to sexuality and destructive anti-social behaviours. Laughter and humour have the power to transform what would otherwise be acts of destructive violence into occasions for laughter, instances of which abound in *Raising Arizona*. The release theory applies particularly to the excesses of 'low' comedy which drive the humour in the film, drawn from early Hollywood slapstick as well as from contemporary cartoon mayhem. Here we should note the proximity of Freud to Bakhtin's theory of humour where Bakhtin stresses that humour is linked to 'the lower stratum of the body, the life of the belly and reproductive organs' (1984a: 21). In his study *Rabelais and His World*, Bakhtin brands this kind of humour 'carnivalesque', a form of comedy derived from the medieval celebration of carnival as a publically sanctioned period of freedom from restraints on social behaviour, a time of farce, masquerade and role reversals. As Bakhtin demonstrates in his analysis of Rabelais' fiction, the carnivalesque puts on display bodily functions otherwise repressed by social taboos, inventing a literary style Bakhtin calls 'grotesque realism'. In this way Rabelais is able to bring the body and its material world into the abstract realm of art, enacting a comic degradation of 'high' art by bringing it 'down to earth'. The degrading humour of the carnivalesque has an important social function too, working to defeat hierarchies of power and class differences by setting aside social divisions, creating a social space of freedom and equality. As residents of the 'white trash' trailer slums, Hi and Ed are surrounded by carnivalesque characters: boorish Glen who lets his tribe of brats run wild and whose idea of adult fun is wife-swapping; the Snopeses who are symbolically reborn in their prison escape but literally emerge into the outside world from the filth of the sewer; the grotesque leather-clad Lone Biker as representative of the outlaw subculture associated with the Hell's Angels motorcycle gangs while simultaneously evoking the savage post-apocalyptic bikers of the *Mad Max* movies. The Lone Biker's death by grenade also has a carnivalesque quality, playing the gross-out effects of violent corporeal dismemberment found in horror movies for 'low' comic pleasure.

Despite its reliance on carnivalesque humour, not all of the joking in *Raising Arizona* is 'low'. Among its more cerebral jests, the film includes several jokes relating to Freud. The first one occurs during the McDunnough's visit to a gynecologist who explains to them the cause of Ed's infertility using a Freudian sight gag. To illustrate Ed's 'barrenness' the doctor uses his cigar – an obviously Freudian phallic symbol – to point out the female reproductive organs on his anatomical chart. Other Freud jokes are made in passing comments by Evelle, as when he gives Ed parenting advice on breast-feeding: 'Ya don't breast feed him, he'll hate you for it later. That's why we wound up in prison' – alluding to the reductive Freudian cliché that childhood trauma leaves an indelible mark on the psyche. This cliché is repeated visually for comic emphasis in a close-up of Smalls' tattoos, one of which bears the inscription 'Momma Didn't Love Me'. The jesting with Freud is elevated to another level in the mythic symbolism attending the Lone Biker of the Apocalypse, who in Freud's terms represents Hi's *doppelgänger,* his psychic 'double' or dark alter-ego. As Freud explains in his essay 'The Uncanny', the *doppelgänger* is a manifestation of 'the return of the repressed,' an event arousing in us 'dread and creeping horror' (1955: 217). Freud illustrates his theory of the uncanny with a fictional story by German writer E. T. A. Hoffmann entitled 'The Sandman', where in keeping with Freud's oedipal theory, the uncanny *doppelgänger* (the titular 'Sandman') is symbolic of the protagonist's dread at the return of his castrating father. In a broader sense, the Freudian *doppelgänger* represents any repressed or disavowed conflict that returns to consciousness, typically as a dangerous and destructive force. The eruption of the *doppelgänger* from the unconscious breaks through the barriers of repression, releasing pent-up psychic energy in acts of violent destruction.

A central theme of *Raising Arizona* is the tension between Hi's desire for domesticity and his compulsion to rob 7-Elevens. Hi wages a war between his civilised self and the outlaw *doppelgänger* inside him. The Snopes brothers (themselves a literalised form of the 'double') serve to remind Hi that the outlaw is his 'true nature'. Gale and Evelle (whose name suggestively conflates both 'evil' and Eve, the biblical temptress) are humorous embodiments of Hi's dark side, agents of the *doppelgänger* risen from Hi's unconscious to draw him back into a life of crime. As Hi's psychic twin, the Lone Biker is frightening precisely because he represents the return of Hi's repressed yearning for the outlaw life. As such, he presents a threat to the happy idyll of marriage and family Hi hopes to create. As if rising from Hi's unconscious, the Lone Biker appears out of nowhere, a figure rising from the darkness of Hi's dreams to become a mythic embodiment of Hi's repressed criminal and self-destructive tendencies. *Raising Arizona* parodies this release of destructive energy in comically intensified images, as when the Lone Biker appears in Hi's dream-vision bursting through a wall of hellish flames, erupting into life as a force of ruthless devastation destroying every creature that crosses his path, especially the 'little creatures' – cute bunny rabbits, tiny colourful lizards, even the house fly Smalls snatches out of thin air.

When *New York Times* film critic Vincent Canby accuses the Coens of over-quoting other movies, complaining that the copious references in *Raising Arizona* 'seem mostly a film-school affectation', he echoes a number of critics who found the movie's central fault in its over-reliance on the kind of postmodernist pastiche that Jon Lewis has labeled 'in-jokes for a new in-crowd' (2002: 110). Again, the critics assume that this kind of referential play indicates the filmmakers' attitude of superiority toward their viewers. Certainly, the humour in Arizona is a different kind of joking. But if not an expression of intellectual elitist superiority, what then?

Philosopher Ted Cohen offers several alternatives to the superiority theory of humour that detractors attribute to the Coens. In his study *Jokes: Philosophical Thoughts on Joking Matters* Cohen theorises that jokes have two basic functions. The first function, rooted in the Freudian release theory, is to give expression to psychic energies that have been repressed by cultural taboos. Cohen's second, more useful definition of humour concerns the joke's capacity for creating a relationship between teller and listener. In contrast to the comedic clowning of slapstick comedy, which relies mainly on pranks and sight-gags that have a direct and visceral impact, jokes – understood as verbal texts – make us think. Several jokes of this variety are told in the movie, for example, the simple joke Hi tells Ed as a way of flirting: 'Hear about the paddy-wagon collided with a cee-ment mixer, Ed? … Twelve hardened criminals escaped.' To get the humour of such a joke the listener must understand the punch line, which requires the listener to join the teller in a thought process that establishes what Cohen calls 'a special kind of intimacy' in the recognition of the humour. When the joke is told badly – as when Glen tries to tell Polack jokes – the intimate relationship fails. In Bakhtinian terms, all jokes foster a 'dialogical community' by creating a shared understanding between joke teller and recipient. Such a dialogical approach to jokes is useful in explaining how postmodern pastiche generates humour. When the reader or viewer recognises a quotation and its source, a relationship of intellectual familiarity is established. Like the punch line of a common joke, the so-called 'in-joke' produces the gratification of shared recognition. For this reason postmodern pastiche is often characterised in general as 'jokey'. Fundamental to the aesthetics of postmodernism is the production of texts that generate the most referential *resonance*, maximising the dialogical exchange between texts and between texts and audience. In the 1980s some might have still considered such 'in-joking' an elitist practice, but from today's perspective, referential humour has become conventional, even mainstream, practiced not just by elite artists but in every form of mass media, especially television advertising.

By embedding in-jokes from a wide spectrum of sources, literary as well as filmic, *Raising Arizona* engages its viewers in an entertaining game of recognition. Thus, the biker-bounty-hunter's name, 'Lenny Smalls', is an allusion to John Steinbeck's *Of Mice and Men*, a novel featuring a dim-witted giant-of-a-man named Lennie Small who, like the Coens' Lenny Smalls, takes perverse pleasure in hurting small creatures. Smalls himself is likened to a creature when he says, 'I'm a tracker. Some say, part hound-dog.' Ed calls the biker a 'warthog from hell', an appellation borrowed from Southern writer Flannery O'Connor, whom the Coens name as a point of reference for *Raising Arizona* (Allen 2006: 26). The name of Hi's jailbird buddies, the Snopses, signals the Coens' referential play with another Southern writer, William Faulkner. The surname 'Snopes' is pirated from Faulkner's so-called 'Snopes Trilogy', which includes the novels *The Hamlet* (1940), *The Town* (1957) and *The Mansion* (1959). Set in the fictional rural county of Yoknapatawpha, Mississippi, Faulkner's trilogy narrates the family history of the Snopes clan, rural Southerners who speak a regional dialect rich in American vernacularisms and whose quirky first names (Flem, Lump, Mink and I. O.) resemble characters' names in *Raising Arizona*, in particular 'H. I.' McDonnough. Populating his stories with a grotesque assortment of provincials, Faulkner exploits these human oddities and their eccentricities to create trenchant black humour. These are ready-made models for the rubes of the Coens' Arizona-of-the-mind. The same can be said of O'Connor's characters who also have unusual names, like Hazel Motes, the atheist preacher in her first novel *Wise Blood* (1952), a man on a mission to spread the 'gospel of anti-religion'. (*Wise Blood* was adapted in 1979 by John Huston, one of the Coens' favourite filmmakers.) More than just sources of odd-ball names, the fiction of these Southern writers offers itself as a rich source of darkly comic narratives that comment satirically on the moral and social injustices of an earlier period of American culture, though in many ways not so different from the world of *Raising Arizona*.

Along with these literary citations there are abundant references to cinematic texts. For instance, when Hi says 'Sometimes it's a hard world for little things' he is quoting lines spoken by actress Lillian Gish in *The Night of the Hunter* (1955), Charles Laughton's Gothic tale of a sinister Southern preacher (Robert Mitchum) who stalks little children in the night. Hi recites these very words just after awaking from his night-mare vision of the boogie-man biker stalking Nathan Jr., seen in a cut-away blowing up a harmless little rabbit with a grenade. The Lone Biker also references the Australian *Mad Max* movies by George Miller, set in a post-apocalyptic world populated by savage motorcycle thugs. The image of the Lone Biker's burning boot – all that remains after Hi, with no little poetic justice, has blown him to bits with a grenade – presents a direct (and darkly humorous) visual quotation of the first film in the series, *Mad Max* (1979), where the footwear left on the highway belongs to Max's brutally murdered wife. Surely one of *Raising Arizona's* most obscure 'in-jokes' references Stanley Kubrick's *Dr. Strangelove* (1964). In the scene following their jail break, as the Snopes brothers clean up and slick their hair in a public toilet, we see written on the washroom door the letters P.O.E., reverse-reflected in a mirror as E.O.P. Those familiar with Kubrick's movie will recall that these letters are abbreviations for the phrases 'purity of essence' or 'our precious essence' – the secret code needed to stop a catastrophic nuclear attack in Kubrick's dark satire on the Soviet-American Cold War. Later, on the trail of Nathan Jr., the Lone Biker's mythical aura as avatar of the Apocalypse is visually emphasised when he too visits the encoded washroom, linking his image with Kubrick's vision of nuclear apocalypse.

In *Problems of Dostoevsky's Poetics*, Mikhail Bakhtin introduces the concept of the 'hidden polemic' in artistic discourse, arguing that every artistic text, regardless of apparent intent, refers to or anticipates a dialogue with a plurality of responses. Without exception, every artistic text 'senses its own listener, reader, critic, and reflects in itself their anticipated objections, evaluations, points of view' (1984b: 107). The artistic text 'senses alongside itself another discourse, another style' – the style of peers, rivals and precursors, which it may reject or try to replace, or to which it might also pay tribute, honour and seek to emulate. The text's sensitivity to its potential inter-locutors also has socio-political consequences. As Linda Hutcheon explains in *The Politics of Postmodernism*, the self-reflexive parody of postmodernism underscores 'the realization that all cultural forms of representation – literary, visual, aural – in high art or the mass media are ideologically grounded' and thus 'cannot avoid involvement with social and political relations and apparatuses' (1989: 3). Any work of art, particu-larly one as self-consciously situated in the history and culture of American society as *Raising Arizona*, is inherently aware of its audience and reception; it is constructed to anticipate and invite dialogical responses and readings. Ethan and Joel Coen might disavow any intention to make political, moral or philosophical statements, claiming that their films, especially an absurd comedy like *Raising Arizona*, have been emptied of 'serious' meaning. Whether intended or not, the film has nevertheless stimulated numerous socio-political readings, ranging from Erica Rowell's broad assessment of the movie as an 'indictment of capitalist greed' (2007: 59), to Richard Gilmore's more tentative observation that it offers a 'fairly piquant critique of America' (2009: 21). Like these interpreters and others, I think one can reasonably discern in *Raising Arizona* varying degrees of social consciousness, however elusive and hidden beneath its layers of comedic farce. The voice of critique might be nearly drowned out by the movie's cartoon zaniness, but here as in all their subsequent films, the Coens drop hints, often obscure, insinuating but never fully enunciating a submerged commen-tary on American society. Speaking of *Raising Arizona*, one interviewer observed that the Coens like popular culture, yet at the same time take an ironic stance toward it. The Coens responded: 'Yes, we have that relationship with American popular culture. We have *an attitude, a commentary* with regard to the material. We make *jokes* with it' (Allen 2006: 32; emphasis added). If we take them at their word, *Raising Arizona* does appear to convey an 'attitude' towards popular culture, even if it is all but smoth-ered by silly jokes. Like their favourite filmmaker Preston Sturges, whose comedies examine the social conventions and mores of American culture with cynical wit, the Coens understand that comedy, parody and satire are often more effective forms for purveying commentary than the explicitly ideological social problem drama.

With a southwest desert setting as the stage for its characters' cowboy/gunslinger antics, *Raising Arizona* first invites a reading as a parody of the Hollywood western. A cartoon version of the cinematic Wild West, the Coens' filmscape is shaped fundamen-tally by the tropes of the western, including outlaws, gun fights and bank robberies, culminating in a final *High Noon* (1950) showdown between Hi and Smalls in the dusty street fronting the 'hayseed bank' of La Grange. The generic parody is embellished with the appropriate details such as the long-coat dusters worn by the Snopes brothers during the bank robbery and their use of the old-time word 'scatter-gun', as well as the long-barrel Colt revolver that Nathan Sr. (who also wears a cowboy hat) brandishes when he catches Hi and Ed returning Nathan Jr.

Within and beyond the generic parody of the Hollywood western, *Raising Arizona* reads as satire on the mythology of national identity. Among other things, it lampoons the American love affair with firearms. In the Coens' vision of America, everyone seems to own a gun and is anxious to use it. Hi, the Snopes brothers and the Lone Biker all serve as cartoonish send-ups of the American outlaw, and the police are caricatured as reckless, state-authorised gunslingers. Even average folks like convenience store clerks and grocery store managers are armed to the teeth and eager to pull the trigger. This comically exaggerated depiction of American gun culture also contributes to a reading of *Raising Arizona* as spoof of the American romance with the outlaw as the dark side of the American pioneer spirit. Hi confirms the myth when he claims, in defense of his criminal tendencies, that he comes from 'a long line of frontiersmen and outdoor types'. In the Coens' contemporary 'Wild West' story Americans are still gun-toting frontiersmen and contemporary American society is just as violent as the imaginary Old West inscribed in the national imagination by the motion picture industry for over a century. As Gilmore observes, the Wild West violence so relentlessly satirised in *Raising Arizona* 'reflects something deep in the nature of capitalism' (2009: 21) linked with its underlying ethos of cut-throat competition. This American spirit of competitiveness is most clearly brought to expression in Nathan Arizona, the shamelessly self-promoting merchandising tycoon who typifies the aggressively competitive attitude needed for success in a free enterprise economy. His contentious attitude is evident in his blustery egotism and in his hostile arrogance toward other people, especially toward his employees whom he berates as incompetent fools. His motto is: 'Do it my way or watch your butt.' His advertising slogan epitomises his compulsive self-promotion: 'And if you can find lower prices anywhere, my name ain't Nathan Arizona.' In truth, his name *ain't* Nathan Arizona, but Nathan Huffhines, a Jewish name he had changed in order to market himself more effectively in the furniture business. A send-up of the American businessman, Nathan Arizona is the first in a series of bad bosses that become familiar fixtures in the Coens' body of work.

The kidnapping and the repeated attempts by various parties to re-kidnap little Nathan drive the plot, but also function as (comically exaggerated) instances of the competition for commodities that drives market capitalism. The purloined baby becomes the most valuable asset in the marketplace and as such a metaphor for the material goods Americans ruthlessly compete for in their pursuit of the American Dream. To Ed and Hi's way of thinking, Nathan Arizona, the rich business tycoon, has more than his share of the wealth, so why not steal one of his babies? 'We thought it was unfair,' Hi comments, 'that some should have so many while other should have so few.' Thus, the crime of kidnapping is morally justified as a Robin Hood method of redistributing wealth, and Hi and Ed's simple-minded rebellion against economic injustice can be ideologically sanctioned as an act of 'underground socialism' (Gilmore

2009: 22). In the struggle between the haves and the have-nots in *Raising Arizona* the McDunnoughs are not the only couple who covet the Arizona's wealth of offspring. Glen and Dot are also greedy consumers, conniving to possess the baby, even though they already have more than they can handle. The Snopes brothers join the competition for Nathan Jr., initially seeing the child's value only in terms of a monetary reward, but quickly growing fond of him. The biker bounty hunter sees the 'little critter' strictly as a market commodity, to be sold to the highest bidder, if not to Nathan Sr., then on the black market, where Smalls himself had been brought and sold when he was just an infant.

Set in 1983, early in the two-term presidency of Republican conservative Ronald Reagan, the story of the McDunnoughs and their attempts to realise the American Dream can be read broadly as a comically satirical comment on capitalism in the era of 'trickle-down' economics and its ideological commitment to the 'free market' as the 'natural' way of distributing wealth in a capitalist democracy. To sharpen the satiric point, *Raising Arizona* targets specific political figures who conceived and promoted the market philosophy of Reaganomics. Remarking on his efforts to find a place in the current economy, Hi complains that he tried 'to stand up and fly straight, but it wasn't easy with that sumbitch Reagan in the White House. I dunno, they say he's a decent man, so maybe his advisors are confused.' If this isolated reference, mentioned in passing, were the only jab at American politicians in *Raising Arizona*, it would do little to support a reading of the movie as political satire. There are, however, additional hints embedded in the movie's *mise-en-scène* that point to extra-textual contexts.

Historically speaking, the state of Arizona is the appropriate setting for a critique of neo-conservative political ideology. In the 1960s Arizona senator Barry Goldwater was instrumental in forging a new, more aggressive Republican strategy. Goldwater, who ran for president in 1964, did much to bolster the resurgence of the Republican Party after the Kennedy-Johnson administration, making possible the eventual success of Richard M. Nixon, elected to the presidency in 1968 and again in 1972. Significantly, Goldwater's portrait appears in several scenes, silently presiding over the proceedings in the parole room of the Maricopa County jail, where the wax-like figures of the parole board meet to assess Hi's fitness for social reintegration. Later we hear from the Snopes brothers that they got the idea for the La Grange hold-up from 'a guy in the joint named Lawrence Spivey, one of Dick Nixon's undersecretaries of agriculture', in jail for soliciting sex from a state trooper – a reminder that America's elected officials are often no better (perhaps worse) than common criminals.

The Coens have said, somewhat axiomatically, that they can't make a movie, even a dark or serious one, without adding a little comedy. Perhaps this axiom also applies in reverse: They can't make a comedy without at least a substratum of seriousness. They may hide their seriousness behind a cartoonish façade, disguising cultural critique as silly slapstick, but inevitably they take an 'attitude' toward their stories and characters, an attitude congruent with the fictions of William Faulkner, Flannery O'Connor and Preston Sturges, and for that matter, with the *Road Runner* adventures of Wile E. Coyote.

CHAPTER THREE

# Miller's Crossing: 'A Handsome Movie about Men in Hats'

Pursuing their desire to do something different with each film, the Coens followed the zany comedy of *Raising Arizona* with a sombre take on gangster movies. According to Joel, 'we didn't want to do another out-and-out comedy, like *Raising Arizona*. We wanted to do something that was a little bit morbid. Less of a comedy, more of a drama. We've always liked gangster movies, so it was what we started to think about when we did another script' (Allen 2006: 37). The result is a film that tips its hat to gangster movies but moves beyond familiar generic formulas to create a story and characters more accurately classified as film noir. In their third feature film the Coens return to the dark world of crime introduced in *Blood Simple*, but instead of the desert wasteland of 1980s Texas, the setting of *Miller's Crossing* shifts to the Prohibition era to tell the story of a cynical and enigmatic gangster, Tom Reagan (Gabriel Byrne), who knows all the angles and how to play them to his advantage. The intricate and elaborately imagined filmstory, inspired by the novels of Dashiell Hammett, chronicles the clash of two crime bosses, the contentious Italian underboss, Johnny Caspar (Jon Polito), and the ruling Irish mob chieftain, Leo O'Bannon (Albert Finney), who both vie for control of a corrupt municipal government that fronts the criminal subculture of an unnamed east-coast city, circa 1929.

The intricate plot is driven by the conflict caused by Leo's ill-advised decision to protect a small-time bookie named Bernie Bernbaum (John Turturro) who crosses Caspar by selling information on fixed boxing matches. When Caspar demands that Bernie be 'bumped' for violating the code of ethics which, he argues, ensures the stability of the underground criminal economy, Leo balks, not, as he claims, because Bernie has bought Leo's protection, but because the crooked bookie's sister, Verna (Marcia Gay Harden), has become the object of Leo's romantic affection. Tom, who serves as Leo's advisor and confidant, disagrees with his boss, but fails to convince him that he is

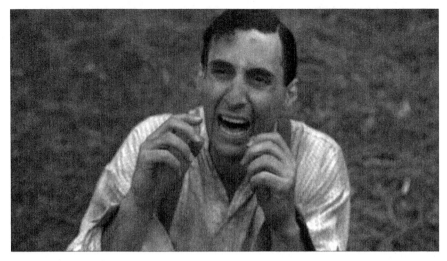

Bernie begs for his life.

making a 'bad play'. Meanwhile, Tom is having an affair with Verna, which he later confesses to Leo, breaking the bond of trust between them and forcing Tom to side with Johnny Caspar against his partner and friend in the impending gang war.

To prove his loyalty to Caspar, Tom must reveal Bernie's whereabouts and is subsequently forced by Caspar's gunsels, Frankie (Mike Starr) and Tic-Tac (Al Mancini), to execute the chiseling bookmaker at a secluded forest killing ground known as Miller's Crossing. When Bernie begs Tom to spare his life with dramatic pathos, Tom relents and lets Bernie live. Later, Tom's failure to murder Bernie leads to unexpected complications when the bookie returns to blackmail him. Additional complications arise when Caspar's henchman Eddie Dane (J. E. Freeman) insists on double-checking for Bernie's corpse, which, fortunately for Tom, has been replaced by another belonging to Mink (Steve Buscemi), one of Bernie's 'amigos'. Amid the increasing violence of the warring gangster factions, Tom engineers a complicated intrigue. First he persuades Johnny Caspar that the Dane and 'his boy' Mink were in cahoots and they, not Bernie, had been double-crossing him, whereupon Caspar murders the Dane brutally, saving Tom from the Dane's stranglehold. Tom then tells Caspar that he has arranged a meet with Mink that night at his apartment, giving Caspar an opportunity for revenge. Tom also arranges a coinciding parley with Bernie. When Caspar shows up at Tom's apartment to murder Mink, he is ambushed and killed by Bernie. Tom arrives later to meet Bernie, who believes that with his nemesis out of way, he is no longer in danger. What Bernie has not reckoned with is Tom's plan to double-cross *him* and 'tie up loose ends'. Saying that someone has to take the fall for Eddie Dane's death, Tom pulls the trigger on Bernie, despite Bernie's pathetically disingenuous reprise of his woodland pleading. In the film's final scene, set at a cemetery in a wooded locale much like the killing ground of Miller's Crossing, Verna and Leo, now engaged, attend Bernie's burial. Arriving late, Tom is scorned by Verna, who exits with the only car, leaving Tom and Leo to walk back to town. Leo now realises that Tom had made a 'smart play' by pretending to cross over to Caspar and forgives him, offering Tom renewed friendship and his former job. Tom rejects Leo's bid for reconciliation, and when the two men part ways, we sense that something important is still unsaid.

Premiered at the 1990 New York Film Festival, *Miller's Crossing* hit theatres at a time when gangster movies were enjoying renewed popularity. Possibly because commentators too were overwhelmed by the surfeit of neo-gangster films also released that year, including Martin Scorsese's *Goodfellas*, Francis Ford Coppola's *The Godfather III* and Abel Ferarra's *King of New York*, the popular critical response to the Coens' third feature was underwhelming. A few critics praised *Miller's Crossing* for its intelligent genre deconstruction and for its astute adaptation of Dashiell Hammett. Geoff Andrew of *Time Out* wrote that the film 'operates both on the surface, as a genre film, and on a deeper level, as an ironic commentary on that genre which, though witty, never lapses into simple parody'. Steve Jenkins thought that *Miller's Crossing*'s 'particular strength derives from a sense that the filmmakers have tapped a kind of essence of Hammett, outside any specific theme or plot'. Other reviewers questioned the filmmakers' motives; as with their previous two movies, the critics took issue with the Coens' presumed emphasis on style over substance. Writing for the *New Yorker*, Terrence Rafferty sums up this view: 'The picture seems to have no life of its own, and the Coens' formal control and meticulously crafted ironies become, after a while, rather depressing.' Objecting to the movie's pastiche aesthetic, Rafferty observes that the film 'is not so much a gangster movie as an extended, elaborate allusion to one'. Roger Ebert agreed, focusing his critique on visual stylisation: 'This doesn't look like a gangster movie, it looks like a commercial intended to look like a gangster movie.' Sheila Benson of the *Los Angeles Times* thought the Coens' 'empty formalism' made the movie 'emotionally remote', as did Gary Giddins of *Village Voice*, who wrote that 'Joel and Ethan Coen may represent the apotheosis of classroom cinema [but] *Miller's Crossing* is so clever about its sources [...] that it has little life of its own'.

In contrast to the frenetic cartoon-like exuberance of *Raising Arizona*, *Miller's Crossing* moves at a stately, almost languid pace, winding its way through a plot that relies less on fast-paced action than on quick-witted dialogue and the complexities of the story's emotional entanglements. With careful attention to production design and period accuracy, the story unfolds in a fictional gangland milieu where style is paramount and fashion, especially in men's apparel, takes precedence over the violent action of a generic gangster movie. When asked by cinematographer Barry Sonnenfeld how to conceptualise the movie's visual style, the brothers answered, somewhat cryptically, 'It should be a handsome movie about men in hats' (DVD Extra, 'Shooting Miller's Crossing'). Ultimately, *Miller's Crossing* is about much more than that, but many of the movie's commentators focused on its elegant style, overlooking the psychological depths explored in the film's astute study of masculine friendship. If we take the Coens at their word and dismiss *Miller's Crossing* as merely 'a handsome movie about men in hats', we risk falling into a hermeneutic trap set for the unwary viewer. Despite what the Coens invite us to assume, the film is more than a retro gangster pastiche. Closer study of its intertextual dynamics shows that the 'handsome' surface masks a subversive undercurrent challenging established notions of the gangster genre. Like its characters, *Miller's Crossing* is a film with hidden motives which are best uncovered by studying the filmmakers' creative rewriting of Dashiell Hammett's *roman noir*.

### 'A Shameless Rip-Off of Hammett'

Rafferty's comment that *Miller's Crossing* is 'an extended, elaborate allusion' to gangster movies articulates a misperception that the Coens do little to discourage. No doubt, the movie's self-conscious use of generic conventions gives the appearance of a gangster pastiche constructed from established conventions of setting, narrative and iconography: Prohibition-era mobsters wearing expensive pin-striped suits and fedora hats, driving vintage Model-T autos and drinking bootleg whiskey (called 'paint'); corrupt city officials upholding a façade of legality while gangsters run the political machine behind the scenes; violent gun fights between warring criminal factions and cold-blooded assassinations. Add to these elements a visual style that replicates the cinematographic realism of 1930s gangster movies and it's easy to see why some commentators could mistake *Miller's Crossing* for 'an abstract distillation of the gangster genre' (Brown 1991). But the film is more than a pastiche of gangster movie clichés embroidered with clever 'hard-boiled' dialogue. In fact, apart from stock generic trappings, the Coens incorporate relatively few recognisable citations actually meriting the derogatory label of pastiche. Some have suggested that the opening scene is a gloss on the opener of Coppola's *The Godfather* (1972) (Mottram 2000: 65–66). The low-key lighting and dark wooden décor of Leo's office is thought to resemble the room where Vito Corleone, surrounded by advisors, receives supplicants asking 'favours' on the day of his daughter's wedding. The Don's homily about friendship and loyalty is echoed in Johnny Caspar's opening speech on the necessity of ethics, and in his request that Leo grant him a favour by giving him permission to kill a crooked bookie. Analogously, it has also been suggested that the final shot of Tom at Bernie's burial recalls the image of Michael Corleone in the final scene of *The Godfather II* (1974), even as the forest setting of the final scene of *Miller's Crossing* glosses the final scene of Carol Reed's film noir *The Third Man* (1949) (Mottram 2000: 67).

Other possible references to genre precursors prove equally random and insubstantial. When Tom strikes a match on the police chief's badge, for instance, we might recall a similar gesture of defiance by Tony Camonte in Howard Hawks' *Scarface* (1932). Naming Caspar's henchman 'The Dane' could be an allusion to the protagonist of Robert Siodmak's *The Killers* (1949), called 'The Swede'. These instances and others are plausible points of reference, but compared with *Miller's Crossing*'s extensive and fully integrated adaptation of Hammett, these incidental referential in-jokes do not figure prominently in the movie's overall intertextual design. An intentional reference to Hitchcock's *Rear Window* (1954) – on a poster in Drop Johnson's room naming his boxing opponent 'Lars Thorwald' – epitomises the Coens' trivialization of movie citations and their view of cinematic precursors as secondary to the film's central project of mounting a highly literate and fully-realised adaptation of Hammett's fiction.

The Coens freely acknowledge their homage to Hammett, saying with boastful self-irony that '*Miller's Crossing* is pretty much just a shameless rip-off of Hammett, mostly his novel *The Glass Key* [1931], but to a lesser extent *Red Harvest* [1929]' (Allen 2006: 120). Emphasising the primary importance of the literary intertext, Joel explains in the film's production notes: 'We weren't thinking so much of gangster pictures, just novels.' *'Miller's Crossing,'* says Ethan, 'is a gangster story because it's a genre we're attracted to – a literary rather than a cinematic genre, by the way' (Allen 2006: 44). Building on the foundation of Hammett's early novels *The Glass Key* and *Red Harvest*, *Miller's Crossing* appropriates the narrative of the former almost wholesale, along with the central characters and a host of minor roles, infusing the dialogue with copious quotations of the novel to shape a unique adaptation that is true to its source, yet playfully inventive in its reimagining of the writer's fictional world. Hammett's influence is immediately evident in the dialogue-heavy script, which cribs shamelessly from Hammett's hard-boiled idiom. Indeed, much of the dialogue is taken directly from *The Glass Key*, and little is lost in translation. There is, for instance, a chapter in the novel in which the bootlegger Shad O'Rory and political boss Paul Madvig exchange differing views on the state of the underground criminal economy. Shad wants assurance of Madvig's protection, a service that costs the bootlegger plenty: 'Politics is politics and business is business,' says Shad. 'I've been paying my way and I'm willing to go on paying my way, but I want what I'm paying for' (1999: 648). Johnny Caspar voices similar concerns in his heated conversation with Leo: 'It's gettin' so a businessman can't expect no return from a fixed fight. [...] Listen Leo, I pay off to you every month like a greengrocer – a lot more than the Shmatte – and I'm sick a gettin' the high hat.' Neither O'Rory nor Caspar is satisfied with the answer he gets. O'Rory's warning to Madvig, 'I'm too big to take the boot from you now' (1999: 649), is echoed in Caspar's contentious response to Leo: 'You think I'm some guinea fresh off the boat and you can kick me, but I'm too big for that now.' When Eddie Dane calls Tom 'half-smart,' he is quoting Jeff Gardner, O'Rory's thug, who tells Ned Beaumont: 'What a half-smart bastard you turned out to be' (1999: 758). As the Dane drives Tom out to Miller's Crossing to check for Bernie's corpse, he assures Tom that he has pegged him correctly as a traitor, describing Tom as 'Mr. Inside-Outsky, like some Bolshevik picking up his orders from Yegg Central'. The term 'Yegg' (in criminal slang meaning safecracker or thief, but used by Hammett to mean Communist) was in Hammett's time loaded with ideological venom. In *The Glass Key* 'yegg' is used to characterise the senator Madvig is supporting for re-election, implying that the politician is morally corrupt and cannot be trusted (1999: 596).

As James Naremore points out, Hammett was 'an unusually "movie-like" author, who possessed an ear for American speech and a strong sense of the texture of modern life, including the tunes people sang, the clothes and hairstyles they wore, the furnishings in their rooms, and way they posed in magazine photographs' (1998: 63). Hammett's characters, especially his protagonists, speak in a quirky, unorthodox manner, an act of creative writing that Naremore calls 'making art out of the vernacular' (1998: 50). The Coens have studied Hammett's artful slang and take delight in impersonating the writer's gangster argot with expressions like 'dangle' and 'drift' (meaning 'to leave, make an exit'), and 'frail' or 'twist' (both meaning 'woman'). The dialogue is peppered with phrases like 'What's the rumpus?' (meaning 'what's going on?') and 'giving the high hat' (meaning 'to show disrespect'). Paradoxically, the fact that most of this slang is borrowed from Hammett is precisely what differentiates the Coens' hard-boiled idiom from that of prior gangster movies, giving it the ring of authenticity that is lacking in classic Hollywood adaptations of Hammett, such as Howard Hawks' *The Maltese Falcon* (1941) and Stuart Heisler's *The Glass Key* (1942), where Hammett's unique idiom is largely neglected and replaced with a bland movie version of tough-guy slang, presumably in the interest of making the dialogue seem more 'realistic' or at least more palatable for mainstream audiences. Clearly, one of the most notable achievements in *Miller's Crossing* is the Coens' faithful restoration of Hammett's vernacular artistry.

The narrative of *Miller's Crossing* also emulates Hammett's typically complex and convoluted plots. Like *The Glass Key*, the plot of *Miller's Crossing* is structured, in Joel's words, like 'a big jigsaw puzzle', providing a supporting structure for the character development, which the Coen brothers considered the most important aspect of the story (Robson 2007: 77). It was perhaps the puzzle-like complexity of the labyrinthine plot that caused the Coens to experience a rare case of writer's block as they struggled to complete the screenplay, breaking off at one point to 'take a vacation' during which they penned, somewhat miraculously, the entire script for *Barton Fink* in several weeks before returning to finish *Miller's Crossing*. To replicate the jigsaw complexity of *The Glass Key*, the screenplay imports and synthesises numerous plot points from Hammett's novel. Like *The Glass Key*, *Miller's Crossing* begins with a mysterious murder that initiates and drives the action but turns out to be of minor consequence. More important, Tom Reagan's duplicitous scheming, as he pits two warring factions against each other, pretending to switch loyalties as he crosses over from one side to the other, is a tactic used by the protagonist in both *Red Harvest* and *The Glass Key*. In *Red Harvest*, Hammett's Continental Op resorts to a double-cross scheme as part of a calculated strategy to cleanse a city poisoned by corruption. With a different motive, Ned Beaumont, the political fixer in *The Glass Key*, shifts his allegiance from his boss, a political powerbroker named Paul Madvig, to Paul's adversary, the bootlegger Shad O'Rory, with the hidden motive of protecting Madvig. The emotional conflict that ensues between Paul and Ned in *The Glass Key* is mirrored in *Miller's Crossing* by the troubled relations between Tom and Leo, as is their romantic rivalry for the affection of a woman. In all three stories the protagonists are in some way forced to use violence against their better judgement to attain outcomes that benefit others more than themselves.

The principal characters in *Miller's Crossing* are drawn almost entirely from *The Glass Key*. Tom Reagan's conflicted relationship with Leo is a slightly altered version of the troubled masculine friendship at the centre of *The Glass Key*. Ned Beaumont is, like Tom Reagan, the right-hand man and advisor of Paul Madvig who, like Leo O'Bannon, is the crooked political boss of a city where the power is divided between bootlegging gangsters and corrupt municipal authorities. Much like Tom's actions on behalf of Leo, Ned involves himself, at considerable personal risk, in the investigation of a murder. The murder victim is the son of a senator whom Madvig is supporting for re-election and Madvig has become a prime suspect. Analogous to the triangulated relationship of Tom, Leo and Verna, Madvig is in love with the senator's daughter, Janet Henry, who resists his romantic overtures but eventually begins an affair with Ned. The protagonists of both stories are key advisors to their shady bosses. Like Tom Reagan, Ned Beaumont is, to invoke Johnny Caspar's words, 'the man behind the man who whispers in his ear'. Both Ned and Tom are obsessive gamblers, accustomed to taking risks and prepared to lose. If they lose and fall into debt, as both Ned and Tom do, they accept the consequences without complaint. Neither Ned nor Tom is a private detective, but they both think and act like detectives, using reason and calculation instead of violence to solve problems and achieve their ends. Like Tom Reagan, Ned Beaumont is an inscrutable thinker. His inscrutability reflects Hammett's insistence on the privacy of his characters' inner life. In *The Glass Key*, as in all of Hammett's mature fiction, the reader is never given access to the protagonist's unspoken thoughts. Any knowledge of his motives must be gleaned from spoken dialogue. Tom Reagan is conceived as a similarly enigmatic figure. A master of language given to witty and often sarcastic repartee, Tom's carefully chosen words are calculated to hide his real intentions. Like his model Ned Beaumont, Tom is a wise-cracking smarty who uses verbal superiority to maintain a permanent state of ironic detachment. Tom keeps his thoughts 'under the hat', a metaphor Ned uses in *The Glass Key* to signify confidentiality (1999: 695). Literary scholar George J. Thompson advises readers of Hammett who hope to understand Beaumont's inner life and motivation to pay close attention to 'the nuances of Hammett's diction' and to 'develop an ability to surmise intention from what is not said but merely implied' (2007: 147).

Like *The Glass Key*, *Miller's Crossing* is a study in moral ambiguity, a theme emphasised in Johnny Caspar's frequent return to 'the question of ethics'. As a man whose loyalties are easily shifted to accommodate changing circumstances, Tom Reagan duplicates Ned Beaumont's questionable code of ethics. Tom proclaims loyalty to Leo but sleeps with Verna right under Leo's nose. Then, knowing it will hurt Leo, he confesses his infidelity and apparently defects to Leo's enemy, Johnny Caspar. The Dane is the only one who has insight into Tom's duplicity, commenting aptly that Tom is 'as straight as a corkscrew, Mr. Inside-Outsky'. When Caspar demands that Tom shoot Bernie Bernbaum to prove his loyalty, Tom 'looks in his heart' and decides not to execute Bernie, putting himself at great risk, perhaps more for the sake of Verna than for her unethical and unsympathetic brother. His motives are uncertain. Later, he contradicts himself, reversing his previous judgement and coldly murdering Bernie, as he says, in the interest of 'tying up loose ends' and restoring the status quo. Is it just that Tom is an ethical pragmatist who regards social codes of morality with a practical sense of indifference? Or is Tom a nihilist who believes in nothing, like his counterpart in Hammett's novel who claims 'I don't believe in anything' (1999: 744). Tom's only true belief is that it is impossible to 'know' anyone and therefore no one can be trusted. His deep mistrust of others is summed up in the terse dictum: 'Nobody ever knows anybody, not that well.' As in Hammett's fiction, where the universal principle of mistrust goes unquestioned, the relationships depicted in *Miller's Crossing*, particularly all forms of friendship, are informed at a deep level by suspicion and fear of betrayal. According to Joel Coen, Tom Reagan is 'the quintessential Hammett guy. You're not let in on how much he knows and what exactly he's up to. He tests the other characters to see what they want and uses that to his advantage' (Robson 2007: 77). As Leslie Fiedler observes, Hammett's protagonist is typically defined by 'a stoic masculine individualism' which does not permit social and sexual entanglements; 'Sometimes misogynistic and homophobic,' Fiedler writes, Hammett's protagonists exhibit a deep 'hostility toward bourgeois marriage' which he thinks 'often results in latently homosexual narratives about male bonding' (Naremore 1998: 52–53).

Thematically, both *Miller's Crossing* and *The Glass Key* can be described as meditations on the vicissitudes of masculine friendship, loyalty and betrayal – common themes in the gangster genre but, interestingly, absent in Hammett's fiction until he wrote *The Glass Key*. Previously, Hammett's stories had focused on the tough-guy detectives typically associated with classic pulp fiction. In this regard, *The Glass Key* represents a significant departure. After perfecting the hard-boiled male in *The Maltese Falcon* with Sam Spade, Hammett felt he had developed the tough private eye as fully as possible and was anxious to write a story engaging what he thought was the more mature theme of male friendship. Literary scholar William Marling considers *The Glass Key*'s portrayal of masculine friendship among 'the classic friendships' of American literature (1995: 94). More to the point, as a kind of 'male melodrama', *The Glass Key* is thematically unique among Hammett's writings, a circumstance of particular interest for the Coens. Throughout their development as cinematic storytellers, the Coens take a special interest in changing conceptions of masculine identity. Although *Miller's Crossing* might look to many like a gangster pastiche, many of its generic attributes identify it as film noir, in particular the concern with male identity and transgressive representations of masculinity. According to Richard Dyer, classic film noir is often characterised 'by a certain anxiety over the existence and definition of masculinity and normality'; although seldom directly expressed, this anxiety is, in Dyer's analysis, related to 'an implicit set of issues and problems that the films seek to come to terms with without ever addressing them explicitly' (1998: 115).

It is often noted that classic film noirs feature a detective whose investigations ultimately become self-examinations, raising questions of masculine identity and its troubled relationship to a corrupt patriarchal order. In his analysis of male identity in film noir, Frank Krutnik observes that the narratives of classic film noir are typically structured by a 'testing of the hero's prowess – not merely testing his ability as a detective, but also how he measures up to more extensive standards of masculine competence' (1991: 86). By solving the crime and thus asserting mastery and control, the noir protagonist rehearses his 'tough' masculine identity. In some cases his toughness is measured by the amount of physical punishment he can take, as in the case of Ned Beaumont, who at one points brags to Paul, 'I can stand anything I've got to stand' (1999: 593). This kind of toughness is a trait that Tom Reagan shares with Hammett's male protagonists, for like Ned, Tom's prowess is measured by the number and severity of the beatings he can survive. During the course of the story, Tom endures enormous physical abuse. He is beaten by mob goons for refusing Caspar's offer to take sides against Leo. After he has confessed his affair with Verna, Leo gives Tom 'the kiss-off' with his fists, which Tom accepts without protest, refusing to fight back. In fact, each time he is beaten, Tom accepts his punishment with stoic passivity. When the book-maker Lazarre presses Tom to pay off his gambling debt, Tom tells him to send his muscle over to break his legs, saying 'I won't squawk'. Later, when Lazarre's enforcers show up to collect their pound of flesh, Tom accepts his punishment with cavalier nonchalance, asking the collectors to tell Lazarre that there are 'no hard feelings'. For Tom, suffering physical abuse is part of doing business in the underworld. In this scene and many others, Tom's masochistic passivity recalls Ned Beaumont's motto: 'Might as well take your punishment and get it over with' (1999: 593).

## 'The Hat Trick'

When French interviewer Jean-Pierre Coursodon suggested that the hat image in *Miller's Crossing* is more than a costume accessory and asked about its significance, Joel answered, 'Everybody asks us questions about that hat, and there isn't any answer really. It's not a symbol, it doesn't have any particular meaning. [...] It's an image that came to us, that we liked, and it just implanted itself. It's a kind of practical guiding thread, but there's no need to look for deep meanings' (Allen 2006: 44). Typically, the Coens shy away from questions concerning the meaning of their films, for reasons Joel makes clear in the same interview with Coursodon: 'Apparently nobody wants to be satisfied with the movie, as if they absolutely need explanations beyond the images, the story itself. That always surprises me. But if you don't comply, journalists get the impression that you're hiding something from them' (Allen 2006: 43). Nevertheless, if the hat is indeed just an image that came to the Coens and ignited their creative imagination, it seems certain that it came to them by way of Hammett's *The Glass Key*, where the hat is a prominent iconic motif, but also serves an important narrative function. When Ned Beaumont says, 'I'm only an amateur detective, but [the hat] looks like a thing that might have some meaning, one way or the other' (1999: 606), he verifies the hat's meaning as a clue which will eventually help him solve the riddle of Taylor Henry's homicide.

*The Glass Key* begins with Ned's discovery of Taylor's dead body, which, as Ned duly notes, is hatless. As the story approaches its conclusion, Ned resurrects this fact and uses it to contradict Madvig's false confession to Taylor's murder, forcing Madvig to admit he has lied to protect the senator and win the affection of the senator's daughter. Hammett focuses particular attention on the hat image in an early chapter entitled 'The Hat-Trick', where Ned uses Taylor's missing hat as a ruse for collecting his winnings from Bernie Despain, a bookie who has skipped town owing Ned a consider-able debt. After acquiring one of Taylor Henry's hats from his sister, Ned tracks down Bernie and, 'wearing a hat that does not fit him', Ned visits the bookie and plants Taylor's hat in his rented room. Later he extorts his winnings from the bookie by threatening to lead the police back to Bernie's room, where they will discover Taylor's hat and, based on that material evidence plus the fact that Taylor owed him money, arrest Bernie for murder.

Generally speaking, hats and masculine apparel receive inordinate attention in *The Glass Key*. In accordance with the fashion of that period, all male characters wear hats, but the particular emphasis Hammett puts men's headwear hints at a significance that goes beyond mere fashion. Hats and overcoats are mentioned at the beginning and end of nearly every scene in *The Glass Key*. When characters enter and exit interior spaces they almost invariably put on or remove hat and overcoat. In a dialogue-heavy novel like *The Glass Key*, otherwise notably lacking in descriptive details, the focus on hats invites hermeneutic curiosity. The persistent presence of the hat in *The Glass Key* is not lost on the Coens, who reproduce this iconic leitmotif in *Miller's Crossing* with the same attention accorded to it by the novelist, but for different purposes.

Despite its frequent appearances in *The Glass Key*, the hat image seems to lack discernible symbolic significance. This is how the Coens would have us view the hat in *Miller's Crossing*. But the film text contradicts its writers, providing abundant evidence that the hat's range of signification is greatly expanded in *Miller's Crossing*. The film's first image, a black fedora falling to the ground and being swept away by the wind, is auspicious and arouses suspicion. As the story develops, this recurring image assumes an important function in the shaping of character identity. Primarily, hats function in the male-dominated criminal underworld of *Miller's Crossing* as signifiers for masculinity. All male characters wear hats, and most of them consistently wear the same type of hat marking their individual and social identity. In an earlier era, a gentleman of the privileged upper class would have worn a 'high hat', fashion signifier for wealth and superior social standing. That is roughly its connotation in *Miller's Crossing*, when Johnny Caspar tells Leo he's sick of getting 'the high hat' or looked upon as inferior and lower in the hierarchy of power. When Caspar angrily announces to Leo and Tom, 'Youse fancy-pants, all of yas', he is making more than a fashion statement, in effect saying that the expensive clothing they take pride in wearing represents an attitude of superiority that does not intimidate him. A change of hat style signals a shift in social identity. In the final scene, for example, Leo is seen wearing the Jewish *yarmulke* at Bernie's burial, a sign that he intends to marry Verna, a Jew, thus surrendering his Irish-Catholic identity and assuming that of his wife-to-be, who, as Leo sheepishly admits, was the one who proposed marriage. Bernie's duplicitous nature is evident in his ever-changing hat fashions. In his first appearance on screen he wears a bowler, which, along with his flashy suit of clothes, presents a dandified image conveying the self-confidence he enjoys at that point in the story, when he can still assume that he is under Leo's protection. Later, after Tom frees him at Miller's Crossing and he goes into hiding, Bernie shows up wearing the nondescript clothes of a working-class nobody. Clearly, his shifting fashion styles are correlated with his shifty personality. As Caspar is at pains to show Leo, Bernie has no ethics. He will do what circumstances dictate and play whatever hand he is dealt.

When characters lose their hats in *Miller's Crossing*, they are usually in mortal danger. Bernie is bare-headed when seized at the Hotel Royale and taken to the forest for execution. The significance of a hatless pate is introduced in *The Glass Key* with the death of Taylor Henry, whose bare-headedness when found dead is a key to the mystery of his murder. The mystery of 'Rug' Daniels' stolen wig goes unsolved, serving only as an opportunity for an irreverent in-joke on Taylor's bald-headed death. Men without hats are likely to suffer a lapse in rational thinking. Leo and Caspar are seen bare-headed in their first encounter, as they argue heatedly over Bernie's fate, allowing emotions rather than intellect to determine their decisions. Significantly, as the opening scene comes to an end and Tom tells Leo he ought to start thinking about the pros and cons of protecting Bernie, he punctuates his admonition by donning his hat and pointedly adjusting its brim to the proper angle. As characters ruled by their hearts rather than their heads, Leo and Caspar are seen most often without their hats. Tom Reagan is almost never without his hat, an elegant black fedora he wears with stylish panache. On those occasions when he does lose it momentarily, he is anxious to retrieve it. After a night of drinking and gambling, he wakes up to find his hat missing; he has lost it in a card game, to Mink or Verna; he doesn't remember. He visits Verna, demanding its return. Here, chasing his hat equates to chasing Verna, an action which will subsequently make him seem a fool when Leo shows up asking about Verna, who listens next door from Tom's bedroom. Later, when Tom accuses Verna of 'Rug' Daniels' murder (because he was tailing her and thus knew she was cheating on Leo with Tom), the scene ends with Verna removing Tom's hat and tossing it onto a chair as they fall into an erotic embrace.

The dream about his hat that Tom relates to Verna promises symbolic significance. Verna guesses that he chased the hat, and when he caught it, it turned into 'something wonderful'. Tom corrects: he didn't chase the hat and it stayed a hat. His only comment is a condemnation: 'There's nothing more foolish than a man chasing after his hat.'

Still, Tom spends a lot of time chasing his hat. Every time Tom takes a beating (which is often), he is separated from his headwear. When, for instance, Tom is about to be beaten by the apish Frankie, he is hatless, but still manages to fend off the assault momentarily, only angering Tic-Tac, who retaliates swiftly. In a memorable moment that mixes comedy and drama, the smaller man avenges his gorilla-sized partner, storming into the room and tossing his hat aggressively in the air, as if to say that his anger has relieved him of all rational self-control. Tom loses his hat (and nearly his head) after confessing his affair with Verna to Leo, who gives Tom the 'kiss-off' in the form of a merciless beating, to which Tom passively submits. Each time Leo delivers a vicious body blow, Tom loses his fedora, and each time he bends to pick it up again. Finally Leo brings the one-sided brawl to its conclusion by thrusting Tom's hat into his stomach (a gesture that recalls a similar incident in *The Glass Key*).

When characters die in *Miller's Crossing* they are invariably hatless. Eddie Dane loses his hat as he is beaten to death by Caspar for his betrayal. Caspar loses it when ambushed and murdered by Bernie. Bernie, in turn, loses his hat when cruelly dispatched by Tom. In each of these scenes the camera is positioned at floor-level to show a hat lying next to a bare-headed corpse. When the Dane escorts Tom to Miller's Crossing to verify Bernie's execution, he removes Tom's hat just before the gunman takes aim at his head. Significantly, this scene reconnects the viewer with the film's opening credits sequence which introduces the hat – a black fedora identical to Tom's – that will become the central image of the story. In this enigmatic establishing shot, a languid low-angle tracking shot, looking upward to the sky through a network of tree branches, ends with a close-up of a black fedora hat falling into the foreground, where it is wafted away on a breeze into an autumnal forest. This is the hat and the scenery of Tom's dream, as told to Verna: 'I was walking in the woods. I don't know why. Wind came whipping. Blew me hat off.' Although Tom's dream may not be, as he insists, meaningful to him, it is nevertheless the portent of an event yet to come. The dream becomes reality at Miller's Crossing, as Tom is about to be executed by the Dane.

Visionary rather than symbolic, the dream and its central image do not sustain a psychoanalytic reading as a product of the dreamer's unconscious which, according to Freudian dream analysis, produces dreams as coded expressions of repressed conflicts and desires. Tom's dismissive reading of the hat dream and the later revelation of its premonitory function essentially foreclose a Freudian reading. Erica Rowell sees the hat as a symbol of 'the indeterminate', like Tom's unknowable inner thoughts and desires: 'We cannot know for sure what's going on in that furtive place underneath his hat' (2007: 75). Losing the hat, as Tom frequently does, precipitates a descent into irrational dream states alluded to by Bernie at Miller's Crossing as he pleads with Tom that 'it is a dream'. 'The hat and its symbolism,' writes Rowell, 'point to a dichotomy between the known, represented by the city, and the unknown, symbolized by the woods,' marking the 'boundary between real and surreal, truth and lies, order and disorder, masculinity and femininity – in other words, the threshold of the "other"' (ibid.). Tom's hat is as a 'cover-up' literally and metaphorically, and 'all signs point to the implicit wild card of love as the unrevealed secret, the thing that Tom keeps under his hat' (2007: 78).

### 'The Kiss-Off'

The conclusion of *The Glass Key* stages a final meeting of Ned Beaumont and Paul Madvig. Like Leo in *Miller's Crossing*, Paul has given Ned 'the kiss-off' because they disagreed about Paul's commitment to Senator Henry, motivated by his affection for the senator's daughter, Janet Henry. In the final scene of the novel Paul, like Leo, tries to defuse their antagonism and make peace. Ned has solved the murder mystery that drives the novel's plot and in doing so, he has won the affection of the woman Paul had hoped to marry. Ending the novel with an uncharacteristic outcome, Hammett allows Ned to emerge as a triumphant romantic hero who solves the mystery and gets the girl – something that otherwise never happens to Hammett's tough-guy loners. As Ned and Janet Henry are making preparations to leave town, Paul appears at Ned's apartment, surprised to see them together. Seeking reconciliation, Paul tells Ned, 'I'd like to think that whether you went or stayed you weren't holding anything against me, Ned.' Ned assures him that he harbours no resentment, then, in an act of unexpected desperation, Paul implores Ned: 'Don't go, Ned. Stick it out with me. Christ knows I need you now. Even if I didn't – I'll do my damndest to make up for all that.' Ned assures him that he hasn't got anything 'to make up for', but insists that his decision to leave is final. At that point Janet enters the room and Ned announces that she is going with him. Paul, practically speechless, mumbles something unintelligibly, and exits, leaving the door open behind him. The final lines of the novel read: 'Janet Henry looked at Ned Beaumont. He stared fixedly at the door' (1999: 777).

The Coens reconfigure this parting of ways in the final scene of *Miller's Crossing*, where the men's roles are reversed: Leo and Verna are to be married and Tom has been dealt out of the romantic triangle. Like Ned Beaumont, Tom has resolved the conflicts that threatened to topple his boss from power; but unlike Ned, Tom does not win the woman's affection, although throughout the narrative it has seemed clear that Verna favoured Tom and was exploiting Leo's affections as a 'grift' to protect Bernie. In all other respects, however, the movie mirrors the novel, where Paul first asks for forgiveness, then implores Ned to stay. The Coens alter little of this exchange. Leo acknowledges Tom's loyalty and expresses gratitude, saying 'It was a smart play all around.' And, like Paul, Leo offers a heartfelt plea for reconciliation: 'Jesus, Tom, I'd do anything if you'd work for me again.' Then, in words that ring with the sentiments of lovers rather than friendly business associates, Leo begs Tom: 'I need you. Things can be the way they were.' Now it is Tom's turn to give Leo 'the kiss-off'. When Leo forgives Tom for his indiscretions with Verna, Tom's response is cold: 'I didn't ask for that and I don't want it.' Tom utters a final 'Good-bye.' As the two men stare at each other, the distance between them seems unbridgeable. Like Paul Madvig, Leo is speechless; he turns and walks away. As Tom watches him leave, the camera captures a highly stylised gesture: Tom pulls the brim of his hat down over his face then slowly raises his head to reveal his eyes and, translating the final words of *The Glass Key* into cinematic imagery, Tom stares 'fixedly' at Leo's departing figure, the close-up of his face capturing the intensity of a gaze that wordlessly voices his emotional desolation.

Where the Coens' rewriting of Hammett gradually becomes apparent is in their subtle excavation of the novel's homoerotic subtext, as the revisionists search for the key to unlock the enigma at the heart of *The Glass Key*. Their investigation into this mystery is guided by clues which the novelist disguises by a clever use of misdirection and displacement, projecting the repressed homoeroticism of his principal characters onto secondary characters. In *The Glass Key*, Ned Beaumont's disavowed homosexuality

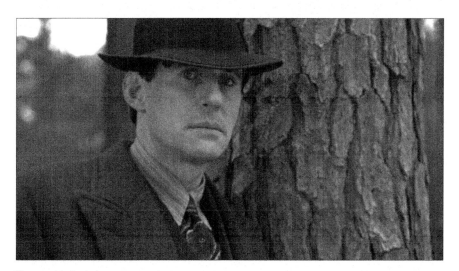

Tom watches Leo's departure.

is projected onto Jeff Gardner, a brutish thug who takes perverse delight in beating Ned. Ned endures numerous assaults in the course of the story, but none as vicious as the beating he takes in the chapter entitled 'The Dog House', where Ned is held hostage by bootlegger Shad O'Rory who, like Johnny Caspar, uses primitive methods to coerce the protagonist to betray his loyalty. Thus, to persuade Ned that he should sell out Madvig and cross over to him, O'Rory subjects Ned to a series of torturous beatings, dealt out by his sadistic enforcer, Jeff. Ned tries repeatedly to escape, and each time he is subdued by Jeff, who attacks him so savagely that his partner finally shouts, 'Jesus, Jeff, you'll croak him.' To which Jeff replies: 'He's tough. He's a tough baby. He likes this.' Then, holding Ned on his knee like a child (or a frail), Jeff asks him: 'Don't you like it, baby?' (1999: 665–666). The pleasure Jeff so obviously derives from dealing these repeated 'body blows' signals an ulterior motive for his violence as a sublimation of repressed (or just unspoken) sexual desire. Pushing the perversity of these assaults to the limit, Hammett veers close to exposing the homoerotic subtext with almost pornographic explicitness. At one point, Jeff pushes Ned down on a bed and says 'I got something to try', whereupon he scoops up Ned's legs and tumbles them onto the bed, after which, as Hammett suggestively words it, 'he leaned over Ned Beaumont, his hands busy on Ned Beaumont's body. Ned Beaumont's body and arms and legs jerked convulsively and three times he groaned. After that he lay still' (1999: 667).

Hammett gives equal time to Ned's masochistic tendencies, which are brought out in fairly explicit terms, as when Jeff says of Ned: 'I never seen a guy that liked being hit so much' (1999: 668). Unable to resist teasing, Jeff says to his partner: 'You see, he likes it. He's a God-damned massacrist.' Leering at Ned, Jeff then asks, 'You know what a massacrist is?' Ned answers simply, 'Yes' (1999: 751). In *Miller's Crossing*, Jeff Gardner's sexualised sadism is transferred to Eddie Dane, Caspar's menacing enforcer, who, like his model in *The Glass Key*, recognizes his victim's latent masochism and mockingly calls attention to it, labeling Tom 'little Miss Punching Bag'. In a climactic scene late in the movie, as the Dane is about to strangle Tom to death, he makes his sadistic intentions explicit, telling Tom, 'I'm gonna send you to a deep, dark place, and I'm gonna have fun doing it.' Taking their cue from Hammett, the Coens recreate the apish Jeff in Eddie Dane, the sadistic complement to Tom's passive masochism. Interestingly, Tom and the Dane are both cast in the role of trusted advisors to their respective bosses. They are both men 'who walk behind the man and whisper in his ear', a wording that insinuates an intimacy exceeding mere confidentiality. Even though he outwardly expresses deep mistrust and dislike for Tom, the Dane has a grudging respect for him, articulated in their sarcastic verbal back-and-forth. When Tom, for instance, asks the Dane, snidely: 'Is there a point? Or are you just brushing up on your small talk?' the Dane replies, 'I like that. Cool under fire. I'm impressed.' The Dane takes pleasure in their verbal intercourse, sensing perhaps an affinity with Tom, a connection that goes beyond their shared identity as right-hand men. More than anyone, the Dane seems to understand Tom, who is to all others an enigma. He expresses his insight clearly in a speech delivered en route to the Miller's Crossing to check for Bernie's corpse:

You're so goddamn smart. Except you ain't. I get you, smart guy, I know what you are. Straight as a corkscrew. Mr. Inside-Outsky. Down is up. Black is white. Well, I think you're half-smart. I think you were straight with your frail and queer with Johnny Caspar. And I think you'd sooner join the Ladies' League than gun a guy down.

The Dane knows 'what' Tom is. He figures him for a guy who will sometimes play 'straight' but also 'queer' a deal and cross over from one side to the other, suggesting that Tom has no genuine loyalties or moral commitments. More to the point, the Dane insinuates with telling rhetoric that Tom 'goes both ways', playing it 'straight' with his frail, but also playing it 'queer' with Caspar, using terms that can be construed either as Hammett-like gangster talk or as sexually-charged innuendo. His crack that Tom is more at home in 'the Ladies League' than in the hyper-masculine underworld of gangsters punctuates the Dane's insinuation. Leo seems also to sense Tom's duplicity when he says, 'Goddamn kid is just like a *twist*', slang for female, but with hidden connotations brought out in the Dane's 'corkscrew' metaphor. In the scene immediately following Leo's 'twist' reference, Tom tells the bartender, 'Gimme a stiff one.' The barman quips, 'No small talk, huh?' Innocent enough, perhaps, in another context, but here such an exchange invites speculation.

*Miller's Crossing* not only works subtly to uncover the psycho-sexual dynamics of the conflicted male friendship at the centre of *The Glass Key* but also expands the novelist's treatment of homoeroticism to create a larger, more visible network of homosexual men, suggesting that the gangster underworld is a homo-social hideout from the sexual prohibitions of straight society. Thus, along with the friendship of Tom and Leo, there is another set of interconnected 'friendships' involving Bernie, Mink and Eddie Dane, which adds a homosexual romantic triangle to the heterosexual triangle of Tom/Verna/Leo. Of these characters, Bernie is most openly identified as gay. The suspicion that he is homosexual is implicit in Caspar's nickname for him, 'The Shmatte Kid'. In Yiddish, *shmatte* means rags or shabby clothing, but in this context a 'lowlife' or degenerate, thus establishing a link between clothing fashion and sexual identity that is reiterated and developed in other parts of the story. Bernie's sexual preference is also implicit in Verna's defense of her brother: 'Yeah, sneer at him like everyone else. Just because he's different. People think he's degenerate. People think he's scum. Well, he's not.' Bernie himself comes close to admitting his sexual preference when he tells Tom that Verna once tried to seduce him, implying that it was an attempt to convert him to heterosexuality. 'She'll sleep with anyone, you know that,' Bernie tells Tom. 'She even tried to teach me a thing or two about bed-artistry. Can you believe that? My own sister. Some crackpot idea about "saving me from my friends".' Bernie's 'amigos' – Mink and Eddie Dane – are more discretely suggested to be lovers. Caspar is the only main male character portrayed as unequivocally heterosexual. With a wife and child, Caspar is a strong believer in the traditional family. He is aware of his associates' preferences, but appears to be tolerant. When Tom tries to persuade him that Mink and the Dane have been cooperating with Bernie to 'queer' the fixed boxing matches, Caspar says: 'I know Mink is Eddie Dane's boy, but still, I don't make it like that.' Caspar believes the Dane wouldn't cross him, saying 'We go back.' Nevertheless, as Tom reminds Caspar, there is always a 'wild card' when love is involved.

*'Running Wild'*

Among the many clues pointing to homoeroticism in *Miller's Crossing*, one of the most revealing (but still well concealed) is planted, significantly, in the ladies' room at the Shenandoah Club. Seeking out Verna, to discuss her relationship with Leo, Tom enters the women's lounge with the odd announcement, 'Close your eyes, ladies, I'm coming through' (as though he, rather than the ladies, might have something to hide). As he enters, we catch a momentary glimpse of Leo dressed in drag as a maid. Reinforcing the visual cue, the soundtrack plays the song 'Running Wild' which was Marilyn Monroe's first musical number in Billy Wilder's cross-dressing gangster comedy *Some Like it Hot* (1959). Accompanied by the song, this brief shot exposes Leo's psycho-sexual duality, suggesting that he occasionally likes to 'run wild', a metaphor linked with the animal motifs that also run wild in *Miller's Crossing*. Character names are identified with animals: Leo (the lion), Eddie (the great) Dane, Bernie (referred to by Tom as 'Saint Bernard'), and, of course, Mink. Significantly, these characters are all active in the hidden socio-homo community, thus their relationships are also described in animal metaphors: Bernie and Mink are said to be 'cozy as lice' and 'jungled up together'. Other characters are linked to animals by analogy, as when Leo says of Johnny Caspar, 'Twist a pig's ear, watch him squeal.' In his long opening speech on ethics, Caspar warns that if Bernie's chiseling is allowed to go unpunished, 'then you're right back with anarchy. Right back in the jungle.' As Caspar goes on to explain, 'That's why ethics is important. It's the grease that makes us get along, what separates us from the animals, beasts of burden, beasts of prey.' Bernie Bernbaum, however, is 'a horse of a different colour, ethics-wise'. Later, as Bernie begs for his life, he confesses his chiseling to Tom, saying 'I couldn't help it, Tom, it's in my nature.' He then beseeches Tom, 'I can't die! Out here in the woods! Like a dumb animal!' Tom rarely resorts to physical violence, even if it means, as it usually does, that he must submit to a terrible beating. Tom is a pure strategist, a thinker who, for the most part, disapproves of violence as a solution to problems. Bernie reminds him of this as he begs for his life, saying 'Tommy, you can't do this. You don't bump guys. You're not like those animals back there.' Bernie's claim that 'they can't make us different people than we are' carries several implications: that Tom and Bernie are not cut out to be gunsels, but also that Bernie (a homosexual) and Tom belong to a 'different' breed altogether.

There is much to suggest that the proliferating animal imagery in *Miller's Crossing* constitutes another instance of intertextual dialogue with Hammett, whose protagonist in *Red Harvest* characterises the citizens of 'Poisonville' variously as monkeys, pigs and wolves. In *The Glass Key*, the poison of corruption and criminal violence has spread to all levels threatening to infect the entire social body, which is slipping into the primitive anarchy of the jungle. Hammett was fascinated with the hidden social structures of the criminal underworld, and particularly obsessed with the idea that criminal gangs could take over an entire community or society and operate as a covert government, as seemed to be the case in the 1920s and 1930s. Hammett's fascination with hidden regimes is preserved in *Miller's Crossing*, but instead of offering social commentary on organised crime, the Coens shift the focus to the culture of homosexuality within the criminal underworld, where 'running wild' assumes a quite different set of connotations and presents an alternative image of hard-boiled masculinity previously missing in the gangster genre. The ideological critique in *Miller's Crossing* is not of the economic politics of capitalism, but about the economy of sexual relations – the hidden politics of homosociality. Usually addressed obliquely in classic gangster movies, if at all, only a few pre-code Hollywood films imply homosexual themes, as in Warner Bros.' *Little Caesar* (1932), where it is suggested that the jealous attitude of gangster Rico Bandello toward the girlfriend of his best friend and partner, Tony Massara, signals his repressed homosexual desire. A reference to this gangster classic is perhaps implied with Mink's surname, LeRouie, which may allude to Mervyn LeRoy, who directed *Little Caesar*. In any case, the depiction of homosexuality in *Miller's Crossing*, however ambiguous, departs from the typical treatment of male homosociality in the gangster genre, where it is generally considered simply another immoral perversion complementing the outlaw's already criminally transgressive nature. Revising genre, *Miller's Crossing* takes the representation of hard-boiled masculinity an important step farther, expanding the scope of Hammett's social critique to examine themes of male homosexuality that had hitherto been suppressed.

Interestingly, a queer reading of *The Glass Key* is noticeably absent in the scholarly writings on Hammett. In fact, many commentators consider *The Glass Key* Hammett's least successful novel, mostly because the motives of its main character, Ned Beaumont, are never adequately explained. Philip Durham argues that 'other than for certain loyalties, [Beaumont's] motions are mechanical and his emotions were not there. What he did, or how, seemed not to matter' (Thompson 2007: 134). Even George J. Thompson, considered by many the pre-eminent interpreter of Hammett, skirts the issue of homoeroticism, observing that 'the bleakness of Hammett's vision is not due to his protagonists' lack of moral feeling, but instead to the modern social condition, a world in which the protagonists' *great depths of feeling cannot find expression*' (2007: 135; emphasis added). How these 'great depths of feeling' might be understood seems to be the question that interests the Coen brothers most. There is abundant textual evidence that *Miller's Crossing* achieves more than a skillful simulation of gangster movies, instead exploring the depths of emotion in *The Glass Key* and bringing to light its unspoken secrets by de-sublimating Hammett's homoerotic subtext. The fact that they chose to adapt *The Glass Key* rather than *Red Harvest* (which has never been adapted for film) indicates the Coens' sense that something unspoken in the novel should come to expression.

# CHAPTER FOUR

# Barton Fink: 'For the Common Man'

Released in 1991, the Coen brothers' fourth feature premiered at the Cannes Film Festival, where it was greeted with enthusiastic acclaim, winning three top prizes: the Palme d'Or for Best Film as well as Best Director and Best Actor (John Turturro). No film had won this many top prizes in over forty years, a circumstance that prompted Cannes officials to introduce a new rule prohibiting any future film from winning more than two of the highest awards.

Written during a three-week 'vacation' from work on the script of *Miller's Crossing* (which the Coens were having trouble finishing), the story of *Barton Fink* takes us back to 1941 Hollywood to chronicle a bizarre episode in the life of Barton Fink (Turturro), a left-wing New York playwright who wants to establish 'a new living theatre of, about, and for the common man'. Although he has doubts about selling his talent, he is tempted by a lucrative salary to do a stint as screenwriter for a Hollywood movie studio, where Barton soon discovers he is out of his element and experiences a nightmarish bout of writer's block.

Upon his arrival in Hollywood, Barton Fink checks into the ghostly Hotel Earle where he is greeted by pale, vaguely uncanny desk clerk, 'Chet' (Steve Buscemi) who ascends to meet the new guest from a trapdoor in the floor. Chet directs Barton to the sparsely furnished rented room where the writer will live and work, comforted only by the painted image of a bathing beauty hanging over his desk. The only other tenant Barton meets during his sojourn is Charlie Meadows (John Goodman), an insurance salesman with whom Barton occasionally wrestles and discusses 'the life of the mind'. Charlie has stories he wants the writer to hear, but Barton is so pompously self-absorbed he doesn't listen.

When Barton meets the Capitol Pictures studio boss, Jack Lipnick (Michael Lerner), and his assistant Lou (Jon Polito), they proclaim that 'the writer is king at

Capitol Pictures', and promptly inform Barton that his first assignment is a 'Wallace Beery wrestling picture', a movie genre Barton has trouble imagining. He seeks guidance from producer Ben Geisler (Tony Shalhoub) and from W. P. Mayhew (John Mahoney), whom Barton considers the greatest novelist of the time. Unfortunately, the great novelist is an alcoholic and of little help to Barton, who in desperation turns to Mayhew's secretary and personal assistant Audrey (Judy Davis) to help him get his wrestling picture started. Audrey, its turns out, is well suited to the task of script-doctoring, having ghost written much of Mayhew's Hollywood output. She seems to have a neurotic compulsion to seduce writers and ends up sleeping with Barton.

The next morning Audrey is inexplicably dead, gruesomely murdered in Barton's bed. Charlie, the friendly neighbour, intercedes and removes the corpse, then vanishes, saying he is going on a business trip to the head office and leaving a box with Barton for safe keeping. During Charlie's absence, Barton is suddenly inspired to write the screenplay for the wrestling movie, completing it in a burst of creative energy. Meanwhile, police detectives visit the Hotel Earle questioning Barton about Charlie, whom they accuse of being Karl 'Madman' Mundt, a serial killer who decapitates his victims. Barton hurries off to a meeting with Lipnick, who angrily rejects Barton's work as 'fruity' nonsense, announcing that Barton's script will not be produced, nor will anything he writes for Capitol Pictures until he 'grows up' enough to comprehend that movies produced by his studio are entertainment products designed for mass consumption and maximum profit, and not to raise the social consciousness of Hollywood's consumer audiences.

Meanwhile, the police detectives' allegations against Charlie now prove to be true when his alter-ego returns to the hotel, which has mysteriously burst into hellish flames, violently murdering the detectives and repeatedly shouting 'I'll show you the life of the mind!' After Charlie frees Barton, who had been shackled to his bed by the cops, he explains that he murdered the detectives because Barton, the champion of the common man Charlie clearly represents, had failed to 'listen' to him. Dazed by the absurd events that have just taken place, Barton collects the box, which Charlie now claims does not belong to him after all, leaves the Hotel Earle, which is still a raging inferno, and wanders onto a sunny beach where he sees a beautiful young woman who looks exactly like the bathing beauty in the picture that hung in his room at the Hotel Earle. 'Are you in pictures?' Barton innocently asks her. 'Don't be silly,' she laughs, turns her back to him, and assumes exactly the same pose as the woman in the painting.

The critical response to *Barton Fink* was, somewhat surprisingly, very positive. Despite the fact that many considered the film, as Geoff Andrew words it, 'perversely weird', the critics generally had good things to say about it. Vincent Canby of the *New York Times* called it 'an exhilarating original' and considered it proof that the Coen brothers could do something 'significant'. Rita Kempley sang her usual praises, calling *Barton Fink* 'rapturously funny, strangely bittersweet, moderately horrifying' – 'a cineaste's landmark on a par with [David Lynch's] *Blue Velvet*'. Writing for the *Daily Mail*, Shaun Usher judged *Barton Fink* 'a film of the decade', but still harbored doubts about its meaning, calling it 'a house of in-joke trump cards' which the Coens 'burn down, leaving the viewer to sift through the ashes for message and moral'. Searching for meaning, Roger Ebert speculated that the relationship between Barton and Charlie was 'an emblem of the rise of Nazism', writing that the Coens 'paint Fink as an ineffectual and impotent left-wing intellectual, who does not understand that for many common men fascism had a seductive appeal'. Stanley Kaufmann was less impressed, writing that 'not since Robert Altman has any American filmmaker been as overrated as this pair'. Terrence Rafferty of the *New Yorker* voiced the familiar complaint that *Barton Fink*, like all of the Coens' films, is 'an empty tour de force'. What Rafferty thought most 'dismaying' about the movie, however, was that 'the filmmakers seem inordinately pleased with its hermetic meaninglessness'.

Much of the confusion about the meaning of *Barton Fink* is likely caused by the sheer complexity of its intertextual design. Previously, the Coens had limited their intertextual dialogue to a single authorial source (Cain in *Blood Simple*, Hammett in *Miller's Crossing*). *Barton Fink* breaks from this pattern to borrow from a multiplicity of sources including historical accounts of old Hollywood, author biographies and a wide range of literary, cinematic and cultural sources. Many critics loved the film for the very reason that it did not serve a mass audience. A complex intertextual pastiche, it relies heavily on literary sources that might seem obscure to today's viewer, making it difficult to see the oblique humour of the Coens' highly referential in-joking. With *Barton Fink* the Coens continue to showcase their knowledge and appreciation of the American literary tradition. In addition to their main sources, which include the biographies and writings of playwright Clifford Odets and novelists William Faulkner and Nathanael West, all important literary figures in old Hollywood, they also incorporate an impressive array of other literary sources, ranging from Shakespeare to the Holy Bible. Generically, *Barton Fink* is a departure from films like *Blood Simple* and *Miller's Crossing*, both shaped predominantly by film noir. It is also a genre pastiche – a hybrid mix of noir, horror, surrealism and comedy. In this regard, it has been compared with Stanley Kubrick's *The Shining*, whose story of a writer living in a haunted hotel and his descent into madness has obvious affinities with Barton's stay at the Hotel Earle and whose signature tracking shots down long hotel corridors are mimicked by the Coens' cinematographer Roger Deakins. Roman Polanski's early films *Repulsion* and *The Tenant*, which like *The Shining* portray hotels and rented rooms as horrifying, degenerate entities corrupted by an unknown evil, have been suggested as close relatives. 'It's kind of a Polanski movie,' admits Ethan. 'It's closer to that than anything else' (Allen 2006: 56). Such filmic points of references notwithstanding, the most prominent and potentially meaningful sources for the Coens' intertext are drawn from literature. If there is a way to construct meaning in *Barton Fink*, it must begin with an understanding of literary elements that form the basis for much of the film's elaborate pastiche.

*The Writer in Old Hollywood*

Many commentators thought *Barton Fink* was intended as a satire on old Hollywood as a commercial trap that ensnared some of the greatest American authors of that time: William Faulkner, Clifford Odets, Nathanael West and many others. Thus Jami Bernard wrote for the *New York Post* that the film is 'a vicious satire of how Hollywood grinds creative minds to pulp in the service of an audience it barely understands'. One could say, somewhat differently, that as a pastiche *Barton Fink* functions much like the classic Hollywood movie mill, grinding up the texts of prior talents, both literary and cinematic, combining them to create a pulp sublime that its audience barely understands. While the Coens admit that Odets and Faulkner provided models for the characterisations of both Barton and Mayhew, generally the filmmakers claim not to have done much research into the history of old Hollywood. They do, however, mention Otto Friedrich's *City of Nets* (1986), a history of Hollywood during the 1940s, as an inspiration: 'It was one of the things that started us thinking about Hollywood as a setting,' they say, 'but we didn't go out and do research beyond it' (Allen 2006: 60). Despite such claims, the setting, characters and scenes depicted in *Barton Fink* present an accurate, if satirically distorted, portrait of the Hollywood movie business in the classic era of the 1930s and 1940s when the major studios operated like industrial factories with the 'mogul' executive producer at the top of the power-pyramid and the screenwriter close to the bottom.

Another prominent literary author who worked as a scriptwriter in the Hollywood industry was Raymond Chandler, one of the Coens' most admired writers. Although they make no specific mention of Chandler in relation to *Barton Fink*, many of Chandler's thoughts on the Hollywood movie industry in the classic era apply to the predicament of the film's central character, a playwright turned studio scriptwriter. Chandler's best and most concise thinking on Hollywood as the 'dream factory' is found in his 1945 essay 'Writers in Hollywood', where Chandler, with measured sarcasm, shares his impressions of the old studio system and its treatment of screenwriters. As a novelist who made his living for a while as screenwriter, Chandler had first-hand experience of the Hollywood writer's plight. He was one of many literary authors lured to Hollywood by the promise of lavish salaries offered by the major studios. Lamenting that the motion picture industry, with its vast financial resources and 'magic techniques', ought to produce 'an art which is capable of making all but the very best plays look trivial and contrived, all but the very best novels verbose and imitative', Chandler describes the movie-making process as 'an endless contention of tawdry egos, some of them powerful, almost all of them vociferous, and almost none of them capable of anything more than credit-stealing and self-promotion' (1995a: 993). The inflated egos he refers to belong mostly to the 'mogul' producers who fancy themselves the real creators of the motion picture because they think that the writers, knowing next to nothing about 'making pictures', cannot possibly know how to write them properly and thus that the producer must teach the writer how to do his job. These producers, whom Chandler dubs 'the showmen of Hollywood', exert absolute control over the creative process and, in Chandler's view, 'thereby degrade it', As a result, argues Chandler, 'there is no art of the screenplay, and there never will be as long as the system lasts, for it is the essence of this system that it seeks to exploit talent without permitting it the right to be a talent', The studio system, he concludes, 'can only destroy the talent' (1995a: 994).

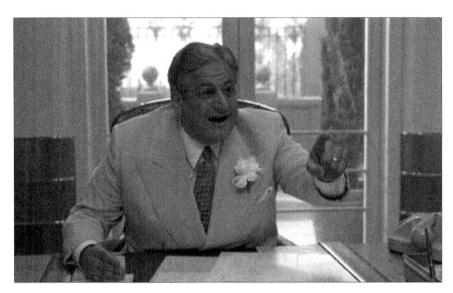

Jack Lipnick: 'The writer is king here at Capitol Pictures!'

These Hollywood moguls who thwart literary talent imported from the East Coast intelligentsia tend to be, in Chandler's words, 'low-grade individuals with the morals of a goat, the artistic integrity of a slot machine, and the manners of a floor-walker with delusions of grandeur' (1995a: 997). This stereotype is roundly parodied in *Barton Fink* with the character of Jack Lipnick, head of Capitol Pictures, who the Coens say is a composite caricature based on studio bosses Louis B. Mayer, Harry Cohn and Jack Warner. As portrayed by Michael Lerner, Lipnick bears a physical resemblance to Mayer, has the vulgar mouth of Cohn and the bombastic manner of Warner, who inspired the idea to have Lipnick appear at the end wearing a military uniform (which Warner was actually reported to have done). Lipnick is also a Jew (another Hollywood stereotype) who brags to Barton: 'I'm bigger and meaner and louder than any other kike in this town.' Stereotype or not, it is well known that many studio heads in old Hollywood were of Jewish descent, born in Central or Eastern Europe, but, anxious to assimilate into American culture, they often disavowed their heritage. Louis B. Mayer was a Russian Jew from Minsk, a fact that makes its way into the Coens' script when Lipnick tells Barton: 'I'm from New York myself – well, Minsk if you wanna go way back, which we won't if you don't mind and I ain't askin'.' Harry Cohn, a Jew but also openly anti-Semitic, liked to boast that the only Jewish actors he hired at Columbia Pictures played Indians, a historical anecdote parodied in *Barton Fink* when Barton introduces himself to producer Ben Geisler (also Jewish) who immediately asks the (obviously Jewish) Barton: 'Ever act? We need Indians for a Norman Steele western.' When Barton declines the offer, Geisler insists: 'Think about it, Fink. Writers come and go; we always need Indians.'

It is also well known that these mogul producers who asserted almost dictatorial control over the artists and technicians were unbelievably ignorant of the actual movie-making process. As Lipnick admits to Barton, he is the boss of Capitol Pictures, but that doesn't mean he understands the techniques of filmmaking, much less the aesthetics: 'I run this dump and I don't know the technical mumbo-jumbo. Why do I run it? I've got horse sense, goddamnit. Showmanship!' In his flamboyantly bombastic style, Lipnick parodies the autocratic businessmen who ran the Hollywood studios like factories. His relationship with Barton presents a comedic version of the constant struggle between producer and writer over control of the creative product, a struggle which continues to this day in the movie industry.

One writer whose Hollywood experience epitomises the writer's loss of control over his artistic work is William Faulkner, represented in *Barton Fink* by Mayhew, the alcoholic Southern novelist. The Coens admit that Faulkner was on their mind when they created the character. Actor John Mahoney was chosen for the part largely due to his physical resemblance to Faulkner. At the same time, the brothers stress that although Faulkner is the basic model, in the details Mayhew is very different. Mayhew has the same disdain as Faulkner had for Hollywood, but unlike Mayhew, Faulkner's alcoholism did not paralyse his creativity and as a screenwriter he was continuously productive. Nevertheless, the parallels are relevant. As Raymond Chandler observes, in that early period of filmmaking 'no part of the vast body of technical knowledge which Hollywood contains is systematically and as a matter of course made available to the new writer in a studio. They tell him to look at pictures – which is to learn architecture by staring at a house' (1995a: 1002). This, we recall, is precisely what the producers tell Barton to do when, claiming unfamiliarity with the genre, he asks Geisler what a wrestling movie is supposed to be and is sent off to view clips of other wrestling pictures, specifically dailies of another being made at that same time, allowing the film to riff on the presentation of these genre works as idiotically, mindnumbingly and scarily repetitive. This particular scene may also allude to Faulkner, whose first assignment for MGM was to write a draft for a remake of *The Champ* (1931), the story of a boxer played by Wallace Beery. The follow-up, titled *Flesh* (1932), was to feature Beery again, this time as a wrestler. In Otto Friedrich's account, when Sam Marx, MGM's story editor, sent Faulkner to a projection room to watch Beery in *The Champ*, Faulkner reportedly watched only a few minutes of the reel then asked, 'How do I get out of here?' (1986: 237). Suffering a fate similar to Barton's, Faulkner did not finish the script, which was reassigned to another screenwriter. As is the case with Barton's failed wrestling script, many of the screenplays Faulkner worked on for MGM were never filmed. In contrast to the fictional Barton, however, the real-life Faulkner was never discouraged by such setbacks and went on to work on more than forty scripts, labouring for years as a scriptwriter under Jack Warner who bragged about 'employing America's best writer for peanuts' (Woods 2000: 107).

The powerlessness of the screenwriter is further emphasised in *Barton Fink* by the sign on Mayhew's studio office door announcing the title of the movie he is currently writing: 'Slave Ship', the title of an actual movie from 1937 directed by Tay Garnett, the script for which was an adaptation of a Faulkner story (starring Wallace Beery). Like Barton, Faulkner didn't like working at the offices provided by the studio, preferring to live and write in cheap hotel rooms. Once, when Faulkner informed studio executive Hal Wallis he wanted to go home to Mississippi to work on a script, Wallis rudely reminded him: 'You're under contract and you'll work here!' (Friedrich 1986: 238). This incident is replayed in *Barton Fink* when, after deciding that Barton's screenplay is too 'fruity', Lipnick informs the writer: 'You're under contract and you're gonna stay that way. Anything you write will be the property of Capitol Pictures. And Capitol Pictures will not produce anything you write.' Concluding his tirade, Lipnick tells Lou: 'Get him out of my sight. Make sure he stays in town, though; he's still under contract.' In the old studio system that Capitol Pictures represents, writers were treated like slaves, presumably why Bill Mayhew is fond of singing the Stephen Foster plantation song, 'Old Black Joe'.

The character of Lou Breeze, Lipnick's subservient factotum, also satirises the institutionalised enslavement of studio personnel. Lou does everything his master bids from fetching coffee to reading scripts for Jack, who, as Ben Geisler tells Barton, can't read: 'You gotta *tell* it to him.' It is reported that the semi-literate Louis B. Mayer never read scripts either; the film story had to be acted out for him by an assistant (Friedrich 1986: 16). The caricature of Lou seems to draw substantially on Otto Friedrich's depiction of Harry Rapf, a producer who worked for Mayer at MGM. According to Friedrich, Rapf was 'one of MGM's embarrassments'. Like Breeze, Rapf had once owned a share of the studio but, in Friedrich's words, 'had been squeezed out during the reorganizational power plays of the 1920s' (1986: 339). Before his demotion, Rapf had been a top studio manager, but was subsequently reduced to insignificance as a lower-level producer. In *Barton Fink* Lipnick tells Barton that Lou 'used to have shares in the company. An ownership interest. Got bought out in the twenties – muscled out according to some. Hell, according to me. So we keep him around, he's got family. Poor schmuck.' Another instance of the Coens borrowing directly from Hollywood lore also concerns Rapf. Once, when Rapf had a disagreement with a director currently in Mayer's favor, the mogul reportedly cursed his subordinate, saying: 'You stupid kike bastard – you ought to kiss this man's shoes – get on your knees' (Friedrich 1986: 340). After more belittling, Mayer suddenly declared, 'Get out of here, you're fired, get out of your office. You had your last chance, you son of a bitch.' When, toward the end of the movie, Lou Breeze reprimands Barton for not delivering an acceptable scenario, reminding the writer of his contractual obligations to the studio, Lipnick's angry (and inexplicably capricious) reaction to Lou is almost a verbatim quotation of Mayer's tirade: 'Get down on your knees, you sonofabitch! Get down on your knees and kiss this man's feet! – OK, get out of here. You're fired, you understand me? Get out of my sight!'

## Clifford Odets

The character of Barton Fink is based in part on Clifford Odets, a successful New York playwright in the 1930s and a member of the Group Theatre, which included Lee Strasberg and Elia Kazan. After initial success on New York stages, Odets went to Hollywood to write scripts so that he could raise money for his New York theatre group, still believing that 'great audiences are waiting now to have their own experiences explained to them' (Mottram 2000: 81). Odets was a committed left-wing intellectual who in early plays promoted a social realist aesthetic glorifying working-class heroes. Fink's 'Bare Ruined Choirs' alludes to Odets' early play *Awake and Sing!* Indeed, Barton's speech about his vision of a theatre dedicated to 'the common man' could have come from the mouth of Odets:

> The hopes and dreams of the common man are as noble as those of any king. It's the stuff of life – why shouldn't it be the stuff of theatre? Goddammit! Why should that be such a hard pill to swallow? Don't call it new theatre, Charlie, call it real theatre! Call it our theatre!

The Coens say they wrote *Barton Fink* with John Turturro in mind for the leading role. In preparation for the part, Turturro committed himself enthusiastically to exploring the character of Barton Fink, including reading a book on the origins of the socially engaged writers of the 1930s titled *Jews Without Money*, as well as Odets' plays to get a better sense of the playwright's speech patterns. Among these sources, the playwright's 1940 journal *The Time is Ripe* is possibly the most significant. In it, Odets begins to question the efficacy of openly political art, writing that in the world of the theatre 'leftism as understood by the Communists is impossible'. 'Any excessive partisanship in a play defeats the very purpose of the play itself,' he writes, and 'an attempt to reach as broad an audience as possible should always be taken into consideration'; 'I once thought that it would be enough to play in a small cellar,' confesses Odets, 'but I soon saw that those who would come to the cellar were not the ones in need of what I could say' (1988: 15).

Furthermore, 1940 was a turning point for Odets' writing career. After the initial success of his early plays there was widespread suspicion that his later writings for the stage betrayed the Hollywood influence, utilising situations and story motifs that mimicked popular fiction and movies. Among the left-wing intellectuals of his theatre group there was a feeling that Odets was retreating from the political arena to express a personal vision that neglected his ideological commitments. While others from the New York group went on to greater prominence, many thought Odets failed to develop after the early plays. He had already moved to Hollywood, where for two decades he enjoyed moderate success as a screenwriter. The idea of a promising New York playwright who loses his soul in Hollywood is fundamental to the story of *Barton Fink*, but it is clear that Odets did not inspire the Coens to homage. Although they may respect his political idealism (the film is particularly ambiguous about this), if any character represents the artistic point of view of the filmmakers, it is probably Mayhew, whose whimsical retort to Barton's pompous speech on the artistic necessity of 'plumbing the depths, to dredge up something from inside' reveals an ironic detachment closer to the Coens' sensibility: 'Me, I just like making things up – escape.' Barton seems intended to parody the younger Odets, in his early, ideological period, and Mayhew perhaps an older, chastened Odets, who has realised that artistic endeavors aiming for political effect must first appeal to the masses, 'the common man', who is the ostensible focus of Fink's socialist art.

*Nathanael West*

If the Coens' source for the setting of old Hollywood is Friedrich's *City of Nets*, and their inspiration for characterisations derived largely from biographies of Odets, Faulkner and the studio moguls, the primary source for the story of *Barton Fink* appears to be Nathanael West's novel *The Day of the Locust* (1939). More than Odets or Faulkner, whom the Coens might admire but still parody mercilessly, West appears to be the central literary influence on *Barton Fink*. When questioned about the influence of West, Joel claimed not to have read his fiction but mentioned that Ethan had read *The Day of the Locust* and West's *Miss Lonelyhearts* (1933) with great interest. As we have seen in previous chapters, the Coens typically acknowledge important influences, especially literary authors. The fact that West is mentioned only in passing is a significant omission, perhaps an act of denial consistent with Harold Bloom's contention that authors must repress the voices of precursors who threaten to rob them of their unique creative identity. Nevertheless, a general comparison of the Coens with Nathanael West reveals key affinities. Much like the Coens, whose early films before *Barton Fink* had fallen well short of achieving mainstream success, West's literary work (consisting of four published novels) received little recognition in his own lifetime. Prior to the publication of *The Day of the Locust*, West wrote to a friend 'how difficult it is to go on making the effort and sacrifices necessary to produce a novel only to find nowhere any just understanding of what the book is about' (Martin 1970: 335). In this context, another letter written to Edmund Wilson in 1939 is worth quoting:

> Somehow or other I seem to have slipped in between all the 'schools'. My books meet no needs except my own, their circulation is practically private and I'm lucky to be published. And yet, I only have a desire to remedy all that *before* sitting down to write, once begun I do it my way [...] and go on making what one critic called 'private and unfunny jokes'. (Martin 1970: 793)

Despite praise from the best writers of his age, including F. Scott Fitzgerald, Dashiell Hammett and William Carlos Williams, West's fiction never reached a wider readership during his lifetime, remaining obscure and widely misunderstood. West's uncontrollable urge to indulge in 'private and unfunny jokes' finds a contemporary parallel in the Coens' dark humour and obscure referential in-joking, on ample display in *Barton Fink*. Though highly regarded by a relatively small group of critics and intellectuals, *Barton Fink* was considered by many the least accessible of their films to date and, as such, it epitomises the Coens' disinterest in box-office success. In this respect, as R. Barton Palmer has written, *Barton Fink* provides 'a telling comment on the Coens' indifference to being properly understood [since] their references have proved too obscure to decode for most reviewers and commentators' (2004: 112).

Like the other literary figures included in *Barton Fink's* pastiche, West worked as a Hollywood screenwriter in the 1930s. Lured to Hollywood in 1933 by 20th Century, who paid him several thousand dollars for the rights to his second novel, *Miss Lonelyhearts*, West got his first scriptwriting job with Columbia Pictures, where, like Barton, the first two scripts he wrote were not filmed. West could not make a living on his novels and thus continued to work on unproduced screenplays because the studio salary supported his literary work. Like other authors who worked in the Hollywood studio system, West objected to the factory-like working conditions, complaining that 'all the writers sit in cells in a row and the minute a typewriter stops, someone pokes his head in the door to see if you are thinking' (Friedrich 1986: 9). For the last five years of his life (1935–1940) West labored as a scriptwriter for Republic, RKO, Universal and Columbia, but he never considered screenwriting anything more than a day job supporting his literary art.

The text by West that proves to be most essential for *Barton Fink* is *The Day of the Locust*. Set in Hollywood of the 1930s, the novel concerns a young artist named Tod Hackett, a painter classically trained at the Yale School of Fine Arts, who moves to Hollywood to work as a set designer. There he lives in a run-down apartment building and makes the acquaintance of a bizarre assortment of characters: an aging vaudeville comic and his attractive but untalented daughter who dreams of becoming a movie star, a dwarf bookmaker, a cowboy (named Earle) who works occasionally in 'horse-operas' and a screenwriter whose house is an exact reproduction of a Southern mansion in Biloxi, Mississippi. West's Hollywood is not the Hollywood filled with glamour and movie celebrities. Instead, the writer depicts Tinsel Town as a provincial village filled with pensioners from the mid-West who come to sunny California seeking a few years of repose after a lifetime of labour. As West describes them, they are 'savage and bitter, especially the middle-aged and old, and had been made so by boredom and disappoint-ment. All their lives they had slaved at some kind of dull, heavy labor, behind desks and counters, in the fields and at tedious machines of all sorts, saving their pennies and dreaming of the leisure that would be theirs when they had enough' (1997: 380).

The setting of *The Day of the Locust* is the seedy side of the 'city of dreams' where the cheated and betrayed looking for glamour find nothing but the dumping ground of civilisation, what West calls in the novel 'a Sargasso of the imagination' (1997: 326). While living and working in Hollywood as a screenwriter, West collected material for his novel from his experiences living in a low-rent apartment building off Holly-wood Boulevard where, as he calls them in *The Day of the Locust*, an assortment of 'screwballs and screwboxes' lived illusory lives in the shadow of the movie studios that mass-produced the imagery of their illusions. West's shabby apartment building in Hollywood became the basis for Tod Hackett's residence, renamed the San Bernardino Arms, and perhaps the inspiration for the Hotel Earle. But while Tod socialises with his colourful neighbours whose strange lives he observes with detached irony, Barton remains isolated, his social contact limited to the hotel staff and his apparently friendly neighbour, Charlie Meadows. Most of the characters in *Barton Fink*'s storyworld are in the movie business, but they are as bizarrely caricatured as West's human oddities. Although Tod the painter has come to Hollywood for the same reasons as Barton the writer, there is a crucial difference. Tod separates his creative art from his commercial day-job at the studio. Like West, he spends his free time collecting material for his paintings by observing the people around him. Barton, on the other hand, cannot free himself from his noble artistic calling to do what should be the simple task of writing a

B-picture screenplay. Like Barton, Tod is a populist devoted to the common man. His paintings are composed of images of the common man, but Tod's notion of the average working man is not the figure of nobility Barton imagines him to be, but instead the 'savage and bitter' refugees from the mid-West, whom he calls 'the cream of America's madmen' (1997: 309).

In his letter to Edmund Wilson, West also laments the problematic reception of his writings, particularly by the political left wing: 'The radical press, although I consider myself on their side, doesn't like it, and thinks it even fascist sometimes, and the literature boys, whom I detest, detest me in turn. The highbrow press finds that I avoid the important things and the lending library touts in the daily press think me shocking' (1997: 793). The leftist critics thought that his stories lacked sufficient attention to their ideological concerns and thus that his dark satire failed to achieve the correct political effect. In fact, West was, like Odets, a committed critic of the capitalist system; and like Odets, he distanced himself from the doctrines of American Communists and their emphasis on the class struggle. Instead, he shifted his focus to the growing threat of right-wing fascism. Unlike many of that era, West was convinced that if fascism emerged in the United States, it would not be caused by an external threat from abroad but rather from within American society itself, manifested as the angry mob depicted in *The Day of the Locust*, or more specifically, in the figure of the raging 'mass man'. The violent rage that West thought could erupt in American society is enacted in *Barton Fink* by Charlie Meadows, a common man who feels anger and resentment toward his job as insurance salesman and because, as he finally tells Barton, his voice from below cannot be heard. The joke on Barton, as a writer who professes solidarity with the proletarian working man, is that, presented by Charlie with the opportunity of learning about the common man firsthand, through Charlie's stories ('stories to curl your hair'), the writer doesn't care to listen and cannot take anyone but himself seriously. That is why, when Charlie, now 'Madman Mundt', returns to the Hotel Earle in a homicidal rage, he tells Barton his savage murders were the price for Barton's refusal to listen to him; ironically, for being the kind of writer Barton had previously claimed to despise, 'writers [who] do everything in their power to insulate themselves from the common man – from where they live, from where they trade, from where they fight and love and converse and so naturally their work suffers, and regresses into empty formalism'.

For West, the rise of fascism in America was the real threat to internal political stability, rather than the external threat of European communism thought by many in the 1930s to be the greatest menace to American national security. In his view, the disillusionment of the masses with the dehumanising effects of a culture of consumption rapidly replacing the industrial production of the capitalist economy would eventually lead to a violent revolt of the masses. In *The Day of the Locust*, the protagonist-painter visualises the fascist mob in a painting he is working on called 'The Burning of Los Angeles', described as follows:

> Across the top [of the canvas], he had drawn the burning city, a great bonfire of architectural styles, ranging from Egyptian to Cape Cod colonial. Through the

center, winding from left to right, was a long hill street and down it, spilling into the middle foreground, came the mob carrying baseball bats and torches. For the faces of its members, he was using innumerable sketches he had made of the people who come to California to die – all those poor devils who can only be stirred by the promise of miracles and then only to violence. [...] No longer bored, they sang and danced joyously in the red light of the flames. (1997: 387–388)

In the novel's final chapter this vision becomes frightening reality. Standing outside Kahn's Persian Palace Theater, a crowd has gathered, awaiting the premiere of a new movie and hoping for a glimpse of some movie-star celebrities. 'At the sight of their movie heroes,' writes West, 'the crowd would turn demoniac.' Growing restless and bored, the throng of thousands outside the movie palace suddenly transforms into the angry mob carrying bats and torches that Tod has already envisioned in 'The Burning of Los Angeles'. 'Then,' Tod says to himself, 'nothing but machine guns would stop it' (1997: 379). Earlier Tod had questioned the prophetic vision of his painting, but refusing to give up the role of Jeremiah, he feels certain Los Angeles will end in flames. 'He was amused,' writes West, 'by the strong feeling of satisfaction this dire conclusion gave him. Were all prophets of doom and destruction such happy men?' (1997: 309).

The collective rioting of Tod's apocalyptic vision is narrowed in *Barton Fink* to focus on the individual madman, Charlie 'Mundt' Meadows, who represents not the revolutionary 'masses' of the proletarian class, but the alienated, angry 'mass man' of a consumer-oriented capitalist society. The surreal burning of the Hotel Earle can thus be read as a variation on the 'Burning of Los Angeles' imagined in *The Day of the Locust*, as a vision of society on the brink of violent collapse. To underscore the idea that a seemingly harmless commoner such as Charlie Meadows can quickly transform into

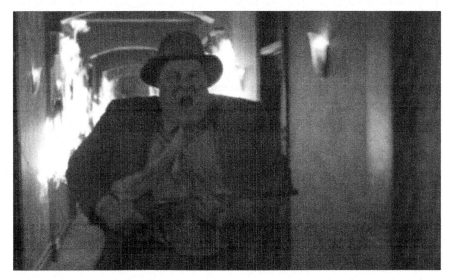

'I'll show you the life of the mind!'

a violent fascist, the Coens incorporate two crypto-fascist police detectives, Deutsch and Mastrionotti, one German, the other Italian, representing the fascist powers that sprang up in Europe and drew America into the global apocalypse of World War II. Their openly anti-Semitic remarks confirm the fascist profile. The associations with the European fascism are further strengthened when, as Mundt is about to execute Detective Deutsch with a point-blank shotgun blast to the head, he says with casual irony, 'Heil Hitler'.

### 'A Particular Kind of Joking'

Some would consider such a casual reference to Hitler in bad taste, a jokey reference to a particularly unfunny historical villain. Equally tasteless are Charlie's numerous references to 'heads', a macabre joke that only reveals its dark punch line in the revelation that Charlie, aka Madman Mundt, is a serial killer who decapitates his victims. When Barton suggests, for instance, that Charlie see a doctor for his ear infection, Charlie responds: 'Ah, doctors. What's he gonna tell me? Can't trade my head in for a new one.' Assuring Barton he'll overcome his writer's block, Charlie says: 'You've got a head on your shoulders. What is it they say? Where there's a *head*, there's hope.' Barton corrects with unknowing irony: 'Where there's *life* there's hope.' Leaving on a business trip, Charlie informs Barton that 'things have gotten all balled up at the Head Office'. After Charlie assists Barton in the disposal of Audrey's dead body, he repeatedly admonishes Barton: 'You gotta act as if nothing's happened. Put this totally out of your head.' When Barton panics, Charlie insists: 'We just gotta keep our heads and we'll figure it out.' This tasteless joke is pushed to the limit of absurdity by its nearly constant repetition throughout the screenplay where the word 'head' occurs more than seventy times, achieving its final degree of intensification in Charlie's going-away gift to Barton, the mysterious box which invites speculation that its contents might be Audrey's head (or perhaps Mayhew's).

Such macabre joking is very much in the spirit of West's humour, politely described by Norman Podhoretz as a 'particular kind of joking' (1971: 155). Podhoretz suspects that West's brand of cynical black humour was motivated by a deep-seated pessimism and for this reason he finds West's grotesque humour 'unpolitical', arguing that it implies humanity's striving for nobility invariably results in absurd failure (1971: 160) – a common criticism of Coen brothers movies, especially *Barton Fink*. Indeed, West's self-assessment of his 'particular kind of joking' resonates with the Coens' comments on their own politically incorrect humour. Of himself, West said: 'I'm a comic writer and it seems impossible for me to handle any of the "big things" without seeming to laugh or at least smile' (Martin 1970: 335). The Coens have made similar self-observations, such as the following from an interview on *Barton Fink*: 'It seems we're incapable of writing a movie which, in one way or another, doesn't get contaminated by comic elements' (Allen 2006: 51).

The Coens' Westian sense of humour is also apparent in their irreverent joking with the Holy Word of God set forth in the Hebrew Bible. Underscoring the apocalyptic tone that builds to a climax in the burning of the Hotel Earle, the Coens steer Barton into an unlikely intertextual detour (already adumbrated in the title of Mayhew's novel – *Nebuchadnezzar* – which he presents to Barton as a 'little entertainment' to divert him during his 'sojourn among the Philistines'). Searching for inspiration, the stymied writer turns to the Gideon Bible in his hotel room drawer. There, Barton comes upon the Old Testament Book of Daniel and the story of Daniel, a Hebrew wise man and spiritual advisor in to the Babylonian King Nebuchadnezzar. The specific passage that draws Barton's attention tells of the king's disturbing dream, the exact contents of which the king refuses to share with his wise men, but nevertheless commands them to decipher:

> And the king, Nebuchadnezzar, answered and said to the Chaldeans, I recall not my dream; if ye will not make known unto me my dream, and its interpretation, ye shall be cut in pieces, and your tents shall be made a dunghill.

Confronted with an apparently impossible task of interpretation, Daniel finds the solution in a divine vision which reveals to him both the content and meaning of the king's dream, which Daniel interprets as a revelatory prophesy of apocalypse. In relation to Barton's story, the reference to Daniel and his vision of apocalypse precedes Charlie's appearance as Madman Mundt, giving special resonance to his predilection for decapitation. As it turns out, cutting people to pieces and destroying their homes is Charlie's other job. And like the biblical king, one might say that Charlie also has a dream in need of interpretation: his story of the Common Man, which Barton is incapable of hearing and properly interpreting. The biblical reference to Nebuchadnezzar might also apply to Jack Lipnick, the 'head' of Capitol Pictures, who commands Barton to tell him the contents of his 'dream', namely, the wrestling movie he tasks Barton to write, while refusing to offer any specifics. In Lipnick's words, 'Wallace Beery is a wrestler. I wanna know his hopes, his dreams.' When Barton fails to deliver the right story Lipnick sentences him to the figurative death of a writer without an audience. Lipnick's absurdly obsequious kissing of Barton's shoe also has a parallel in the Book of Daniel, where King Nebuchadnezzar prostrates himself before Daniel for delivering the divine prophesy. Unlike Daniel, however, Barton can satisfy neither of his rulers – not Charlie, the idealised working man he supposedly worships, and not Lipnick, the tyrannical ruler of Capitol Pictures. And with the vengeance of an Old Testament God, they both punish him.

## The Fulfillment of a Prophesy

Turning once again to the reception of *Barton Fink*, we note that even though the film collected numerous awards and garnered high critical praise, many expressed doubt and confusion about its meaning or purpose. To reiterate Terrence Rafferty's complaint, what is most bothersome about *Barton Fink* is the impression that the filmmakers were 'inordinately pleased with its hermetic meaninglessness'. Playwright Arthur Miller responded to this complaint, writing: 'I'm not sure there is a problem with *Barton Fink*. It may be perfect. Maybe I'm not supposed to be sure.' Comparing the film with the notoriously inscrutable work of David Lynch, Miller hedged, admitting that perhaps *Barton Fink* was not *about* anything in particular, just another example of what he calls the 'genre of mere chaos'. Nevertheless, he concludes that it is a film that 'cannot be easily dismissed, since it might reflect the stage at which we have truly arrived – whether in our rise or our decline' (1991). Asked about the meaning and message of *Barton Fink*, the Coens simply balked: '"That question about a larger purpose always stops us," says Joel, who insists that "there is no larger purpose outside the story itself"' (Johnston 1991). This lack of a larger purpose, particularly evident, even flaunted, in *Barton Fink*, marks the film as the product of a postmodern aesthetic, or in Miller's phrase, 'the stage at which we have truly arrived'. As postmodernists, the Coens take no fixed position on any issue and refuse to attribute any profound meaning to their film art. Their diffident response to such critiques might be considered an instance of what French philosopher Jean Baudrillard calls 'the cool smile' of the postmodernist, which no longer merely signifies ironic detachment, but instead a stance of radical indeterminacy, wary of political commitment and hence passively complicit with the dominant socio-political ideology (1998: 121). For Baudrillard the 'cool smile' of the postmodern parodist is 'not the smile of critical distance', but rather 'the smile of collusion', signaling indifference and passive capitulation to a dominant and insurmountable socio-economic system. Thus Baudrillard reaffirms Jameson's condemnation of postmodern parody as 'blank pastiche' lacking critical purpose and thereby colluding with the aims of capitalism.

No doubt, the oft-repeated criticism that Coen films have no valid points of reference outside the world of cinema and are therefore the self-indulgent amusements is particularly salient for *Barton Fink*. The Coens' reconstruction of the historical moment of Hollywood circa 1941 is fabricated, as we have seen, by raiding an extensive archive of textual sources, announcing itself as a postmodern pastiche *par excellence* and an illustration of Jameson's conception of pastiche as a 'neutral mimicry' of fashions and styles associated with a certain time period (here the classical studio era), replacing historical reality with the history of aesthetic styles. Jameson attributes postmodernism's loss of connection with empirical history to a nostalgic longing for an imagined past that never existed. Arguing against this reading of *Barton Fink*, R. Barton Palmer contends that 'it is not the intention of the Coens to provoke some false sense of nostalgia through this kind of parody. [Their] films do not in any sense flatten out the past, eliminating the depth of its otherness for comic effect' (2004: 106). In Palmer's reading, *Barton Fink* is not located in 'a present ever looking backward' but in a past that is carefully reconstructed but simultaneously marked as a fictional construct with the aim of provoking a 'historiographic curiosity about a bygone era whose depths have yet to be fully explored' (2004: 112).

Foremost among the historical depths explored in *Barton Fink* is the era of classic Hollywood and the workings of the movie industry in the 1930s and 1940s. The film's elaborate intertextuality and highly stylised visual presentation encourage reviewers to the assume that in *Barton Fink* historical reality has been reduced to a set of codes and fashions culled from the history of film and literature. Stylisation aside, the film does deliver a potent lampoon of Hollywood's vulgar commercialism. However reductive it might be to say that *Barton Fink* is a satire on the Hollywood industrial complex, the film does render a realistic (if comically distorted) picture of the major Hollywood studios as prototypical sites of industrial manufacturing, vertically integrated systems controlled by top-down management and dedicated to the profitable mass-production of entertainment commodities. The idea that the Hollywood dream factory is based on capitalist principles of commerce is openly implied in the name of Lipnick's movie studio: Capitol Pictures. As we have seen, Lipnick himself is a composite character based on the lives of the top business managers of classic Hollywood studios, represented as super-wealthy barons of monopoly capitalism. Here we should recall that in the 1930s and 1940s five major studios (Paramount, MGM, Warner Bros., Twentieth-Century Fox and RKO) controlled a large share of the hugely profitable American movie market, and that the moguls who owned controlling shares of the studios' stock were in charge of all major decisions concerning production. As head of Capitol Pictures, Lipnick controls every aspect of the studio's operations. He thinks of himself as the commander-in-chief of Capitol Pictures, an image parodied by the army colonel's uniform he wears in his final meeting with Barton, who is shocked when Lipnick dismisses his inspired wrestling scenario out-of-hand. It seems the self-absorbed writer has not heeded the producer's warning about 'fruitiness': 'This is a wrestling picture; the audience wants to see action, drama, wrestling and plenty of it.' Capitol Pictures, in other words, produces entertainment, not art. 'They don't wanna see a guy wrestling with his soul,' Lipnick explains, '…well, all right, a little bit, for the critics, but you make it the carrot that wags the dog.' Aside from his hilariously mixed metaphor, Lipnick's critique offers a succinct formula for highly profitable action movies that is still relevant today. The parody of Hollywood's market-driven capitalism reaches its apex when Lipnick instructs his underling Lou to inform Barton that 'the contents of your head are the property of Capitol Pictures'. The producer's final blow to the writer's ego comes when Lipnick takes possession of Barton's creative identity: 'You think you're the only writer who can give me that Barton Fink feeling?! I got twenty writers under contract that I can ask for a Fink-type thing from.' Hollywood owns Barton's 'head' as it owns many others, any of them capable of reproducing 'the Fink-type thing'. Like everything else in a capitalist economy, the artist's style can be bought, duplicated and sold as a mass-marketable commodity.

Another historical depth usefully explored in *Barton Fink* concerns the representation of early 1940s Hollywood and the debt this representation owes to West's *The Day of the Locust*. Although the Coens' pastiche borrows substantially from biographies and writings of Clifford Odets and William Faulkner (who are made to look ridiculous), West's novel proves a more significant source. In fact, the extent of intertextual borrowing from *The Day of the Locust* is such that it might be fair to consider the Coens' screenplay a disguised adaptation of the novel. West's central importance is evident in the Coens' reworking of the writer's darkly humorous vision of Hollywood as a microcosm of consumer capitalism. At the same time, the intertextual dialogue with West constitutes a substantial rereading of *The Day of the Locust*, correcting previously common misreadings of his work as nihilistic and validating him as an important author of the 1930s with a prophetic vision of American society. Interestingly, the Coens' revisionary reading is affirmed by the scholarly analysis of Jonathan Veitch, whose reassessment of West's writings counters the long-standing view that his novels are cynical and pessimistic and therefore politically suspect. Instead, Veitch discovers an undercurrent of cultural critique in West's darkly satirical portrayal of American society, brought to expression in a style heavily influenced by the European surrealists, which Veitch calls 'superrealism'. As its name implies, 'superrealism' is an excessive realism, without the depoliticised connotations generally associated with later American surrealists. In West's hands, this 'superrealism' becomes a distinctly different mode of fictional representation capable of transforming the writer's 'particular kind of joking' into a form of social criticism by intensifying and grotesquely distorting his vision of reality far beyond the conventional bounds of literary realism to expose the terrifying *reality* of the real. In an effort to deconstruct the mimetic forms of representation that constitute traditional art, West modified the surrealist dream reality to create a grotesque 'hyper-reality'. Against the grain of his surrealist contemporaries, West refused to move beyond representation and embrace the aestheticism of pure abstraction, believing that 'representation or similitude constitutes the sum total of what can be known', allowing the writer to explore 'the ways reality is constructed – literally or figuratively – under capitalist modernity' (Veitch 1997: 22).

While West's Communist contemporaries focused their writings on the disintegration of a production-oriented capitalist economy, West took a different view of post-Depression America enabling him to foresee the beginnings of a consumer-oriented capitalism. West understood that the liberal left-wing faith in the revolutionary working class was historically out of step. The proletarian industrial workforce was rapidly being replaced by middle-class consumers thoroughly co-opted into an economy increasingly predicated on the consumption of mass-produced products. In the place of the heroic factory worker, the social figure of greatest importance is now the unheroic 'mass man', whose unheard voice of resentment and frustration is the harbinger of fascist reaction. As previously discussed, such a fascist scenario comes vividly to life in *The Day of the Locust*:

> Every day of their lives they read the newspapers and went to the movies. Both fed them on lynchings, murder, sex crimes, explosions, wrecks, love nests, fires, miracles, revolutions, wars. This daily diet made sophisticates of them. The sun is a joke. [...] Nothing can ever be violent enough to make taut their slack minds and bodies. They have been cheated and betrayed. They have slaved and saved for nothing. (West 1997: 381)

Anticipating the media-saturated hyper-reality of postmodernism, West depicts a world flooded by the debased, mass-marketed products of journalism and Hollywood kitsch, which displace and finally supplant the real. Tod describes the Hollywood movie industry as 'the final dumping ground' for detritus of American culture, a junkyard for used-up dreams. As he explains, there isn't a dream that's been dreamed that doesn't sooner or later turn up in the Hollywood dump, 'having first been made photographic by plaster, canvas, lath, and paint' (1997: 326). Motion pictures are simulations *par excellence*, dreams that appear as the real. Indeed, the way movies are consumed and tossed aside is paradigmatic for the wider consumption of media. The contemporary world now consists of mass-mediated representations of real that have replaced reality. The older economy of industrial production based on the manufacture of material goods gives way to the production and consumption of media culture. In a world so totally mediated, we gradually lose the ability to distinguish between the real and its artificial representation.

The critique of representation West mounts in *The Day of the Locust* is subsumed and rearticulated in *Barton Fink* with the implication that much if not all of the narrative unfolds in Barton's over-active imagination, that it is the story of a dreamer lost in his dream. With its surrealist atmosphere, notably on display in the decor of the Hotel Earle, *Barton Fink* invites viewers to imagine that its story could be a dream that takes place 'in Barton's head'. The dream trope is introduced early in the dialogue of his stage play: 'Daylight is a dream if you've lived with your eyes closed,' says Barton's imaginary proletarian hero. From the very beginning it is suggested that Barton has lived with his eyes closed, incapable of seeing past the self-enclosing dream world of his ideologically blinkered imagination. This is illustrated by his naïve view of the working class, which he represents in his stage play as noble and heroic but of which he possesses neither genuine knowledge nor understanding. He knows them only as imaginary figures. For this reason Barton fails to recognise that Charlie Meadows *is* the wrestler, the 'burly man' of his movie script – a common man whose story begs to be told but remains unheard because Barton simply won't listen. The distinction between reality and illusion is also put in doubt that Mundt is a manifestation of Barton's savage unconscious. He and Charlie appear to be the only residents of the Hotel Earle, which according to the filmmakers is designed to reflect the mind of Charlie/Mundt as rotten and decaying (Allen 266: 110). 'At the end,' says Ethan, 'when [Charlie] says he's a prisoner of his own mental state, that it's like a hell, the hotel has already taken on that infernal appearance' (Allen 2006: 52).

At the end of the story it is made clear that Barton cannot distinguish between reality and representation. In the movie's final scene Barton is finally confronted with the paradox of representation, namely that now the representation of the real constitutes the limit of what can be known about reality. As Barton wanders onto an empty beach, he is confronted with what appears to be the living embodiment of the bathing beauty represented in the painting that hung over his writing desk. Confused, Barton asks her if she is 'in pictures' and, after replying 'Don't be silly', the bathing beauty casually assumes exactly the same pose as the painting. Bathing Beauty has accompanied Barton throughout his hellish ordeal as an image, the kind of cheap mass-produced representation of the real one finds in any cheap hotel room. Because the copy or representation has preceded the real, Barton can no longer distinguish between original and simulated copy. *The Day of the Locust* provides an analogous moment when Tod is caught in the rioting mob outside the picture palace. Stunned and injured by the sudden eruption of violence, Tod retreats into his imagination, where he resumes work on his prophetic painting 'The Burning of Los Angeles':

He had almost forgotten both his leg and his predicament, and to make his escape still more complete he stood on a chair and worked at the flames in an upper corner of the canvas, modeling the tongues of fire so that they licked even more avidly at a Corinthian column that held up the palmleaf roof of a nutburger stand. (West 1997: 388)

As if to remind us that their their films are never about 'the real' but instead the reworking of received cultural texts as a form of creative re-presentation, the Coens embed a 'private and unfunny' joke that only the most observant viewer will see and comprehend. When Bill Mayhew signs a copy of his novel 'Nebuchadnezzer' for Barton, we notice that the publisher is 'Swain and Pappas'. Marshall Swain and George Pappas were philosophers who wrote on epistemology and metaphysics in *Essays on Knowledge and Justification*, a study on the limits of knowledge. If *Barton Fink* can be said to have any message of import beyond its story, it would appear to be the post-modern dictum that the representation of the real constitutes the limit of what can be known about reality.

# CHAPTER FIVE

# The Hudsucker Proxy: A Comedy of Reinvention

The Coen brothers' fifth feature film, *The Hudsucker Proxy*, was released in 1994, but the screenplay, co-scripted with Sam Raimi, had already been written before the release of *Blood Simple*. Due to projected high production costs the project was put on hold until, a decade later, the Coens teamed with high-profile producer Joel Silver who arranged the financing for the movie at a cost of $25 million, considerably more than any of the Coens' previous films. Perhaps unsurprisingly, considering the minimal appeal of its throw-back homage to Old Hollywood comedy, the movie was a box office bust, earning only $2.8 million in theatrical release. The film's financial misfortune likely had much to do with its arcane generic form, for *The Hudsucker Proxy* is a clever reinvention of the classic 'screwball' comedy popular in the 1930s and 1940s as exemplified in the movies of Frank Capra and Preston Sturges. Its fairy tale story revolves around Norville Barnes (Tim Robbins), a naïvely ambitious young man from Muncie, Indiana, who arrives in New York City hoping to launch a successful career in business. Although his first job at Hudsucker Industries as mail clerk puts him at the bottom of the corporate hierarchy, he soon makes a miraculous rise to the top when he is chosen for the role of 'proxy' to replace the recently deceased company president, Waring Hudsucker (Charles Durning). Against all expectations, the seemingly simple-minded proxy enjoys immediate success by inventing a kid's toy that becomes the craze of the nation – the Hula Hoop. Under the heady influence of sudden success and power, however, Norville quickly loses his small-town innocence and slips into a downward spiral of depression, ending in suicidal despair.

Set in New York City, 1958, Norville's rise-and-fall narrative also reflects a trend in Hollywood movies of the 1950s such as *The Sweet Smell of Success* (1957), a noirish story written by Clifford Odets (a model for the Coens' *Barton Fink*) about a ruthlessly ambitious newspaper man named J. J. Hunsecker (Burt Lancaster) who climbs to the top but ends up, like Norville Barnes, contemplating a death leap from the top of a skyscraper. The similarity of the name Hunsecker with Hudsucker suggests a kinship, although the Odets-penned story was clearly intended as a sober critique of American big business, while the intentions of *The Hudsucker Proxy* are less transparent. Another movie of this era with similar concerns is Robert Wise's drama *Executive Suite* (1954), a cynical tale that opens with the death of a top executive, which, as in *The Hudsucker Proxy*, initiates a battle for control of the company. One of contenders for corporate power schemes to profit from the old boss's death by selling a large share of his stock to destabilise the company and lower stock values so that he can later buy back the stocks at a deflated rate, a scheme very similar to that of Sidney J. Mussberger (Paul Newman), who installs Norville as president of the Hudsucker Corporation hoping that the 'proxy' (whom Sid considers 'a jerk we can really push around') will shake the confidence of Wall Street and push down the price of company stock. In both *Executive Suite* and *The Sweet Smell of Success* the moral message is clear and meant to be taken seriously: Men who value career and material success above all else, even above personal relationships, are fated to live empty lives and ultimately to suffer despair.

Despite such affinities with movies that openly indict American big business, the Coens insist that their primary aim was not to critique capitalism but to create a 'modern-day fairy tale' set in the corporate culture of the 1950s. A far cry from the down-beat social dramas of the 1950s, *The Hudsucker Proxy* mimes the popular comedies of the 1930s and 1940s, and certainly, much of its fun derives from the enjoyment of the film's complex and cleverly wrought pastiche, which offers a feast for the film-literate viewer, quoting heavily from the comedies of Capra and Sturges, as well as from Fritz Lang's science-fiction masterpiece *Metropolis* (1927), Terry Gilliam's dark satire *Brazil* (1984), and a rich array of additional cultural sources.

The movie's initial reviews were mixed. Roger Ebert called it the 'best-looking' movie he had seen in a long time. Otherwise, he voiced the view, shared by many, that *The Hudsucker Proxy* was 'all surface and no substance'. Todd McCarthy wrote that the Coens' new movie was 'one of the most inspired and technically stunning pastiches of Old Hollywood pictures ever to come out of New Hollywood', but otherwise little more than sterile pastiche, lacking emotion and human warmth. Geoff Brown thought the Coens' new film praiseworthy, 'a brilliant film about archetypes and movie ghosts', but was also forced to admit that 'for something with heart and a cast of humans, you must go elsewhere'. Christopher Tookey condemned *The Hudsucker Proxy* as 'one of the worst movies of this, or any, year', faulting the Coens especially for their failure to critique capitalist big business and insisting that the movie should have created a more realistic image of big capitalism instead of the 'fairy palace' the Coens had built from the ruins of a dead genre. Considering the high production costs for such a movie, Tookey concludes that 'a multi-million dollar budget has been wasted on film-school thinking'.

As the critics rightly emphasised, style *does* trump content in a film that recreates the look of old studio movies but playfully exaggerates and distorts that cinematic vision of reality with a style of monumental proportions. In terms of scale, the film's overbuilt production design pushes the realist aesthetic far beyond conventional limits,

its decorative excess serving to parody rather than replicate the naïve studio realism of its classic models. Production designer Dennis Gassner reports that he and the brothers 'agreed that *Citizen Kane* had the scale and perspective we wanted, but we wanted to do it much better than they did it, to do it the Coen way, not the Welles way' (Allen 2006: 68). To rival the visual monumentality of *Citizen Kane*, elaborate sets were constructed in super-sized sound stages large enough to house the enormous Hudsucker board-room with its improbably long meeting table as well as Sid Mussberger's palatial pent-house office atop the Hudsucker skyscraper (which Gassner compares to the office of fascist Italian dictator Mussolini). One of the most ambitious sets was the cavernous mailroom in the bottom floor of the Hudsucker Building which, in Gassner's words, 'looks as if it might have been designed by Albert Speer', the Nazi architect Hitler commissioned to plan a new Berlin to be the greatest imperial city since ancient Rome (Robson 2007: 140). The design for the Hudsucker mailroom also takes a cue from Gilliam's *Brazil*, where a horrific vision of totalitarian rule and its domination of the lower classes is conjured as a bureaucracy of absurd proportions, symbolised by a work-place which in its colossal dimensions overwhelms the oppressed workers, visually reducing them to ant-like images. Extravagant special effects sequences and spectacular action set-pieces such as Waring's leap from the Hudsucker boardroom and Norville's near-fatal plunge at the end also contribute to the movie's overall sense of monumen-tality. Co-writer Sam Raimi directed the second unit needed for filming these and other technically complex sequences which, according to Joel, have a 'cartoon element' comparable to the animated *Road Runner* series where Wile E. Coyote can fall off a cliff and get up unharmed (Mottram 2000: 104). Combined with the film's otherwise exaggerated production design, the cartoon-like action pieces lend the story world of *The Hudsucker Proxy* an air of faux-grandiosity, staged with such anti-realistic excess that ultimately its intended effect is alienating. In R. Barton Palmer's view, 'the self-conscious grandiosity of image in *Hudsucker* expresses the filmmakers' detached view of the diegetic world they have conjured into existence' (2004: 135). Style functions in *The Hudsucker Proxy* to distance audiences, as well as the filmmakers themselves, from the characters and the transparently 'made-up' world they inhabit.

## A Capra Film Written by Sturges

Generally, the Coen brothers state their preference for rewriting literary sources (Cain and Hammett in their early films, Odets and West in *Barton Fink*), rather than doing remakes of antecedent films. This makes *The Hudsucker Proxy*, a film devoted entirely to recreating cinematic precursors, something of an oddity, and all the more interesting because it is one of the Coens' earliest screenplays. As homage, *The Hudsucker Proxy* is proof of the brothers' enduring affection for classic Hollywood genres, especially for the kind of comedies known as 'screwball'. In its restoration of screwball comedy, *The Hudsucker Proxy* draws on a cluster of films from the 1930s and 1940s, in particular those by Frank Capra and Preston Sturges, sampling plots and characters from Capra films like *Mr. Deeds Goes to Town* (1936) and *It's a Wonderful Life* (1946) and infusing them with a darker, more cynical humour substantially derived from Sturges' comedies of the 1940s. Like its historical models, *The Hudsucker Proxy* uses screwball antics to lighten its treatment of weightier themes, painting a picture of corrupt corporate capitalism with the brush strokes of a cartoon illustrator. In its reinvention of Capra-style screwball *The Hudsucker Proxy* pursues one of Capra's most characteristic conceits: the hero's failure and the temptation of suicide, typically prevented by the intervention of some last-minute *deus ex machina*. Probably the best-known version of this narrative occurs in *It's a Wonderful Life* where one of Capra's most memorable heroes, George Bailey (James Stewart), contemplates suicide to alleviate the humiliation and despair he has suffered in his failed struggle against Mr. Potter (Lionel Barrymore), a greedy, heartless capitalist who schemes to profit by purchasing and controlling all the local real estate. In his fight against Potter's take-over, George makes great self-sacrifices for his community, staying home to manage the small-town savings and loan bank established by his father instead of following his dream of travelling and exploring the greater world. Only when a guardian angel sent from heaven intervenes to show him the error of his suicidal intent, does George relent, finally to be redeemed by his previous good deeds and saved from financial ruin by the generosity of friends and patrons, proving (Capra-style) the karmic principle that 'what goes around, comes around'.

Another instance of the suicidal hero is found in Capra's *Meet John Doe* (1941), the story of a down-and-out ballplayer named Long John Willoughby (Gary Cooper) who is hired by a local newspaper for a sensational hoax intended to boost circulation by running a fake story on 'John Doe' predicting that he will leap to his death from the top of City Hall on Christmas Eve. The hoax does indeed increase newspaper sales, but it also makes the John Doe proxy a populist hero. When the scam becomes public knowledge, the shame drives Long John to contemplate actual suicide. The suicide motif is also prominent in several of Sturges' early screenplays, written in the 1930s, two of which concern financially successful men driven to commit suicide because their success leaves them with empty lives. In *The Power and the Glory*, scripted in 1934 for Warner Bros., the central character Tom Garner (Spencer Tracy) rises to the top as a ruthless railroad tycoon, but after a series of personal tragedies, shoots himself to death. In *Diamond Jim* (1935) the eponymous hero (Edward Arnold), rejected by the woman he loves, decides to eat himself to death. The Coens resurrect the suicidal tycoon in the character of Waring Hudsucker, whose leap from the top of the Hudsucker Building reenacts the suicides of Sturges' tragic anti-heroes, but who returns in a Capraesque ending as Norville's saving angel, confessing that he jumped to his death because, like Tom Garner and Diamond Jim, his professional success had ruined his personal life, causing the woman he loved to reject him and marry his Machiavellian business associate, Sidney Mussberger.

The opening sequence of *The Hudsucker Proxy* finds Norville Barnes on the brink of repeating Waring Hudsucker's fatal leap from the top of the Hudsucker skyscraper. Off-screen, the omniscient narrator, Moses (Bill Cobbs), poses the story's central question: 'How'd he get so high, and why's he feelin' so low?' In the end, like George Bailey, Norville is saved by Waring Hudsucker's angelic intervention and given a second chance, but for very different reasons. Bailey's near-demise is, ironically, the consequence of his moral virtue. By helping his fellow working-class citizens resist the domination of big capital, Bailey represents the populist ideal mythologised in Capra's vision of American democracy. Norville, on the other hand, can hardly be held up as a hero of the working class. Instead of using his power to help the workers of Hudsucker Industries, his miraculous and unearned ascension to power goes to his head and as chief executive he soon shows himself to be little better than his antagonist, Sid Mussberger. As president of Hudsucker Industries, Norville leads a princely life of luxury in his penthouse office, while below he has decreed big layoffs from the workforce to boost profits. When Amy (Jennifer Jason Leigh) confronts him with this, Norville replies matter-of-factly, 'Well yes, we're pruning away some of the dead wood', whereupon she scolds him angrily, accusing him of 'sitting up here like a sultan not doing a lick of work'.

Norville Barnes also recalls Jefferson Smith (James Stewart), the hero of Capra's *Mr. Smith Goes to Washington* (1939), who, like Norville, journeys from backwater to the big city where he is chosen by corrupt powers to serve as a kind of proxy, selected by devious politicians to fill the term of a deceased senator because they think he can be easily manipulated. In the ethical conflict that ensues, Jefferson Smith emerges as a symbol of moral integrity in a corrupt world, a mythic incarnation of patriotic virtue and the American belief in the power of a strong democracy to counter political graft. Norville's journey to the big city is a somewhat different story, with a very different outcome. Like Mr. Smith, Norville triumphs over the powers of greed and corruption, but not for the sake of the utopian ideals of populist democracy and moral virtue. The only ideal Norville pursues is success in business, which he achieves more as the result of dumb luck than of moral strength. Norville never questions the capitalist ideology implicit in the corporate culture of big business and happily carries out his duties in service to the American Dream of material success.

The most extensively quoted film in *The Hudsucker Proxy*'s Capra pastiche is *Mr. Deeds Goes to Town*, from which the filmmakers recruit another of Capra's populist heroes whose story develops the familiar theme of provincial 'little man' fighting big-city corruption. Longfellow Deeds (Gary Cooper) is a small-town rube who unexpectedly inherits a large fortune which, of course, powerful big-city businessmen and lawyers scheme to take from him. With the help of Babe Bennett (Jean Arthur), an ambitious newspaper reporter who at first tries to expose the protagonist as a 'Cinderella Man' but then joins his noble cause, Deeds is able to outsmart his scheming antagonists, retain his inherited millions and become the heroic benefactor of the working class, freely redistributing his windfall fortune to bankrupt farmers during the Great Depression. In addition to the obvious borrowings in narrative structure and characterisations from *Mr. Deeds Goes to Town*, *The Hudsucker Proxy* references numerous scenes directly, notably the scene in which muck-raking reporter Amy Archer stages a con designed to deceive and expose Norville as an 'imbecile'. The scene's referent in *Mr. Deeds Goes to Town*, a 'lady-in-distress' scenario, stages a similar deception. Hoping to get the inside scoop on the overnight millionaire, Babe Bennett schemes to meet Deeds on a rainy night outside his urban mansion, posing as an unemployed and homeless waif. Accompanying Babe on her mission to swindle Deeds are two snide photographers

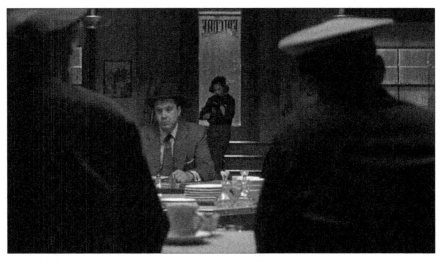

'Enter the dame.'

from the newspaper who observe from a parked taxi as Babe works her magic on the unsuspecting mark. To gain his sympathy and assistance she feigns poverty and finally pretends to faint from hunger, forcing Deeds to take her to a nearby restaurant for sustenance.

This comedic routine is replayed by Amy and Norville in a scene entitled 'Enter the Dame', but with a fundamental revision. In *Mr. Deeds Goes to Town*, the role of the observing photographers is minor, their sarcastic commentary on Babe's deception intermittent and mostly insignificant. In the Coens' parodic reinvention, two veteran cab drivers, Benny (John Seitz) and Lou (Joe Grifasi), replace the tag-along photographers in *Mr. Deeds Goes to Town* as witnesses to Amy's swindle, narrating and commenting on her scam in the style of a Greek chorus (if the chorus was composed of veteran New York cabbies). The entire scene is shot in one long take from the cabbies' point of view. Thus, instead of dialogue between Amy and Norville, we hear only the cabbies' cynical off-screen narration, as they knowingly anticipate Amy's every move, mocking the well-worn clichés she uses to deceive a gullible Norville. As Amy seats herself next to Norville, the veterans begin their commentary:

> Lou:  Enter the dame.
> Benny:  There's one in every story.
> Lou:  She's looking for her mark...
> Benny:  She finds him.
> Lou:  She sits down.
> *Norville, meanwhile, is not noticing her presence, prompting Lou to speculate...*
> Lou:  Maybe he's wise.
> Benny:  He don't look wise.
> *To get Norville's attention, Amy resorts to Plan 2, pretending to cry.*
> Lou:  Here come the water works.

Benny: Yellowstone.

Lou: Old Faithful.

Benny: Hello Niagara.

Having finally been noticed, Amy proceeds to lament her predicament. She has family problems, her mother needs an operation. Benny speculates: 'adenoids'. Lou corrects: 'lumbago' – then exclaims: 'That gag's got whiskers on it.' Just as the cabbies begin to think her act is failing to reach Norville, she pretends to pass out from hunger. The cabbies look on in disbelief. Lou can only say: 'She's good, Benny.' Benny agrees: 'She's *damn* good, Lou.' As if to emphasise the nauseating transparency of Amy's con artistry, the narrators conclude their commentary by ordering a 'bromo'. For the most part, the sob story Amy feeds Norville is cribbed directly from the Babe Bennett routine. Presenting the scene exclusively from the cabbies' perspective, however, not only highlights its referential status as movie cliché, but also has the effect of distancing the viewer, whose experience of the scene is mediated entirely by the cab drivers' sarcastic voiceover.

Capra's *Mr. Deeds Goes to Town* is not the only movie this scene references. Benny and Lou's commentary also brings to mind a scene in Sturges' *The Lady Eve* (1941) in which the con artist Jean Harrington (Barbara Stanwyck) observes from afar a group of women trying to impress the wealthy eligible bachelor Charles Pike (Henry Fonda), whom she herself has targeted as a mark. 'Holy smoke,' she exclaims at one point, 'the dropped kerchief! That hasn't been used since Lily Langtry,' echoed in the cabbie's remark: 'That gag's got whiskers on it.' Although the content of this scene is straight out of Capra, the ironic framing of the cabbies' off-screen commentary lends it a distinctly Sturgean point of view, subverting Capra's sentimentality with Sturges' cynical irony. Thus, the Coens playfully resurrect an antiquated subgenre, but at the same time render what is arguably a more authentic version of screwball, as exemplified by the movies of Sturges. Not surprisingly then, the Coens cite Sturges as the bigger influence on *The Hudsucker Proxy*: 'There is Capra in the film,' says Joel, 'but there's more Sturges'; the difference, as he explains, is that 'Sturges had a more satirical undertow [and] his relationship to business and society is much more sympathetic to our view than Capra's' (Robson 2007: 133). No doubt, there are crucial differences between these two filmmakers that shape their worldview and their conception of characters. Capra's heroes are truly heroic; they fight for justice, and though they generally fail, they are redeemed for their virtuous actions. Sturges prefers the comic fool whose redemption is granted not for his altruistic motives but in spite of his character weaknesses. Sturges also takes a rather different view of morality. *Contra* Capra, Sturges' comedies commonly portray self-interest and monetary gain as more important than traditional ethical values. Accordingly, the material qualities of personal success and external beauty are rewarded.

Norville Barnes is not a sympathetic populist hero in the mold of Capra. The only ideal he seems to embrace is the American Dream of getting rich quick, a feat Norville achieves not on the strength of his moral virtue or work ethic, but as the result of accidental good fortune bestowed on him simply because he is a gullible fool. In this way, Norville is closer to the naïvely vacuous figures typical of Preston Sturges' movies such as *Christmas in July* (1940), where the protagonist, Jimmy MacDonald (Dick Powell), is tricked into thinking he has won a national advertising contest. His false success so impresses his boss that he is awarded an unearned promotion to advertising executive. When the truth comes out, Jimmy is allowed to keep the promotion and given a chance to prove himself. If *Christmas in July* mocks the American mythology of success and wealth for all, *Hail the Conquering Hero* (1944), Sturges' satire on patriotism during World War II, travesties the myth of the warrior-hero in its farcical tale of a returning war veteran mistakenly celebrated for heroic deeds he did not perform. As his name indicates, Norville Barnes is a direct descendent of Norval Jones (Eddie Bracken), the hero of *The Miracle of Morgan's Creek* (1944), Sturges' satire on small-town morality in 1940s America. Like many of Sturges' characters, Norval is an accidental hero. A nerdy weakling unfit for military duty, Norval is miscast in the role of the archetypal all-American boy in love with the girl-next-door, mischievously named Trudy Kochenlocher. As Trudy's surname suggests, she too does not conform to the conventional notion of the chaste and virtuous all-American girl. Going against type, she is portrayed instead as a 'loose' young woman whose idea of patriotism is partying with the soldiers going off to war. When one of her soldier friends gets her pregnant before shipping out, Norval steps in to offer assistance to the 'lady in distress'. While at first Trudy cannot take Norval seriously, eventually his genuine love and devotion win Trudy's heart and the story concludes with their marriage and with Trudy giving birth to not one baby but sextuplets. The news that he is suddenly the father of six causes the surrogate father to pass out and the movie ends with an ironic title card:

> But Norval recovered and became increasingly happy for, as Shakespeare said: 'Some are born great, some achieve greatness, and some have greatness thrust upon them.'

His belated 'greatness' thrust upon him, Norval once again proves that the heroism of Sturges' protagonists is illusory, in this case, as much the outcome of the hero's weakness as of his strength. Lacking a clear moral message, *The Miracle of Morgan's Creek* does more to undermine than uphold a conventional code of ethics and propriety thought to be the provenance of small-town Americans.

The Coens borrow much from Sturges to fashion their reinvention of screwball comedy, but nothing so much as his style of writing dialogue. In its time, Sturges' highly stylised dialogue established, as film critic Andrew Dickos describes it, 'the standard of eloquence' for Hollywood screenwriting in its poetic rendering of 'a cacophony of Euro-American vernacularisms and utterances, peculiarly – and appropriately – spoken with scandalous indifference' (1985: 56). The fast-paced wit of Sturges' dialogue is most effectively imitated in *The Hudsucker Proxy* by the speeches of Amy Archer, whose character appears to be shaped primarily in the mold of Babe Bennett, the fast-talking, ruthless journalist bent on exposing the incompetence of Longfellow Deeds. Most viewers identify Amy's cinematic model as Katherine Hepburn, famous for her roles in such films as Howard Hawks' *Bringing up Baby* (1938) and George Cukor's comedies,

*The Philadelphia Story* (1940) and *Adam's Rib* (1949). But, as actor Jennifer Jason Leigh told the *Los Angeles Times*, 'It's not just Hepburn. Amy is very reminiscent of all those 1930s and 1940s heroines in the screwball Capra and Preston Sturges movies, Howard Hawks, Cukor.' 'Actually,' says Leigh, 'I'm doing everybody' (Anderson 1994). Thus, while Leigh's performance is a studied impersonation of Jean Arthur's Babe Bennett, it also recalls Rosalind Russell's performance as Hildy Johnson in Howard Hawks' *His Girl Friday* (1941) and Barbara Stanwyck's memorable rendering of the con-lady Jean Harrington in Sturges' *The Lady Eve*. A composite pastiche of acting styles, Leigh's delivery reflects and amplifies *The Hudsucker Proxy*'s multi-voiced dialogue with classic Hollywood comedies.

Critics complained that such denaturalised acting, which forces the actors to speak their lines in a peculiar, stilted way, reduces the characters to a set of stylised mannerisms. For this reason Jeff Shannon of the *Seattle Times* called *The Hudsucker Proxy* a 'sleek machine that just doesn't work', because 'not one minute of it registers even the slightest hint of emotional involvement'. As R. Barton Palmer points out, however, the Coens' approach to the film may be better understood in relation to the theory of drama advanced by German playwright Bertolt Brecht, whose so-called 'epic theatre' utilises a variety of 'alienation effects' to suspend spectator empathy and promote critical thinking and ideological engagement. As a practical function of his theory of estrangement, Brecht instructed his actors to speak as if they were quoting their lines. Thus, the arch anti-realism of *The Hudsucker Proxy* is in accord with Brecht's aim to discourage identification with characters in order to create the critical distance required for the audience to reflect intellectually on ideological themes. Other practices of Brechtian dramaturgy designed to deconstruct the illusion of reality are on display in the film as well. The breaking of the 'fourth wall' separating on-stage reality from audience is invoked, for instance, when Moses, searching for a way to save Norville from his fatal leap from the 44th floor, addresses the viewer directly, saying 'I'm really never supposed to do this, but do you have a better idea?'

The general use of comedic farce to counteract elements of melodrama lends the entire film story a sense of cool detachment that disturbed both audiences and reviewers. Viewed from this perspective, *The Hudsucker Proxy* offers itself as a Capra story as it might have been written by Sturges (under the influence of Brechtian aesthetics). Indeed, one of the central creative concerns in the movie is the filmmakers' attempt to orchestrate a contentious duet between Capra and Sturges, juxtaposing the differing styles and themes of these two filmmakers to commemorate their works but also to examine the values their movies convey. Simply put, the major difference that emerges in such a comparison is ideological. Capra has an unclouded moral vision; the division between good and evil in his fictional universe is clear and unequivocal. Sturges, in contrast, is wary of closed belief systems and his attitude toward inherited cultural values is typically ambivalent and critically distanced. Capra was a sentimentalist dreaming nostalgically of the return of an America based on cultural myths that likely never existed. By filtering Capra's 'corny' mythology of America through the lens of Sturges' more cynical comedies, *The Hudsucker Proxy* works to subvert Capra's sentimentality with an ironic, 'alienated' sensibility consistent with the self-reflexive artificiality characteristic of postmodernist art, rather than with Capra's antiquated notions of sincerity and earnest altruism.

*Circular Thinking*

According to Joel Coen, *The Hudsucker Proxy* is, 'in a weird kind of way, almost an exception to the other movies we've made. It was almost calculated to prove what people thought about our previous movies but actually I don't think was ever the case' (Mottram 2000: 93) – namely, that their previous films were 'all style and no substance'. Describing the film's narrative as 'a very simple story with a rather banal moral', Ethan admits that, in his words, the movie is 'anally constructed' according to strict principles of design (Woods 2000: 134). As the Coens go on to explain, the geometric figure of the circle is the movie's most basic design element and every aspect of the film is coordinated with it. The image of the circle is of course prominently displayed as the design for Norville's inventions, the Hula Hoop and the Frisbee, but circular imagery infuses the film's *mise-en-scène* from beginning to end. In the opening sequence the camera tracks through the New York cityscape on New Year's Eve, 1958. Gliding among the skyscrapers, the camera registers their high-rise vertical linearity, which, geometrically, stands in sharp contrast to the circularity of the huge clock atop the Hudsucker Building where the camera eye finally comes to rest. In voiceover, Moses speaks of the celestial order that keeps the planets in circular orbit around their solar fulcrum: 'Daddy Earth fixin' to make one mo' trip around the sun.' Thus commences a retrospective narrative that begins at its end point and circles around to tell in flashback the story from its beginning as Norville arrives in New York City. Eager but inexperienced, he seeks employment in the 'help wanted' ads at the Nidus Employment Agency, only to find that he is unqualified for any of the jobs available due to his inexperience. Discouraged, Norville enters the 'Epicure Diner',

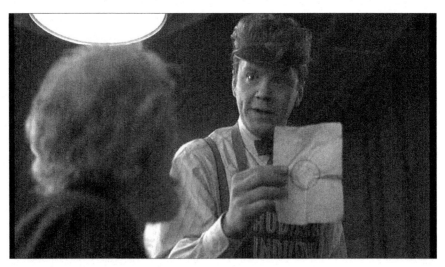

Norville's invention: 'You know, for kids!'

where the camera focuses on the counter, panning casually from a circular ashtray to the circular saucer under Norville's coffee mug. As he leaves the diner, we see (but Norville does not) that the coffee cup has left a circular stain on his abandoned newspaper, inscribing a perfect brown ring around an ad for a job in Hudsucker Industries' mailroom. Blown by the wind of some inexplicable fate, the newspaper follows Norville out the door and down the street until it finally plasters to his leg and he sees the coffee-stain circle announcing the beginning of Norville's quest for business success. As Norville enters the Hudsucker Building to apply, he walks, appropriately, through a circulating revolving door – at the very moment when Waring Hudsucker leaps to his death.

Although circularity is featured prominently in the film's visual design, most of the design elements are in fact angular – the skyscraper cityscape dominated by the modernist architectural styles of Manhattan and Chicago, the interior spaces of the Hudsucker Building (where most of the story takes place) featuring improbably high ceilings braced by enormous columns, windows rising up from floor to ceiling, and oversized wooden doors large enough to accommodate a giant astride another giant. Appropriately, angularity is the dominant design element in the construction and décor of Sidney Mussberger's extravagant office, which brings to mind the control centre of Joh Frederson, mastermind of a fully mechanised super city of the future in Fritz Lang's science fiction classic *Metropolis*. Reminiscent of the austere executive suite from which Frederson rules over his city, the offices and boardroom atop the Hudsucker skyscraper are extravagantly spacious, with high ceilings, oversized doors and a minimalist décor that emphasises the enormity of the set's spatial dimensions. In both films, the monumental *mise-en-scène* serves the same purpose, aggrandising and accentuating the power and control of those who sit atop the economic pyramid.

In opposition to the 'square' aesthetic of capitalism conveyed by the grand urban monoliths of corporate power, the circular iconography articulates a different philosophy of life, symbolised in the figure of Norville Barnes, for whom the circle becomes a constant visual motif. In every scene he is associated with and surrounded by circular objects and shapes. Circular lamp shades appear whenever he is in the shot; in the coffee shop he is surrounded by circular coffee cups and plates; he is seen wearing a scarf featuring white circles set against a dark field, creating the impression of tiny luminous globes. His executive desk has an oval shape and the décor of his office space is generally more organic, its edges rounded and softened. Even when Norville is not present but being discussed by others, for instance by the chief editor of the *Manhattan Argus*, the motif is continued in the circular desk lamps, ashtrays and furniture decorating the editor's office. The thematic relevance of the circular design is on full display at the Hudsucker Christmas gala where, in a Capraesque romantic scene, Norville and Amy share an intimate moment on an outdoor terrace high above New York City. As Norville nurses a black eye inflicted by an incensed stockholder, applying a circular ice pack to his injury, he waxes philosophical, invoking the Hindu concept of *karma*. Looking down from the skyscraper balcony, Amy comments that the people below look like ants. 'Well,' Norville replies, 'the Hindus say – and the beatniks also – that in the next life some of us will come back as ants. Some will be butterflies. Others will be elephants or creatures of the sea.' Norville imagines Amy in a previous life as a gazelle and himself as an antelope (or an ibex) and goes on to explain that 'the whole thing is what your beatnik friends call "karma" – the great circle of life, death, and rebirth'. Amy puts it in more common terms: 'What goes around, comes around.' With the circular bulbs of a Christmas tree shining in the background, Norville exclaims, 'That's it! A great wheel that gives us each what we deserve.' What Norville alludes to here is the Hindu belief in the cycle of reincarnation called *samsara*, based on the cause-and-effect morality of *karma*. For Hindus, the ultimate goal of human existence is liberation from the circle of *samsara* and the merger of the individual soul with the great cosmic spirit, *Brahman*. In Hindu religious thought, the *mandala* (Sanskrit for 'circle') is a sacred symbol representing cosmic order and unity. Norville's comment, seemingly innocent, invites a reading of the film as religious allegory in which the circle serves as a universal symbol for unity and infinity – the unbroken line with no beginning and no end. When Norville succumbs to the temptations of materialism, the karmic wheel spins him into despair. The realisation that he has, in Amy's words, 'outrun his soul chasing after money and ease', drives Norville to the brink of self-annihilation, but at the last moment he is saved – Capra-style – by an angelic Waring Hudsucker, who returns from heaven wearing a glowing round halo to give Norville a second chance, or, one might say, a reincarnation.

To supplement allusions to Hindu beliefs, the Coens also sneak in a reference to the Jewish *Cabala*, a book of mysticism based on the idea that divine truths are encoded in religious scripture. The biblical Moses (probable namesake of Moses, the story's narrator and Norville's secret guardian) is said to have initiated the tradition of cabalistic interpretation which, like Hinduism, teaches that those who understand the mysterious codes of sacred scripture can break free from the 'enchanted circle of life' that traps the unenlightened. Appropriately, a cryptic reference to the *Cabala* is suggested when Amy says to office mate Smitty, 'There's a real story here, some kind of plot, a set-up, a *cabal, a* – oh.' Using a fancy word (Amy's standard way of showing off her verbal finesse), she ponders the possibility of a 'cabal' or secret intrigue within the power structure of Hudsucker Industries, but ends her thought with an added 'a', thus casually rendering the quite different, though oddly related term: 'cabal-a' – which gives her cause ('oh') to ponder another mystery. Combining Eastern religious mythologies of spiritual enlightenment with the Western quest myth, the Coens create a fairy tale narrative *à la* Capra populated by archetypal figures: the good king who dies at the beginning (Waring Hudsucker), the evil regent (Sidney Mussberger) and the callow youth (Norville Barnes) who replaces the dying king. By transporting this mythic material to 1950s corporate America, *The Hudsucker Proxy* implies that the noble quest of ancient legend has degenerated into an ignoble conquest of the material world, reflected in the empty-minded materialism of a consumer society for which the Hula Hoop is emblematic and precisely the opposite of the wisdom of Eastern religious thought which stipulates detachment from worldly desires as the path to true enlightenment and escape from the circle of *samsara*, the great circle of life, death and rebirth.

Further elements in *The Hudsucker Proxy*'s production design point to the influence of Lang's *Metropolis*. Noted for its monumental architectural visualisation of the urban future, Lang's film provided a rich conceptual model for the Coens' fairy-tale vision of New York City. Lang had in fact visited New York before making *Metropolis* and reported that its impressive modern skyscrapers had inspired his grandiose vision of a technologised future world. Instead of a utopian vision, however, Lang challenged the modernist faith in technological progress, presenting a dystopian view of a fully-technologised mega-city. In this respect, *Metropolis* is a forerunner for the critique of techno-bureaucracy and its relationship with capitalism depicted in futuristic films like *Brazil* and Ridley Scott's *Blade Runner* (1982). Using elaborately crafted models and advanced visual effects techniques, Lang envisioned the urban future as a dense cluster of towering high-rise structures, the scale and complexity of which are reconstructed in *The Hudsucker Proxy* with a set of miniature models based on various well-known New York structures such as the Chrysler Building, the Chanin Building and the Bank of New York, as well as famous Chicago buildings like the Merchandise Mart. Due to its division of society into an elite ruling class and an underclass of exploited workers, Lang's *Metropolis* has often been read as a Marxist allegory. In this regard, Palmer's comments on the implied politics of *The Hudsucker Proxy* are of particular interest:

> Dominating both its narrative and visual design is the monolithic Hudsucker Corporation, an organization identified with its impressive New York edifice, where most of the narrative unfolds. True to the American myth of the 'robber baron,' its founder has built this company through the ruthless pursuit of profit. [...] Those at the top exploit underlings with the unconcern of the factory owners in *Metropolis*, Fritz Lang's horrifying vision of end-stage capitalism, which seems to have provided the Coens with a model both architectural and ideological. Seldom has the gulf between management and labor loomed wider than in the depiction of modern economic relations featured in *The Hudsucker Proxy*. (2004: 138)

This reading of *The Hudsucker Proxy* as political allegory is affirmed by others, like Erica Rowell, who asserts that the movie presents 'a sweeping indictment of power and greed' (2007: 154). Similarly, Paul Coughlin argues that an important part of the film's agenda is its parodic engagement with ancestral cinematic forms as a way of reexamining interrelated socio-historical issues: New Deal politics, the myth of small-town America and contemporary corporate practices (2009: 209). To say, however, that political satire is the essential tenor of the movie contradicts the filmmakers who insist that in making *The Hudsucker Proxy* their primary aim was not to critique capitalism, but simply to create a 'modern-day fairy tale' (Romney 1994). After all, at the end of Norville's rainbow there is a pot of capitalist gold and a permanent position at the top of the economic pyramid. In his epilogue the narrator Moses tells us that Norville 'went on and ruled with wisdom and compassion', seemingly reaffirming Capra's myth of American democracy with an optimistically 'Capra-corny' note. 'Wisdom and compassion' are characteristic for Capra's humanist heroes, but Sturges' characters are seldom heroic in such a simplistic way, and they are even less often wise or compassionate. Neither are the Coen brothers' protagonists typically heroic and a Coen-penned story does not typically have a happy ending. Norville Barnes may be the only Coen character to approach the stature of a hero, and only then because he stars in a fairy tale. Furthermore, saying that Norville went on to 'rule' Hudsucker Industries is a telling choice of words. Indeed, we are left at the end to imagine that under Norville's benevolent reign Hudsucker Industries continues to manufacture and mass-market trendy but frivolous leisure products to the unquestioning 'Silent Generation' of 1950s America, whose increasing demand for vacuous entertainment fueled the beginnings of the consumer society that emerged fully in subsequent decades. As with everything else in *The Hudsucker Proxy*, the happy ending of Norville's triumph over Sidney and the continued success of his inventions seems artificial, not just a clichéd Hollywood ending or the customary positive resolution of conflict at the conclusion of a fairy tale, but also a refusal to draw conclusions about potentially relevant social issues raised in the narrative. If anything, *The Hudsucker Proxy* seems to reinforce the conservative values of capitalist society in a way not unlike Capra's movies like *It's a Wonderful Life*, where the message is not that the system of capitalism is evil because it spawns villains like Potter, but rather that the power of democracy and the perseverance of people like George Bailey are sufficient to counterbalance and correct the faults of capitalism, without any need for structural reform.

As Ethan Coen once said, disingenuously, all of their movies are 'frameworks on which we can hang cheap jokes' (Woods 2000: 127). Comments of this kind excusing the Coen brothers from social responsibility and serious content are familiar, but not all of the jokes in *The Hudsucker Proxy* are 'cheap'. Beyond the slapstick pratfalls, sight gags and witty banter one expects in a screwball comedy, there are, as critics have noted, signs of engagement with socio-political themes, especially with the corrupting power of material success and the social inequities caused by capitalist economics. Indeed, certain citations, buried in the film's abundantly citational pastiche, begin to accumulate and form a polemical undercurrent. There are, for instance, repeated references to Communist Russia, notably in the film's musical score, which borrows heavily from the works of Armenian composer Aram Khachaturian, noted for his musical celebrations of the Soviet laborer. A loyal Communist ideologue, Khachaturian was devoted to making art relevant to the common worker. Elements of Carter Burwell's score are taken from the Khachaturian ballet *Spartacus and Phrygia,* which depicts a slave uprising in ancient Rome. Erica Rowell suggests that like Spartacus, Norville opposes and eventually triumphs over the tyrannical rule of corporate greed represented by Sidney Mussberger (2007: 151). Khachaturian's 'Saber Dance' accompanies the lengthy Hula Hoop montage depicting the toy's highly efficient industrial development from design stage to manufacture and distribution, finally ending up on the hips of an All-American youngster who magically discovers the joys of Hula Hooping and ignites a craze that swept the US in the 1950s. The juxtaposition of Khachaturian's Marxist aesthetics and the capitalist mass-production of the Hula Hoop insinuates ideological commentary, equating corporate business with totalitarian communism, suggesting that both socio-economic systems operate in similar ways and ultimately result in the same constellation of power – top-down control of the masses. Further references reinforce the juxtaposition of opposing ideologies. Outside the 'Creative Bullpen' where the 'Hudsucker Brainstormers' search for a name to call Norville's 'dingus', we see a secretary reading Tolstoy's *War and Peace* and *Anna Karenina*, novels that champion the worker. Much of the interior décor of the Hudsucker Building reflects Communist values and icons, such as the struggle of the working class depicted in a base relief decorating the wall of the Hudsucker boardroom. As a whole, the filmic text is presented in a Brechtian style, alienating the viewer with its ostentatious visuals, its archly mannerist style of acting and its anachronistic confusion of period styles in clothing and setting (1930s story and acting set in the late 1950s) in order to stimulate critical thinking. Taken in aggregate, these minor, seemingly insignificant elements begin to suggest that *The Hudsucker Proxy* might be, in Palmer's words, an 'engaged reinvention' of the past (2004: 158), an excavation of historical forms as commentary on contemporary life.

Assuming the Coens were (at some uncertain level of consciousness) aware of the inherent ideological implications of the capitalist tropes they summon to create their story world, such awareness does not force the conclusion that social commentary is the film's primary thematic agenda. It is just as reasonable to assume that the characters and corporate setting are simply tropes borrowed from Capra, whose stories typically pit an Everyman underdog against big business or big government. Perhaps the agenda of *The Hudsucker Proxy* is not thematic at all, but rather to showcase the filmmakers' superbly crafted orchestration of an intricate pastiche in which every element can be read as a quotation. As a complex pastiche, *The Hudsucker Proxy* bears further comparison with Lang's *Metropolis*, which provided the Coens with an aesthetic as well as architectural-visual model. Conceived as a mixture of cinematic spectacle and popular kitch, *Metropolis* is a movie, as one commentator writes, 'jammed almost to the point of incoherence with ideas, references, allusions, and visualizations' (Rutsky 2005: 180). The screenplay, written by Lang's wife Thea von Harbou, based on her popular novel, was clearly intended as the script for a profitable blockbuster that would, with its multitude of references to popular culture, be assured of widespread appeal. The German movie studio UFA invested heavily in the production of *Metropolis*, hoping it would compete on the international market with big-budget Hollywood movies of the time, but its relatively weak box-office performance helped drive the studio into bankruptcy. A similar, though less drastic production history attends *The Hudsucker Proxy*. Executive producer Joel Silver's confidence in the movie's potential for success as a mainstream movie product was not rewarded at the box office, where his $25 million investment returned a mere $2.8 million in US distribution. Despite its initial financial failure, Lang's *Metropolis* has over the years retained its aesthetic appeal. According to R. L. Rutsky, contemporary viewers 'enjoy the film less as a serious parable about modern life than as an amusing, often campy pastiche that mixes striking scenes with naïve ideas, cinematic virtuosity with comically over-the-top acting' (2005: 194), which is not a bad description of *The Hudsucker Proxy*. Perhaps, like *Metropolis*, the enduring worth of the film resides in the appeal of its pastiche aesthetic – the very element for which it was initially condemned.

With *The Hudsucker Proxy* the Coens had attempted the impossible: reinventing a dead style that cannot be brought back, even as sincere homage. Screwball, unlike other classic film genres, has long been moribund. Perhaps its style and ethos are too antiquated, its historical moment too far removed from contemporary concerns. Unlike the western, which, despite a waning popularity in recent years, still continues to be reinvented, screwball is now relegated to the museum of cultural artifacts, with few, if any, legitimate 'neo-screwball' equivalents (although the Coens' *Intolerable Cruelty* [2003] can be considered precisely that). As R. Barton Palmer puts it, screwball is 'an outmoded regime of representation that can only be displayed, not reinvented' (2004: 137). The awareness of this impossibility shapes the Coens' ironic approach to the generic material. No doubt, *The Hudsucker Proxy* reflects the filmmakers' affection for the classic period of film history and their appreciation of the exemplars of classic screwball comedy, Capra and Sturges. Perhaps the only certain purpose of the film is to offer the pleasure of experiencing a dead genre, returned briefly to life in a gaudy flourish of pastiche. Indeed, in keeping with the circle motif, the film demonstrates that in art as in life, 'what goes around, comes around', stressing the intertextual processes of recycling in which all texts are generated by repetition in an endless discursive continuum with no certain point of origin.

# CHAPTER SIX

# Fargo: In the Land of Tall Tales

*Fargo* (1996) presents itself as a true crime story based on incidents that occurred in Minnesota in 1987. As such, the narrative recounts events set in motion by car salesman Jerry Lundegaard (William H. Macy), whose staged kidnapping of his wife Jean (Kristin Rudrud) has unintended and ultimately horrific results. To carry out the fake kidnapping Jerry hires two low-life criminals, Carl Showalter (Steve Buscemi) and Gaear Grimsrud (Peter Stormare), who grab Jean and hold her captive in a backwoods cabin while Jerry negotiates with his wealthy father-in-law, Wade Gustafson (Harve Presnell), for a $1 million ransom. As always in the Coens' fictional universe, something can and does go very wrong. En route to their hide-out, the kidnappers are stopped by a state trooper, whom Carl attempts to bribe. When the policeman refuses the bribe and demands to inspect their vehicle, Gaear murders him in cold blood and then pursues and shoots down two passers-by who had witnessed his crime. Now, instead of a fake kidnapping where no one would come to harm, Jerry is suddenly, absurdly an accomplice to a triple homicide. The local police chief Marge Gunderson (Frances McDormand) is called in to investigate. As the body count increases to include the senseless deaths of Jean and her father, Marge's investigations begin to reveal a horror beyond her comprehension. How could such things happen in the quiet little town of Brainerd, Minnesota, in the heart of the heartland?

For the most part, the Coen brothers' earlier films had garnered considerable critical acclaim, but were largely box-office disappointments. Then came *Fargo*, the break-out film that catapulted the Coen brothers into the industry mainstream, grossing more than $25 million in the US alone and establishing them as prominent American film-makers. The brothers were somewhat mystified by its box-office success. According to Joel, '*Fargo* was the final straw in trying to figure out why certain things are popular and others aren't. Its success was a complete surprise to us' (Mottram 2000: 115). The

Coens' dark comedy had apparently struck a chord with reviewers; nearly everyone had something good to say about *Fargo*. Roger Ebert, not always an ardent admirer, called *Fargo* 'one of the best films I've ever seen'. Many thought that despite its grim story, the film was, as Leonard Klady wrote in *Variety*, 'strikingly mature'. Geoff Brown of the *Times* praised it for its warmth and humanity, writing: 'No previous film from the Coen brothers has contained such human characters.' Philip French observed that *Fargo* 'essentially reworks their film noir *Blood Simple*, but with greater depth of character and a new respect for human decency'. Tom Shone of the *Sunday Times* wrote: 'Far from being their coldest film, it's *Blood Simple* with snow on top but with a few warm gusts of genuine feeling down below.' Even Christopher Tookey, who had disliked the Coens' previous movies, was pleasantly surprised by what he took to be the film's 'morality', writing: 'This is the Coens' most generous-spirited effort yet.' Comparing *Fargo* with similar contemporary crime dramas, Tookey lamented that the film is, regrettably, 'out of tune with our times' by virtue of its 'civilised detachment and unpretentious moral rectitude' – words, one imagines, the Coen brothers never expected to hear as a description of their movies.

In addition to its generous reception by critical commentators, *Fargo* received more nominations and awards than any previous Coen brothers movie, including seven Academy Award nominations, for Best Film, Best Director, Best Original Screenplay, Best Actress (Frances McDormand), Best Supporting Actor (William H. Macy), Best Cinematography and Best Editing; and winning Academy Awards for Best Actress (McDormand) and Best Original Screenplay. At the Cannes Film Festival Joel Coen was named Best Director, and the New York Film Critics' Circle also honoured him with Best Director, as well as Best Film. Not surprisingly, *Fargo* also swept the Independent Spirit Awards that year, walking away with top honours for Best Feature Film, Best Director, Best Original Screenplay, Best Actor (Macy), Best Actress (McDormand) and Best Cinematography (Roger Deakins).

*True Crime Fiction*

The claim that *Fargo* is based on a 'true story' bears some examination. The title card tells the audience that the story is based on real events that took place in Minnesota in 1987, but as the Coens subsequently admitted, this was a ploy misleading viewers to believe that the story is based on historical fact. 'If they're told up front that it's true,' says Joel, 'the audience gives you permission to do things that they might not if they're essentially coming in expecting to watch a fictive thriller' (Allen 2006: 81). 'Generally speaking,' says Joel, 'the movie is based on a real event, but the details of the story and the characters are invented. It didn't interest us to make a documentary film, and we undertook no research on the nature or details of the murders. But, by telling the public that we took our inspiration from reality, we knew they wouldn't see the movie as just an ordinary thriller' (Allen 2006: 72). As it turns out, the Coens were playing a con game with their audience. When first released, the brothers avoided answering direct questions about the story's veracity. Asked, for example where, exactly, the crimes took place, Ethan would only say: 'I could tell you, but then I'd have to kill you' (Robson 2003: 163). When the questioning persisted, the Coens eventually came clean and confessed that the events depicted in the movie were mostly based on hear-say: 'We heard about it through a friend who lived near to where the drama took place in Minnesota,' says Ethan (Allen 2006: 72). Finally, the whole truth about the 'true story' was disclosed: 'Not being acquainted with any true crimes that seemed sufficiently compelling,' Ethan admits, 'we made up our own "true crime" story' (Mitchell 2000).

*Fargo*'s false claim to truth finds its visual equivalent in the statue of legendary giant woodsman Paul Bunyan, which appears intermittently to remind us that the movie, like the legend, is actually a 'tall tale' and not the true story it pretends to be. Indeed, many of *Fargo*'s characters are tellers of tall tales. Jerry Lundegaard is the biggest liar, deceiving family and friends while spinning a string of falsehoods with fatal outcomes. Carl Showalter is also given to tall tales. He lies about the amount of the ransom money and pays for it under the blade of Gaear Grimsrud, an 'axe man' whom other characters refer to as a 'big fella'. Even minor characters are prolific liars, like Mike Yanagita (Mike Parks), Marge's pathetic suitor who claims to be married to an old high school friend but in reality (as we later find out) is unmarried and living at home with his parents.

The pretence of truth calls for realistic presentation. In this regard, *Fargo* is a significant departure from the Coens' previous films, much criticized for their lack of 'realism'. According to Joel, after the excessively stylised artificiality of *The Hudsucker Proxy* they 'wanted to make a new start from a stylistic point of view, to make something radically different from our previous movies' (Allen 2006: 75). Elaborating, Joel explains: 'What was interesting to us in the first place about doing this movie was the fact that from every point of view, stylistically, the architecture of the narrative, the way the characters came across, it was an attempt to do something very far from what we'd done before. It's more naturalistic generally in terms of everything: unembellished sets, real locations' (Allen 2006: 81). It helped that the brothers grew up in Minnesota, near Minneapolis, and thus had the advantage of being familiar with the region and its inhabitants, though clearly they don't identify culturally with Minnesotans and the culture of 'Minnesota Nice', characterised by a humble and unpretentious sincerity that could not be farther from the Coens' hip irony.

Compared with their previous films, *Fargo* lacks the flashy visual style usually associated with the Coens. There are no complicated tracking shots (as in *Blood Simple*), no kinetic camera movements (as in *Raising Arizona*) and no elaborate, ostentatious visual effects (as in *The Hudsucker Proxy*). Instead, in keeping with the story, *Fargo* affects a streamlined semi-documentary visual style. 'In *Fargo*,' Joel explains, 'we attempted a very different stylistic approach, tackling the subject in a very dry manner. We also wanted the camera to tell the story as an observer' (Allen 2006: 73). Thus the Coens' cinematographer Roger Deakins drew on his earlier work in documentary films to create a distanced, more objective visual approach. To emphasise the static bleakness of the landscape in this region, camera movements were kept to a minimum. Intentionally bland locations were for chosen for much of the action, a challenge for Deakins, who remarks on the difficulty of creating an image that treads a fine line between bland

and boring. 'In fact,' Deakins reports, 'we chose some of the locations because they were particularly bland. Both the designer [Rick Heinrichs] and I would say, "Well, that's *really* nothing"' (Probst 1996). Interiors were likewise selected for their bland appeal: Jerry's middle-class suburban home, his workplace at the car dealership, the restaurants and coffee shops where characters meet – all were chosen to convey a sense of the ordinary. Here Joel recalls earlier experiences in Minnesota, while raising money for *Blood Simple*: 'I remember having meetings with these hardened businessmen who would hang out in the local coffee shop and then put their parkas and galoshes on and slog out into this Siberian landscape' (Fuller 1996). Ethan concurs, describing Minnesota in winter as a 'bleak windswept tundra, resembling Siberia, except for its Ford dealerships and Hardee's restaurants' (Coen and Coen 1996: x).

In the vast empty expanses of the northern Mid-West they found what they most wanted: 'a covered sky, no direct sunlight, no line on the horizon, and a light that was neutral, diffused [...] These landscapes were really dramatic and oppressive. There were no mountains, no forests, only flat, desolate stretches of land. It's just what we wanted to convey on the screen' (Allen 2006: 79). But unexpectedly, the snow-covered setting, the low wintry ceiling with no horizon where the line between sky and land is blurred, creates an almost abstract visual impression. 'Curiously,' says Joel, 'starting from real events, we've arrived at another form of "stylization"' (Allen 2006: 75). The abstract quality of this indeterminate landscape is introduced in the opening credits sequence where, against the backdrop of an all-enveloping blizzard whiteout, Jerry drives toward the city of Fargo towing the Cutlass Ciera he will give to the hired thugs as a down payment for their services. The image of Jerry's car pulling its load, slowly, laboriously, from distant horizon toward visible foreground, establishes the visual density of this incommensurable wilderness, devoid of life except for the isolated traveler, whose insignificant figure is engulfed in the vast expanses of white. This shot and many others like it throughout the movie create, as R. Barton Palmer words it, 'the perfect visual correlative not only to the harsh monochrome environment, but also to the characters' embodiment of those northern European Protestant values (especially the dislike of ostentation in all its forms) that define the culture of the American Middle West' (2004: 104).

*Fargo*'s characters are modeled on the plain-spoken, emotionally reserved rural Minnesotans whose customs and values reflect a culture of modesty, politeness and honesty. In all of their films the Coens take a special interest in regional dialects, which they studiously replicate in the movie's dialogue. In *Fargo*, the brothers say 'that flat, Midwestern effect' was what they found most interesting (Biskind in Woods 2000: 146). Although some viewers found the Scandinavian-influenced Minnesota idiom exaggerated or improbable, it was in fact intended to enhance the quotidian realism of the characters. Jerry and Marge were of particular interest to the Coens, who imagined them as 'very ordinary people with ordinary sensibilities' who get involved in circumstances that are 'anything but ordinary'; 'Marge and Jerry are both very banal, like the interiors and landscape' (Robson 2003: 163). To heighten the sense of naturalism, the plot is episodic and digressive. Certain scenes seem not to serve any narrative function. According to Joel, 'Our intention was to show the story had a relationship to life rather than to fiction, setting us free to create a scene that had no relationship to the plot' (Allen 2006: 75). Thus we see Marge and Norm sharing lunch as they discuss worm bait; we accompany Carl and his hooker to a Jose Feliciano show where Carl struggles awkwardly to make small-talk; and, particularly notable for its irrelevance to the plot, we sit in on Marge's lunch date with Mike Yanagita, which if anything suggests a divergent plotline the film fails to follow.

The humour of *Fargo*'s noir comedy, so pleasing to critics and audiences alike, owes much to the folksy mannerisms of the Minnesotans, especially their manner of speech. In the scene with Mike Yanagita the underlying humour results from the incongruity of a visibly Asian man speaking with a Minnesota accent. But the Coens are not just playing ethnic stereotypes for laughs. As the brothers have noted, for many Americans this regional dialect is unfamiliar and therefore might seem exotic. 'In fact,' Joel explains, 'the Scandinavian influence on the culture of that region, the rhythm of the sentences, the accent, are not at all familiar to the rest of America; it might as well have happened on the moon!' Ethan continues the thought: 'All the exoticism and strangeness of that region comes from the Nordic character, from it politeness and reservation. There's something Japanese in that refusal to show the least emotion, in that resistance to saying no! One of the comic wellsprings of the story comes from the conflict between that constant avoidance of all confrontation and the murders gradually piling up' (Allen 2006: 74). As is generally true of the Coen brothers' comedy, much of the humour is generated by such incongruities. By juxtaposing contrasting elements, in particular, the conflict between the Minnesota culture of denial and the intrusion of gangster violence, the Coens create an off-beat brand of noir comedy.

The filmstory's most fundamental incongruity is, of course, the clash between the 'abnormality' of serial homicide committed by the criminals and the 'normality' of the law-abiding citizens of Brainerd, who are dumbfounded by the discovery of outrageous evil in their quiet provincial community. This bewilderment is on full display when Marge, already faced with a triple homicide, discovers Gaear feeding his partner into the wood chipper. The unlikely casting of Marge, a pregnant woman, as chief of police, representing the Law (in slang parlance 'the Man'), is a particularly salient illustration of comic incongruity, further enhanced by its potential for thematic messaging. One of the funnier aspects of Marge's character is the reversal of gender stereotypes. In many ways Marge represents the maternal (her name is the colloquial short form of Margaret, patron saint of expectant mothers), yet she acts more like a 'man' than the men around her. Palmer suggests that Marge uses logic and common sense (stereotypically considered masculine traits) to contain the emotional instability (a feminine attribute) of the men around her (2004: 81–82). Thus, when confronted with the bloody aftermath of Gaear's highway rampage, she calmly investigates the crime scene, pausing only a moment to relieve her morning sickness, which we falsely assume is her reaction to the dead bodies, matter-of-factly applying the rule of rational analysis to determine the logistics of an irrational, and for Marge morally imponderable, act of violence.

Marge and her appropriately-named husband 'Norm' figure as the chief representatives of small-town normality. But in many ways the out-of-town thugs are just as

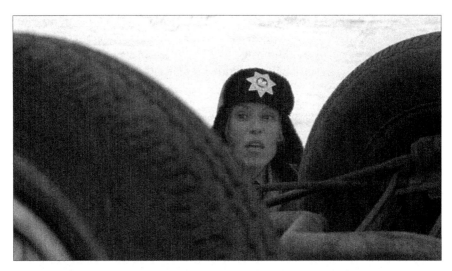
Marge investigates the crime scene.

normal and banal. Carl and Gaear engage in the same trivial routines as their 'normal' counterparts and, in a comic way, they often interact like a married couple. Making the long car trip from Fargo to Minneapolis, for instance, Carl gets bored and bickers with his morose partner about the lack of conversation, parodying the stereotypical marriage in which the wife talks too much and the husband too little. They argue about what to eat (Gaear demands that they eat at a 'Pancakes Hause'); they stop to rest at a motel and after a romp with prostitutes they settle in bed like husband and wife to watch late-night TV. More than just off-plot interpolations enhancing the story's reality effect, these digressions slyly comment on contemporary American culture. The import of such commentary is especially apparent in a scene at the kidnappers' wood-land hideout, where Carl struggles to get clear reception on an cheap portable TV. Gaear sits and watches impassively while Carl bangs on the television set in a futile attempt to eliminate the static or 'snow' that disrupts the screen images. Suddenly, the snowy blur of the TV screen resolves into a vivid close-up of a bark beetle. At first glance, we are meant to see the insect image as the successful outcome of Carl's thumping. But, as a quick shift in point-of-view reveals, we are now viewing the television screen in the Gundersons' bedroom, where Marge and Norm are snuggled up watching a nature show. Using an editing technique that has become a Coen brothers signature, the opposition between the law-abiding normalcy of Brainerd's Middle Americans and the aberrant criminality of the outsiders is visually deconstructed by suturing together domestic scenes of the happily married Gundersons with shots of the oddly-coupled hit men. Not only does this editorial trickery materialise the movie's implicit discourse on epistemological themes (how belief and perception can stabilise but also limit the parameters of human knowledge), it also makes a rather pointed statement on the blurred and porous boundary separating normality and abnormality, making sardonic commentary on the illusionary safety of ordinary citizens from extraordinary criminal threats. In contemporary America, even in the mostly unlikely places, there is a savage verminous underworld that can emerge suddenly and reach into the most distant provinces (a subtext, incidentally, that resonates with David Lynch's *Blue Velvet* [1986], where a similar image projects a closely related symbolism).

## Blood Simpletons

Along with the pervasive humour of incongruity, the Coens include the usual grab-bag of in-jokes. There is, for instance, an off-colour reference to Stanley Kubrick's *A Clockwork Orange* (1971) in Carl's tasteless witticism in answer to his escort's query about why he is in Brainerd: 'Just here on business, in and out, you know, "the old in-out"' (in *A Clockwork Orange*, a euphemism for sexual intercourse). There is also an oblique nod to the Coens' actor friend Bruce Campbell, famous for his roles in Sam Raimi's *Evil Dead* series. Campbell had appeared previously in *Crimewave*, the Coens' early collaboration with Raimi, after which he took a bit part in *The Hudsucker Proxy*. The soap opera Gaear watches at the cabin hideout is a clip taken from the actual low-budget TV show called *Generations* which aired on a Detroit channel in the 1980s and featured Campbell. An equally obscure tribute to a friend and collaborator is found in the end credits, which identify the unfortunate motorist Gaear shoots in the back with the symbol for 'The Artist Formerly Known as Prince', a native of Minneapolis, but actually played in the film by J. Todd Anderson, the Coens' storyboard artist. Another obscure but perhaps more meaningful insider's joke concerns Marge's long-lost admirer, Mike Yanagita, whose name has been interpreted by some as a reference to the Japanese cultural anthropologist Yanagita Kunio, whose research focuses on folk tales and legends narrated in regional dialects (Rowell 2007: 193).

Entertaining as such in-jokes might be, a fundamental and certainly less subtle source of humour in *Fargo* is based on the astonishing stupidity of the criminals. Indeed, much of the comedy in the film results from the absurd simple-mindedness of its hapless bad guys. 'One of the reasons for making [the criminals] simple-minded,' Ethan explains, 'was our desire to go against the Hollywood cliché of the bad guy as a super-professional who controls everything he does. In fact, in most cases criminals belong to the strata of society least equipped to face life, and that's the reason they're caught so often. In this sense too, our movie is closer to life than the conventions of cinema and genre movies' (Allen 2006: 80). Joel elaborates: 'We were trying to bring both the villains and the hero down to a recognizable, ordinary scale. The hero isn't a super-cop; she's a very real ordinary person with ordinary and mundane concerns' (Allen 2006: 82). Two years after *Fargo*'s release, Sam Raimi made *A Simple Plan* (1998), a *noir blanc* set in Minnesota featuring Billy Bob Thornton in a Coenesque story of ill-fated criminal scheming by backcountry dim-wits. Like Raimi's bunglers, none of the players in the Coens' crime farce can carry out a simple plan. Jerry's plot is initially undermined by Carl's absent-minded inattention to the Ciera's license plate. His failure to handle the problem by bribing a state trooper results in Gaear's impulsive violence and the deaths of three innocent people. Wade's obsessive need to control compels him to change Jerry's game, resulting in his own death at the hands of Carl who, after murdering Wade on the parking deck, recklessly calls attention to himself by killing the parking attendant for overcharging. Likewise, Carl's mindless greed compels him to cheat Gaear out of most of the ransom, just as his uncontrolled anger and wounded pride push him to insist on taking the Ciera, resulting in his own gruesome death. As Joel sums it up, 'People who do these kinds of crimes generally, in reality, are not rocket scientists. There's a tendency in movies to make criminals much smarter than they are in real life. If you read about how these things usually happen it's incredible stupidity that usually trips these people up' (ibid.).

*A Lighter Shade of Noir*

The American Film Institute lists *Fargo* among the hundred greatest American movie comedies, yet it is also recognisable as a variant of film noir. Like *Blood Simple*, which many critics considered a dark comedy, *Fargo* blends noir's realistic crime drama with comedic stylisations to produce a lighter shade of noir. Some would say that 'noir comedy' is a contradiction in terms, that film noir and comedy are generically incompatible, if not mutually exclusive. Historically, that may have been true, at least until Robert Altman's 1973 adaptation of Raymond Chandler's *The Long Goodbye*, perhaps the first postclassical film noir to take an explicitly self-parodic approach which, despite its humorous tone, does not devolve entirely into burlesque. In the wake of Altman's film, the noir/comedy hybrid enjoyed increasing popularity, spawning quirky neo-noirs like Martin Scorsese's *After Hours* (1985), Quentin Tarantino's *Reservoir Dogs* (1992) and *Pulp Fiction* (1994), as well as Oliver Stone's *U-Turn* (1997). In the classic period of film noir the idea of noir comedy might have seemed oxymoronic, but in the post-classical cycle of noir the comedic element has become a predictable consequence of a postmodern aesthetic privileging parody and satiric wit. Christopher Sharrett argues that the general 'tone' in *Fargo* 'is not Expressionist grimness, but sitcom joviality' (2004: 61).

Satire and parody aside, *Fargo* qualifies in several important ways as bona fide film noir. To be sure, the setting in wintry rural Minnesota is a significant departure from the typically urban milieu of classic noir. Here, as in *Blood Simple*, the Coens give the genre a new spin, moving the narrative to an ordinary rural setting far from the ominous 'dark city' of classic film noir. The nocturnal labyrinth of narrow alleyways, dead-end streets and shadowy street corners shaping the cityscape of classic noir give way in *Fargo* to open highways winding through limitless expanses of snowy tundra, where under leaden skies the horizon vanishes into a landscape that, for all its openness, is as opaque and existentially oppressive as the claustrophobic urban spaces of its classic noir forerunners. The drifting fog and steam rising from rain-slick streets in classic noir serve as metaphors for psychological disorientation and moral malaise. These are replaced in *Fargo* with the blinding haze of blizzard whiteout. The claustrophobic hotel rooms, shadowy, atmospheric bar rooms, and all-night diners that constitute the urban interiors of classic noir become in *Fargo* the bland, florescent-lighted dining rooms of chain restaurants and car dealership showrooms. One surviving vestige of classic noir is the 'lost highway' trope, featured in *Fargo* as a recurring establishing shot and as the site of Gaear's multiple homicides, reminiscent of the dark highway in

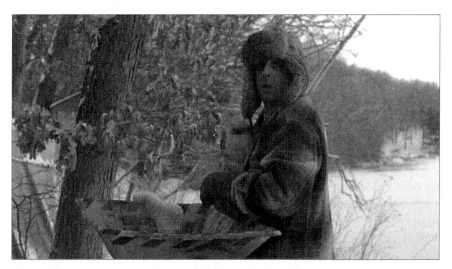

Wood chipper burial.

*Blood Simple* where Marty's perversely comical burial takes place. Both films exhibit a macabre fascination with the disposal of dead bodies, as Gaear's wood-chipper disposal of Carl's corpse grimly demonstrates, exploiting the grotesquery of low-budget horror to forge Hitchcockian black humour.

Casting Marge, a woman, as the story's chief detective gives the noir genre another humorous spin. Without exception, the principal investigators of crime in classic film noir, whether private eye or public law officer, are gendered masculine. The fact that this female sheriff is also noticeably pregnant heightens the incongruity, while her unshakable self-confidence and down-to-earth lack of pretension mock the myth of the neurotic and emotionally vulnerable men propagated in classic film noir. The story, however, and its putative protagonist Jerry, are definitively noir. Jerry's lapse into crime is driven less by malicious intent than by garden-variety psychological weaknesses – lack of self-confidence and willful self-deception – and by a desire to realise by any means the American dream of economic success. His weakness makes him a liar; he deceives everyone, including himself, and his self-delusion prevents him from seeing beyond present circumstances to anticipate what might go wrong with his simple-minded plan. Jerry's pressing need for money may have to do with an ill-conceived accounting fraud, but beyond that, he sees his ransom plot as a clever nostrum for achieving a higher economic status with which he can reclaim his social standing as husband and father, a status constantly challenged and thwarted by his antagonistic father-in-law. This, too, is a commonplace of classic noir: the oedipal son's conflict with patriarchal authority over possession of the maternal object of desire.

Unlike previous Coen brothers movies, *Fargo* does not appear to rely heavily on intertextual sources, nor is it a re-composition of any discernible precursor text. There are, however, certain elements in *Fargo* that indicate a return to the Cain-influenced narrative of *Blood Simple*. Taking narrative cues from the Cainian *ur-text*, both *Blood Simple* and *Fargo* presuppose a fatal misfortune, summed up in Loren Visser's pessimistic axiom: 'Something can always go wrong.' Also essential in Cain's fiction is the idea of 'tabloid murder', the sensationalised newspaper stories said to be the pulp novelist's favourite real-life source. Like Cain's tabloid stories, *Fargo* purports to be the 'true' story of ordinary people who become the perpetrators and victims of bizarre and inexplicable violence. But while Cain accorded the everyday crimes of the common people the pathos of tragedy, the Coens exploit the stupidity of these crimes and their perpetrators for dark comedy, reducing Cain's pathos to pathetic bathos.

The plots of *Blood Simple* and *Fargo* are similarly driven by the frustrations of impotent men who scheme against their wives. Jealousy is a motive in both cases. But while Marty is jealously possessive of Abby, Jerry's jealousy is directed at Wade, the domineering father-in-law. Indeed, both Jerry and Marty are trying to re-possess their masculinity, but to do so these emasculated weaklings must hire shady hit men to act out their repressed desires. In this way, both Marty and Jerry become *hommes fatal,* or 'fatal men', the masculine counterpart of film noir's *femme fatale.* Driven by jealousy and pathological rage, Marty coldly plots fatal revenge on his adulterous wife and her lover. Jerry is fatal in a different way. His animus is aimed more at Wade, his castrating father-in-law who seizes every opportunity to undermine Jerry's self-esteem and claims to paternal authority. Trapped in a job he performs at the discretion of his wife's father, hobbled by his own weakness and inability to assert himself, Jerry hatches a plan he thinks will provide both the economic means to achieve autonomy and self-respect, plus the satisfaction of revenge on the tyrannical patriarch. In the absurd farce that ensues, Jerry ends up playing the sad clown. As several characters say, Jerry is already 'kinda funny-lookin''. His round, mostly expressionless face, his big eyes and protruding ears enhance his oddly comical appearance. He rarely smiles, and when he does, it reveals more than disguises his underlying anxiety and defeatist attitude. Jerry is a mundane car salesman and boring husband; in just about every sense, a fool. Nobody takes him seriously. In the eyes of everyone who knows him (including his son), Jerry is a joke. Like Carl, his evil twin (also 'kinda funny-lookin''), Jerry is a little man who wants respect and never gets it. In this way too, his character has more in common with Cain's small-time proletarian characters than with the slick private eyes and criminal masterminds glamorised in Hollywood noir.

*Existentialism in the Snow*

Pursuing themes prefigured in Cain, *Fargo* depicts the greed, deceit and sudden brute savagery that can erupt even in what are thought to be the safest recesses of provincial America. In its Cain-inspired narrative, *Fargo* explores one of the novelist's central themes: the loss of meaning and certainty in the modern world and the increasing sense of personal alienation in a society quickly losing its traditional collective values. As often noted, Cain's fiction has marked affinities with the writings of the existentialists, in particular, with Albert Camus and Jean-Paul Sartre who, like Cain, took as their primary concern the meaninglessness of human existence or what Camus calls 'the absurd'. Like Cain, whose novel *The Postman Always Rings Twice* inspired Camus' *The Stranger* (1942), the existentialists explored in their philosophical fiction the anxiety, alienation and pessimism resulting from the awareness that life is no longer given meaning by transcendent beliefs. In his foundational essay, 'No Way Out: Existential Motifs in the *Film Noir*', Robert Porfirio offers a concise definition of their thematic preoccupations:

> Existentialism is an outlook which begins with a disoriented individual facing a confusing world that he cannot accept. It places its emphasis on man's contingency in a world where there are no transcendental values or moral absolutes, a world devoid of any meaning but the one man himself creates. (1996: 81)

The dark vision of human experience projected by film noir is shaped precisely by this profound loss of meaning and certainty, in consequence of which, everything in the noir universe is contingent, everything happens by chance. This vision of the world engenders in film noir a mood of fatalism, the pessimistic belief that all human effort is doomed to failure and all one can reasonably do is postpone an inevitable and possibly brutal end. Without the hope for salvation in an eternal afterlife, the continual striving of which life consists becomes senseless and futile; without a divine authority to legislate and adjudicate moral values, the formerly clear distinction between good and evil becomes subjective, contingent. In such a world, unable to give meaning to his experiences, the noir protagonist's actions are pointless. He loses his moral compass; indeed, he no longer qualifies as moral or heroic because, as Porfirio explains, 'his world is devoid of the moral framework necessary to produce the traditional hero' (1996: 83). Lacking meaningful purpose, moral or otherwise, film noir's un-heroic protagonists are paralysed, trapped in circumstances beyond their comprehension and control. When the film noir protagonist does take action, it is the result of desperation rather than reasoned decision, his action merely a reaction to a capricious and intractable reality ruled by chance.

Such are the characteristics of Jerry Lundegaard. In his desperate pursuit of money and power, Jerry rejects the traditional values of family and community, which (in his thinking) limit him and keep him weak and insignificant. He approaches his stingy father-in-law Wade and his yes-man Stan Grossman (Larry Brandenburg) with what he thinks is a solid investment plan; but when rejected, he is driven to take desperate action, lying to family and friends and recklessly putting his wife's safety at risk for a phony kidnapping scheme which only results in further, increasingly bloody complications he could not foresee and cannot control. His attempts to resolve these complications are futile.

Throughout the film Jerry is typically framed in doorways, car windows, or in his cubicle at work behind slatted blinds, which visually telegraph his feeling of confinement and the futility of his attempts to break free from the entrapments of job and family, which in his case are practically one and the same. Jerry's sense of futility comes to lucid expression just after the unsuccessful business meeting with Wade and Stan in which Jerry tries and fails to sell them his investment deal. Disheartened, Jerry returns to his car. Shot from extreme high angle, the camera looks down first at his car parked in an otherwise empty, snow-covered lot, then down on Jerry as he treads wearily over the deserted parking lot, a tiny cipher. Like everything in the Minnesota winter, his car is blanketed in snow and ice, which, as he tries to scrape it from the windshield, gives hostile resistance. In an act of sheer frustration expressing his resentment and anger at Wade, he suddenly attacks the icy windshield in a frenzied rage. The tantrum passes; Jerry stands panting, staring at nothing in particular; then he goes back to work on the windshield, a defeated little man crushed by a world indifferent to his puny existence.

In contrast to film noir protagonists like Philip Marlowe, whom Raymond Chandler could still call a hero and who was still thought to have dignity and a code of ethics, Lundegaard lacks redeeming qualities, including 'strength' of any kind.

Above all, he lacks the tragic pathos of his film noir precursors. We feel little sympathy for him; he is just a buffoon – foolish, but fatally so. The mood of fatalism that haunts film noir hangs heavy over Jerry. His honest efforts to make something of himself have led him to a dead end; as a way out, he resorts to dishonest means, and these too are inevitably doomed.

In the film noirs of the 1940s and 1950s the aura of fatalistic doom was typically mediated by a visual design wrought with chiaroscuro lighting and post-expressionist *mise-en-scène*. Another, less common technique of capturing the mood of oppressed entrapment is deep focus which, with the use of a special lens, permits the cinematographer to approximate natural human optics, presenting to the viewer a unified space in which all planes of vision are equally in focus, thus simulating the object-density of physical reality. In the classic film noir, set design, *mise-en-scène* and lighting are constructed and photographed to render the cluttered, claustrophobic density of a reality devoid of meaning from which there is 'no exit'. The fatalistic mood projected by such techniques finds its philosophical analogue in the writings of the existentialists, whose emphasis on the meaningless absurdity of life is reflected in the brooding pessimism of film noir. The density of the real simulated by deep focus thus becomes the cinematic articulation of a basic existentialist premise: the separation of the human mind from the physical universe.

Both Camus and Sartre postulate that the objects of the material world are independent and indifferent of human consciousness; that is, they have no inherent meaning or natural connection to the human mind. Camus defines the absurd as the awareness that the human mind and the world beyond it are fundamentally disconnected. In consequence of this awareness, the objects of the external world become distant, alien, inimical in their indifference to man. The resulting incomprehensibility endows even ordinary objects with an excessive, oppressive presence, in Sartre's terms, a 'density' or 'viscosity'. A stone, a beer glass, a tree – the presence of any of these can cause the protagonist of his novel *Nausea* to sicken, oppressed by the estrangement of matter from mind. In *The Myth of Sisyphus*, Camus observes that this alienation from material reality is compelled by the loss of transcendent meaning, knowledge of which produces a heightened perception of the 'strangeness' of the physical world forcing us to acknowledge, in Camus' words, 'to what degree a stone is foreign and irreducible to us, with what intensity nature or a landscape can negate us' (1991: 14).

Returning to the opening sequence of *Fargo*, we can observe an interesting variation on classic noir's deep-focus rendering of nature's oppressive viscosity. Instead of deep focus, however, cinematographer Roger Deakins utilises a foreshortening focal lens to protract and distort the long travelling shot that tracks Jerry's path through the snowstorm. In this lengthy establishing shot, the intractable density of reality, its viscosity, is mediated by the opaque haze of a blizzard: an optical void where there is light but nothing to see, where vision is occluded just as effectively (and symbolically) as in the dark night of classic film noir. Emerging from the frozen void, Jerry's car breaks through the wind-blown curtain of snow, gradually approaching the foreground. Finally we discern a tiny figure hunched over the steering wheel, a vague shadow, surmised as human only by vague estimation, struggling toward a safe destination in a coldly indifferent universe.

In such an inhospitable world, humans are isolated, cut off from the real and from each other, reduced to 'anxious stutterers' who, like actors in a drama with no meaning, are 'unscripted', pathetically staging the universal failure of communication afflicting modernity. Such is the reading of Jerold J. Abrams, who borrows the notion of 'unscripted stutters' from philosopher Alasdair MacIntyre's study *After Virtue*. As we have seen, the failure to communicate is a major theme in the Coens' movies, given special emphasis in noir-inflected films like *Blood Simple* and *Miller's Crossing*. In *Fargo* Jerry is the most recognisable among the unscripted stutterers. Often at a loss for words, he barely manages to formulate a single meaningful utterance throughout the entire movie. Not only does he have trouble expressing himself, he also has trouble getting anyone to listen and take him seriously. This becomes obvious in his first meeting with Carl and Gaear, a travesty of miscommunication that terminates with Carl's frustrated statement: 'You're tasking us to perform a mission, but you, you won't, uh, you won't – aw, fuck it, let's take a look at that Ciera.' Later, at home Jerry tries uselessly to make conversation with Wade who, absorbed in watching a hockey game on TV, rudely ignores him and will only respond to Jerry with non-verbal grunts. Jerry suffers a further, more urgent breakdown in communication when he tries to cancel the fake kidnapping. Shep Proudfoot (Steven Reevis), the ex-con auto mechanic who first put Jerry in touch with Carl and Gaear, flatly refuses to give up their phone number, stifling Jerry's attempt to abort the mission. Later, under the pressure of Marge's interrogation, Jerry suffers a complete verbal breakdown. Her insisting on seeing an inventory of the cars at the dealership quickly reduces Jerry's stonewalling to stutters and disjointed sentence fragments: 'I'm not, uh, I'm not arguin' here. I'm cooperatin' ... There's no, uh – we're doin' all we can.' Finally, Jerry can say no more. In a speechless panic, he flees the interview.

Carl has similar experiences, especially in his partnership with Gaear, whom Carl futilely tries to engage in conversation. As they drive to Minneapolis to kidnap Jean, for instance, Carl, a compulsive talker, gives a lengthy speech about Gaear's obtuse refusal to talk. 'Would it kill you to say something?' he complains. Gaear replies with monosyllabic sarcasm: 'No.' Having said nothing in the last four hours, Gaear sits in morose silence, barely acknowledging Carl's presence, except with an occasional baleful stare. Carl threatens to give Gaear the silent treatment but, comically, he just can't shut up. Carl needs to communicate badly, but usually fails, as he does when he tries to make conversation with his 'escort' in the Carlton Celebrity Room. 'Ya find the work interesting, do ya?' Carl asks the prostitute. 'What're you talking about?' she responds coldly. Obviously, she has misread his intention, thinking he is being condescending. Carl is just trying to make small talk, to make a connection, the irony of which is underscored as they listen to Jose Feliciano sing 'Let's Get Together Tonight'. A similar scene plays out when the plot digresses to Mike Yanagita. A miserably alienated man, Mike pretends to lead a normal life, but desperately wants to connect with Marge, an old acquaintance who hardly remembers him. He too is a 'stutterer', barely able to carry on a simple conversation before breaking down and weeping lugubriously as he confesses: 'I been so lonely.'

Near the end of the film, after she has taken Gaear into custody, Marge tries vainly to establish meaningful communication. When she tries to reason with the taciturn thug, however, she is met with the same menacing silent treatment given to Carl. Sitting in the police prowler, Gaear caged in the back seat, Marge holds forth on the dire moral implications of his crimes: 'So that was Mrs. Lundegaard on the floor in there? And I guess that was your accomplice in the wood chipper … And those three people in Brainard. And for what? For a little bit of money. There's more to life than a little money, you know. … Don't you know that?' Gaear's response is nothing more than a chilling stare, then he resumes staring out the window at the winter gloom. But his eyes are far from vacant. He greets her pious homily with silent indifference, yet his eyes signal a perverse sense of superiority, suggesting that he, at least, can see and comprehend the existence of the human evil Marge deplores in him and he accepts it, in himself and in others, without judgement or moral condemnation. Perhaps, as Jerold Abrams (2009) suggests, Gaear is a reincarnation of Alex Delarge, the incurably psychopathic 'droog' of *A Clockwork Orange*. Both Gaear (the 'big fella') and De-*large* are violent psychopaths of mythic dimensions, both immune to societal mechanisms of repression, their psychopathology too 'large' to be deterred by conventional moral or legal constraints, indeed beyond any appeal to human decency. The existence of such human wickedness is a reality Marge simply refuses to acknowledge: 'I just don't understand it.'

Sartre would call Marge's disavowal of Gaear an instance of 'bad faith', manifest not only in the moment she contemplates the absurdity of Gaear's crimes, but equally in her unreflective acceptance of a provincial life, itself a form of denial that sanctions a retreat into empty routines and prescribed modes of behaviour, humorously parodied in the folksy dialect of the locals where vacuous clichés are substituted for meaningful dialogue: 'Yah, you betcha, okey dokey, you're darn tootin'!' In his essay on the existentialist themes in neo-noir, Richard Gilmore references Jean-Paul Sartre's concept of 'bad faith', defining it as 'a refusal to *see* that becomes an unconscious blind spot, a blind spot that haunts us with feelings of hypocrisy and alienation' (2009: 123). For all her apparent virtues, Marge is willfully oblivious to the darkness of the human psyche, blinded to the reality of events she has witnessed with her own eyes, recalling Camus' existential paradox of 'the mind's retreat before what the mind itself has brought to light' (1991: 50). Her denial of reality is made humorously literal in her comments on the weather. Even though, as she preaches ethics to Gaear in the cruiser, it is just another miserable winter day in Minnesota, she is moved to exclaim: 'And here ya are, and it's a beautiful day!' Outside it is snowing. Road, earth and sky have merged once more in the blizzard whiteout, conjuring a visual metaphor for the haze of confusion and disbelief that clouds Marge's perception. The snowstorm's blinding opacity evokes Marge's blind spot on a greater scale, blankly signifying her refusal to see the evils that exist even in the remote province of Brainerd, Minnesota.

Lying, deception, self-deception – all are equally acts of bad faith, the Coens seem to say, unless those lies are the fictions of a formative myth which, by acts of calculated deception, may lead the blind along the path to enlightenment. But what enlightenment does *Fargo* offer, itself a deception that purports truth? Perhaps Sartre can help. At the end of his lengthy treatise *Being and Nothingness*, Sartre concludes that to live an authentic life one must reject the 'spirit of seriousness' ('l'esprit de serieux') that assumes the existence of absolute values beyond human comprehension (1966: 766). If human existence lacks a divine purpose to give it meaning, the universe is ultimately absurd and every human project is doomed because it aims for an unobtainable goal. To counteract the pessimism that results from this worldview, personal freedom and choice become the central themes of Sartre's writings. To lead an authentic life requires a rejection of the facile assurances of truth offered by orthodox systems of belief, but also demands the discovery of one's own subjective values. As Sartre writes, 'For human reality, to be is to *choose oneself*' (1966: 538; emphasis added). As we have seen, much of the humour in *Fargo* arises from the juxtaposition of conflicting opposites. In existentialist terms, what could be said to produce the film's pervasive tone of dark irony is the fundamental incongruity between a 'serious' attitude toward life which stipulates values that exist independent of or beyond human reality (exemplified by Marge), and the 'absurd' awareness that true knowledge is impossible and therefore that nothing is meaningful, rendering all human actions equal and indifferent to moral valuation (represented by Gaear).

Philosophers such as Thomas Nagel suggest that the only adequate response to the absurdity of life is its ironic acceptance. 'If a sense of the absurd is a way of perceiving our true situation,' Nagel argues, 'then what reason can we have to resent or escape it? We can approach our absurd lives with irony instead of heroism or despair' (1980: 163). If the Coens can be said to embrace any philosophical attitude in their films, the ironic celebration of the absurd in *Fargo* would certainly qualify.

CHAPTER SEVEN

# The Big Lebowski: 'The Dude Abides'

Following the success of *Fargo*, in 1998 the Coen brothers released *The Big Lebowski*, a modest box-office earner that would later become a cult hit and spawn an enduring subculture with far-flung legions of fans, some of whom elevate their devotion to the movie's unlikely hero, 'the Dude', to a quasi-religious faith. It is, indeed, the story of the Dude (Jeff Bridges), a post-hippie stoner living in early 1990s Los Angeles who devotes his life to Mary Jane, vacant meditation and the art of bowling. His is the story of an adventure; it begins with a case of mistaken identity. It seems the reckless wife of a certain millionaire named Jeffrey Lebowski (David Huddleston) is in debt to local gangster Jackie Treehorn (Ben Gazzara), who sends out his thugs to collect. Now, the Dude's given name also happens to be Jeffrey Lebowski, and Treehorn's thugs mistakenly pay the Dude an unfriendly visit, demanding payment of the debt. Clearly the victim of a 'wrong man' scenario, the Dude explains that it is a case of mistaken identity and sends the enforcers on their way. On the way out, however, one of the intruders urinates on the Dude's favorite rug, 'the one that ties the room together'. This wanton destruction of the Dude's prized possession must be compensated, and thus his quest for justice commences.

His adventure takes him on a magic carpet ride through greater Los Angeles, where he encounters a series of colourful characters: a scheming millionaire, his nympho-maniac wife and his snobbish daughter; a trio of kidnapping nihilists; a sullen teen-aged car thief; the car thief's father (entombed in an iron lung); a seedy local crime boss looking to recover a gambling debt; and seemingly endless numbers of hostile goons who frequently ambush the Dude in his modest bungalow. On his quest the Dude is accompanied by his best friends and bowling partners: Walter Sobchak (John Goodman), a loud and aggressive Vietnam vet, and Donny (Steve Buscemi), a simple-minded fellow bowler whom Walter constantly silences by yelling, 'Shut the fuck up,

Donny. You're out of your element!' In the farce that ensues, the Dude is cast in the role of accidental hero as he is drawn ever deeper into a criminal underworld where he is, like Donny, truly out of his element.

As its title announces, *The Big Lebowski* comes packaged as a film noir parody, but it is much more than that. Parody can connote many things: imitation, homage or critique, and *The Big Lebowski* is all that. It is also a pastiche, not in the Jamesonian sense ('without laughter'), but rather in a Bakhtinian sense – a densely layered intertext assembled from citations gathered from widely disparate cultural sources, common-places and not-so-commonplaces, and orchestrated to produce a resonant dialogical humour. To complement its parodic rewriting of Raymond Chandler's pulp fiction, *The Big Lebowski* incorporates a montage of real-life stories and 'characters', culled from eccentric acquaintances and their anecdotes and designed to create an off-beat comedy that appeals to a certain taste that we shall call, in the parlance of our times, postmodern.

The initial critical response to *The Big Lebowski* was ambivalent, and complicated by the almost unanimous admiration bestowed on the Coens' previous hit, *Fargo*. Indeed, as film critic Eddie Robson notes, 'It's very difficult to find a review of *The Big Lebowski* that doesn't feature an unfavorable comparison to *Fargo*' (2007: 202). 'Another *Fargo*, it is not,' agrees Alexander Walker, who chastised the filmmakers for having 'let their fondness for pastiche run away with them to the extent that they are pastiching themselves'. Critics enamored of the Coens' previous 'true crime' story found *The Big Lebowski* silly and pretentious, and essentially vacuous. Todd McCarthy wrote in *Variety* that although *The Big Lebowski* does offer many funny scenes, it nevertheless 'adds up to considerably less than the sum of its often scintillating parts, simply because the film doesn't seem to be about anything other than its own cleverness.' Writing for the *Independent*, Ryan Gilbey observed that 'the Coen brothers make films about nothing. Really, nothing, and does that matter? Well, people said similar things – and worse – about Orson Welles. The truth is, though, their films may convey nothing, examine nothing and demonstrate nothing, their particular brand of meaninglessness is so keen, so inimitable, so rib-crackingly funny that their work can be quite exhausting to watch.' Presumably, many of these critics were looking for signs of the 'human warmth' they thought distinguished *Fargo* from previous Coen brothers films where humanity is generally depicted either as moronic or mentally ill, and often both. Veteran reviewer Roger Ebert of the *Chicago Sun-Times* wrote that 'some may complain *The Big Lebowski* rushes in all directions and never ends up anywhere', an assessment of the film the Coens did little to refute. As Joel admits, 'the story, if you reduced it to plot, would seem rather ridiculous or uninteresting' (Allen 2006: 96). In Ebert's view, however, 'that isn't the film's flaw, but its style', pointing out that the wandering, seemingly aimless storyline correlates perfectly with the Dude's state of mind. He smokes a lot of pot, guzzles White Russians and, in consequence, in Ebert's words, 'starts every day filled with resolve, but his plans gradually dissolve into a haze of missed opportunities and missed intentions'. Thus, the film's 'style' corresponds to the Dude's incoherent experience of life which is, as the Dude likes to boast, sustained by 'a strict drug regimen'.

Despite others' misgivings, many critics gave *The Big Lebowski* high marks. Writing for *Time Out*, Geoff Andrew thought the movie 'truly terrific', exclaiming that 'it's almost impossible to think of a recent movie more thoroughly enjoyable than this exhilarating comic update of the world crystallised by Raymond Chandler'; 'Far from being shallow pastiche,' he adds, 'it's actually about something: what it means to be a man, to be a friend, and to be a "hero" for a particular time and place.' In his review for *Empire* Ian Nathan rose to poetic heights in his praise, writing that in *The Big Lebowski* 'the leisurely pursuit of ten-pin bowling is transformed into something lyrical and wondrous in a stream of elegant longeurs'. A few critics took a second look and changed their assessment. Peter Howell, who had initially panned *The Big Lebowski*, subsequently published an article reversing his previous judgement: 'The things I considered flaws upon first encounter, namely the episodic plot and the out-there eccentricities of the characters, are now what I consider to be the chief virtues of *The Big Lebowski*.'

### 'The Most Worshipped Comedy of Its Generation': Cult Status and Big Lebowski Subculture

Perhaps the most remarkable response to *The Big Lebowski* has come from its large and faithful fan base. Indeed, in the years since its first release it has acquired a robust second life as a cult film. In a retrospective article for the *New York Times*, Dwight Garner (2009) describes how *The Big Lebowski* 'became, stealthily, the decade's most venerated cult film'. To determine what qualifies as a *bona fide* cult film we can refer to Umberto Eco's well-known essay 'Casa Blanca: Cult Movies and Intertextual Collage'. There Eco defines a cult movie as the cinematic object of affection for a particular sub-cultural group, a film that provides 'a completely furnished world, so that its fans can quote characters and episodes as if they were part of the beliefs of a sect, a private world of their own, a world about which one can play puzzle games and trivia contests, and whose adepts recognize each other through a common competence' (1985: 3). Among the 'furnishings' of the world presented in *The Big Lebowski*, the spoken dialogue figures prominently as an area of common competence. *Big Lebowski* fans are known for identifying themselves and each other by quoting lines from the movie's script. Walter's one-liners rate especially high with fans. 'Mark it 8, Dude' and 'Nothing fucked here, Dude' are favorites quotes, as are 'Shut the fuck up, Donny!', 'That's very un-Dude, Dude' and 'This is not 'Nam, this is bowling. There are rules!' Scott Hertzog, a college English professor, confided in a *USA Today* blog that while grading student essays he often recites to himself his own variation of Walter's injunction: 'This is not 'Nam. This is *grammar*. There are rules!' The fans' passion for quoting can get frenetic during public screenings, where 'Achievers', as they call themselves, loudly recite lines of script, joining each other in a communal chant of reverently memorised dialogue.

Some of the more prominent Achievers have incorporated *Lebowski* citations into mainstream media texts, like animator Craig McCracken, creator of the TV cartoon *Powerpuff Girls* and ardent *Lebowski* fan, who frequently inserts *Lebowski* quotes and allusions into his cartoons. The opening sequence of his feature-length *Powerpuff Girls* movie (2012), for instance, pays homage to the opening sequence of *The Big Lebowski*. Another Achiever, Joe Forkan, contemporary painter and associate professor of art at California State University, Fullerton, was inspired to create 'The Lebowski Cycle', a series of oil paintings and drawings that explore the idea of layered narratives by reproducing masterpieces of European art as scenes from *The Big Lebowski*. Thus Forkan re-renders Michelangelo da Caravaggio's 'The Supper at Emmaus' (1601), which portrays the Holy Jesus telling parables to a small gathering of common men, with a frame-grab from *The Big Lebowski* depicting the Dude, Donny and Walter sitting at the bowling alley bar discussing Bunny's kidnapping. The Dude's pose and gesture in the painting match those of the Jesus figure in Caravaggio's composition, suggesting by visual analogy the Dude's quasi-divine status. Another canvas, titled 'The Death of Marat (After David)', re-renders Jacques Louis David's 'The Death of Marat' (1793) with a frame shot of Uli, the nihilist, floating in the Big's swimming pool in an alcohol-induced stupor. Again, as in 'The Supper at Emmaus', the repetition of a specific posture, here of total physical and spiritual dissipation, creates an interesting symbolic affinity.

The movie's cult popularity can also be measured by the emergence of so-called Lebowski Fests, gatherings of fans united by their desire to celebrate the fictional world of *The Big Lebowski*, about which, as Eco says, 'one can play puzzle games and trivia contests'. The first *Big Lebowski* celebration took place at a bowling alley in Louisville, Kentucky in 2002. Since then, hundreds of fests have been celebrated annually, in big cities like Las Vegas, New York and Los Angeles, as well as in numerous cities around the world, large and small. Typically, a Lebowski Fest is a two-day event. The first day focuses on live music, followed by a midnight screening of the movie. The second day celebrates *The Big Lebowski* with festivities such as a costume contest for which Achievers dress as characters from the movie, as well as 'ringer-tossing', 'marmot-flinging' competitions and a trivia contest. In honour of the Dude, fans imbibe White Russians and, of course, roll a few. The proliferation of Lebowski Fests worldwide attests to more than the movie's popularity. As a cultural event, the Lebowski celebrations illustrate what Mikhail Bakhtin calls the 'carnivalesque', referring to a long social history of carnival festivities extending back to the ancient Greeks and Romans and reaching its zenith in the medieval carnival. In its historical sense, carnival denotes a brief holiday period when festive celebration supersedes daily work routines and inhibitions are loosened, permitting behaviour otherwise prohibited including the mockery of religious, social and state orthodoxies. In *Rabelais and His World* he analyses how the carnivalesque is given literary expression by tapping the resources of popular vulgar culture, using the diverse genres of 'marketplace speech' and the 'common' settings of folk festivals to create a fictional world that serves the same purpose that carnival did in the medieval world, namely, the creation of a 'second world' where the rules of the 'first world' – social hierarchies, class differences and moral codes – are temporarily invalid and open to comic travesty.

According to Robert Stam, when applied to literature and art, the carnivalesque exhibits certain general attributes including: 'the constant presence of the comic element,' 'an extraordinary freedom of plot', 'the fusion of the fantastic, the symbolic, and slum naturalism' and a special 'fondness for scandal and violations of decorum' (1989: 97, 98). As a parody of film noir, *The Big Lebowski* generates much of its humour by transgressing generic rules, illustrated by casting the Dude in the improbable role of 'tough' noir detective. The filmstory also features an unusually 'free' plot in the manner of Chandler's episodic narration, recalling Eco's prescription for the cult movie, which, as he puts it, 'should not exhibit a coherent philosophy of composition' but should exist instead 'in and because of its glorious incoherence' (1985: 4). As such, *The Big Lebowski* presents a carnivalesque fusion of the fantastic (magic carpet rides), the symbolic (surrealist dream sequences) and slum naturalism (the subculture of bowling as well as mob-financed pornography), all of them ultimately orchestrated in a musical number called 'Gutterballs'. The Coens' carnivalesque fondness for scandalous violations of decorum is evident in the almost constant use of profanity and crude sexual insults (the word 'fuck' and its variations occurs 281 times in the film), as well as in the deviant behavior of its scurrilous characters, perversely illustrated by 'the Jesus'.

According to Bakhtin, the carnivalesque generates both overt and hidden polemics critiquing religious, philosophical and ideological thought systems and mocking the 'masters' of such orthodoxies. In this vein, it has been said that the *The Big Lebowski*'s parody of Raymond Chandler is an attempt 'to *deface* the work of the greatest of the "old masters" of the American detective story' (Tyree and Walters 2007: 43; emphasis added). This may be an exaggerated view of the Coens' stance *vis-à-vis* an 'old master' of pulp fiction whom they otherwise venerate, but beyond the affectionate ribbing of Chandler, *The Big Lebowski* does offer oblique commentary on a range of social and political issues, in particular, the Vietnam War and US military interventionism, the modern malaise of social alienation and problems of identity, especially the crisis of masculine identity in the new age of feminism. As Linda Hutcheon has suggested, the carnivalesque quality of much contemporary art indicates that 'medieval and modern sensibilities may not be as fundamentally different as we might like to think' (1985: 73). Contemporary culture has developed its own 'popular-festive' forms to celebrate the anarchy of the carnival, of which the festivals celebrating *The Big Lebowski* are most exemplary.

Pronounced by *Rolling Stone* magazine 'the most worshipped comedy of its generation' (Greene 2008), it is hardly surprising that a pseudo-religion called Dudeism has emerged in the wake of *The Big Lebowski*'s rise to cult status. Dudeism was initiated by Oliver Benjamin, author of the essay 'What is Dudeism?', where he explains the basic premise: 'Life is short and complicated, and nobody knows what to do about it. So don't do anything about it. Just take it easy, man.' Along similar lines, Wayne Eutsey, 'Arch Dudeship of the Church of the Latter-Day Dude', has published 'The Take It Easy Manifesto' in which he likens Dudeism to Buddhism. The Dude himself, Jeff Bridges, has also been inspired to co-author a book entitled *The Dude and the Zen Master* (2013), which in turn inspired *The Dude De Ching*, a flippant parody of the sacred Taoist text, *Tao Te Ching*, translated into Dudespeak by members of the Church of the Latter-Day Dude. A more serious effort to unravel the religious mysteries of the Coen brothers is Cathleen Falsani's *The Dude Abides* (2009), in which the author takes on the task of interpreting the underlying 'gospel' encoded in the Coens' films. In a chapter on *The Big Lebowski* she likens the Dude to the Jewish-kabbalistic myth of the *lamed-vavnik* – righteous people on whom the fate of the world depends. Calling the Dude 'righteous', however, may only be possible in the slang parlance of the Dude's formative era in the 1960s when righteous meant 'good' or 'genuine'. If Dudeism can be considered a religion in any sense, it would have to be as a counter-religion. The Dude's ethos of 'takin' it easy' is a sensibility most orthodox religions (predicated on human obedience to a set of transcendent moral imperatives) would discourage. The film's narrator, the Stranger, who occasionally appears on-screen as a one-man Greek chorus in a Stetson, takes comfort in the idea that the Dude is 'takin' it easy for all us sinners', evoking a central tenet of the Judeo-Christian orthodoxy: that humans are by definition sinful. In the Stranger's pagan logic, the Dude is a non-sinner by virtue of his supreme laziness, or what Christopher Raczkowski calls his 'immaculate leisure' (2009: 99). Paradoxically, the Dude's lack of Christian work ethic is precisely what makes him a saint.

### *'I Think Those Guys Owe Us Money': Real-life Sources*

As Ethan Coen has pointed out, *The Big Lebowski* is, to a surprising extent, based on actual events and real-life people: '*Fargo*, which was allegedly based on real events, in truth contains mostly made-up stuff, whereas *The Big Lebowski*, which purports to be fiction, actually is based on real people and events' (Robertson 1998: 38). A book entitled *I'm a Lebowski, You're a Lebowski: Life, The Big Lebowski, and What Have You* (2007), edited by Bill Green, Ben Peskoe, Will Russell and Scott Shuffitt (foreword by Jeff Bridges), provides a wealth of interesting interviews with these real-life sources. The interviews with Pete Exline, John Milius and Jeff Dowd are of special interest. Walter Sobchak, the Dude's improbable bowling buddy, is an amalgam of these three Coen brothers' acquaintances. Pete Exline is a film producer and professor at USC whom the Coens have known since the 1980s. According to Exline, when he first met the Coens he told them some funny life-stories and completely charmed them with his sense of humour. Later, Exline invited the Coens to a dinner at his home during which he recounted a personal anecdote about his car being stolen and how he got it back. Exline recalls that evening and that story in great detail for interviewers (Green *et al* 2007: 98ff), confirming not only that many of the characters in *The Big Lebowski* are based on real-life models, but also how much of the plot is a retelling of actual incidents.

In retrospect, what is most striking is that the Coens were not merely listening to Exline's stories, they were studying him – his comic deadpan delivery, his deft use of the 'hook' (an utterance reiterated for comic effect, such as 'that rug really tied the room together'). Apart from his style, Exline's storyline must have also had great appeal for the Coens; much of it ends up in their script. The similarities between Exline's anecdote and the Dude's misadventures are unmistakable, and because they are so similar, certain particulars of Exline's tale merit retelling. After Exline's car was stolen, he phoned a friend, named Lew Abernathy, who had worked as a private investigator, to ask for advice. Lew, better known as 'Big Lew', told Exline he'd never see his car again, but several days later it turned up in the police impound. In the impounded car they found an assortment trash left by the car thieves, in particular, dozens of fast-food wrappers. As Exline tells it: 'So Lew makes this big pronouncement. He's determined that three guys stole the car. He said there are three of them and the guy in the backseat is really big. Like the only guy who ate any food was the guy in the backseat. And the other two just drove him around to Burger King' (Green *et al* 2007: 99–100). Among the Whopper wrappers littering the stolen car, Lew finds a piece of paper, an eighth-grader's homework, belonging to one Jaik Freeman. Exline does some quick detective work and manages to track down Jaik, who happens to live nearby, and arranges a meeting with Jaik and his parents, taking Big Lew along. Strangely, in the Freeman family living room they find 'a hospital bed and a guy in the hospital bed – seventy-five, eighty years old – chain-smoking unfiltered Camel cigarettes, reading underneath a rack of track lighting' (Green *et al* 2007: 101). During the meeting with the Free-mans, Big Lew flips open a brief case and pulls out a baggie containing a Whopper wrapper, 'like he's Perry Mason in front of a jury', says Pete. Then he pulls out another baggie, this time with Jaik's homework. According to Exline, 'when I told this part at the dinner party, Joel and Ethan almost gagged' (ibid.). Exline is relishing their reaction so he embellishes his story with the random fact that he had just acquired an old 'faux-Persian' rug, which he thought 'tied the room together'. As he narrated his adventure, Exline would intermittently repeat the phrase, 'And doesn't this rug really tie the room together?' 'And every time I said it,' reports Exline, 'I got a laugh' (Green *et al* 2007: 98). Exline portrays himself as a skillful raconteur, milking his story for every drop of humour. Such was the impression he made on the Coens that they gave him the honourary title 'Uncle Pete, the Philosopher King of Hollywood'.

A few years later at another dinner party with the Coens, during a discussion of the Gulf War, Exline (a Vietnam vet) felt it necessary to 'explain things to them' and said: 'All right, guys, you gotta understand. It's a lot easier to fight a war in the desert than it is to fight in *canopy jungle*.' The brothers liked that line so much they gave it to Walter. The first time Exline heard his own words coming from Walter's mouth was at a screening of *The Big Lebowski* at the Writers' Guild. When John Goodman says, 'Dude, you gotta understand, it's a lot easier to fight a war in the desert than it is in triple canopy,' Exline's first thought was: 'What the fuck?' As he turned around, he saw Joel standing near the door, looking right at him and laughing. A few more years pass and Exline gets a phone message from Lew in Texas, who has just seen *The Big Lebowski* for the first time. 'I just rented *The Big Lebowski*, and I think those guys owe us money,' said Big Lew. 'So I'm sitting there watching [*The Big Lebowski*],' recalls Lew, 'and it starts to become eerily familiar. Did I read this script at one point? Did I work for the Coen brothers and I don't remember it?' Lew's first thought: 'This stinks of Exline.'

Abernathy's version of these events (documented in a lengthy interview in Green *et al* 2007: 106–112) lends credence to Exline's story and adds a few salient details. Among his recollections, Abernathy relates several real-life stories which seem also to have made their way into *The Big Lebowski*. One of them takes place in Malibu, where Abernathy, working as a private investigator, was reported to the police, arrested and

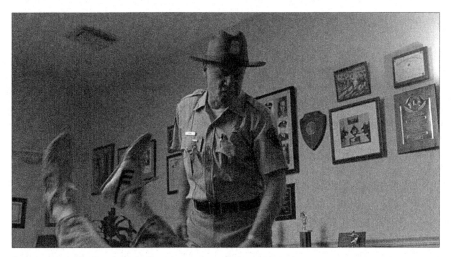

'Stay out of my beach community!'

'dragged to the Malibu sheriff'. When Abernathy crudely refused to answer questions about his activities, the sheriff (in Abernathy's words) 'bounced a coffee cup off my head and threw me out of town'. And, adds Big Lew, he did use 'those immortal words: "Stay out of my beach community!"' As with Exline, the similarities between Abernathy's account and the events staged in *The Big Lebowski* are unmistakable.

When Abernathy's friend, filmmaker James Cameron, heard that Big Lew was the inspiration for the Coens' Walter, he emailed: 'Congratulations! After thirty years in the film business, you are the inspiration for one-third of a fictional character.' The third element that completes the composite of Walter Sobchak is noted screenwriter and film director John Milius, whose credits include writing the original screenplay for Francis Ford Coppola's *Apocalypse Now* (1979) and directing such movies as *Conan the Barbarian* (1982) and *Red Dawn* (1984). A gun-loving political anarchist, Milius is something of a misfit in Hollywood where politics lean heavily to the liberal left. As he himself puts it, 'I'm not house-broken.' Asked how he became a 'militarist', Milius replies: 'I probably feel that I didn't get my chance to get killed in Vietnam.' Milius is an ardent supporter of the military, but also a vehement critic of what he considers the capitalist corporate greed that poisons American society. Not a standard right-wing conservative, he calls himself a 'Zen anarchist'. Despite being 'a gun enthusiast and survivalist type', the Coens think Milius is 'a really funny guy, a really good storyteller' (Robertson 1998: 40). Looking back, Ethan comments: 'You know these people and hear these stories and they all sort of figure together in nebulous ways.'

As for the character named Jeffrey Lebowski but known as the Dude, the brothers say he is 'more like Jeff Dowd and Jeff's whole way of seeing things' (ibid.). The Coens first met Dowd around the time *Blood Simple* was released. A film producer, Dowd helped the Coens land a distribution deal for their debut film. Nicknamed 'the Dude', Dowd was a 1960s radical activist, a member of 'The Seattle Seven' and of the Students for a Democratic Society (SDS). Along with being the 'Pope of Dope' he admits to drinking plenty of White Russians during his radical student years.

In his lively retelling of the case of the stolen car, Pete Exline comments on the similarity of the Freeman family meeting with a scene from a Raymond Chandler novel: 'Here's this guy, he lives in a hospital bed, and it's like a Chandler novel, this guy's in a fucking hospital bed in his living room and he's reading screenplays' (Green *et al* 2007: 102). Exline might have been thinking of the opening scene in Chandler's *The Big Sleep*, which introduces the crippled millionaire shut-in who hires Philip Marlowe to investigate a blackmailer. The importance of Exline's off-hand reference to Chandler might be that it sparked the idea to write a Chandler parody. Joel recalls thinking that when Exline told his story there was 'something quintessentially L.A. about it, but L.A. in a very Chandlerian way' (Robertson 1998: 42). Given that the Coen brothers are great admirers of classic pulp fiction, it should come as no surprise that *The Big Lebowski* is a reworking of Chandler, completing a trilogy celebrating James M. Cain (honoured in *Blood Simple*), Dashiel Hammett (paid tribute in *Miller's Crossing*) and now Chandler. As with their previous homages, the Coens stress that their primary inspiration for *The Big Lebowski* was Chandler's fiction, not previous film adaptations like Howard Hawks' *The Big Sleep* (1946). 'With *The Big Lebowski* we were really consciously thinking about doing a Raymond Chandler story,' say the brothers. 'It was more thinking about [Chandler's stories], specifically, than about the subsequent films that were made from them that got us going' (Allen 2006: 137). The Coens say they were thinking mostly of *The Big Sleep*, Chandler's first novel, published in 1939, which features a wealthy wheelchair-bound grandee, General Sternwood, who summons Marlowe to his mansion in West Hollywood and hires the private eye to investigate a blackmailer who claims that the General's sexually promiscuous daughter, Carmen, owes him a gambling debt. Like her Coen counterpart, Bunny Lebowski, Carmen is also mixed up with a pornographer. Sternwood has another, older daughter, Vivian, who, although more sophisticated than Carmen, is nevertheless cynical and manipulative. Lebowski's character of Maude (Julianne Moore) owes much to Vivian. Even Vivian's snobbish manner of speech, described by Chandler as 'cool, insolent, and ill-tempered' (1995b: 693), is humorously recreated in Maude's highly-mannered cosmopolitan idiom, rendered by Moore in what Ethan refers to as 'a vague, non-specific geographically, swell-finishing-school-for-girls-in-Switzerland accent' (Robson 2007: 194).

As the story of the Dude's adventure began to take shape in their minds, the brothers report that they drew loose inspiration from the standard Chandler plot. 'The logic here is more episodic,' says Joel. 'Like in a Chandler novel, the hero sets out to clear up a mystery and while doing so visits a lot of odd characters who spring up like Jack-in-the-boxes' (Allen 2006: 101). In accordance with the Dude's habitual pot smoking, Ethan thinks the storyline is structured by 'the logic of soft drugs'. Indeed, Chandler's plots are famously episodic and convoluted, often little more than a loose framework for Marlowe's adventures, which require him to unravel complicated intrigues and deal with assorted eccentric and dangerous characters. The plotline of *The Big Lebowski* is similarly labyrinthine and, as in Chandler, ultimately of secondary importance. The Dude's encounters with an array of off-beat characters are the primary interest.

Chandler's novels also feature first-person narration, a technique rendered in movie adaptations by the use of subjective voiceover. Not wanting to identify their story too obviously as film noir, the Coens invented the Stranger as a comedic variation on the voiceover narrator, reflecting the film's underlying principle of comic incongruity. According to Ethan, every aspect of *The Big Lebowski* was conceived to generate a sense of clashing ideas, motifs and images: 'Even the things that don't go together should seem to clash in an interesting way,' he explains, 'like, you know, a Cheech and Chong movie, but with bowling' (Robertson 1998: 45). The cowboy narrator who wanders into a crime comedy, the unlikely friendship between the Dude, a former peacenik, and Walter, a militaristic Vietnam vet, the clashing irony of a Polish Catholic becoming a Sabbath-observing converted Jew, the incongruousness of casting a lazy pot-head in the role of the film noir private eye – these juxtapositions and many more shape the Coens' comedic parody of Chandler.

In addition to the meandering storyline introduced by a cowboy, the Chandler parody is most apparent in the clashing personalities of Marlowe and the Dude. In almost every respect, the Dude represents Marlowe's antithesis. Marlowe is a competent professional, well-equipped to do his job; the Dude is, as Ethan says, the 'least equipped' character to deal with the problems that typically beset a private eye (Mottram 2000: 133). Chandler's Marlowe has swagger; he conducts his business with tough self-confidence. The drug-and-alcohol-addled Dude can barely recall what day it is. In the context of cowboys and westerns suggested by the Stranger, we should recall that the term 'dude' denotes an Easterner who is out of place in the 'Wild West', lacking the skills and knowledge to cope with the rigours of frontier life – also called a 'tender-foot'. As the cowboy Stranger wryly remarks, 'Dude' is a name that no one would 'self-apply' where he comes from. Indeed, the Coens have conceived their pot-smoking protagonist as a kind of anti-Marlowe. True, both the Dude and Marlowe consume large amounts of alcohol, but the Dude's somewhat effeminate preference for White Russians (vodka mixed with kahlua, cream and sugar) runs counter to Marlowe's more manly choice of unadorned hard liquor – scotch or bourbon, neat. Both Marlowe and the Dude smoke compulsively, but the Dude prefers weed to tobacco. Even their respective clothing styles are patently antithetical. Marlowe is a sharp dresser, while the Dude is content with a bathrobe and sandals. Above all, Marlowe is articulate and witty; his linguistic prowess is a part of his tough masculine identity. Conversely, the Dude is hilariously inarticulate. After one of his most egregious verbal follies, explaining to his namesake that 'new shit' has come to light in Bunny's case, the Big Lebowski exclaims: 'What in God's holy name are you blathering about?' The Dude's lack of verbal proficiency also produces some comical malapropisms, such as the insult he hurls at the Big Lebowski: 'You're a human *paraquat*' (confusing 'parasite' with 'paraquat', a toxic chemical herbicide used in the 1970s to destroy illegal marijuana fields). When Da Fino, an old-school private eye straight out of Chandler, calls himself a 'brother shamus' (meaning 'fellow detective'), the Dude asks: 'Brother Seamus? Like an Irish monk?' Sometimes though, the Dude does rise to the occasion with a wisecrack worthy of Marlowe: when asked by one of Treehorn's thugs holding a bowling ball, 'What's this?' the Dude quips, 'Obviously, you're not a golfer.'

The Coens also subject specific scenes in Chandler to comedic parody. The so-called 'great-room scene' in *The Big Lebowski* is intended to recall the opening chapter of Chandler's novel depicting Marlowe's first meeting with General Sternwood, reenacted in the Dude's second visit to Jeffrey Lebowski's mansion, where the disabled millionaire tearfully informs the Dude of Bunny's kidnapping. Production designer Rick Heinrichs recalls that in this scene the Coens wanted to convey 'that grand feeling you get when looking at … General Sternwood's place in *The Big Sleep*'. 'You want a bit of a *Citizen Kane* feeling,' says Heinrichs, citing an additional cinematic source, 'to make a strong statement about this pitiful guy in a wheelchair with all this magnificent artwork staring down at him' – 'the detritus of a rich man' (Robertson 1998: 127–129). Umberto Eco refers to such citations as 'intertextual frames', by which he means images or scenes which can be separated from the flow of frames animating a motion picture and stand apart as memorable and repeatable. Eco also calls these frames 'intertextual archetypes', here limiting the meaning of archetype to a 'recognizable topos' that appeals to a given cultural group (1985: 5). The Coens are aware that their *Lebowski* pastiche will appeal to a cine-literate audience which, as Eco puts it, recognises itself through a 'common competence' and takes intellectual pleasure in the recognition of such intertextual framing. One suspects that the Coens' self-consciousness about the film's incessant citational framing finds expression in Walter's rude rant to Donny: 'So you have no frame of reference, Donny. You're like a child who wanders into the middle of a movie.' Indeed, the repeatability of certain memorable 'frames' is itself in a sense parodied through the characters and their obsessive repetition of each other's utterances. Justus Nieland coins the term 'Dudespeak', arguing that the basic mode of 'Dudespeak' is 'mimicry' (2009: 74). 'Dudespeak' connotes a compulsive borrowing of another's utterance which, through repetition, assumes not only exaggerated authority, but a highly subjective personal meaning for its speaker. For example, when the Dude repeats President George H. W. Bush's Gulf War ultimatum, 'This aggression will not stand,' he appropriates a political slogan as his battle cry against the unjust destruction of his private property. Walter repeats the slogan to instigate conflict, his characteristic approach to dealing with problems.

Among its densely textured pastiche of Chandler, elements of *The Big Lebowski* resonate with other works such as *Farewell, My Lovely* (1940) which also features a complicated story in which Marlowe, like the Dude, is repeatedly knocked unconscious. Describing his descent into darkness, Marlowe says: 'A pool of darkness opened at my feet and was far, far deeper than the blackest night. I dived into it. It had no bottom' (1995: 888). Quoting Chandler, the Stranger uses almost the same wording to describe the Dude's black-out after being drugged by Treehorn, with the difference, of course, that the Stranger delivers his description in an incongruous cowboy-idiom: 'Darkness washed over the Dude – darker'n a black steer's *tookus* on a moonless prairie night. There was no bottom.' Another obvious gloss of Chandler stems from his late novel *The Long Goodbye* (1954), where a homosexual houseboy named Candy – a model for the paedophilic Jesus – threatens Marlowe with a knife, warning 'Nobody fools with me' just as the Jesus warns the Dude, 'Nobody fucks with the Jesus.' An additional source for the Jesus might also be the 'boy killer' in Chandler's *Big Sleep* named Carol Lundgren who, when questioned by Marlowe or anyone else, always shouts: 'Go **** yourself' (1995b: 665).

## 'Musical Signatures'

Among the many noteworthy soundtracks in the films of Joel and Ethan Coen, including the Grammy award-winning *O Brother, Where Art Thou?* (2000), *The Big Lebowski* is one of their richest, featuring thirty songs. Unlike *O Brother*'s soundtrack, which draws on the popular music of the Depression era (country, blues and gospel), and can be stylistically identified as American roots revival, *The Big Lebowski* offers a rich and varied tapestry of popular musical styles. An eclectic compilation of songs mainly from the 1960s and 1970s (assembled by noted music producer T Bone Burnett), the soundtrack is not merely a sonic background, but integral to the story, underscoring character identity and amplifying key themes to create what might be called an arabesque pattern, like that of the Dude's Persian rug (the one that 'tied the room together'). In *The Big Lebowski* the music, like the Dude's Persian, gives some cohesion to an otherwise sprawling and amorphous text. At the same time, like the diverse ethnic communities that comprise the Dude's Los Angeles, the soundtrack of *The Big Lebowski* traverses multiple musical genres, moving freely among them to accentuate character identity and articulate major themes. As much as any of their films, *The Big Lebowski* pursues the signature Coen brothers theme of identity, which, in an impressive array of permutations, features prominently in all of their movies. Here they integrate the theme of identity into the soundtrack by giving each character what they call a 'musical signature' (Allen 2006: 107), creating for each a sonic *leitmotif* reflecting, enlarging and commenting on (often humorously) their identity. Thus, the Stranger's voiceover prologue, a standard narrative technique in film noir, is accompanied by the classic western song 'Tumblin' Tumbleweed'. Although this kind of song is typically found in classic Hollywood westerns, thus underscoring the Stranger's cowboy identity, the lyrics are clearly intended to comment on the Dude and his lifestyle. The tumbleweed image that visually accompanies the Stranger's voiceover creates a visual correlative for the Jeffrey Lebowski who calls himself the Dude. Like the tumble weed (and the bowling balls that occupy so much of his time), he rolls through life, carefree and blowing with the wind.

The music that defines the Dude is classic 1960s rock, preeminently the songs of Creedence Clearwater Revival (CCR), which function in the narrative to identify the Dude's time and place in American cultural history. As the name of the band indicates, the music of CCR advocates a return (revival) to authenticity (credence) and purity (clear water). These concepts were integral to the ethos of the 1960s hippie counterculture to which CCR made its greatest appeal. Stuck in the 1960s, the Dude still lives by this ethos. Despite his lazy ways and general disregard for social conventions, he clings to an idealistic hope for the best in fellow man while patiently tolerating humanity's inevitable weaknesses. This is one meaning of his motto, 'The Dude abides'. He 'abides' or perseveres as the naïve antithesis of the nihilists whose claim to 'believe in nothing' merely confounds him. Like the no-frills roots rock of CCR, reflected in the laid-back rural persona projected by its band members, the Dude is relaxed and unpretentious. Interestingly, although 'the Creedence' is mentioned often in the film, only two of their songs are actually featured on the soundtrack. In both instances, their songs play in scenes where the Dude wrecks his beloved Gran Turino. CCR's 'Run Through the Jungle' is heard while the Dude is *en route* with Walter to deliver the ransom to the kidnappers. The Dude listens to 'Lookin' Out My Backdoor' on a Walkman during the prostate exam Maude has scheduled for him, giving the phrase 'back door' a certain humorously anatomical connotation. The song continues as the Dude drives home, smoking a joint. This time the backdoor the Dude looks through is his rear-view mirror, where he catches sight of the VW Bug that has been tailing him. Distracted, he smashes his Gran Torino a second time. As these instances show, the songs of CCR function mainly as comic props.

In contrast to his affection for CCR, the Dude professes a hatred of the Eagles, a point driven home by the inclusion of Eagles' hit 'Peaceful Easy Feeling' immediately following a rude interview with the Malibu police chief. Obviously, the Dude is feeling neither peaceful nor easy after his run-in with the law, so he asks the cab driver to change the music. Irate that someone would impugn his favorite listening, the driver throws him out. Set in the wider contexts of music history, the Dude's antipathy towards the Eagles could be interpreted as a response to their commercial co-optation by a capitalist music industry. As much as any group of that era, the Eagles, who rose to prominence in the 1970s, after the counter-culture had peaked, present a belated and commercially diluted imitation of the roots rock revival led by CCR. The Eagles took the country-rock style of the Creedence and repackaged it as mainstream pop, exploiting its ethos of authenticity for post-counterculture profit. In *The Big Lebowski*, capitalist big business is embodied in the 'Big' Jeffrey Lebowski, whose musical signature is inscribed by Mozart's 'Requiem in D Minor'. Selected from a genre befitting the wealthy elder Lebowski, classical Mozart represents the kind of music one might expect the affluent upper class to prefer. At another level, the choice of Mozart's mournful requiem for this scene heightens the irony of the Big's false identity. Mozart evokes a sombre mood appropriate for the grieving husband whose wife has been kidnapped. But behind this pretentious musical façade, the Big is not at all sad or anxious about Bunny's alleged abduction. He only pretends to be, just as he pretends to be an authentic 'achiever', one who succeeded despite his disability, which seems to be the only thing about him that is authentic.

Many of the characters in *The Big Lebowski* have hidden or falsified identities. They are imposters, or as Walter would say 'amateurs'. Like the 'covers' that copy an original recording, many have double (sometimes multiple) identities. The musical signature of the Jesus, for instance, is 'Hotel California', written by the Eagles but covered (in Spanish) by the Gipsy Kings. Scoring the Jesus's eroticised bowling dance ritual, the Spanish cover of 'Hotel California' links the Hispanic ethnicity of the Dude's bowling nemesis with the Dude's hatred of the Eagles. Like his signature cover, the Jesus has a dual identity as a convicted paedophile, which he compulsively flaunts by wearing a skin-tight lavender Spandex bowling suit and making overtly sexual gestures and homosexual threats. Bunny Lebowski's theme song is 'Viva Las Vegas', a tribute to

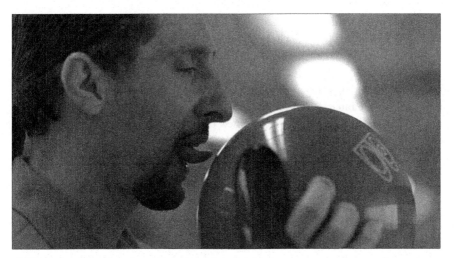

The Jesus

Sin City referencing her sexual promiscuity, originally recorded by Elvis and covered twice on the soundtrack, by Big Johnson and Shawn Colvin. It turns out that 'Bunny', the Big Lebowski's slutty wife, is actually Fawn Knutson, a runaway cheerleader from Minnesota. Her real name, Knutson, is a reference to the actress Peggy Knudsen, who had a minor role in Hawks' *The Big Sleep*, adding to her character a hidden intertextual identity as well.

Appearances by the German nihilists are accompanied by techno-pop, referencing their alter-identity and parodying the 1970s techno band Kraftwerk. The name of Uli's band, 'Autobahn', is the title of Kraftwerk's signature hit song. As it turns out, the nihilists are neither nihilists nor kidnappers, but musicians. Ironically, the theme song of these fakers is the only original composition on the soundtrack. Written by Carter Burwell and entitled 'Wie Glauben' ('How to Believe'), its refrain, 'Wir glauben an nichts' ('We believe in nothing'), blares from a boom-box during the nihilists' parking lot confrontation with the Dude, Walter and Donny. The link with Autobahn is introduced by Maude, who refers the Dude to her record collection to explain Uli's multiple identities. In addition to Uli's album, titled 'Nagelbrett' ('Bed of Nails'), Maude's collection of LPs is an eclectic sampling of distinctly differing styles and artists: the progressive rock of the Alan Parsons Project, the Yiddish swing of the Barry Sisters, the Greenwich Village folk of Eric Andersen and the jazz-pop of Herb Alpert and the Tijuana Brass. Maude's signature song, an obscure experimental piece by Meredith Monk entitled 'Walking Song', scores the sequence in which Maude meets with the Dude in her art loft. Monk's breathy, erotically suggestive delivery reflects Maude's avant-garde artistic persona, given visual expression in her 'vaginal' abstract paintings.

The real-life referent for Maude is Fluxus artist Carolee Schneemann, noted for her proto-feminist art works intended to change the perception and artistic representation of the female body. Schneemann was known for using her own body as the primary instrument in the creative act, a process illustrated by her installation 'Up to and Including Her Limits' (1973–1976), which consists of Schneemann suspended by a harness, drawing random marks on the surrounding walls and floor. This is parodied in *The Big Lebowski* when the Dude is almost bowled over by Maude as she sails past him, naked, like a trapeze artist. Schneemann is associated with the Fluxus movement of the 1960s and 1970s, an approach to art focused on the creative process, rather than the unified end-product of the finished work. As the name Fluxus implies, these artists were interested in the free 'flow' of creativity and poked fun at traditional rule-bound art forms, playfully creating new combinations of objects, images, sounds and texts, blending multiple artistic and cultural media to produce an intermedial pastiche. Perhaps the aesthetics of Fluxus also apply to the soundtrack of *The Big Lebowski*, as well as to the expansive intermedial pastiche shaping the film text as a whole, consisting as it does of a continuous, wandering flow of images, texts and sounds loosely bound together by a narrative seemingly about nothing in particular, other than bowling and weed. Perhaps we can say that the Coens, like Schneemann/ Maude, are filmic 'splatter artists'.

Although *The Big Lebowski* offers a superabundance of jests concerning identity – mistaken or false, dual or multiple, cultural or ethnic – some of the best joking relates to issues of masculine identity. *The Big Lebowski*'s parody of pulp fiction and film noir – literary and filmic genres obsessed with problematic or damaged masculinity – provides a handy frame of reference for jokes mocking conventional models of masculinity. The songs concerned with the problem of masculine identity are found in the film's two major dream sequences. The first of these occurs after the Dude has been knocked unconscious by Maude's thugs, transporting him to a dream world where he flies high over Los Angeles in pursuit of Maude, who speeds ahead on a magic carpet. The song accompanying this sequence is Bob Dylan's 'The Man in Me', which also plays at the very beginning of the film over the opening credits, doubly marking it as a theme song of the Dude. As the lyrics make clear, the central theme is manhood:

The man in me will do nearly any task and as for compensation,
there's a little he would ask.
Take a woman like you,
to get through to the man in me.

The man in me will hide sometimes to keep from being seen,
but that's just because he doesn't want to turn into some machine.

Despite its apolitical sentimentality, perceived by many as out-of-character for Dylan, who was already widely considered the political voice of the counter-culture, 'The Man in Me' nevertheless comments on a model of masculinity defined by the machine-like obedience and tireless labour needed to exist in the culture of corporate capitalism. The man in the Dude 'hides' by dropping out of mainstream society, rejecting the values of corporate America he believes will 'turn him into some machine'. The question of 'what makes a man?' is of central importance in *The Big Lebowski*. It is first raised by the Big when he asks the Dude: 'What makes a man, Mr. Lebowski? Is it being prepared to do the right thing? Whatever the price? Isn't that what makes a man?' To which the Dude replies: 'That, and a pair of testicles.' Reducing it jokingly to its biological function, the Dude is indifferent to socio-cultural definitions of masculinity. The Dude is, after all, a self-avowed pacifist who abhors the use of violence – the antithesis of a common, if questionable, stereotype of American masculinity. This is what makes his friendship with Walter so comical. They are indeed an odd couple: Dude, the peacenik, and Walter, the gun-toting Rambo of the bowling alley. In fact, many aspects of the Dude's character are at odds with conventional notions of male identity. Unlike Walter, who clings (machine-like) to rules even if they don't make sense, the Dude is not rigid or rule-oriented. His approach to life is relaxed and flexible; he rolls through life like tumbleweed. The Dude understands the importance of friendship. He is patient with Walter, even though he sometimes thinks Walter is a 'fucking asshole'. And the Dude has genuine empathy for others, a personal quality Brandt (Philip Seymour Hoffman), Big Lebowski's personal assistant, exploits to ensure the Dude's full participation in the fake kidnapping, reminding him solemnly, 'this girl's life is in your hands,' to which the Dude replies: 'Oh man, don't say that,' fearing that the kidnappers are going 'to kill that poor woman.' In effect, the Dude distances himself from other models of masculinity portrayed in the film, which are based on negative stereotypes of manhood – not just Walter, the aggressive militarist, but also the Big Jeffrey Lebowski, a right-wing fat cat, Treehorn, the amoral playboy and porn producer and the raging Malibu sheriff who throws a coffee mug at the Dude's head.

The film's thematic focus on problematised manhood provides a convenient framework for castration jokes, of which there are many, including the nihilists' 'marmot' (actually a ferret) that attacks the Dude's genitals as he lies naked in his bath, after which the nihilists threaten to cut off the Dude's 'Chonson'. The threat of castration is taken to an absurd extreme in the dream sequence entitled 'Gutterballs', a music/dance number mixing Busby Berkeley choreography with 1960s psychedelic rock. As a result of being drugged by Treehorn, the Dude has a fantastic dream that ends in a nightmare with the nihilists chasing him with gigantic scissors, threatening to make good on their promise to cut off the Dude's 'Chonson'. In the Dude's dream-fantasy he impersonates the macho porn star Karl Hungus (Peter Stormare), alter-ego of the nihilist Uli. Dressed like Hungus in the porn film 'Logjammin'' as a cable repairman with a big 'tool' belt, the Dude's self-image clearly contradicts his waking identity as a burned-out aging hippie whose libido is considerably diminished by his heavy consumption of pot and White Russians. Here, in his dream, he plays out a repressed fantasy of himself as a virile stud like Karl Hungus or Jackie Treehorn (a parody of Hugh Hefner) surrounded by sexy and compliant women.

The music accompanying 'Gutterballs' is provided by Kenny Rogers' 'Just Dropped In (to See What Condition My Condition Was In)', a pop hit in the late 1960s, thought by many to be a hymn praising the psychedelic experience, when actually it was intended as a satire on the 'acid rock' of the counter-culture. Mistakenly understood as an authentic statement on the drug experience, its popular misinterpretation is consistent with the theme of mistaken identity informing *The Big Lebowski*. The 'condition' the lyrics allude to certainly suggest the pharmacological experimentations that were common in the youth culture of the 1960s, but might also, in the context of 'Gutterballs', connote

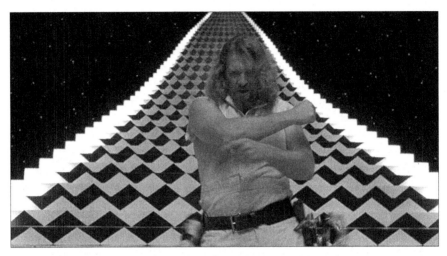

'I just dropped in to see what condition my condition was in'.

another condition, not so much the Dude's drug-altered state of consciousness as the condition of his subconscious mind and, obviously, at a deeper level, he has Maude (and sex) on his mind. Maude, we know, is concerned about the Dude's physical condition, specifically his sperm count, which is subsequently revealed as her hidden motive for sending the Dude for a check-up. It is later revealed that Maude covets the Dude's 'balls' only as a source of the sperm required to impregnate her. In her view, the definition of a man is reduced to his procreative function and nothing more, a belief that ironically reiterates the Dude's earlier smart-ass quip to the question, 'What makes a man?'

The title card introducing the 'Gutterballs' sequence shows a pair of bowling balls and a bowling pin arranged to resemble the male genital parts. These are set up and knocked over, bowling-style to foreshadow Maude's castrating scheme to exploit the Dude's 'balls' for her own selfish purposes. Maude is a Lebowski 'achiever', an assertive woman who knows what she wants and takes a direct and pragmatic path to her goal, characteristics stereotypically considered masculine. If the Dude's visual *leitmotif* is the drifting tumbleweed, Maude's leading iconic motif in 'Gutterballs' is a sharp-tipped trident, bluntly parodying Freudian symbolism. Indeed, Maude might be the answer to the question: Who is the real 'Big' Lebowski? Certainly not her father, who only pretends to be the man of his house, but is actually an impotent figurehead. In the Lebowski family Maude wears the pants. As Maude tells the Dude: 'The wealth is all mother's. We did let father run the companies briefly, but he didn't do very well at it. He helps administer the charities now, and I give him a reasonable allowance. He has no money of his own.' The fact that the Big Lebowski is crippled and confined to a wheelchair literalises his castration: he has been 'cut off' financially and well as physically. Incapable of standing on his own, he compensates by taking an over-sexed younger trophy wife.

The final song of the soundtrack, 'Send Me Dead Flowers', seems intended as a farewell for Donny, whose ashes Walter attempts to commit to the ocean's deep, but instead blow back into the Dude's face. The song's refrain – 'I won't forget to put roses on your grave' – memorialises Donny's tragi-comic death. Thus Donny's musical signature is inscribed posthumously; his belated frame of reference comes too late. He shall be remembered, but we will never know who he was. Compared to his bowling buddies, the Dude and Walter, characters we come to know well, precisely because they are 'characters', Donny might be a case of missing identity. He is a tag-along who is always out of the loop and constantly being told by Walter to 'shut the fuck up!' Even though he is integral to the Dude's story, we never learn much about Donny, except that he's a good bowler (and we do actually see him bowl, while the Dude, oddly, is never shown in the act). But Donny, as Walter repeatedly tells him, has 'no frame of reference'. We have no frame of reference for him either, no stereotype or cultural model to frame his identity. Every other main character has a well-defined identity, either as cultural stereotypes – the Dude, the post-hippie slacker, Walter, the crazy Vietnam vet, the Big as the corrupt big-shot, Bunny, the slutty trophy wife – or as generic movie characters – the Dude as (a parody of) the film noir private eye, the cowboy Stranger, Treehorn as the sleazy mob boss, and so on. Without any frame of reference, Donny's identity remains indeterminate. Even the names stitched on his bowling shirts reveal nothing of his identity. In every scene the name changes. Donny's musical signature, however, does offer at least one identity frame in its relation to the artist who recorded his song, Townes Van Zandt. A veteran alt-country singer, legendary for his alcohol and drug abuse, Van Zandt died in 1997, a year before *The Big Lebowski*'s release, just as the film was set to go into production. Perhaps including Van Zandt's country and western cover of the Rolling Stones' original is a memorial gesture, a way of 'putting roses on his grave' as well as on Donny's.

# CHAPTER EIGHT

# O Brother, Where Art Thou?: The Hayseed Epic

Although *O Brother, Where Art Thou?* was released in 2000, script development for the project had already begun in the mid-1990s. In fact, as early as 1987, the Coen brothers were envisioning a movie set in the Deep South that would complete what they called their 'Hayseed Trilogy' (which includes *Blood Simple* and *Raising Arizona*), but prohibitive production costs kept the project on hold. Set in Depression-era Mississippi, *O Brother* tells the story of three chain-gang convicts who escape to freedom and embark on a homeward odyssey in search of fortune and redemption. The central figure of this trio, Ulysses Everett McGill (George Clooney), takes his name from the heroic protagonist of Homer's epic poem *The Odyssey*, from which the Coens borrow freely to tell the story of a modern-day Ulysses and his crew, Pete (John Turturro) and Delmar (Tim Blake Nelson), who accompany the hero on his homeward journey. Along the way, they encounter an assortment of characters plucked not only from the pages of Homer's poem but also from the history of the Deep South in 1930s America. All of these figures are targets for comic stereotyping, including a bank-robbing gangster (George 'Baby Face' Nelson, played by Michael Badalucco), the good-ol'-boy governor of Mississippi (Pappy O'Daniel, played by Charles Durning) and a black blues guitarist (Tommy Johnson, played by Chris Thomas King), representing the three generic discourses framing the film narrative: crime comedy, period film and musical.

## The Odyssey Homage

Although *O Brother, Where Art Thou?* has structural and thematic similarities to Homer's *Odyssey*, the original premise for the screenplay was, according to Joel, the simple idea of convicts escaping from a chain gang in 1930s Mississippi. 'Homer was an afterthought,' Joel confides, telling an interviewer that halfway through the writing process, the brothers became aware of the similarity of their 'road movie' to the epic poem and from that point pirating from *The Odyssey* became a running joke, an intertextual dialogue with Homer that amused them during the writing of the screenplay (Mottram 2000: 159). Making light of their classical references, the Coens say, 'Whenever it's convenient, we trot out *The Odyssey*' (Allen 2006: 136). Homer's poem, a story of exile and return, recounts the homeward journey of Odysseus (called Ulysses in Roman mythology) after the end of the ten-year Trojan War. Although the mythic hero must endure long years of wandering, he is determined to see once more the shores of the isle of Ithaca. During his journey he encounters many dangers and is constantly beset with trials and tribulation (his Greek name, Odysseus, means 'Son of Pain'), but ultimately Ulysses triumphs and reunites with wife and son, illustrating the Homeric themes of family unity and the affirmation of marriage. In *O Brother, Where Art Thou?* the episodic voyage of *The Odyssey* is recreated by Ulysses Everett McGill's picaresque homeward wanderings and his quest for redemption.

A title card with a citation from *The Odyssey* introduces the film narrative, acknowledging *O Brother*'s debt to Homer:

*O muse!*
*Sing in me, and through me tell the story*
*Of that man skilled in the ways of contending,*
*A wanderer, harried for years on end...*

This, the first sentence of *The Odyssey*, introduces us to the hero of Homer's epic and serves as a description of his contemporary counterpart, Ulysses Everett McGill. Both men are 'skilled in the ways of contending' or adept at the art of rhetorical persuasion, and both are 'harried' by agents of persecution and beset with 'constant sorrow'. Like his Homeric namesake, Ulysses Everett embarks on an odyssey filled with trials and tribulation. His goal is to reclaim his bride, Penny (Holly Hunter), an allusion to Ulysses' wife, Penelope. In *The Odyssey* Penelope waits in Ithaca for the return of her husband, surrounded by a gang of suitors, all hoping in the long absence of Ulysses to win Penelope's hand in marriage. Like his mythic double, Everett must return to Ithaca (Mississippi) to reestablish himself as *paterfamilias* by winning back Penny from an aggressive suitor named Vernon T. Waldrip (Ray McKinnon), whose name does not derive from the ancient Greek epic but, as Joel reports, from the William Faulker novel *The Wild Palms* (Allen 2006: 180). As one of the more obscure literary references in *O Brother*, the name Waldrip may also allude to the contemporary fantasy writer Howard Waldrop, noted for his 'alternate-history stories', in particular for his 1989 novella *A Dozen Tough Jobs*, a retelling of the twelve labors of Hercules transposed to Depression-era Mississippi.

The ancient bard tells us that Ulysses was known as a bold leader of cunning intelligence who always, even in direst straits, had a plan of action. Everett too, fancies himself a leader of men, although Pete may occasionally question his authority. If they find themselves 'in a tight spot' (a phrase Everett uses repeatedly), he always has

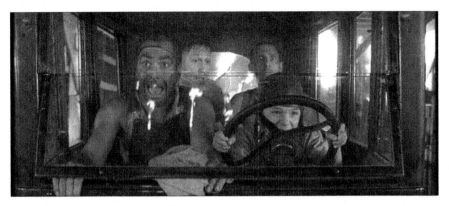

'Damn, we're in a tight spot!'

a plan. The modern Ulysses also shares with his mythic forebear a mastery of deception. Homer calls his Ulysses 'a cheat and dissembler' and 'a teller of deceitful tales'.
The same can be said of Everett. At the outset of his story, Everett is in prison for
misrepresenting himself as a lawyer (without a license); at the story's conclusion he is
contemplating becoming a phony dentist. Like Homer's Ulysses, who upon his return
to Ithaca disguises himself as an aged beggar, Everett wears a fake beard to cover his
identity when he makes his return to Ithaca. As in *The Odyssey*, where Ulysses proves his
real identity by passing a test of knowledge, Everett is tasked with recovering Penny's
lost wedding ring from the flooded valley before she will consent to his reinstate-
ment as rightful husband and father. To facilitate the recording of 'A Man of Constant
Sorrow', Everett misrepresents himself as a black man, using the name 'Jordan Rivers'
(an undisguised reference to the biblical Jordan River, where Jesus was baptised, and
through which Joshua led the enslaved Israelites to freedom). His ultimate deception,
however, is enticing his jail mates to make a dangerous escape with the false promise
of a non-existent fortune.

Homer's Ulysses is stubbornly self-reliant, even defiant of the gods, but even he
must petition the divine powers for assistance. Thus, at the end of *The Odyssey* the
goddess Athena intervenes to save him from the wrath of the citizens of Ithaca seeking
to avenge the deaths of their sons, Penelope's suitors. In the Coens' version, Everett
fancies himself an enlightened rationalist who rejects religious beliefs as irrational
superstition, as he attests in a pompous speech on the socio-cultural advantages of
hydro-electric power that the newly flooded valley will yield:

> Yessir, the South is gonna change. Everything's gonna be put on electricity and
> run on a payin' basis. Out with old spiritual mumbo-jumbo, the superstitions
> and the backward ways. We're gonna see a brave new world where they run
> everyone a wire and hook us all up to the grid. Yessir, a veritable age of reason
> – like the one they had in France – and not a moment too soon…

As Everett's voice trails off, a cow on a cottonhouse roof floats past – a miraculous
vision challenging the logic of mortal rationality. When faced with death by hanging,

however, he prays ardently for salvation: 'I'm sorry I turned by back on you, Lord. I know I've been guilty of pride and sharp dealing.' His confession of pride also harks back to the Homeric Ulysses, known for his vanity and the arrogance of hubris, offending the gods who then hinder his progress with many calamities. Everett's somewhat less cosmic vanity manifests itself in his obsession with a hairstyle that requires copious amounts of a pomade branded 'Dapper Dan'. In Homer's *Odyssey* Penelope's suitors are also said to have 'hair sleek with oil' to make themselves attractive to Penelope. Penny's suitor, Vernon Waldrip, slicks his hair too, prompting a sniffing Everett to query, 'Have you been using my hair treatment?'

Many of the other characters in *O Brother* have Homeric analogues: a blind handcar driver (Lee Weaver) foretells the fate of the wanderers, echoing the blind seer Tiresius; Big Dan Teague (John Goodman), the larcenous, one-eyed Bible salesman, reincarnates the monstrous Cyclops; and the singing woodland seductresses recall the mythic Sirens whose musical temptations threatened the lives of Ulysses and his sailors. *O Brother* begins and ends with appearances by the blind handcar driver who, like the oracle of Homer's poem, foretells great fortune for the escapees, but cautions the travelers that they will endure a difficult and dangerous journey, 'fraught with peril and pregnant with adventure', predicting that the fortune they will find is not the one they seek. The handcar driver claims 'I work for no man' and 'I have no name', recalling Ulysses' cunning trick of telling the Cyclops his name is 'No-man', a ploy that sets up the hero's escape from the Cyclops' lair. After stabbing the Cyclops in the eye with a burning spear, blinding him, Ulysses and his men make good their escape. When the wounded Cyclops shouts to his neighbors 'No-man is killing me', his plea for help is ignored, allowing Ulysses and his sailors to elude a terrible fate. In *O Brother*, one-eyed Big Dan, also a member of the Ku Klux Klan, is similarly dispatched. Revising the Homeric scenario, Everett hurls a sharp-pointed Confederate flagpole at Big Dan's eye, which he snatches in mid-air, only to be struck down the next instant by a burning cross, symbol of the Klan's racist hatred. During the ensuing confusion, Everett and his comrades escape another 'tight spot'.

The episodes of *The Odyssey* chronicling the encounters with the Sirens and the goddess Circe, who bewitches Ulysses' men and turns some of them into swine, are combined in *O Brother* in the Soggy Bottom Boys' seduction by three nymph-like singers washing clothes by the river. Attracted by their unearthly song, the boys join the woodland nymphs who seduce them with corn liquor and feminine charms. Awakening from his alcohol-induced stupor, Delmar notices that Pete is missing and believes he has been turned into a toad by the river singers, who actually just turned Pete in to the sinister chain-gang boss Sheriff Cooley (Daniel von Bargen), who doggedly pursues the three escapees throughout their homeward odyssey. Cooley's counterpart in *The Odyssey* would be Poseidon, the god of the sea, who swears vengeance on Ulysses for harming his son Polyphemus, the Cyclops, and persecutes the heroic sailor and his crew relentlessly with stormy seas. When Cooley finally captures the Soggy Bottom Boys, he tells them: 'You have eluded fate – and eluded me – for the last time,' thus identifying himself as a mythic agent of destiny. The Sheriff's malice is thwarted, ironically, by a flood tide, the very element that Poseidon rules.

Despite the Coens' cavalier treatment of Homer, *O Brother*'s retelling of *The Odyssey* is more than a haphazard collection of mythological clichés. Indeed, some of Homer's most fundamental themes are in evidence, if only to be parodied, as a comparison of the two endings illustrates. Upon his return to Ithaca, Ulysses proves his true identity by detailing to Penelope how he built their marriage bed. By so testing and proving his identity, she authorises Ulysses to reclaim his status as family patriarch and restore his honour and aristocratic position. By acknowledging him as *paterfamilias*, Penelope renews the bonds of marriage and family and restores the social order upset by his absence, bringing narrative closure to the epic. The same cannot be said of *O Brother*, which avoids both narrative and thematic resolution. At the movie's conclusion, Everett has failed to retrieve Penny's wedding ring from the flood, proffering instead a ring belonging to Aunt Hurlene. Insisting that only her own wedding ring will do, she tasks poor Everett with fishing it from the 9,000-hectare lake created by the flood, to which Everett can only retort: 'That is one hell of a heroic task.' Suspended in marital limbo, Everett's patriarchal status is still in doubt as the story ends.

## Sullivan's Travels

While Homer's *Odyssey* lends *O Brother* its episodic structure and furnishes an archive of recognizable tropes, the movie's most essential sources are found in the cinematic tradition. In its wide-ranging dialogue with the history of cinema, *O Brother* glosses numerous filmic precursors such as Stuart Rosenberg's *Cool Hand Luke* (1967), a chain-gang story featuring Boss Godfrey, a cruel lawman in mirrored sunglasses, reflected in *O Brother* as Boss Cooley, the relentless sheriff who, accompanied by a slobbering blood hound, pursues the escaped fugitives like Satan himself. His connection with the Devil is reinforced by the blues musician Tommy, who describes the Devil who bargained with him for his soul at the crossroads as a white man, 'white as you folks, with mirrors for eyes and a big hollow voice and always travels with a mean old hound'. Another cinematic point of reference is Stanley Kramer's *The Defiant Ones* (1958), the story of two prisoners escaped from a chain gang, one white (Tony Curtis) and one black (Sidney Poitier), shackled together and forced to transcend racial differences and cooperate for survival. The latter allusion is cross-referenced in a remark by Everett encouraging Pete to overcome his 'hopeless negativism': 'Consider the lilies of the goddamn field.' *The Lilies of the Field* (Ralph Nelson, 1963) starred Poitier, playing a character named Homer Smith, a role for which Poitier was awarded the first Academy Award given to an African-American actor. Critiques of racism and an unjust penal system unify these antecedents, hinting at an underlying polemic in *O Brother*.

The caricature of George 'Baby Face' Nelson adds another facet to the Coen pastiche, suggesting a broader parody of the gangster genre. Baby Face's trademark line, 'I'm on top of the world!' mimics the famous last words of Cody Jarrett (James Cagney) in Raoul Walsh's gangster-noir *White Heat* (1949): 'Made it, Ma. Top of the world!' which Cody shouts out defiantly moments before he dies in a fiery inferno. Both Cody and Baby Face are 'defiant ones' who taunt the police arrogantly, defying capture and celebrating their superiority over the law, linking them with Homer's

Ulysses and Everett as men guilty of hubris. Nelson's hatred for cows, which he shoots on sight with malicious delight ('I hate cows worse than coppers') parodies the sailors in Homer's *Odyssey* who slaughter Apollo's golden cattle. When, after an exciting bank robbery in the town of Itta Bena, a morose Baby Face parts ways with Everett and crew and wanders aimlessly into the dark night, we hear echoes of the melodramatic final scene of Mervyn LeRoy's classic gangster movie *I am a Fugitive from a Chain Gang* (1932), in which the protagonist, an escaped con played by Paul Muni, drifts off into night, doomed to run endlessly from the law.

The Coens have repeatedly stated their preference for literary antecedents as sources for their intertextual constructs. *O Brother* is an exception to this rule, mainly due to the brothers' special affection for Sturges, whose comedy *Sullivan's Travels* they cite as the main inspiration for their chain-gang epic. Despite openly professing their fondness for Sturges' classic comedies, the Coens approach the question of his influence with cagey reserve. 'There are things in [*O Brother*] that are very reminiscent of *Sullivan's Travels*,' admits Joel. 'But, I would say "reminiscent of" instead of "rip-off"' (Allen 2006: 136). To tell the tale of Ulysses Everett McGill, *O Brother, Where Art Thou?* borrows its narrative premise, the idea of convicts escaping from a chain gang in 1930s Mississippi, from *Sullivan's Travels*, where the protagonist, Hollywood director John 'Sully' Sullivan, otherwise known for directing silly comedies, proposes to make a film with 'social importance' entitled 'O Brother, Where Art Thou?' Tired of directing vacuous comedies with titles like 'Hey, Hey, in the Hay Loft' and 'Ants in Their Pants', Sully decides he wants to make a serious social problem film about the poverty and suffering caused by the Great Depression, hoping, as he says to his skeptical studio bosses, 'to realise the potentiality of film as the sociological and artistic medium that it is'. To research his subject, of which the wealthy and spoiled movie director knows nothing, Sully sets out, in his words, 'to know trouble', going on the road as a hobo to live among the poor and homeless and experience their hardships first-hand. At the end of his travels, he indeed finds enlightenment, but not the enlightenment he had expected. After experiencing the existential plight of the disenfranchised, he decides against making the 'serious' movie, realising that his audiences, who must endure an otherwise harsh and impoverished existence, benefit more from the diversions of comedic entertainment than from the sobering lessons of social realism. 'There's a lot to be said for making people laugh,' he tells the studio execs. 'Didn't you know, that's all some people have?' To emphasise his artistic credo, Sturges dedicates *Sullivan's Travels* 'to the memory of those who made us laugh; the motley mountebanks, the clowns, the buffoons, in all times and in all nations'. This is, in essence, the artistic ethos the Coens have always espoused, expressed by Joel in blunt terms: 'If somebody goes out to make a movie that isn't designed primarily to entertain people, then I don't know what the fuck they're doing' (Allen 2006: 11).

Direct allusions to *Sullivan's Travels* abound in *O Brother*, some of them obvious in any comparison of the two movies, others quite obscure, such as the title of one of Sullivan's popular comedies, 'Ants in Their Pants', which was one of the actual working titles for Sturges' *Christmas in July* (1940). One of the more striking references to *Sullivan's Travels* occurs in the scene where Cousin Hogwallop's adolescent son engineers a daring rescue of Everett and the boys from the clutches of Sheriff Cooley, piloting a getaway car through the hellish flames of a burning barn and yelling 'Come on, boys! I'm gonna run OFF!' This incident tropes director Sullivan's comical attempts to elude the caravan of caretakers sent by the movie studio to protect their star director on his vagabond odyssey. In one of his attempts to ditch the studio's babysitters, Sully hitches a wild ride in a jalopy driven by a thirteen-year-old boy who claims he is studying to be a 'whippet tank driver'.

Another direct borrowing from *Sullivan's Travels* targets a crucial scene in which Sully's chain gang attends a screening of a Walt Disney cartoon as guests of an African-American church congregation. As they watch the silly antics of Pluto on screen, Sullivan looks around at the viewers – an integrated group of blacks and whites, quite uncommon in that era – and has an epiphany, suddenly realising the therapeutic power of comedy to lift, if only momentarily, the burden of hard reality and to bring segregated groups into harmonious unity. In *O Brother*, Everett and Delmar also go to the movie theatre to see a comedy. They are joined at the showing by a gang of convicts, among them Pete, who Delmar had been convinced was now a toad, and who warns his friends, 'Do *not* seek the treasure!' The movie they are watching is the 1933 comedy *Myrt and Marge*, a reference to film history that also affords the Coens an opportunity to flaunt their knowledge of radio history. The movie *Myrt and Marge* is an adaptation of the popular radio program created by Myrtle Vail, based on anecdotes from her career in vaudeville. Among Vail's supporting cast were the Three Stooges. 'Myrt' is also the name Everett chooses to bestow on a non-existent member of the Soggy Bottom Boys to deceive the blind recording engineer at WEZY Radio and collect extra pay for their recording of 'A Man of Constant Sorrow'. Although Everett and Delmar do not experience Sully's revelatory insight about the healing power of comedy, the popular success of their record proves that music, like comedy, has the power to unify, transcending racial and cultural barriers and uniting people in the spirit of democratic freedom. This is borne out at the town gathering where the Soggy Bottom Boys perform 'A Man of Constant Sorrow' to the roaring approval of all, except the racist demagogue Homer Stokes, who is run out of the meeting on a rail.

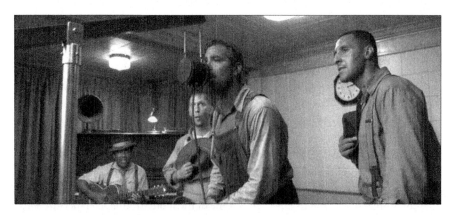

The Soggy Bottom Boys record 'A Man of Constant Sorrow'.

The Coens have said, 'In our minds' [*O Brother*] was presumably the movie [Sullivan] would have made if he'd had the chance. The important movie. The one that takes on the big, important themes' (Allen 2006: 136). As self-contradictory as ever, they also say that *O Brother* 'pretends to be a big important movie, but the grandiosity is obviously a joke. It's a comedy' (Allen 2006: 129). When asked about a political subtext, Joel replied that 'the political undercurrent of the movie functions primarily for dramatic purposes', depicting the politics of *O Brother* as 'frankly pretty primitive' (Allen 2006: 130). Indeed, pitting movie cut-out villains like Sheriff Cooley and cultural stereotypes like KKK Grand Wizard Homer Stokes against a singing trio of clownish but loveable folk heroes, *O Brother* does not ask to be taken seriously as social commentary. The result is a movie that appears to lack the crucial distinguishing attribute of Sturges' comedies – a sharp satirical edge that cuts to the core of important socio-political issues.

For all its emphasis on 'the sunny side', *Sullivan's Travels* also offers an at times starkly realistic picture of abject poverty and hardship, and although the comedic tone is dominant, parts of the movie (shot in faux-documentary style) still manage to portray the reality of human degradation and social malaise experienced by millions of Americans in the Depression years. Despite mounting what Paul Coughlin has described as a 'technically precise and culturally astute recreation of America's Deep South in the 1930s' (2009: 197), the Coens deny having done any background research on the period and insist that their movie is not 'about' the actual history and politics of the 1930s. Instead, the Coens describe their storyworld as 'an imagined world where all those things intersect – real people and made-up people' (Allen 2006: 130). Rather than striving for historical authenticity, the Coens implicitly endorse the postmodern view of history as inexorably mediated by its textual remains, always only a *post facto* reconstruction fashioned from surviving cultural documents. The parodic pastiche giving shape to *O Brother* reminds us of our postmodern condition, implying that, in the words of Linda Hutcheon, 'there is no directly and naturally accessible past "real" for us today: we can only know – and construct – the past through its traces, its representations' (1997: 39).

The search for authenticity and the processes of authentification are central themes in all three of *O Brother*'s principle intertexts. Homer's Ulysses returns home a stranger and must authenticate his identity to reclaim his wife and family. The same is more or less true of Ulysses Everett. Sullivan is similarly required to prove his identity to be freed from the chain gang. A related undercurrent is suggested in both *O Brother* and *Sullivan's Travels* in their implied criticism of Hollywood's willingness to exploit socio-political realities to produce motion-picture profits and artistic prestige. Such was certainly the case in Sturges' day when, after flooding theatres with escapist comedies during the Depression years, Hollywood studios began to veer away from entertainment genres to produce more 'serious' movies which, as one of Sullivan's studio bosses cynically comments, 'stink with messages'. As *Sullivan's Travels* makes clear, the pampered movie director's sudden interest in poverty amounts to little more than a shallow appeal to a new industry fashion. Recalling Barton Fink's dream of establishing a theatre 'for the common man', the Coens join Sturges in satirising aloof artists and intellectuals whose pretentious solidarity with the lower classes merits nothing so much as comedic lampooning.

Oblivious to the message of Sturges' movie – that 'message films stink' – critics sought a deeper meaning or message in *O Brother*, only to find, as did Alexander Walker, that the film 'says everything about the Coens' love of old movie genres and pretty well nothing about anything else'. R. Barton Palmer, who elsewhere champions Coen brothers movies as 'exceptions to the general regime of pastiche in genre filmmaking' (2004: 60), takes back his assessment, viewing *O Brother* as the Coens' 'least serious movie': 'witty and sophisticated, but, true to Sullivan's theory of a filmmaking dedicated to uncomplicated emotional uplift, it avoids serious questions of any kind' (2004: 133). The Coens' contention that *O Brother*'s political undercurrent serves only dramatic purposes confuses the issue even more. Nevertheless, Erica Rowell describes *O Brother* as 'biting social drama' and 'a satirical investigation into America's past' that explores the political and spiritual bedrock of the nation (2007: 244). Given these differing perceptions, how are we to understand *O Brother, Where Art Thou?* Is it merely a postmodern prank on American history? Or is there a hidden polemic in their sepia-toned re-visioning of the past?

Douglas McFarland contends that although it appears to confirm the accusation that postmodern pastiche engages in nothing more than a neutral game of allusionism, *O Brother* shows how even a silly comedy can address social history in progressive ways. In particular, McFarland examines the 'ironic incongruities' built into the film's pastiche and explores how such incongruities convey an ethical challenge to the political complacency of postmodern audiences (2009: 50). The workings of these ironic incongruities are fully exemplified, McFarland argues, in the episode staging a Ku Klux Klan rally at which the Soggy Bottom Boys' accompanist, Tommy Johnson, is about to be hanged for the crime of being black. As the hooded brethren of the Klan assemble, they are greeted by the racist harangue of their 'Imperial Wizard': 'Brothers! We are foregathered here to preserve our hallowed culture and heritage! From intrusions, inclusions and dilutions! Of colour! Of creed! Of our ol' time religion!' The viewer with any knowledge of the Ku Klux Klan and the racist atrocities committed by its members in the 1920s and 1930s is forced to confront the enormity of this historical moment. 'There is quite simply,' writes McFarland, 'no possibility of avoiding the historical setting of the episode and the ethical response that that setting demands' (2009: 48). Even though the sequence is rife with jokey allusions to Homer, Busby Berkeley and *The Wizard of Oz* (1939), it restores to memory a particularly dark moment in American history when society was still poisoned by intractable racist hatred.

Despite the dense and comical cluster of allusions on display, this scene cannot be separated from a time and place in American history that demands moral condemnation. This creates a strange kind of incongruity, where film history intersects with political history. Marching in formations reminiscent of Busby Berkeley as well as Leni Riefenstahl's Nazi propaganda film *Triumph of the Will* (1936), the Klan members are made to look ridiculous as they perform a silly ritualised dance, choreographed to evoke an imagistic fusion of Hollywood escapism and fascist fanaticism in the 1930s. More than one critic has noted *O Brother*'s similarity to *The Wizard of Oz*, comparing Everett's odyssey with Pete and Delmar to the story of Dorothy's journey home to Kansas accompanied by three nitwit companions. Specifically, the KKK rally parodies the 'March of the Winkies' in *The Wizard of Oz*, where guards parade in military style outside the wicked witch's castle. Sounding the depths of *O Brother*'s political undercurrent, Rowell reminds us that E. Y. Harburg, who wrote the lyrics and much of the dialogue for *The Wizard of Oz,* had artfully woven politics into that movie's musical texture. According to Harburg, *The Wizard of Oz* was conceived as a tribute to US President Franklin D. Roosevelt's 'sunny' leadership in dark and troubled times (Rowell 2007: 261). FDR's state-funded socialist agenda for economic recovery included the Tennessee Valley Authority, alluded to in *O Brother* by the flooded valley that proves to be the salvation of Ulysses Everett McGill and company.

The satiric edge of the KKK scene is sharpened with the revelation that the 'Wizard' is none other than Homer Stokes, the would-be governor who campaigns with a midget representing the 'little people' he promises to serve faithfully. Promising reform to help 'the little man' but secretly leader of the KKK, Stokes has a historical model in Huey Long, Louisiana governor and senator nicknamed 'Kingfish', who initially promoted a reformist agenda supporting workers' rights, but eventually succumbed to the evils of political corruption. His campaign slogan, 'Sweep them out of office', is echoed by Homer Stokes' vow to 'sweep this state clean'. Stokes' political opponent, Pappy O'Daniel, takes his name from the corrupt Southern politician of the Depression era, W. Lee 'Pappy' O'Daniel, a Texas governor known for his racist politics who posed as a hillbilly during election campaigns to increase his appeal to 'the common man'. Like the Pappy O'Daniel of *O Brother*, the real-life Texas politician also had a radio show and sang with groups such as the Hillbillies and the Light Crust Doughboys. Despite intervening to pardon the Soggy Bottom Boys, however, Pappy is hardly better than Stokes, a cynical shill for wealthy power-brokers, more interested in promoting his brand of flour and prolonging his incumbency than in representing the interests of his constituents. As a composite figure parodying Southern politicians, Pappy is also reminiscent of Jimmie Davis, Louisiana's 'Singing Governor' who, like Pappy, campaigned with the song 'You Are My Sunshine'.

*Good Ol'timey Music*

Given the filmstory's setting in 1930s Mississippi, the mixture of Delta blues, gospel and early country music (colloquially, 'old-timey music') that comprises the soundtrack of *O Brother* is historically accurate or authentic. Both Coen brothers are long-time fans of country music, so it is not surprising that during the preparation of the screenplay they report that the music 'began to take over the script' (Robson 2007: 236). Music producer T Bone Burnett, who had compiled the eclectic collage of songs for *The Big Lebowski* soundtrack, returned to help select music for *O Brother* that would support the narrative, underscoring thematic elements and giving the film what Joel calls the 'tone and the flavour' (ibid.). On the whole, one has the impression that the soundtrack was compiled with every attempt to preserve the integrity and authenticity of this early country musical tradition. All the music chosen for the film is rooted in the southern regions in the 1920s and 1930s, and all the songs are incorporated as diegetic sound, sourced in the fictional storyworld, creating the generic impression of a musical.

Wherever possible, vocal and instrumental music is performed on-screen by an all-star line-up of musicians including veteran artists like country legend Ralph Stanley and the Grammy Award-winning Cox Family, as well as younger talents like Alison Krauss and Union Station. Some vocals had to be lip-synched, notably, George Clooney's lead vocal on 'A Man of Constant Sorrow', which is sung by Dan Tyminski, a member of Union Station. Several actors performed the music unassisted, including Tim Blake Nelson, who sang the lead vocal for the Soggy Bottom Boys' rendition of Jimmy Rogers' 'In the Jailhouse Now' and Chris Thomas King, who renders the Skip James tune 'Hard Time Killing Floor Blues'. The gravediggers who sing 'You've Got to Walk That Lonesome Valley' are not professional actors but members of a vocal group called the Fairfield Four. 'Keep on the Sunny Side' is sung by the Whites (end title version by the Cox Family) and 'I'll Fly Away' is performed by the Kossoy Sisters. The sirens' lullaby, 'Didn't Leave Nobody but the Baby', is voiced by country singers Alison Krauss, Emmylou Harris and Gillian Welch (who also has a cameo in the film), while 'Angel Band', first recorded by the Stanley Brothers in 1955, was rerecorded for *O Brother* by the Peasall Sisters. Some of the tracks are remixes of archival recordings and new performances. Emmylou Harris and Alison Krauss, for instance, recorded new vocal tracks that were dubbed into archival recordings of 'Big Rock Candy Mountain' (written by Harry McClintock, 1928). The same is true of 'You Are My Sunshine' (written by Jimmie Davis), for which an archival version is refreshed with the voice of Alan O'Bryant.

Roger Ebert views the Coens' imaginative reconstruction of 1930s Mississippi as a reminder of 'a freaky, forgotten, haunted side of American culture'. This supposedly forgotten period of US history is linked in *O Brother* to the image of the railroad, originally a symbol of Manifest Destiny, but in the early twentieth century increasingly associated with the widespread poverty and homelessness of the Great Depression and a new underclass of rail-riding hobos. This phenomenon is reflected musically in the hobo chantey 'The Big Rock Candy Mountain', which plays during the opening credits as accompaniment to the convict trio's escape from the chain gang. At a narrative level, the song's lyrics extend an invitation to the odyssey upon which Everett and crew are about to embark: 'I'm headed for a land that's far away,' an itinerant's paradise where 'all the cops have wooden legs, and the bulldogs all have rubber teeth and the hens lay soft-boiled eggs' – a fantasised candy land that proffers the illusion of escape from the harsh reality of train-hopping vagabonds who often had to dodge railroad police and guard dogs and endure painful starvation.

Also emblematic for this historical period are the chain gangs that built the railways, the image of which is introduced in the movie's opening scene, accompanied by 'Po' Lazarus', a convict work song depicting a crafty fugitive (like Everett) wanted dead or alive. As a work song sung by chain gang prisoners, 'Po' Lazarus' also reiterates the central theme of *O Brother, Where Art Thou?*: artistic entertainment (music, movies) provides some relief from life's unpleasant realities. It is worth noting that the sound used for this scene in *O Brother* is an actual field recording of a chain gang from the Mississippi State Prison made by music historian Alan Lomax and thus a historical document of actual prison life. The documentary quality of this scene is enhanced visually by de-saturating the colour to a near-monochromic level, lending it a heightened air of realism reminiscent of *Sullivan's Travels* and its mixture of comedy with documentary-style images of privation, particularly in its depiction of Sully's sojourn in a prison camp. As both films suggest, the prison camps of the Depression created a new form of social tyranny used to prolong the outlawed practices of slavery. Along these lines, *O Brother*'s references to the 'Parchman Farm' allude to a Mississippi prison of the 1930s infamous for its cruel treatment of the inmates, mostly blacks. Built by racist governor James K. Vardaman, the Parchman Farm was a 'correctional institution' with an ideological agenda aimed at conditioning black prisoners to be subservient to the dominant white culture, while also supplying cheap labour for business and industry.

The sense of disenfranchisement that afflicted the Depression years is revived in 'Hard Time Killing Floor Blues', the lyrics of which stress the plight of the homeless: 'Times is harder than ever before, and the people are driftin' from door to door. Can't find no heaven.' Sung by Tommy Johnson, this early blues classic sets the mood for the escaped convicts' campfire meditations on the uses of the wealth Everett's buried treasure will yield. When asked what he will do with his share, Delmar expresses his desire to buy back his family's farm and ancestral home, saying 'Hell, you ain't no kinda man if you ain't got land.' Besides adding a Sturges-like touch of historical reality, 'Hard Time Killing Floor Blues' frames a scene that modestly restores to memory the hardship of capital foreclosure widely experienced during the Depression era – a hardship humorously highlighted by Cousin Hogwallop, whose farm lurches on the verge of bank repossession, driving him to betray his next of kin. The Tommy Johnson character is of course based on Robert Johnson, early blues singer and guitarist who, according to legend, traded his soul to the Devil for musical genius. Inspired by his role in *O Brother*, Chris Thomas King, a professional musician, not an actor, wrote an album based on Tommy Johnson's character entitled *The Legend of Tommy Johnson, Act I: Genesis 1900s–1990s*, which chronicles the rise of blues music through the twentieth century.

The social tensions caused by racial integration in the old South are roundly satirised in Ku Klux Klan episode. In this historical context, the Soggy Bottom Boys constitute a socially progressive grouping. Like the subculture of chain gangs, which were often racially integrated, the musicians' subculture is inclusive, making no distinction between black and white, creating a racial 'blindness' that becomes the premise for repeated sight gags, for instance, when the Boys misrepresent themselves as black men to the blind music producer at WEZY Radio who records 'A Man of Constant Sorrow'. The recording session and its terms of payment satirise another historical inequity. In the early days of the music record industry producers would pay artists an insignificant fee and sell their recordings for huge profits. One of the best-known instances dates back to 1927 when the Carter Family played for the 'Bristol Sessions', receiving the modest sum of $50.00 per song. Nicknamed 'The First Family of Country Music', the Carters' landmark early recordings of such songs as 'Wabash Cannonball' and 'Keep on the Sunny Side' not only exerted a profound influence on country, bluegrass and gospel music but subsequently earned huge profits for the music producers.

The gospel song 'The Good Old Way (As I Went Down to the River to Pray)' accompanying the river-side baptism of wandering Christians (whom Delmar calls 'a gopher village') introduces another ideological agenda subjected to parodic scrutiny. Besides washing away the sins of Delmar and Pete, the religious symbolism of water as purifying agent anticipates the biblical flood at the end of the story that saves the convicts and, ironically, allows Everett to be 'born again'. Everett sees that 'everybody's lookin' for answers' but he objects to the 'good old way' of finding them promised by orthodox religion, refusing to join his comrades in what he considers the 'ridiculous superstition' of baptism. When, after the flood saves them, Delmar and Pete call their salvation 'a miracle', Everett complains: 'It just never fails; once again you two hayseeds are showin' how much you want for intellect. There's a perfectly scientific explanation for what just happened.' After they pick up the hitch-hiking Tommy Johnson, who says he is going to meet the Devil and sell his soul, Everett exclaims: 'Well ain't it a small world, spiritually speakin'! Pete and Delmar just been baptised and saved! I guess I'm the only one here who remains unaffiliated!' This may be as close as the Coens come to disclosing their own theological position – 'unaffiliated', skeptical of all religious doctrine and generally mistrustful of any systematic claims to meaning and truth.

The original soundtrack for the movie was an unexpected winner of Album of the Year at the 2002 Grammy Awards, and since its initial meteoric rise to the top of the US Billboard chart it has sold millions of copies. It has been said that the *O Brother* soundtrack sparked a widespread revival of interest in old-time country music and blue grass, musical idioms of the 1930s that had almost passed into obscurity. This is a hallmark of the Coens' filmmaking: rediscovering neglected aspects of American cultural history. The sincere presentation of folk music in *O Brother, Where Art Thou?*, apparently without the irony infusing the rest of the movie, implies that its soundtrack, if nothing else, is a piece of authentic culture worthy of being saved from the oblivion of neglect.

CHAPTER NINE

# *The Man Who Wasn't There: Recreating Classic Film Noir*

Released in 2001, *The Man Who Wasn't There* was almost unanimously well received by film critics. Joel was awarded Best Director for a third time at the Cannes Film Festival, although this time top honours had to be shared with David Lynch for his surrealist noir *Mulholland Drive* (2001). Many reviewers rated *The Man Who Wasn't There* among the very best the Coen brothers had so far produced. In the *Guardian* Peter Bradshaw called it 'stunning' and 'mesmeric', praising the Coens' 'originality and playful brilliance' and hailing it as 'quite simply the Coen brothers' masterpiece'. Writing for *Time Out*, Geoff Andrew described it as 'richly imaginative, resonant, rewarding, and of course, admirably weird'. Even *Village Voice* critic J. Hoberman, otherwise a detractor of the Coens' films, found it to be a 'sadder but wiser remake of the Coens' rambunctious debut *Blood Simple*'. Like many reviewers, Jason Caro was particularly appreciative of the Coens' imaginative remaking of classic film noir, not only because they dared to release a black and white film (today considered both a financial and aesthetic risk), but because they had succeeded admirably in recreating classic noir cinema, offering a contemporary film noir that plays like 'a re-discovered noir gem from 1944'. In a film that takes doubt and uncertainty as its central thematic concerns, there can be no doubt that this project, in its consummate reproduction of 1940s film noir, serves the artistic ambitions of its makers, who return once again to their most favoured movie genre to put on full display their considerable knowledge and understanding of historical film noir.

Set in the southern Californian small town of Santa Rosa in the year 1949, *The Man Who Wasn't There* is the story of Ed Crane (Billy Bob Thornton), who in subjective narration recounts his and the crimes of others who struggle to achieve the American Dream of economic success and self-betterment. Ed works as a barber in a shop owned by his brother-in-law Frank Raffo (Michael Badalucco), where he mechanically performs his mundane labours with a deep sense of resignation. But he dreams of a way out of his burdensome life, to take flight from the dissatisfactions of a mindless job and escape his servitude to an unloving and unfaithful wife, Doris (Frances McDormand), who is having an affair with her boss, Big Dave Brewster (James Gandolfini), right under his nose, finally driving Ed to plot a sneaky revenge. The unexpected success of his scheme to extort $10,000 from Big Dave enables Ed to invest in a newly emerging branch of industry: dry cleaning. After his business partner, a shady character named Tolliver Creighton (John Polito), absconds with his investment, Ed faces another threat from Big Dave, who has discovered Ed's secret identity as blackmailer. In an unforeseeable turn of events, Ed must kill Big Dave, only to learn afterward that Doris will be tried for the murder. Ed engages Freddy Riedenschneider (Tony Shalhoub), a fast-talking big-city lawyer, to defend Doris, but she cannot be saved. With no hope for acquittal, she takes her own life while awaiting trial. The story's final twist of fate serves Ed poetic justice when he is convicted of murdering Creighton, whose real murderer was Big Dave, and sentenced to death. As the story comes to its conclusion and the barber sits on death row awaiting execution, he reveals that the tale he has just narrated is actually the text of an article he is writing for a 'men's magazine'. Recounting his story for publication has given Ed Crane a new perspective on his life and imminent death. In his laconic words, 'seeing it whole gives you some peace'.

## Homage to Cain

As they had in *Blood Simple*, the Coens again inhabit the mind of one of their most honoured literary predecessors, this time reconstructing Cain's fictional universe with unusual sincerity. While *Blood Simple* re-examines the Cainian themes of sexual misadventure, greed and betrayal with darkly ironic inflection, *The Man Who Wasn't There* takes a noticeably more sober approach, avoiding the genre-bending revisionism and black humour of their debut to reconstitute Cain's pulp fiction as a gesture of genuine homage. Preserving the downbeat mood of Cain's writing throughout, *The Man Who Wasn't There* generally keeps faith with its source texts, only briefly verging on *Blood Simple*'s dark farce and intensifying, almost to the point of impersonation, the filmmakers' identification with their literary precursor. Indeed, the extent to which they cede authorship to Cain can be measured by the Coens' admission that basically 'it's [Cain's] story' (Robson 2007: 253), as if to say the film story owes its existence so completely to Cain that it no longer belongs to the screenwriters, who surrender authorial voice and artistic ownership to the revered ancestral writer. Like many of their postmodern contemporaries, the Coen brothers, with a few exceptions, as mentioned in the discussion of *Barton Fink*, seem unaffected by any Bloomian 'anxiety of influence'. Disinterested in competing with artistic predecessors in pursuit of originality, the Coens fully embrace the parasitic aesthetic of postmodernist citationality, authorising them to borrow (without debt) from Cain to reinvent his fiction in a way that it never was but could have been.

The basic elements of story and character constituting *The Man Who Wasn't There* are undisguised borrowings from Cain, as is the focus on everyday people caught in a web of crime and betrayal. Ethan describes Ed Crane as an Everyman type who 'inadvertently stumbles' into a drama of mischance set in motion by the actions of others (ibid.), thus emulating Cain's predilection for proletarian stories featuring ordinary people forced either by circumstance or greed to commit extraordinary crimes. 'What intrigues us about Cain,' say the Coens, 'is that the heroes of his stories are nearly always schlubs – loser guys involved in dreary, banal existences. Cain was interested in people's workaday lives, and he wrote about guys who worked as insurance salesmen or in banks, and we took that as a cue. Even though there's a crime in this story, we were still interested in what this guy ... does as a barber' (Allen 2006: 180). *The Man Who Wasn't There* also retains Cain's focus on the loss of communitarian social values and the resulting pervasive sense of personal alienation and pessimistic despair that permeated Depression-era America. Like Cain's doomed protagonists, Ed Crane is thrust into an existential predicament from which there is little hope for escape, teaching us that there is no exit from a world ruled by chance, where anything can, and ultimately does, go wrong.

These concerns along with Cain's special interest in murder for profit and the inevitable failure of the 'perfect plan' are best illustrated in the two principle sources for *The Man Who Wasn't There*: Cain's *The Postman Always Rings Twice* and *Double Indemnity*, both written as confessional narratives of working-class men marginalised by the economic crash of the Great Depression. As we saw in chapter one, *The Postman Always Rings Twice*'s Frank Chambers begins his story as a vagrant attracted to the freedom of the open road, but still searching for something to give his life meaning. He accepts a job working for Nick 'the Greek' Papadakis, a good-hearted restaurant owner, but quickly succumbs to a Cainian *l'amour fou*, lusting after Nick's sexy younger wife, Cora, who rejects her older, unattractive immigrant husband for the more virile and adventurous Frank. At Cora's urging, Frank plots to kill Nick and to acquire his roadside café so that he and Cora can make a new life together. After the failure of what they imagined would be a perfect murder, the adulterous lovers' second attempt succeeds, killing Nick in an auto wreck staged as an accident. An aggressive district attorney quickly sees through their plot and charges Cora with the Greek's murder. However, because Nick had life insurance with three different carriers, all of them seeking to avoid making payment on his death, the insurers' private investigators are instructed to testify before the court that no crime was committed, forcing the district attorney to withdraw his charges and permitting Cora to go 'free as a bird'. This legal trick is masterminded by the high-powered defence lawyer named Katz who, instead of representing his client's best interests, cynically works the justice system for his own benefit. Later, the 'postman' of fate rings a second time, this time killing Cora in a car wreck with Frank at the wheel, repeating with terrible irony the fate of her deceased husband. Although Cora's death is accidental, Frank is convicted of her murder and sentenced to death. In Frank's trial, where no one would benefit from an acquittal, Katz takes Frank for everything he's got, including Nick's restaurant, but is unable to save Frank from the hangman. At the end, the narrative is revealed as Frank's retrospective confession, written in his prison cell on death row, to be given to his priest for eventual posthumous publication.

Cain's later novel *Double Indemnity* features Walter Huff, a young and aggressive insurance salesman, who falls for Phyllis Nirdlinger, the fatally attractive wife of a customer. As in *The Postman Always Rings Twice*, the illicit lovers plot murder for money, staging the murder of her unsuspecting husband as an accident. But it is not just Walter's erotic obsession with Phyllis that motivates his criminal scheme. The insurance man knows his game and has been thinking for some time that he could 'pull something off', beat the insurance game, and cash in. Referring to the insurance business as 'the biggest gambling wheel in the world', Walter thinks of himself as a 'croupier' who knows all the tricks: 'One night I think up a trick, and get to thinking I could crook the wheel myself if I could only put a plant out there to put down my bet. When I met Phyllis, I met my plant' (1982: 382). Thus, Walter's underlying motive is not so much his desire for Phyllis but his secret wish to beat the bosses of the insurance company by rigging the game to his advantage. Although Cain does not address explicitly the socio-political implications of his croupier metaphor, he nevertheless creates a provocative image of American capitalism as a game rigged to benefit the wealthy, thereby reflecting a widespread resentment among Americans in the 1930s who felt they were being excluded from the American Dream.

Cain's protagonists may be losers in the end, but they are at least in the game. Ed Crane's disillusionment has reduced him to a passive onlooker. He leads a life of quiet resignation, accepting a job he secretly loathes from his brother-in-law and acquiescing to the stronger will of Doris who, like her brother, treats Ed as a subordinate. Ed's profound inner disaffection and disconnection from social reality is outwardly evident in his muted, nearly emotionless demeanour. Absent from his own life, he is in this sense truly 'the man who wasn't there'. After Doris's suicide Ed's spiritual malaise deepens: 'I sat in the house, but there was nobody there. I was a ghost. I didn't see anyone. No one saw me. I was the barber.' So insubstantial is his presence that when Ed visits Tolliver to enquire about the dry cleaning venture, the con man doesn't recognise him at first, mistaking him for a hotel porter and exclaiming, 'I didn't recognise you without the smock.' In contrast to Frank Chambers, a man defined by an elemental vitality and naïve self-confidence, or compared with Walter Huff, whose distinguishing quality is his desire to take control of 'the game', Ed is defined by a profound apathy, illustrated by his stoic reaction to the realisation that Doris and Big Dave are two-timing him: 'The signs were all there plain enough – not that I was gonna prance about it, mind you. It's a free country.'

Ed does, however, share one important trait with his Cainian models: he is a working man who feels cheated and dreams of finding a way out of his spirit-numbing routine, searching for, in his words, a way to overcome 'the instinct that kept me locked up in the barbershop, nose against the exit, afraid to try turning the knob'. Opportunity seems to knock when a scam artist appears in his barber chair, promising 'the biggest business opportunity since Henry Ford' to anyone willing to invest in his dry cleaning business. To raise the venture capital Ed blackmails Big Dave for $10,000, thereby also exacting a sneaky revenge on his romantic rival.

Generally, the narrative of *The Man Who Wasn't There* takes its cue from the Cainian romantic triangle, but bends it to a different angle. Ed, the cuckolded husband, is not, as in Cain's stories, targeted for murder by the adulterous lovers. Instead, he is cast in the role of blackmailer and accidental killer of Big Dave who, for his part, suffers the fatal misfortune typically assigned in Cain's fiction to the unsuspecting husband. Ed's criminal plotting does not include a plan to murder Big Dave, whose violent death is more the consequence of his inability to control his own rage than of any criminal calculation on Ed's part. Furthermore, Cain's adulterous couples typically scheme to eliminate the unwanted husband, but in the Coens' variation the crime Doris and Big Dave plot is embezzlement rather than homicide. To comply with the anonymous blackmail demand Big Dave commits himself, and Doris, to the risky conspiracy of 'cooking the books' at Nirdlinger's department store. To be sure, both Big Dave and Doris bear the moral guilt of marital infidelity and the legal guilt of embezzlement, but they do not plot murder. Unlike Cain's *femmes fatales*, Cora and Phyllis, who both assist in the cold-blooded murder of their husbands, Doris is innocent but indicted nevertheless on circumstantial evidence for Big Dave's murder, thus becoming the unintended victim of Ed's extortion scam. This and subsequent outcomes mirror the fate of the adulterous lovers in *The Postman Always Rings Twice* where Frank is not charged with Nick's murder but later condemned for what was actually Cora's accidental death in a car crash. Ed suffers a similar fate. When the police find Creighton's corpse, they falsely assume that Ed had a compelling motive for killing him. The partnership papers Ed had signed with Creighton are found in the dead man's briefcase, proving that Ed had given him $10,000 – circumstantial evidence at best, but enough to send Ed to the chair.

The apparent death of Birdy Abundas (Scarlett Johansson) in an auto accident with Ed in the driver's seat clearly alludes to Cora's unfortunate death with her lover at the wheel. Unlike Cain's Cora, however, Birdy survives the crash relatively unharmed, and unlike Cora, a primary character of the story, Birdy is a secondary player who enters the story after Doris (Cora's true counterpart) has committed suicide. Instead, Birdy plays a role similar to Madge Allen in *The Postman Always Rings Twice*, a minor character with whom Frank Chambers has a brief fling while Cora is out of town. Like Madge, who tames wild jungle cats, Birdy likes animals and professes a desire to be a veterinarian. Birdy's name also recalls Nick's pet name for Cora, whom he calls 'my little white bird'. As a younger, more innocent stand-in for Doris, Birdy also bears comparison with Phyllis Nirdlinger's step-daughter Lola in *Double Indemnity*, in whom Walter Huff sees an innocent purity lacking in her devious step-mother. Like Ed Crane, Walter feels compassion for Lola and wants to help her start a new life. Likewise, Birdy Abundas, whose surname suggests the abundant plenitude of youthful promise, represents a chance for Ed to escape and 'find some peace', and perhaps also a chance to make restitution for his own wasted life. Ed wants to be Birdy's manager and handle her business affairs, but his concern for her professional well-being has a compensatory aspect. As he explains: 'You're young. A kid really, your whole life ahead of you. But it's not too soon to start thinking … to start making opportunities for yourself. Before it all washes away. I can't stand by and watch any more things go down the drain.'

Katz, the conniving lawyer in *The Postman Always Rings Twice*, finds his counterpart in Freddy Riedenschneider. But while Katz is a minor character in Cain's novel, Riedenschneider's role and significance in *The Man Who Wasn't There* is expanded and caricatured, exaggerating the smug self-importance and cynical greed of his Cainian model. In Cain's novel Katz initially works *pro bono* in Cora's case because his victory over the rival district attorney is sufficient reward. But later, when Frank Chambers is put on trial, Katz's steep legal fees cost his client everything he owns, including Nick's roadside burger joint, just as Riedenschneider's billings eventually consume Crane's entire financial holdings, including brother-in-law Frank's barber shop, put up as collateral for a loan to subsidise Riedenschneider's fees and extravagant expenses such as staying in the best hotel in town and ordering expensive meals at upscale restaurants. Eventually, Ed must sign over his house to Riedenschneider, whose tricky legal defence cannot prevent the barber's conviction and death sentence.

As ever, the Coens indulge in citational name-play. Those familiar with Cain's writings will recognise the store name Nirdlinger as Phyllis's married name in *Double Indemnity*. In Billy Wilder's adaptation of *Double Indemnity*, Nirdlinger was changed to Dietrichson. A similar name – Diedrickson – is given to the medical examiner who informs Ed that Doris not only killed herself in prison but her unborn child as well. Notably, the name-play gives prominence to the Cain-texts, while names borrowed from film adaptations like Wilder's are relegated to minor characters. The one exception is Freddy Riedenschneider who takes his name from John Houston's *The Asphalt Jungle* (1950), a classic film noir in which Doc Riedenschneider (Sam Jaffe) is the criminal mastermind who plans the logistics of a complicated armored car heist. The irony of this reference should be obvious: Riedenschneider only thinks he is a mastermind; his faux-philosophical legal discourses are in fact 'gibberish' (a word the filmmakers use to describe Riedenschneider's diatribes). Other character names develop the motif of aviary flight, most prominently with 'Birdy', whose piano playing offers a way to 'fly' from a soul-deadening existence for Ed 'Crane', who shares his name with Marion Crane of Hitchcock's *Psycho* (1960), another character hoping to 'fly away' and start a new life with stolen money.

*Homage to Classic Film Noir*

Undoubtedly, *The Man Who Wasn't There* gives pride of place to Cain's writings, but at the same time the Coens, somewhat uncharacteristically, pay double homage to the cinematic tradition of film noir, exploring the genre as historical form and imitating its signature techniques while reexamining its most basic themes and worldview. Challenging Paul Schrader's claim that film noir is historically determined, 'a specific period of film history, like German Expressionism or French New Wave' (1990: 81) which cannot be reduplicated out of historical context, the Coens dare to render a remarkably convincing recreation of classic film noir – a movie that looks, sounds and feels like 'the real McCoy'. From the outset, *The Man Who Wasn't There* announces its generic identity with recognisable noir techniques, beginning with Ed's voiceover narration. Used in classic film noir to signify the self-enclosing subjectivity of the narrator (particularly in adaptations of Cain's stories where it functions to replicate the protagonist's first-person confessional mode), the Coens insert a continuous voiceover to underscore Ed's alienated detachment while creating the impression that he is telling his story as an extended flashback, thus replicating the retrospective narrative structure of classic film noirs. At the end of the movie, Ed reveals that he is writing down the story he has just told us for a men's magazine and that he is being paid by the word, which accounts for his talkativeness as a narrator, in contradiction to his on-screen character who 'doesn't talk much' and who finds 'gabbers' like his chatty brother-in-law and the loudmouth Riedenschneider tiresome.

Filmed entirely in rich black and white, the visual style of *The Man Who Wasn't There* identifies it unmistakably as a period film noir. This is a movie that strives to achieve what few contemporary filmmakers have attempted: a nearly exact replica of classic film noir visual style. When asked about influences, director of photography Roger Deakins cites several key classic noirs as visual models, including *This Gun for Hire* (Frank Tuttle, 1942), *Kiss Me Deadly* (Robert Aldrich, 1955) and Orson Welles' *Touch of Evil* (1958). Ultimately, however, Deakins and the Coens decided against the so-called 'hard lighting' used in classic noir, opting for more diffusion to soften the high contrast effects (Robson 2007: 257–258). Somewhat flippantly, the Coen brothers also say that the look of the movie is based more on science-fiction movies and cheap documentaries of the 1950s. 'For some reason,' says Ethan, 'it's an object of interest among critics, what our influences are, and you tell them important stuff because that's what they want to hear, but it's really like high school hygiene movies' (Robson 2007: 258). As R. Barton Palmer has noted, the visual style of *The Man Who Wasn't There* departs markedly from the excesses of the classic noir look, featuring 'few striking chiaroscuro effects or deglamorized low-key lighting set-ups, no unbalanced compositions marked by slaked angles, no disorienting disruptions of continuity editing, and no un-motivated camera movements designed to unsettle' (2004: 65). Although I differ somewhat on the frequency of chiaroscuro effects, which are, in fact, pervasive in *The Man Who Wasn't There* and at times quite dramatic, it is generally true that the visual style does not draw attention to itself with the excesses of previous

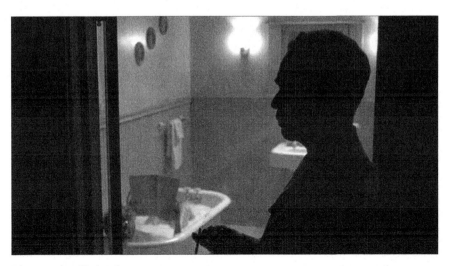

Ed contemplates blackmail.

Coen brothers films. The cinematographic effects are not designed to convey the urban paranoia of classic film noir, instead utilising a balanced spectrum of light and dark to achieve a less strident visual tonality as a cinematic correlate to Ed's monotonous provincial life.

One of the more dramatic uses of chiaroscuro lighting occurs in an early scene as Ed contemplates Tolliver's risky proposition, wondering if the mysterious entrepreneur is a 'huckster' or 'the real McCoy'. In the first of a series of shots, Ed stands motionless in a doorframe, his profile facing right, half in light and half in shadow. A quick cut shows his figure again framed in a doorway. This time his profile, now facing left in full shadow, creates a dark silhouette against a brightly-lit background, enhancing the notion that Ed is a negative presence, a 'ghost'. Here the filmmakers also employ a subtle editing trick to disrupt the continuity of transition from one shot to the next creating the impression that in both shots we are seeing Ed in the same doorframe only from different angles. A closer look at the background of each shot, however, tells us that from one shot to the next, Ed has moved from the doorway of the dining room to the doorway of the bathroom. Because his pose is essentially the same in both shots, his movement from one space to another does not register immediately, evoking in the viewer a vaguely unsettling sense of temporal and spatial disorientation. As he ponders the question of the Tolliver's authenticity, Ed is drawn over the threshold by Doris's request for assistance shaving her legs. Contemplating his own capacity for duplicitous deception, he enters the bathroom, where his inner thoughts assume visual form as his image is doubled in the reflection of a mirror. Shadows and mirrors – stock signifiers of duality in classic film noir – are here employed to good effect, foreshadowing Ed's subsequent shady dealings.

Another striking use of noir visual technique occurs in a scene that takes place in the prison meeting room. As Riedenschneider stands silently in the middle of the confined space about to commence his interview of the defendant, a shaft of sunlight

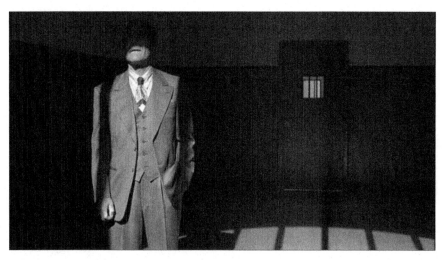

The Uncertainty Principle.

enters from a high window, casting brilliant illumination across the attorney's solitary figure against a background of deep black. The shaft of light cuts a diagonal line across Riedenschneider's face, leaving his eyes and forehead in darkness while brightly illuminating his mouth and beneath it, the lower portions of the lawyer's finely-clad figure. Freddy has assumed the posture of one in deep thought, but he stares upward as if in communication with some higher power. The joke of course is that, represented in this way – eyes covered with a thick veil of darkness, mouth and lower body exposed to harsh light – Freddy is rendered blind, perhaps blinded by his own ego, his image visually signifying a lack of enlightenment commensurate with his total miscomprehension of 'what happened' in the case of Big Dave's murder. The lawyer's mouth, however, is fully visible and fully functional, ready to litigate vigorously as well as consume large amounts of food to satisfy his rapacious bodily needs. Here the lighting set-up vividly recalls a scene from the classic film noir *Phantom Lady* (1944), directed by the German-Jewish émigré Robert Siodmak, an important, if unacknowledged, influence on *The Man Who Wasn't There*. The corresponding scene in Siodmak's movie stages a prison meeting of the story's protagonist, Scott Henderson (Alan Curtis), wrongly accused of murder, and his devoted secretary, Kansas (Ella Raines), who gives her despairing boss hope by promising to find the titular 'phantom lady', the missing witness who can prove the innocence of the accused. Exploiting chiaroscuro stylisation for maximum symbolic effect, the inmate and his visitor are illuminated by a strong back-light made to look like a single shaft of sunlight streaming through a high barred window. As in Reidenschneider's jailhouse scene, brilliant light from above cuts through the darkness of the jail cell's gloom, transforming the actors into shadowy, one-dimensional silhouettes, phantom figures in search of a phantom lady.

Further evidence of Siodmak's influence emerges in comparisons of the Coens' movie with *Criss Cross*, featuring Burt Lancaster as Steve Thompson, an obsessive romantic caught in a vortex of deceit and betrayal. The 'double cross', a common theme in classic noir, is given visual expression in Siodmak's movie by a set design featuring a variety of crisscross patterns, particularly evident in the lattice-work decor of the Rondo, a dingy barroom where Steve and his lover Anna (Yvonne De Carlo) often meet. A similar iconic symbolism is evident in the carefully arranged *mise-en-scène* of Nirdlinger's department store where, during a company party, Big Dave draws Ed aside for a private chat, confesses to an extra-marital affair and confides to Ed that he is being blackmailed for $10,000. As they speak in hushed tones, shadowy images in the background decor form crisscrossing patterns, ironically signifying Ed's secret double-cross – the very cause of Big Dave's suffering. The signifying function of noir *mise-en-scène* is further developed in *The Man Who Wasn't There* by incorporating circular imagery throughout (mirrors, ashtrays, light fixtures, hubcaps), subliminally insinuating the constant unsettling presence of alien flying saucers.

Another distinctive intertext in the Coen brothers' dialogue with classic film noir is supplied by Alfred Hitchcock's 1943 noir thriller *Shadow of a Doubt,* which the Coens acknowledge as a major influence on *The Man Who Wasn't There* (Allen 2006: 179). Like the Coens' movie, *Shadow of a Doubt* transfers its story and characters from the characteristic big-city setting of classic film noir (typically Los Angeles) to the quiet little town of Santa Rosa, where Hitchcock spins a dark tale of a man with a double life, by day law-abiding citizen, by night sinister serial killer. In Hitchcock's Freud-influenced rendering of the *doppelgänger*, the shadow self is never exposed and the killer goes to his grave a respected man, his secret self vanishing as if it had never been there. Something similar happens to Ed Crane, whose crimes go unnoticed (even when he confesses them to Riedenschneider), but must later pay for a crime actually committed by the man he has murdered.

When Ed speaks of his detachment from fellow Santa Rosans, he seems to cherish his secret identity, for it provides him with what he perceives as a higher knowledge. While watching pedestrians on the sidewalk through the window of a moving car, Ed remarks: 'There they were. All going about their business. It seemed like I knew a secret – a bigger one even than what had really happened to Big Dave, something none of them knew.' The staging of this scene seems to acknowledge Hitchcock, who is said to have instructed his cinematographer for *Shadow of a Doubt*, Joseph Valentine, to include in his filming shots of 'everyday people in motion' which the director thought would create 'an atmosphere of actuality that couldn't be captured in any other way' (Spicer 2002: 57). Shot from Ed's point of view as he drives slowly down the main street observing his fellow citizens, this brief scene seems to heed Hitchcock's advice but also to modify and distort the 'actuality' of Santa Rosa by employing a speed aperture change in the camera, thereby slowing down the image of Ed while accelerating the images around him. This effect produces an uncanny visual sense of Ed's disconnection, reinforcing the sense that he had 'made it to the outside' while his neighbours were 'all still struggling way down below'. The omission of ordinary street noise in this scene, replaced on the soundtrack with languid strains of Beethoven, also enhances the viewer's sense of Ed's separation from the ordinary world, the disjunction of sound and image intensifying the otherworldly atmosphere.

In *Shadow of a Doubt* the provincial American town of Santa Rosa feels threatened by sinister 'alien' forces. A similar mood of creeping dread pervades *The Man Who Wasn't There*, articulated visually in the pervasive use of shadow imagery. Departing from film noir's generic preoccupation with the mean streets of the big city, both films choose a small-town setting. Thus, the shadow imagery in both movies is shaped not by the sharp geometrical angles of an urban cityscape, but instead by the flowing contours of a more natural landscape, exemplified in *The Man Who Wasn't There* by the delicate shadows of a waving tree branch that flicker over Ann Nirdlinger's face when she emerges from the night at Ed's door to share with him her paranoid fears of 'alien' extraterrestrials and government conspiracies. The effect of such nature-chiaroscuro is an evocation of silent dread, not the hysterical paranoia of urban noir, but rather a whispering undercurrent of existential angst spooking America's quiet suburbs.

Masculine identity – what it means to be a man – is a recurring concern in the Coen brothers' body of work, evident in one way or another in all their movies, especially in their noir-inflected works. The crisis of gender identity is a basic element of film noir, a common trait of the noir male protagonist who is often depicted as psychologically conflicted, damaged or otherwise emotionally victimised, and thus emasculated. The passive male victim of classic film noir has an important source in the writings of Cain, but variations on this theme are also found in classic noirs like Billy Wilder's *Sunset Blvd.* (1950), where Joe Gillis (William Holden), a down-and-out screenwriter, becomes a gigolo for wealthy silent film star Norma Desmond (Gloria Swanson), who treats him like property and eventually kills him.

Film scholars have linked the male victim-type of film noir with the fear of passive homosexuality, which is thought to have been pervasive among post-war American men (Buchsbaum 1992). It may well have been on the minds of American males at that historical juncture, but any treatment of homosexuality in movies was strongly suppressed by the censorship of the Production Code. As if observing the delicate protocols of the 1940s censors, *The Man Who Wasn't There* makes only cursory overt allusions to male homosexuality, but the film's numerous indirect and disguised references constitute a continuous subtext. Thus the Coens choose not to approach the issue of Ed's sexual orientation directly, instead dramatising it by introducing the ambiguous partnership between Crane and the fancy stranger with a proposition. Hints are dropped early and often. At the beginning of his story we see Ed wearing an apron; at the end, preceding his execution, he is shown having his legs shaved (as he had once done for Doris). During the course of the story, Ed is repeatedly feminised, as when one of Doris's co-workers asks him, 'You in ladies' wear?' Or when Freddy Riedenschneider refers to the cigar trimmer Ed uses to kill Big Dave as a 'dame's weapon'. No wonder then that 'the pansy' (as Big Dave refers to Creighton Tolliver) mistakes Ed for a gay man. Consider the scenario when they meet to consummate their partnership in a cheap hotel room. Tolliver is lying in bed, his toupée a bit ruffled. He gives Ed a heavy-lidded stare, a faint smile on his lips. As Ed returns the stare, the con-man loosens his tie and shoots his new partner an almost imperceptible wink. 'Was that a pass?' asks Ed. 'Maybe,' says Tolliver. Ed's response – 'You're out of line, mister' – seems too subdued, even for Ed, suggesting that his stern but gentle rejection of Tolliver's advances betrays the barber's uncertainty about his real inclinations.

Thus, the question, 'What kind of man are you?' is asked of Ed twice, first by Big Dave after he has discovered that Ed is his blackmailer. Big Dave's query has moral implications: What kind of man would extort $10,000 from another man for sleeping with his wife? The irony of Big Dave's outrage of course is that his own boasts of manliness are a sham based on comic-book fabrications about his he-man exploits in the war. The second time Ed hears the question it comes from his brother-in-law, who after hearing the district attorney's accusations, loses control and attacks Ed, whom he now believes to be guilty not only of Tolliver's murder but of his sister's death as well. This is a secret side of Ed that takes Frank completely by surprise. But this twice-repeated interrogative has larger implications for the problem of male identity permeating *The Man Who Wasn't There*, an issue introduced visually in the opening minutes of the movie as Ed discourses on the entrepreneurial success of Frank's father August Raffo, founding owner of Guzzi's barbershop. After lingering momentarily on Ed at his barber's station, the camera tracks in toward an old photograph of 'old Guzzi' taped to the mirror. Beside it hangs an advertisement from a men's magazine promising to 'make you a new man' in just fifteen minutes a day. Indeed, nearly everything about Ed Crane suggests the need for self-improvement, but the necessity of defining his masculinity, of answering the question, 'What kind of man are you?' seems at times to trump all others. In this context Ed's willing partnership with an effete, dandyish stranger whose business deal offers 'a way out', a way to become a 'new man', assumes added connotations.

Viewed within the larger history of classic film noir, Tolliver 'the pansy' constitutes a belated reimagining of the *homme fatal* – the fatal male, gender-opposite of the *femme fatale*. As such, Tolliver's representation of the noir homosexual offers a less menacing, more openly gay version, compared at least with *hommes fatal* like Bruno Antony (Robert Walker) in Hitchcock's *Strangers on a Train*, or Waldo Lydecker (Clifton Webb) in *Laura* (1944), or with Peter Lorre's memorable characterisation of Joel Cairo in *The Maltese Falcon*. Although such characters were allowed to appear in classic Hollywood noir, their sexual identity was suppressed by censors like Joseph Breen whose policies explicitly prohibited any overt depictions of homosexuality in motion pictures. Proof of such censorship is presented in a Breen Office report on *The Maltese Falcon* sent to Jack Warner, specifying that the Joel Cairo character should not be openly portrayed as 'the pansy type' (quoted in Naremore 1998: 98). By including the character of Creighton Tolliver, the depiction of male homosexuality, largely absent in classic film noir, repressed by censorship and prevailing social attitudes, is restored to importance as part of a larger culture of repression in 1940s America. Perhaps one could say that *The Man Who Wasn't There* is an attempt to mediate (to paraphrase Ed's final words) 'all those things they didn't have words for' in the era of film noir's emergence, disclosing a hidden truth embedded in historical film noir that can only now be spoken.

Ultimately, the question of Ed's masculine identity remains unanswered, just another uncertainty in a world under the shadow of doubt. At the end of his story, Ed Crane begins to imagine a world where doubts about identity (gender or otherwise) become irrelevant, where he might be freed from earthly constraints. Such freedom is connected, weirdly, with improbable science fiction images. Perhaps extraterrestrials in flying saucers can open a path to a world beyond, where the things he doesn't understand on the terrestrial plane will become clearer.

*The Uncertainty Principle*

In his jailhouse discourse on the legal ramifications of doubt and uncertainty the hotshot lawyer Freddy Riedenschneider thinks he has come up with an ingenious defence for Doris. Invoking Heisenberg's Uncertainty Principle as a method of deconstructing the judicial concept of 'reasonable doubt', the legal mastermind explains:

They got this guy in Germany. Fritz something-or-other. Maybe it's Werner. Anyway, he's got this theory, you test something, you know, scientifically – how the planets go round the sun, what sunspots are made of, why the water comes out of the tap – well, you gotta look at it. But sometimes, you look at it, your looking *changes* it. You can't know the reality of what happened, or what would've happened if you hadn't stuck in your own goddamn schnozz. So there is no 'what happened'. Looking at something changes it. They call it the 'Uncertainty Principle'.

According to physicist Werner Heisenberg, the objects of scientific observation are inevitably altered by the human observer, casting doubt on the reliability of outcomes in scientific investigations. Specifically, Heisenberg postulated the impossibility of accurately measuring variables at the subatomic level, arguing that the act of measuring alters what is being measured and concluding that the presence of the observer changes the reality of what is being measured. His theory had far-reaching implications for quantum physics, suggesting that even the nature of light (thought to be a constant) might be indeterminate. Of course, Riedenschneider's gloss is mostly comic gibberish, but he does identify the philosophical crux of Heisenberg's theory: human subjectivity is a source of uncertainty for all forms of investigation.

The lawyer's strategy is to correlate this scientific principle with the legal concept of reasonable doubt. Contrary to the lawyer's idiosyncratic interpretation, however, the Heisenberg Principle (never named as such) was in fact an attempt by the physicist to specify a *provisional form of certainty* for the calculation of probabilities in tracking the position and momentum of subatomic particles. In the lawyer's reductive misreading of Heisenberg, since *nothing* in Doris's case can be known with absolute certainty, since there were no witnesses to Big Dave's murder, there can be no 'what happened', and thus it follows that Doris must be acquitted on the grounds of reasonable doubt. In Riedenschneider's simplistic logic, 'looking at something changes it' and therefore 'the more you look, the less you really know'. His outlandish claim that uncertainty is 'the only fact there is' establishes uncertainty as a universal principle. 'Even Einstein says the guy's on to something,' says Riedenschneider approvingly. 'This heinie even wrote it out in numbers.'

If nothing else, Riedenschneider's excursus on the Uncertainty Principle gives ludic expression to the very serious crisis of doubt afflicting Ed Crane, whom the lawyer in his defence describes as 'a man who has lost his place in the universe'. He calls Ed an example of 'modern man', suggesting that his predicament is an allegory of man's growing uncertainty about his place and meaning in the universe. Ushering in this age of uncertainty, the emergence of quantum physics, and with it the threat of global nuclear destruction, gave profound proof of the contingency of human life. Describing their sense of the dominant cultural mood of the late 1940s, the Coen brothers say they envisioned 'laymen going around saying "Einstein says light is curved" and wondering what it means, where they fit in, feeling like they're cast adrift' (Robson 2007: 274). As film scholars recognised early on, the meaninglessness of human existence is an essential theme in classic film noir, which in its day served as a major point of entry for the new European intellectual import called existentialism. Paul Schrader stresses the significance for film noir of the influx of Germanic filmmakers whose stylistic mannerisms gave shape to a noir universe where, in Schrader's words, 'style is all that separates one from meaninglessness' (1990: 86). No doubt, the rise of existentialist thinking and its entry into the cultural mainstream, not just through motion pictures but via a variety of artistic media, constitutes an important socio-historical context to which *The Man Who Wasn't There* speaks. Thus, in addition to film noir and the writings of

Cain, the Coen brothers address the premiere existentialist writers of that period, in particular Albert Camus, who was inspired by Cain's *The Postman Always Rings Twice* to write his novel *The Stranger*. Although the presence of existentialist ideas is not as prominent in *The Man Who Wasn't There* as Cain's influence, it cannot be said (despite what the Coen brothers might say) that their movie is *just* a 'Cain story'. Perhaps it would be more accurate to call it a Cain story as it might have been rewritten by Camus.

Indeed, important elements that could only derive from Camus' *The Stranger* find their way into the story of Ed Crane. To be sure, *The Postman Always Rings Twice* provides the basic narrative frame for *The Man Who Wasn't There*; but in certain ways the same could be said of Camus' *The Stranger* where, as in Cain's novel, the story and its protagonist come to an end on death row. Other elements, however, such as character traits not traceable back to Cain, are shared by Ed Crane and Meursault, the titular 'stranger' of Camus' novel. Most notably, both share a profound aversion to the spoken word. Meursault's distinguishing trait is his taciturnity. Like the silent barber, he is a man who doesn't waste words on idle conversation. When asked during his murder trial, for instance, if he has anything to say in his defence, Meursault tells the judge, 'I rarely have anything much to say. So, naturally I keep my mouth shut' (1958: 82). Ed Crane is just as loath to verbalise his experience, as he wearily announces at the beginning of his narrative: 'Me, I don't talk much ... I just cut hair.' Most times the only response Ed can manage is his characteristic gesture, the slightest of nods.

The self-estrangement from verbal intercourse that marks these characters has its emotional equivalent in the lack of meaningful interpersonal relationships in both their lives. Meursault gives little credence to notions of love or emotional attachment. He is indifferent to his girlfriend's affections and appears to feel no grief after his mother's death. When asked how he felt after his mother's funeral, Meursault answers that in recent years he had 'lost the habit of noting [his] feelings' (1958: 80). Ed's emotional disconnectedness is reflected in his loveless marriage to Doris, who, only a few weeks after they met asked him to marry her because 'she liked it that I didn't talk much'. Thus the amatory passion of *The Postman Always Rings Twice*'s Frank and Cora, essential to Cain's lovers as the central determinant of their fate, is drained entirely from the relationships of Meursault and Ed Crane. Ed's aloof silence is the outward sign of his refusal to participate in the routine conventions of everyday life and, at a deeper level, of his suppressed spiritual unease. Ed's silence makes him a social outsider. His almost total disinterest in small talk frequently creates awkward silences. Because Ed does not observe the usual conventions of social decorum his behaviour makes an unsettling impression. In this way he is 'alien'. His silence makes him inscrutable, urging others to ask, 'What kind of a man are you?' A similar question of identity haunts Meursault. His murder trial, like Ed's, is in many ways an attempt to establish what kind of man he is.

The hero of Cain's novel is a drifter, a self-professed 'gypsy' and thus a social outsider, but he is far from silent. Moreover, Frank Chambers exudes a primitive vitality and connectedness with physical reality that differentiates him fundamentally from the detached indifference of Crane or Meursault. Accordingly, Frank is at home in the world of things. He hungers for the physical and seems unburdened by metaphysical longings. Frank is never granted that 'leap of consciousness' into the lucid awareness of the absurd that in *The Stranger* happens suddenly, almost involuntarily, at the moment Meursault shoots his Arab antagonist. Meursault's violence seems to lack any clear motive; he kills a stranger on impulse and later tells the judge that he could think of no particular reason for his action. The crucial difference between these two outsiders resides in Meursault's transformation from detached, unreflective passivity to active reflection and self-awareness. Even though he appears to kill without reason, his act finds purpose in its consequences as it initiates Meursault's evolution from common man to existential man. Whatever else Camus may have borrowed from Cain, this transition, Meursault's leap of consciousness, constitutes a significant philosophical renovation of *The Postman Always Rings Twice*, restoring to Cain that oft-noted absence of a philosophical framework and giving back to Cain's characters what their author had denied them: an awareness of their absurd condition. Ed's feeling of the absurd begins when he is forced to murder Big Dave in self-defence. From that point on Ed feels a growing awareness, the sense that he knows some big secret that the others do not.

Allusions to Sartre and his 1938 novel *Nausea* are also incorporated into the Coens' existentialist pastiche. The bouts of nausea suffered by Sartre's protagonist, Antoine Roquentin, caused by the stifling awareness of life's meaninglessness and absurdity, find their equivalent in the distaste with which Ed Crane confronts his reality. Roquentin's disgust is triggered by the overwhelming presence of a physical reality unmediated by human thought and indifferent to human subjectivity. The unintelligibility of the real that causes Roquentin's nausea is, as Sartre explains in an essay on Camus' *The Stranger*, the consequence of an 'inability to think, with our words and concepts, what happens in the world' (1957: 33). Without the mediating illusions of language and conceptual thought, external reality begins to lose its comfortable familiarity. The real becomes viscous, thick with the density of a world now crowded with a mass of 'things divorced from their names'. Of these nameless things Roquentin says: 'They are there, grotesque, headstrong, gigantic, and it seems ridiculous … to say anything at all about them: I am in the midst of things, nameless things' (2013: 125). This crisis of language forces him to confront a reality stripped of causality and revealed as absurd. Ed Crane's Sartrean disgust manifests itself in his shared aversion to the viscous density of the real. Presumably, it is Ed's hope for deliverance from the messy entanglements of material reality that motivates the barber's interest in the new method of laundering called 'dry' cleaning. As Ed enters the bathroom to shave Doris's legs, a task he no doubt regards as an unpleasant reminder of his barber's duties, he thinks of dry cleaning, describing its attraction in terms that emphasise its sterile purity: 'Clean. No water. Chemicals.' The promise of quick riches in dry cleaning offers him a 'way out' not only from the economic enslavement of being a lowly barber but from the nauseating materiality of the real, which Ed, the barber, confronts ceaselessly in the tangles of human hair he cuts off that go 'down the drain' but that won't stop growing. His friendship with 'Birdy' promises another clean getaway. Listening to the ethereal strains of Beethoven she rehearses gives Ed a sense of transcendent peace, momentarily enabling him, as Birdy's name reminds us, to 'fly away.'

The full extent of the Coens' existentialist rendering of Cain becomes evident in a comparative reading of the endings of *The Postman Always Rings Twice*, *The Stranger* and *The Man Who Wasn't There*, where in all three stories the condemned protagonist re-examines his life from a cell on death row. Facing the certainty of death, Frank Chambers' final thoughts give shape to a longing for 'another life after this one'. Uncertain whether Cora, before dying, understood that he didn't kill her intentionally in the car crash, Frank hopes for an afterlife so that he can convince her of his innocence: 'I didn't do it, I know that. That's what I'm going to tell her, if I ever see her again.' Frank quells his fear of death with memories of himself and Cora united, floating on the gentle swells of the ocean where they had once experienced a fleeting glimpse of transcendent harmony: 'Whenever I can make it, I'm out there with Cora, with the sky above us, and the water around us, talking about how happy we're going to be, and how it's going to last forever.' When Frank is with Cora in this remembered moment he has hope for a life beyond: 'Out there with Cora, that's when it seems real, about another life' (Cain 1982: 101). But Frank's notion of transcendence as 'out there' lacks conviction. His vision of a world beyond, where he will be reconciled with Cora seems little more than a doomed man's desperate fantasy. If anything, Frank's imagined reunion with Cora recalls the Freudian concept of 'oceanic feeling', a sense of self-dissolution associated with regressions to the maternal origin of the womb.

By contrast, Meursault's story ends without hope for an afterlife. Asked by the prison priest how he imagines the afterlife, Meursault shouts at the clergyman that he has very little time left and he is not going 'to waste it on God' (Camus 1958: 150). His leap of consciousness has washed him clean and emptied him of hope. Gazing up at the darkened sky, 'spangled with its signs and stars', Camus' existential anti-hero is now able to 'open his heart to the benign indifference of the universe' (1958: 154).

Like Meursault, Frank Chambers is also visited by a priest promising the afterlife, but Frank remains skeptical of the priest's vision of Kingdom Come. Only when he thinks of being 'out there' with Cora does it seem possible: 'That's when it all seems real, about another life, not with all this stuff how Father McConnell has got it figured out. When I'm with her I believe it. When I start to figure, it all goes blooey' (Cain 1982: 101). In other words, when Frank applies human reason to 'figure' or calculate the universe's unintelligible mysteries, he fails. In his final speech Ed Crane likewise expresses a hope for a reunion with Doris in another world:

> I don't know where I'm being taken. I don't know what waits for me, beyond the earth and sky. But I'm not afraid to go. Maybe the things I don't understand will be clearer there, like when the fog blows away. Maybe Doris will be there. And maybe there I can tell her ... all those things ... they don't have words for here.

In their proximity to those of Frank Chambers, Ed's final words might seem merely a re-inscription of the ending of Cain's novel. Frank's dream of being 'out there' with

Cora and his desire for reconciliation are reiterated in Ed's departing monologue. But, whereas Frank has naturalised the idea of transcendence as 'out there' in the ocean, reducing the transcendent to the elemental, Ed cannot give material shape or location to the afterlife. It's just somewhere 'beyond the earth and sky'. Throughout his story, Ed has given no indication of religious beliefs. Apparently, Ed no more believes in an eternal afterlife than Doris, who believes, according to Ed, 'that our reward is on this earth and bingo is probably the extent of it'. Ed shares neither Frank's naive agnosticism nor Meursault's unapologetically atheistic repudiation of the eternal hereafter. What distinguishes Ed's parting words most notably from those of his literary models is his hope for communion with Doris somewhere *beyond words*, where they are freed from the prison-house of language. Ed has followed Meursault in taking the leap into the absurd, but he has also accepted the linguistic consequences of his leap: the world 'beyond' must be beyond language. It must make possible what Camus calls the 'odd state of soul in which the void become eloquent,' creating space for the raw experience of 'lucid' awareness that results from the existentialist's heightened consciousness of the absurd (1958: 12).

In his final hours on death row, Frank Chambers reveals he has been writing down his story and that his priest has promised to find for it a publisher. Likewise, Ed Crane confesses that he is writing the story he has just told for a 'men's magazine'. In revealing that he has been writing for a cheesy pulp magazine (and being paid by the word), Ed casts suspicion on the reliability of his story. Perhaps, like Frank's dream of Cora 'out there', Ed's story is an elaborate fantasy fabricated to escape the terrible reality of his impending death. Perhaps, in Riedenschneider phrase, there is no 'what happened' in Ed's story. Perhaps the tale Ed has just told us is a fiction, no more credible than Big Dave's war stories or Creighton Tolliver's promise of a fortune to be made in dry cleaning. This uncertainty makes Ed an unreliable narrator, and his story merely an illustration that the world of imagination, like the 'real' world itself, is always a subjective construct, its meaning subject to doubt and the vagaries of human interpretation. Nevertheless, by putting his life story into words, Ed has been able to get some distance and now he can see his life as a whole and realise that 'all those twists and turns are the shape of your life'.

When he 'pulls away from the maze' and perceives the larger pattern of his life, Ed finds a 'way out' in the act of storytelling. In doing so, Ed finds salvation in the human imagination, which makes possible an escape into alternate dimensions of consciousness, where anything is possible, even UFOs and extraterrestrial intelligence. Thus, on the eve of his execution Ed is inexplicably free to wander from his prison cell (despite being on 'death watch') and mysteriously drawn to the prison yard where a flying saucer hovers, perhaps communicating with Ed, who nods ambiguously. What are we to make of this alien visitation? Significantly, Ed's UFO encounter takes place just after the disclosure that he is writing his story for a men's magazine like those littering Ed's prison cell with titles like 'Muscle Power', 'Stalwart' or 'The Unheard-Of', which features an article entitled 'I Was Abducted by Aliens'. Like Frank's imaginary voyages 'out there' with Cora, perhaps Ed's encounter with an unidentified flying object is nothing more than the fantasy of a narrator who wasn't really ever there.

# CHAPTER TEN

# No Country for Old Men: Darkness in the New West

Based on the 2005 novel by Cormac McCarthy, *No Country for Old Men* gives vivid expression to the novelist's nihilistic vision of the darkness in the new West. Set in west Texas, 1980, its narrative concerns the destinies of three men whose paths cross and collide, altering the course of their lives irrevocably. The first of these is Llewelyn Moss (Josh Brolin), a working-class cowboy who by chance stumbles upon an abandoned fortune of drug money and decides to risk its theft. Moss is pursued by Anton Chigurh (Javier Bardem), an enigmatic hit-man engaged by the drug cartel to retrieve the money Moss has stolen. Moss is a skilled ex-military marksman, a hunter, but to protect his stolen fortune he must go on the run, become the hunted instead of the hunter. Chigurh is also a hunter, pursuing Moss relentlessly, an unstoppable force, menacing in his cold and methodical purpose. A third hunter, local sheriff Ed Tom Bell (Tommy Lee Jones), investigates the gangland shoot-out that put the money into Moss's hands, following the chase, always one step behind, and always dreading the moment of fatal confrontation. One of these three meets his fate in violent death, another is inexplicably spared. The third has no fate, for he is fate itself, or the shape it assumes in these times when 'signs and wonders' have again become the sole reliable codex of a civilisation in decline.

In the years immediately preceding the release of *No Country for Old Men*, the Coen brothers had enjoyed moderate box-office success with two comedies, *Intolerable Cruelty* (2003), a contemporary screwball, and *The Ladykillers* (2004), a remake of Alexander MacKendrick's 1955 British comedy. The critics had few kind words for these films and during this period it was generally thought that the Coens weren't living up to the promise of their earlier achievements. The critics' ill mood passed in 2007 with the premiere of *No Country for Old Men*. After *Fargo* more than a decade earlier, *No Country for Old Men* became the Coens' second break-out hit, a film that generated significant box-office returns as well as garnering top accolades and awards including Academy Awards for Best Picture, Best Direction, Best Adapted Screenplay and Best Supporting Actor (Javier Bardem). Upon its theatrical release, *No Country for Old Men* was almost unanimously acclaimed as a major cinematic achievement. In Peter Travers' estimation the film was nothing less than 'a new career peak for the Coen brothers'. *New York Times* reviewer A. O. Scott praised the movie's 'brilliant technique', citing the Coens' 'ruthless application of craft' to shape a film that is, for formalists, 'pure heaven'. Roger Ebert thought it was 'as good a film as the Coen brothers have ever made'. Comparing it with *Fargo*, he writes: 'To make one such film is a miracle. Here is another.' There was generally high praise for the Coens' adaptation of McCarthy. Writing for *Time Out*, Geoff Andrew considered the screenplay so attuned to McCarthy's novel it seemed like an original written by the Coens. Peter Rainer thought that *No Country for Old Men*'s 'dizzying alternations of comedy and horror' branded it unmistakably as a Coen brothers movie. From a somewhat different vantage, Lisa Schwarzbaum thought the Coens had finally surrendered the 'hyper-controlling interest in clever cinematic style' that had marred their previous films. Geoffrey O'Brien echoed this thought, describing the film as one that draws its power precisely from the filmmakers' stylistic restraint, 'deliberately holding in check the invention that flourishes so exuberantly elsewhere in their work'. In *No Country for Old Men*, thinks O'Brien, 'the Coens rigorously deny themselves most of the gratifications associated with the phrase "a Coen brothers movie"'.

Despite widespread acclaim, some reviewers still had doubts. Veteran reviewer David Denby of the *New Yorker* wrote that '*No Country for Old Men* is the Coens' most accomplished achievement in craft' but he thought there were 'absences' in the movie that 'hollow out the movie's attempt at greatness'. These absences seem to consist of gaps in character credibility and the unceremonious elimination of Moss without the dignity of a proper death scene. Stephen Hunter was completely unimpressed, admitting bluntly, 'I just don't like it much', although like many he praised the film for its flawless cinematic craftsmanship. Hunter's main complaint concerned character development, of which he thought there was very little. In his view the Coens had reduced their characters to one-dimensional stereotypes, assigning to each a simplistic moral or symbolic attribute: Chigurh as the menace of death or evil, Carson Wells (Woody Harrelson) as pride and Sheriff Bell in the part of 'Melancholy Wisdom'. Andrew Sarris, another veteran movie critic, seventy-eight years old when he wrote his review, expressed strong disapproval, refusing to take the film seriously because that would be, in his words, 'an exercise in cosmic futility'. Perhaps *No Country for Old Men* is no movie for old men.

*Adapting McCarthy*

Unlike their previous screenplays which draw, often indiscriminately, on a multiplicity of literary and cinematic sources, *No Country for Old Men* is a direct adaptation of McCarthy's novel, honouring a writer many consider the greatest living American author. Here for the first time the Coen brothers exchange their postmodern technique of 'free adaptation' for conventional fidelity to a single literary source. The Coens must have seen something of themselves in McCarthy's writing, a kindred storyteller with an approach to crime fiction that matched their own philosophy and worldview. As a direct adaptation of a contemporary literary source, the Coens' *No Country for Old Men* is an anomaly among their works. McCarthy is one of only two living writers the Coens have chosen to adapt (the other is Charles Portis, author of *True Grit*). Otherwise, the brothers have not expressed interest in filming contemporary literature, though McCarthy can be considered a special case. By the time the Coens got around to adapting his novel in 2007, he had already become a kind of institution among the literati, the recipient of many awards, including the National Book Award for his novel *All the Pretty Horses* (1992) and the Pulitzer Prize for Fiction for *The Road* (2006), and therefore eligible for inclusion in the Coens' pantheon of ancestral writers, joining the likes of Hammett, Cain, Chandler, Odets and West, all of them writers of the 1930s and 1940s.

In choosing to adapt McCarthy, the Coen brothers forego their characteristic ironic detachment and, via McCarthy, assume a more earnest stance toward the story. Generally, the Coens avoid displays of seriousness, deflating any hint of sincerity in their works with irony and comic absurdity. But in the case of *No Country for Old Men* they surrender authorial control to the literary source (which takes itself seriously enough), allowing them to assume another's view of American society without claiming it as their own. Further reasons for choosing to adapt McCarthy are rooted in the strong affinity between McCarthy and the Coens as storytellers, a unique attraction that can be traced to a number of shared authorial preoccupations. The first of these is no doubt their shared interest in the 'dark side' of the human spirit, made frighteningly real in McCarthy's nihilistic saga of human iniquity. We have seen it before in Coen brothers films, this darkness, especially in *Blood Simple* and *Fargo*, two closely related precursors of *No Country for Old Men*. We have seen characters very much like Sheriff Bell, too, whose mystified incomprehension of human degeneracy differs from that of police chief Marge Gunderson only as a matter of geography.

McCarthy's is a vision of darkness in the West, the American southwest, a region that has long had exotic appeal for the Coen brothers dating back to the early days of *Blood Simple*, making McCarthy's barren desert landscape familiar territory for the Coens. The chase unfolds in the towns and cities of west Texas along the southern border traced by the Rio Grande: Sanderson, Del Rio, Eagle Pass, Odessa and El Paso. Shooting on location in the barren expanses of west Texas and New Mexico, the filmmakers found settings and imagery suited to rendering McCarthy's concrete and detailed descriptions of topography, terrain and climate. The desert backdrop for Sheriff Bell's opening voiceover is a striking visualisation of McCarthy's landscape, revealing the rugged Texas outland in a tableau of eleven stationary shots surveying the countryside, each one an extreme long shot isolating a different perspective of the barren and formidable Texas back country, but taken together forming an image of vast emptiness inhospitable to human life. This is a view of the world as it had been for thousands of years, as it was in the days of the 'old timers' and still is, despite all human efforts to tame it – a country unchanged and unconquered by man.

In the Coens' imagination Texas assumes a set of mythological connotations. Recalling the setting of *Blood Simple*, Joel Coen stresses that it was not intended to represent Texas as it exists today, but rather 'something preserved in legend, a collection of histories and myths' (Allen 2006: 26). The Texas of McCarthy's story also suggests something legendary preserved in its far western territories, where vast desert expanses are rimmed by distant mountains to shape a landscape of heroic dimensions in which myth and legend are readily born and nurtured. McCarthy's novel evokes the aura of myth potently in the figure of Anton Chigurh, but it also tells with blunt realism the story of the people of Texas, tough survivors in a 'hard country' that grinds its weaker inhabitants into the hardened *caliche*. Beyond the territories of McCarthy's Texas a much bigger story unfolds, the story of the 'hard country' of contemporary America and the new hardships its belated western settlers must endure, casting a rueful eye on the historical growth of the nation and its cultural deterioration in the late twentieth century. In this sense, the decision to adapt *No Country for Old Men* is perfectly consistent with the Coen brothers' oft-repeated self-description as 'American filmmakers' dedicated to making films in and about the United States of America.

The Coens' adaptation of *No Country for Old Men* maintains a respectful degree of fidelity to the original. Most of the novel's narrative as well as its central characters and themes have been preserved. Originally conceived and written as a screenplay, the novel has a fundamentally cinematic structure well suited to adaptation and well matched with the interests and talents of the Coen brothers. As an adaptation, the Coens' movie renders McCarthy's novel with admirable economy. The density and pace of the novel's narrative is smoothly translated to the screen with skillful editing, done as always by the brothers themselves (still credited to their fictional film editor of long-standing, Roderick Jaynes). Some of the movie's most memorable dialogue is transcribed unaltered from the novel, such as Sheriff Bell's folksy comment on the aftermath of the desert drug deal gone wrong: 'If this ain't the mess, it'll sure do til the mess gets here.' The regional dialect, so prominent in the dialogue of the novel and always fascinating to the Coens, is reproduced in the movie with careful attention to authenticity. McCarthy's tough westerners are also given shape and life by intelligent casting. Tommy Lee Jones was chosen for the role of Sheriff Bell because his aging, weathered face (seen previously in many westerns) and earthy gravitas brought dignity to the part, and because, as a native of west Texas, he speaks the local dialect naturally. Josh Brolin, also a native of west Texas where he grew up on a horse ranch, seemed equally well suited to play the cowboy-adventurer Moss. In his Academy Award-winning performance as Chirgurh, Javier Bardem brings uncanny menace to his characterisation of a rogue hit man who is, in Joel's words, 'like the man who fell to earth', so alien is his presence in the story's setting. His accent and ethnic identity are not readily identifiable, his hairstyle odd and unsettling, his clothing somehow out-of-place. 'He's the thing,' remarks Joel, 'that does not grow out of the landscape' (Hirschberg 2007).

Though for the most part faithful to the novel, the Coens embellish McCarthy's story with additional narrative elements, such as the pit bull that chases Moss in the river and nearly kills him. The Coens' imprint is particularly noticeable in the touches of humour added to McCarthy's tale, like the cranky mother-in-law with cancer, prone to obtuse utterances like: 'It's not often you see a Mexican in a suit,' or the substitution of Mexican street musicians improbably serenading a wounded Moss in the early dawn, instead of the solitary street sweeper of the novel who encounters Moss on his morning rounds. The filmmakers' presence is also evident in minor flourishes, like the facial expressions of actor Bardem as he admonishes the frightened gas station owner to keep his lucky quarter separate, otherwise it just becomes another coin, 'which it is'. As if he can think of no other words to convey his profundity, he simply raises his eyebrows in a gesture that says, 'Think about it. This is meaningful.' One of the most noticeable editorial nuances occurs at the very end of the movie with the clock that ticks ominously after Bell finishes recounting his dreams, reminding him that (as he says himself and knows perfectly well) 'time is not on my side'.

Another allure of McCarthy's novel is its reliance on (and departures from) the generic structures of crime fiction, which play to the Coen brothers' preference for adapting pulp fiction. Generically, *No Country for Old Men* is a notable departure from McCarthy's previous work, although the novelist had previously explored neighboring territory in his masterpiece *Blood Meridian* (1985), another story of criminal violence and inhuman savagery along the Tex-Mex border, anno 1849. As a crime story McCarthy's *No Country for Old Men* may even owe something to Coen favorite James M. Cain. The similarities with Cain's fiction are noticeable in McCarthy's terse, 'hard-boiled' dialogue that translates Cain's southern California vernacular into cowboy slang. The novel's fast-paced plotting also resembles Cain's technique, as does the focus on Moss, an ordinary guy tempted by greed to enter into dangerous circumstances that quickly spin out of control. The Coens called it an action movie, or at least as they said, 'it's the closest we'll ever come to making an action movie' (DVD extra, 'The Making of *No Country for Old Men*'). Pressed by interviewers to specify its genre, the brothers vacillated. They and some cast members suggested various possibilities: chase, western, noir. Because of the film's excessive violence and its light treatment thereof, Tommy Lee Jones called it a 'comedy horror'.

Among the generic models suggested, two distinguish themselves most: film noir and western. Clearly, these are the operative terms defining the movie's hybrid form. Despite the contemporary time frame, the desert setting of west Texas and the images of lawmen on horseback recall stock elements of the Hollywood western. Ed Tom Bell is a Texas sheriff in pursuit of outlaws who threaten the citizens he is sworn to protect. As a lawman on the eve of retirement who has lost his self-confidence and feels 'overmatched' by the outlaws, Sheriff Bell evokes Marshal Will Kane (Gary Cooper) in Fred Zinnemann's classic western *High Noon* (1952). Chigurh recalls the classic villain: a sinister hired gunman dressed in black and given to sadistic violence in the tradition of Jack Wilson (Jack Palance), the psychopathic gunslinger in *Shane* (George Stevens, 1953). The style of clothing clearly identifies the characters as westerners. Cowboy hats, saddle boots and Wrangler jeans are *de rigeur*. In *No Country for Old Men*, as always, the Coens pay special attention to wardrobe, especially to the boots worn by male characters. Moss wears Larry Mahans, not flashy, but very durable and functional, like Moss himself. Chigurh wears alligator boots because, as costume designer Mary Zophres explains, they wanted his boots to look 'bumpy, gross, and pointy, [like] they could kill somebody' (DVD extra, 'Working with the Coen Brothers'). Carson Wells wears expensive and stylish Lucchese crocodile boots as befits a 'day trader' whose interest in his work is strictly economic and opportunistic, unlike Chigurh, whose only interest seems to be dealing death to all in his path.

Weapons are another indispensable part of the western's iconography. In the old West they used six-shooters and Winchester repeating rifles. In the new West these are replaced with an impressive military arsenal: Tec 9 automatic machine guns, short-barreled Uzis, automatic shotguns with drum magazines. Moss hunts antelope with a .270 Mauser equipped with a telescopic sight, the type of rifle used by snipers in the Vietnam War. Sheriff Bell prefers the old-style lever-action Winchester model 97, but expresses great admiration for the old-timers who didn't need to carry a firearm. Chigurh's weapons are exotic customised killing tools, the most unusual being the captive bolt pistol, a tool used to slaughter cattle, which he applies to his human victims as if they are nothing more than animals. Yet, for all this attention to weaponry, the gunfights in *No Country for Old Men* are limited. Gunfights (referred to by Moss as 'shootouts') occur onscreen only twice – once when drug dealers pursue Moss across the desert at night and again when Moss and Chigurh shoot it out at Eagle Pass. We do witness the aftermath of the 'colossal goat fuck' in the desert, or what Bell's deputy refers to as the 'Wild West' (and are thus invited to imagine the carnage), and we see, very briefly, the cartel shooters fleeing from Moss's murder at the El Paso motel, but for a movie that plays like a western, actual gun battles are relatively few. The most explicit and egregious acts of violence are carried out by Chigurh in his executions. Indeed, the first scene of the movie in which he strangles a deputy with handcuffs is probably the most visceral violence in either book or movie. As at least one commentator has suggested, this scene and other acts of cold-blooded murder add an element of horror, created by the film-makers' unblinking portrayal of excessive violence (Landrum 2009: 200).

The Coen brothers have said that what they like best about McCarthy's novel is its subversion of the western genre. One of several major breaches of genre convention concerns 'the showdown'. In the typical western a final showdown is the dramatic climax in the struggle of good versus evil, where the good ultimately prevails. *No Country for Old Men* thwarts the genre's promise of a final showdown between Chigurh and Bell. In fact, they never meet face to face. The sheriff, always a step behind, fails to track down his man, whom he believes to be a 'ghost'. Even the show-down between Moss and Chigurh in Eagle Pass ends in a draw, both of them wounded and limping from the scene – Moss to a Mexican hospital, Chigurh to a cheap motel room where he tends to his wounds unassisted, acquiring the necessary medications by coolly staging a car explosion outside a pharmacy and casually strolling off with stolen drugs. Chigurh displays several key attributes that subvert generic expectations for the western villain. The generic outlaw is driven by lust for money (a bank robber or bandit) and, lacking a moral code, will resort to violence and murder to get what he wants. Chigurh is not interested in money or material things. He uses violence as a tool for administering his twisted sense of justice. As Carson Wells describes him, 'He's a peculiar man. You could even say he has principles. Principles that transcend money or drugs or anything like that,' adding, 'He's not like you. He's not even like me.' Chigurh adheres to a code of ethics which, though incomprehensible to others, he upholds with the dedication and personal integrity conventionally associated with the western hero. In a sense, Chigurh defines himself as a lawman, an agent of some quasi-divine constabulary authorised by some unknown power to administer punishment to those who violate his cryptic principles. Moss, the character we would like to imagine as the hero, is an opportunistic thief who has taken advantage of the cartel's criminal blunder. As narrator, Bell is authorised to deliver the moral of the story and thus positioned to fulfill the genre's demand for a strong patriarchal hero who intervenes to rescue Moss and defeat Chigurh. But as the story unfolds it becomes increasingly apparent that Bell's efforts to protect 'his people' are futile. In the end he seems little more than a worn and defeated relic of old-fashioned law enforcement who hopes to avoid rather than capture his formidable antagonist and who in the end cannot protect Moss (whom he calls 'his boy') from the fatal consequences of his actions. All in all, Sheriff Bell does not cut a very heroic figure.

*What Makes a Man?*

The question of manhood – 'What makes a man?' – is posed repeatedly in the films of the Coen brothers. It is one of their most central thematic preoccupations, explicit or implied in every one of their stories. It is asked of the Dude in *The Big Lebowski*, where the problems of masculine identity are given parodic scrutiny, and in *The Man Who Wasn't There*, where the question becomes an accusation: 'What kind of a man are you?' In *No Country for Old Men* the question of manhood is linked with the western genre's focus on violence and domination as defining features of masculinity. To be a man in the old West one had to fight – fight to defend the innocent from villainous outlaws, fight off attacks by indigenous tribes, subdue the harsh wilderness and bring it under human control. Victory over the forces of adversity by violent means is a defining feature of the western male hero. In the inimical world of the western frontier, the power to subdue and control adversarial forces is the male hero's greatest virtue. As Stacy Peebles writes, based on themes of conquest and control, the western genre is 'the ultimate venue for the display of male power' (2009: 125). Similar preoccupations with masculine identity are definitive of film noir, another classic American genre that defines manhood in terms of violence and control. Indeed, the private detectives of classic film noir provide models of masculinity distinctly similar to the western hero. Like the rugged protagonists of the western, noir detectives are tough, hard-boiled; they can take a beating as well as give one. Incarnated in characters like Hammett's Sam Spade and Chandler's Philip Marlowe, these are rough and ready men not easily intimidated by the threat of violence. They keep their cool and control the situation. Certainly, Moss fits this description. A mixture of self-reliant cowboy and battle-hardened soldier, he possesses abundant physical strength and cunning and, like his adversary Chigurh, Moss is possessed of a single-minded determination; once set on a path, he is undeterred. Perhaps this is why the pit bull attack on Moss was added to the screenplay, establishing a symbolic connection between Moss and the 'beast' (Chigurh) who pursues him so doggedly. When wounded by Chigurh, however, Moss

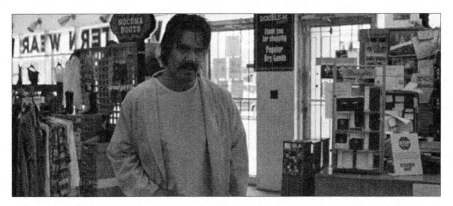

'You have a lot of people come in here without any clothes?'

loses control. As he convalesces in a Mexican hospital, cared for and protected by a staff of female nurses, Moss is temporarily robbed of his masculine strength, powerless to protect himself or his wife from Chigurh's lethal threat. The crippling wound is the outward sign of his emasculation. Thus, when he leaves the hospital he wears only a hospital gown, which gives him the feminising appearance of wearing a woman's dress. After awkwardly explaining to a border guard his reasons for appearing in public 'undressed', Moss immediately goes to a Western clothing store and buys the garments appropriate for a man of the West: Mahan boots, Wrangler jeans and a Stetson hat.

The loss of manly power and control played out in *No Country for Old Men* parallels the crisis of male identity commonly portrayed in classic film noir, where, unlike the western's splitting of male identity into good men and bad men, we find a wider spectrum of alternative models of masculine identity. Indeed, noir protagonists are often weak and powerless anti-heroes, either the 'dupe' who is manipulated and betrayed by a deceitful *femme fatale,* or the 'wrong man', an innocent victim of circumstances beyond his control. Other models of masculinity in film noir include the psychopathic killer and the damaged or traumatised man, often a veteran of war, who in his various forms exemplifies the crisis of male identity symbolised by Moss's crippling wound. During the shoot-out in Eagle Pass Chigurh also suffers a wounded leg, which in contrast to Moss he doctors himself, thus asserting his masculine claim to autonomy, but also demonstrating his preternatural indestructibility. Chigurh's coldly rational, machine-like manner and his total lack of emotion or sympathy are all stereotypically masculine. In this regard, his favourite weapon, the cattle-gun, is emblematic of his mechanical method of thinking and killing – pragmatic, efficient and emotionless. Anton Chigurh is also machine-like in his inflexible commitment to his so-called principles. Above all, Chigurh wants to maintain control, by whatever means necessary. As he tells Carla Jean after she insists that 'you don't have to do this', Chigurh cannot make himself 'vulnerable'. 'I have only one way to live,' he says. 'It doesn't allow for special cases.' As much as Chigurh enjoys demonstrating the uncertainty of life to others, he himself is possessed of a supreme certainty. Thus, when Wells tries to save himself from Chigurh by revealing the location of the satchel containing $2 million, saying, 'I know where it is,' Chigurh replies, 'I know something better. I know where it's going to be.' 'Where's that?' asks Wells. 'It will be brought to me,' answers Chigurh, 'and placed at my feet.' When Wells protests, 'You don't know that to a certainty,' Chigurh retorts: 'I *do* know that to a certainty.'

Sheriff Ed Tom Bell represents the traditional ideal of masculinity. As a patriarchal protector he assumes responsibility for defending his community. His resolve, however, is weakened by an underlying fear of his inability to stop Chigurh and eliminate the threat the killer presents to the people he is sworn to protect. More than his own weakness, Bell fears the failure of patriarchal authority, the breakdown of the old system and its values, a breakdown he cannot comprehend and thinks he can no longer fix or control. There are indications that he no longer takes himself seriously as an active agent of the law. At various points in the story Bell mocks himself and the stereotypes associated with masculinity. When, for instance, he and Deputy Wendell (Garret Dillahunt) prepare to enter Moss's abandoned trailer home to investigate, Bell says to his younger partner, 'You go in first. Gun out and up!' The deputy asks, 'What about yours?' 'I'm hiding behind you,' says Bell with a cynical grin. During their previous investigation of the desert shoot-out between rival drug dealers, Bell's coolly rational assessment of the crime scene prompted Wendell to compliment the sheriff on his 'linear thinking'. Bell's off-hand quip is openly self-deprecating: 'Old age flattens a man.' In the voiceover prologue that begins the film Bell gives a brief history of his family as lawmen: 'My grandfather was a sheriff, my father, too. Me and him was sheriff at the same time, him up in Plano and me out here. I think he was pretty proud of that. I know I was.' He notes in particular his admiration for the 'old-timers', wondering how they might have 'operated these times', thus establishing an unbroken succession and a strong sense of identification with the patriarchal tradition. Bell's prologue also includes an anecdotal recollection of a boy he sent to the gas chamber for killing a fourteen-year-old girl who said he'd do it again if he could and that he knew he was going to hell. Bell's mystified comment, 'I don't know what to make of that. I surely don't,' establishes him as the voice of an older generation no longer able to take the measure of declining moral values in a rapidly changing and increasingly secular and permissive society.

Bell is depicted as a frightened man confronting his worse fears. It isn't death he fears so much as being defeated in his struggle against the rising tide of pathological evil embodied in Chigurh, of whom he says 'I don't want to push my chips forward and go out and meet something I don't understand. A man would have to put his soul at hazard. He'd have to say "Okay, I'll be part of this world".' Bell never actually accepts his part in this world. He longs for a past when police officers protected their flocks as gentle shepherds and had no need to carry firearms. In his long years of law enforcement he has seen the worst in humanity, but still refuses to acknowledge its existence. The world he once knew, the world of his forefathers, is disappearing and he cannot comprehend or control the forces of change.

*No Country for Old Men*'s similarity to *Fargo* is often cited, with good reason. The basic premise of both films is the same: a small-town sheriff must confront psychopathic killers whose violent intrusion into an otherwise peaceful provincial locale seems inexplicable to local law enforcement. Chigurh has a precursor in the figure of

Gaear Grimsrud, who is but one in a series of psychopaths populating Coen movies including Loren Visser of *Blood Simple*, Eddie Dane of *Miller's Crossing* and Karl 'Madman' Mundt of *Barton Fink*. In both *Fargo* and *No Country for Old Men* the story centres on a provincial law officer who cannot comprehend the motives for the outrageous acts of violence they commit. Like Marge Gunderson, Sheriff Bell is at a loss to explain the bodies that keep piling up. Discussing the shootout at the motel and Moss's death, Bell's colleague exclaims: 'It's beyond everything. Who would do such a thing? How do you defend against it?' When Deputy Wendell asks 'Who the hell are these people?' Bell comments laconically, 'I ain't sure we've seen these people before. Their kind. I don't know what to do about them even.'

When asked how dangerous he thinks Chigurh is, Carson Wells replies, 'Compared to what? The bubonic plague? He's bad enough that you called me. He's a psychopathic killer, but so what? There's plenty of them around,' punctuating his statement with a slight, self-satisfied smirk indicating that he would probably consider himself one of the 'plenty around'. Measured strictly by his actions, Chigurh fits the standard profile of the psychopathic serial killer. His total lack of emotion, even during ultra-violent acts of murder, and the complete absence of empathy for his victims are textbook symptoms of criminal psychopathy. When, in the opening scene, he strangles a deputy brutally, or later when he executes the cartel associates point blank, not a hint of emotion shows on his face. Chigurh performs his murders in ice-cold blood, like the teenage boy Sheriff Bell describes in his opening monologue who, after killing a teenage girl said 'there wasn't no passion to it'.

But *No Country for Old Men* presents us with something more than the garden-variety psycho-killer, conjuring instead a mythic, vaguely supernatural aura around Chigurh, reinforced by Bell's superstitious belief that he is chasing a 'ghost'. Fully reproducing the mythic dimension in McCarthy's writing, the Coen brothers recreate the tricky realism of the novel where reality continually threatens to reveal itself as a nightmare, evoking an atmosphere of dread rivalling that of a horror movie. As a mythic figure, Chigurh is not allegorical. He does not merely represent Death or Fate, or any abstract concept. He is far too real, too plausibly human, if only as an aberration of humanity. The mythic or supernatural aura surrounding him is created by his seeming indestructibility, but also, more significantly, by his serene transcendence of earthly concerns and his single-minded dedication to 'higher principles'. Bell's fear of the new kind of criminal that Chigurh represents drives him into retirement: 'Now I aim to quit and a good part of it is knowin' that I won't be called on to hunt this man. I reckon he's a man.' The Coens further enhance Chigurh's ghostly aspect in the scene at the Desert Sands motel when Bell returns at night to revisit the crime scene. Knowing that the killer has returned to the scene of his crime before, Bell senses that Chigurh could be there. Indeed, we see him briefly in a dark reflection, waiting inside, hidden behind the door. Mysteriously however, when the sheriff enters to inspect the darkened room, Chigurh has vanished. No explanation, in cinematic terms, is given for his disappearance. The viewer is abandoned to speculation and uncertainty.

Each of the three central male characters – Moss, Chigurh, and Bell – presents a differing image of masculinity based on control and mastery. It begins with the early

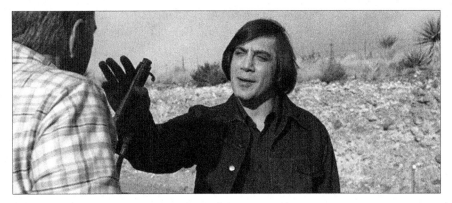

'Will you hold still, please?'

scene in which Chigurh, driving a stolen police cruiser, stops a lone driver and asks him politely, 'Step out of the car sir, please.' When the confused driver sees Chigurh's cattle gun and asks, 'What's that?' Chigurh repeats his request with a friendly demeanor. Raising the deadly bolt to the driver's forehead in a gesture that suggests a priest giving his supplicant a blessing, Chigurh asks, gently, 'Will you hold still, please?' Immediately after the killer's victim collapses and falls to the ground the film cuts to Moss looking through the scope of his rifle, targeting an antelope far off in the distant desert plain. Moss's first words, directed at his prey, are: 'You hold still.' He shoots but only wounds the animal, which he must now track and finish off. His failure as a marksman proves fatal as it forces him to follow the antelope which eventually leads him to the scene of the desert shoot-out and to 'the last man standing' and the fortune in drug money. Although he perceives the risk of taking the money, Moss believes he can master the odds and control his fate. Moss's arrogance leads ultimately to his downfall. He thinks he is smart enough and tough enough to take on Chigurh, scoffing at Carson Wells' warning: 'What's this guy supposed to be? The ultimate bad-ass?' Moss is angered by Wells' presumption of Chigurh's superiority and threatens: 'Maybe he's the one who needs to be worried.' For both Moss and Chigurh, identity depends on their power to master and control, to make things 'hold still'. Chigurh insists on controlling every situation, or as he puts it, remaining 'invulnerable', but denies all others such control, sometimes introducing the element of chance. In the end, Chigurh too is subject to the whims of chance, as dramatically illustrated by the unexpected car crash following Carla Jean's murder. Bell promises to 'make Moss safe' but fails to prevent his death. The lawman works to save a dying social order, but fails to make the forces that threaten it 'hold still'.

In her reading of *No Country for Old Men* Stacy Peebles uncovers an underlying value system opposed to the ethos of masculine power and mastery that the main characters represent, suggesting as alternatives renunciation and surrender to forces beyond individual control. The voice that speaks most directly to this alternative model of masculinity is given to a minor character, Uncle Ellis (Barry Corbin), who shares some hard-won wisdom with his nephew Sheriff Bell. When the aging sheriff expresses feelings of self-doubt and fears about his inability 'to stop what's comin'', Ellis reassures him: 'You can't stop what's comin'. It ain't all waitin' for you. That's vanity.' He implies that Bell should not assume personal responsibility for protecting 'his people' from a criminal element that has outmatched him. There are forces in this world, Ellis seems to say, that cannot be controlled by force. To think otherwise is vain, and dangerous. Likewise, the past cannot be changed. Regrets about how we have lived our lives are useless and crippling. Uncle Ellis is a living illustration of his quietist philosophy. Wounded in the line of duty as a sheriff's deputy, Ellis is confined to a wheelchair for life, but feels neither anger nor desire for revenge. As he reasons: 'All the time you spend trying to get back what's been took from you, more's goin' out the door. After a while you just have to get a tourniquet on it.'

### Existential Uncertainty

Chigurh's will to control is intensified by the sadistic pleasure he derives from tormenting the condemned. This is most evident in his pre-execution ritual where he poses a final agonising question: What meaning does your life have, now that it has brought you to this? Or in Chigurh's precise formulation: 'If the rule you followed led you to this, of what use was the rule?' In McCarthy's novel, just before he ends Wells' life with a point-blank shotgun blast, Chigurh presses him to consider the meaning of his existence: 'It calls past events into question. Don't you think so?' (2005: 175). Here Chigurh seems to espouse a philosophy of fatalism: the future is always already prefigured in the past and the past cannot be altered. When Chigurh executes Carla Jean (Kelly Macdonald), however, his logic is somewhat different. In her case, it is a matter of moral imperatives. Chigurh promised Moss that his wife would pay the price if he did not return the drug money. Now he has come to make good his promise. As he had in his encounter with the gas station owner, Chigurh offers Carla Jean a last-chance coin toss to decide her fate. She refuses, compelling Chigurh to take responsibility for his actions, saying 'The coin didn't have no say. It was just you,' to which Chigurh replies coolly: 'I got here the same way the coin did.' McCarthy elaborates Chigurh's enigmatic reasoning, explicating more fully his philosophy of fatalism, when in the novel he explains to Carla Jean, 'I had no say in the matter. Every moment in your life is a turning and every one a choosing. Somewhere you made a choice. All followed to this. The accounting is scrupulous. The shape is drawn. No line can be erased.' 'The shape of your path,' he concludes, 'was visible from the beginning' (2005: 259). It is only during these existential inquisitions that Chigurh shows any genuine interest, however perverse, in the life he is about to extinguish. These are the moments in which we see a glimmer of life behind his malicious smile. The ritual coin toss with which he invites unwilling participants to wager their lives is little more than an amusement to Chigurh, a game to impress on his victims that their lives are ruled by chance and nothing else.

Chigurh is fascinated with the uncertainty of the human condition, a fascination he shares with the Coen brothers who return to this theme frequently in their films, notably in *The Man Who Wasn't There*, their existentialist rewriting of Cain's *The Postman Always Rings Twice*, and in *A Serious Man*, where college physics professor

Larry Gopnick teaches his students about Heisenberg's Uncertainty Principle. Heisenberg's theory also appears in *The Man Who Wasn't There*, where, as we saw in the previous chapter, defense attorney Freddie Riedenschneider exploits it to prove the legal principle of 'reasonable doubt'. Although the Uncertainty Principle is invoked in both these films, its thematic importance is undermined by an ironic humour that disguises its potential seriousness. In *No Country for Old Men* the Coens drop their mask of ironic detachment and for once, through McCarthy, give serious voice to the existentialists' insistence that the only certainty in life is the rule of uncertainty. In McCarthy the Coens have found a writer of philosophical fiction akin to Albert Camus, whose novel *The Stranger* rendered an existentialist reading of Cain and, as we have seen, provided a model for the Coens' rewriting of Cain in *The Man Who Wasn't There*. In *No Country for Old Men* the philosophical implications of a world ruled by uncertainty are made palpable in the figure of Chigurh.

Bell's encounter with Chigurh, whose inexplicable savagery defies comprehension by the moral standards Bell takes to be true, triggers an existential crisis. Faced with the incomprehensibility of Chigurh's crimes, Bell lacks reliable categories for understanding him and thus effective strategies for combating him. Ultimately, the defeat handed him by Chigurh forces the sheriff to confront the meaninglessness and futility of his actions and indeed the meaninglessness of the world at large. Bell's sense of failure shakes his belief in himself as a lawman, but also his belief in God, whom he believes has abandoned him. As he tells Uncle Ellis, 'I always figured that when I got older, God would come into my life.' After a pause, Bell admits, 'He didn't. And I don't blame him.' Bell's crisis of religious faith is symptomatic of a larger existential crisis which, according to Camus, Bell can only resolve by learning to accept 'a life without consolation'. The question is whether or not Bell can live a life 'without appeal' (Camus 1991: 60).

What Camus means is that we must learn to live not only without hope for salvation in an eternal afterlife promised by religion, but also without the belief in truth or absolute knowledge and certainty of any kind. For existentialist philosophers like Camus, the old truths or certainties based on metaphysical concepts had become unreliable. Thus, reasons Camus, we must learn to accommodate ourselves to what *is*, to that which exists in the immediate present, and bring nothing into our perceptions that we can not be certain about. And if nothing is certain, at least that is a certainty. Camus claims that the acceptance of the fundamental uncertainty of human existence produces a 'lucid awareness' he calls 'the absurd', entailing the recognition of life's meaninglessness which then facilitates a 'leap' of consciousness that frees us from traditional metaphysical illusions of unity, meaning and purpose. Throughout the story there are signs that Bell is entering a lucid awareness of the absurd, for example, in his commentary on a newspaper article concerning a Californian couple who tortured and killed old folks for their social security income. It seems no one took notice of these crimes until an old man was spotted in their back yard wearing nothing but a dog collar. 'You can't make up such a thing as that,' says Bell to Wendell. 'I dare you to try.' 'But that's what it took,' Bell continues. 'All that hollerin' and diggin' in the yard didn't bring it.' When Wendell starts to laugh, then apologises, Bell consoles him: 'That's okay. I laugh myself sometimes. There ain't a whole lot else you can do.' Bell's wisdom is rooted in the existentialist notion that the conflict between the seriousness with which we live our lives and the ultimate meaninglessness of human existence renders all human endeavor futile, absurd, and therefore a joke. Laughter is all that remains. The colourful anecdote Bell tells Carla Jean about Charlie Walser and the 'beef' he tried and failed to kill has a vaguely parabolic message, its point being, as Bell explains, 'that even in a contest between man and steer, the issue is *uncertain*'.

In the dark uncertainty of the new West there can be no happy ending, no triumph of good over evil, no resolution of the story's philosophical questions. Moss, a sympathetic and potentially heroic figure, dies unceremoniously, while his antagonist makes good the promise to hold his wife 'accountable' for her husband's arrogance. Later, Chigurh, the villain, survives a car crash that should have been fatal and manages to walk away. Bell is powerless to prevent any of this and ends the story in melancholy retirement, still anxious and confused about the social and moral decay that surrounds him. The darkness of this ending extends into the epilogue, in which Bell relates a cryptic dream of his father slipping into the night, leaving his son to find his way through a barren wilderness alone. In his final monologue, Bell recounts to his wife Loretta two dreams about his father, one in which he is supposed to meet his father in town to receive some money which he promptly loses, and a second, longer dream of a horseback journey with his father through a cold, dark night in desolate and unknown lands. His father, riding ahead, carries fire, which promises light and warmth in the frigid darkness. In the dream, says Bell, 'I knew that he was goin' on ahead and that he was fixin' to make a fire somewhere out there in all that dark and all that cold and I knew that whenever I got there he would be there.' The symbolism of the dual dream narrative suggests that Bell may feel he has squandered his father's gift, the money symbolising the value of the life given to him by his father and what he has done with it, a question that troubles him deeply, now that he is retired and forced to contemplate the path he has taken through life.

The second, longer dream seems almost biblical in its parabolic tone and imagery. The images of Bell and his father riding on horseback through darkness and cold assume an archetypal quality, reinforced by the image of the 'horn' his father carries 'the way people used to do'. This is a trope resonant with meanings: a primordial image of ancient fire as the means of survival for primitive ancestors, but also conceivably a religious symbol of the divine spark of human life and the eternal soul as it journeys toward reunion with the heavenly Father. Perhaps, in relation to the imminent apocalypse imagined by Sheriff Bell, the fire in the horn is closer in meaning to the image of fire in McCarthy's post-apocalyptic novel *The Road* (2006), which tells the story of a father and son struggling to survive in a world gone mad. The father tells his son that they are 'the good guys' who 'carry the fire'; that is, those who guard and preserve the small remainder of man's dwindling humanity in a world of inhuman savagery. In his dream Bell is left out in the cold, following after the father, who passes by, head down, as if in his passing unaware of the son's existence. The horn of fire has not been handed down to the son who still wanders in the darkness seeking the light of the father. Bell has lost his connection with the ancestral patriarchal order he had hoped to conserve and 'carry on' and now must acknowledge his failure to do so. We are left with the sense that Bell is losing his belief in an afterlife where he would be reunited with his father, joining him in the light and safety of his fire, finally satisfying the all-too-human 'nostalgia for unity' described by Camus as 'that appetite for the absolute that illustrates the essential human impulse of the human drama' (1991: 17). Bell's final words – 'And then I woke up' – are perhaps a call for 'lucidity', for an awakening to and acceptance of man's absurdity in a universe indifferent to his existence, a call to 'live life without appeal'.

*No Country for Old Men* ends on a dark note, leaving the meaning of Bell's dreams uncertain – an ending perfectly consistent with the absence of narrative and interpretive closure in all Coen movies. At the end of the film the viewer is left in darkness too, left to puzzle the meaning of a story that even its narrator fails to understand, proving nothing, except perhaps that uncertainty is the only 'principle' the filmmakers themselves might trust.

CHAPTER ELEVEN

# *A Serious Man: Parable and Paradox*

Following the exceptional success of *No Country for Old Men*, the Coen brothers made *Burn After Reading* (2008) and quickly thereafter released in 2009 a comparably modest, low-budget movie entitled *A Serious Man*. With a cast of little-known actors and a story written in a more personal, autobiographical vein, *A Serious Man* plays more like an independent film one would expect to see in a festival competition than a movie by filmmakers now considered by many to be amongst the preeminent auteurs of their time. In the words of film critic Todd McCarthy, '*A Serious Man* is the kind of picture you get to make after you've won an Oscar.' Roger Moore echoes this thought, writing that *A Serious Man* is 'exactly the sort of film [the Coens] release after some dazzling success'. Although these critics seem to have overlooked *Burn After Reading*, which despite its sizeable budget might also qualify as the kind of off-beat movie the Coens make after a big success like *No Country for Old Men*, *A Serious Man* does prove what the brothers have often said: that they can and will make any kind of film they like. The Coens have made it clear that they do not seek popular success and auteur celebrity, which they have nevertheless achieved, one might say, in spite of themselves.

The Coens are notoriously reluctant to speak of their personal lives to interviewers and carefully skirt anything even remotely autobiographical in their writing. In this regard, *A Serious Man* is an exception. Set in a suburb of Minneapolis in 1967, the film's period-milieu and characters are based on recollections of their upbringing in St. Louis Park, a Minneapolis suburb and an ethnic enclave for American Jews in the 1960s. In 1967 Joel was thirteen, the age of *bar mitzvah*, suggesting that Danny's storyline draws on personal experiences of the director. Danny's obsessive pot smoking also has a basis in historical fact. In a moment of rare candor, the Coens have admitted that they smoked a lot of weed in the late 1960s, indulging in one of the 'new freedoms' introduced by the emerging hippie counterculture. The summer of 1967 was famously labelled 'the Summer of Love', and events of that summer initiated the dissemination of the hippie counterculture into the social mainstream, particularly through the rock music emerging in the West Coast scene, represented in the movie soundtrack by the Jefferson Airplane and Jimi Hendrix. In June 1967 Hendrix made his North American debut along with Janis Joplin, Santana and many others at the Monterey Pop Festival, the first major rock festival to be staged in the US. But the revolutionary spirit of 1960s counter-culture had yet to reach St. Louis Park, Minnesota, where among the Jewish families of the community the traditions of Judaism were still piously observed. Indeed, the rich heritage of the Jewish cultural tradition is the story's most important cultural source and, like every other ethnicity represented in the movie, it is subjected to acerbic stereotyping. In addition to the film's *dybbuk* prologue spoken entirely in Yiddish, the dialogue is peppered with Yiddish expressions, like *gett* (a divorce under Jewish law), *agunah* (a woman whose husband is unwilling to grant her a *gett*), *tsuris* (aggravating trouble), and *naches* (pride and joy, or more specifically, the pleasure parents receive from their children). *Hashem* (literally translated from Hebrew as 'the name'), a term for God used in casual conversation when uttering His real name would not be permissible, comes up often and contributes to the mystery that the story insists we should simply accept.

*A Serious Man* chronicles two weeks in the life of Larry Gopnick (Michael Stuhlbarg), a Jewish physics professor up for tenure. Not knowing what the outcome will be, this is time of anxious uncertainty in Larry's life, during which he teaches his students about Heisenberg's Uncertainty Principle. Gopnick's middle-class suburban life seems at first quiet and secure, but suddenly it all starts to fall apart. For no apparent reason, his wife Judith (Sari Lennick) asks for a divorce so that she can marry Sy Abelman (Fred Melamed), a self-important friend of the Gopnicks. Larry's home life is further complicated by his shiftless brother Arthur (Richard Kind) who is unmarried, unemployed and free-loading at Larry's house. Larry's children are annoyingly self-absorbed. His son Danny (Aaron Wolff), who is supposed to be studying Hebrew scripture in preparation for his *bar mitzvah*, instead smokes pot at every opportunity, listens to rock music during his Hebrew classes, and constantly whines about the poor TV reception that interrupts his favorite comedy show, *F Troop*. Larry's daughter Sarah (Jessica McManus) complains about Uncle Arthur hogging the bathroom (spending a lot time attending to his cyst) and steals money from her father, which she is saving for a 'nose job' (a joke on Jewish self-loathing). At the university, a mysterious Korean student named Clive Park (David Kang) tries to bribe Larry for a better grade on his mid-term exam. When Larry accuses Clive of bribing, the student's father threatens him with a defamation suit. Meanwhile, Larry's department head informs him that an anonymous letter-writer is trying to sabotage his promotion. Judith and Sy add to Larry's travail with the demand that he move out of his own home and take up residence (with his brother Arthur) at a sleazy motel, the Jolly Roger. Arthur, who likes to gamble, is subsequently arrested for sex solicitation, forcing Larry to hire another expensive lawyer, in addition to the one already handling his impending divorce. Then, in an event that should have worked in Larry's favour, Sy is killed in a car accident and Larry, ironically, is asked to pay for his funeral expenses. Later, we are given to understand that Sy was the anonymous letter-writer subverting Larry's bid for tenure. While all this is going on, Larry is busy trying to figure out 'what it all means' by visiting a series of rabbis, none of whom can offer any useful advice. To make a bad situation worse, a routine visit to the doctor reveals that Larry might have a serious illness (probably cancer; we never know for sure). At the end of the story, crushed by mounting debt, Larry appears to take the Korean's bribe, changing the student's grade from F to C-. As if in punishment for his moral transgression, a tornado blows into town threatening the life of his son who, as the film comes to its abrupt end, stands directly in the path of the whirlwind.

The initial reviews of *A Serious Man* were mixed. Some critics loved it. In the *Guardian* Peter Bradshaw thought it was 'sublimely funny… a superb and intelligent comedy.' The Coen brothers, he writes, 'always operate on a spectrum between broad, bright comedy and bitter darkness, and when their creations are pitched just the right distance between each, the resulting film is a marvel. So it is here.' Ben Walters of *Time Out* commented that *A Serious Man* tells a story that is 'sincerely engaged with the challenge of unjust suffering', noting that what emerges from the protagonist's struggles is 'the sensibility the Coens have unobtrusively espoused throughout their work: reject worldly status, bear trials with humility, find joy in fellow-feeling'. Calling *A Serious Man* 'a darkly funny, affectionate homage to their Jewish roots', Ann Hornaday thinks the film succeeds 'because it engages questions worth asking. What is integrity? What does it mean to be good?' Owen Gleiberman of *Entertainment Weekly* considered *A Serious Man* 'a landmark in the Coen canon' primarily because it deals in an autobiographical mode with the Coens' Jewish heritage. The movie is not perfect, thinks Gleiberman, who finds himself still 'grappling with the powerfully offbeat ending', but it is 'cathartic to see the Coens finally show you a bit of who they are, or at least where they came from'.

Other critics had serious reservations. David Denby wrote: 'As a piece of filmmaking craft, *A Serious Man* is fascinating; in every other way, it's intolerable', particularly in the way the Coens make their characters so 'drably unappealing'. Peter Rainer of the *Christian Science Monitor* focused on the brothers' penchant for stereotyping, writing that 'the Coens stereotype this Jewish milieu to a fare-thee-well, and the stereotypes seem to function for them as a form of Yiddish Theater … Since the Coens have always been misanthropic,' he writes, 'it's not enough to say that *A Serious Man* makes fun of Jews. The Coens make nasty fun of everybody. This is what they do.' Although they poke fun at Jews and the Judaic tradition, they are still a part of it, thinks Rainer, making *A Serious Man* another contribution to 'the ancient storehouse of Jewish black humour that takes off from the question, "What did I do wrong?"'. Dana Stevens of *Slate Magazine* proclaims *A Serious Man* 'an exquisitely realized work' in which 'the filmmakers' technical mastery of their craft, always impressive, has become absolute'. The degree of control the Coens exert over their audience's aesthetic experience, however, 'can feel almost claustrophobic'. Control issues aside, Stevens thinks the film is 'a funny and nuanced exploration of chance, justice, and faith'. A. O. Scott of the *New York Times* couldn't decide whether the Coens were making a case for atheism or looking at the world from a 'divine' point of view. Despite confusion and despair among some movie reviewers, *A Serious Man* made it onto the 2009 Top Ten lists of the American Film Institute and the National Board of Review, as well as receiving Academy Award nominations for Best Picture and Best Original Screenplay. There were many more awards and nominations too numerous to recount here, but it is worth noting that *A Serious Man* was chosen for Best Original Screenplay by both the National Board of Review and the National Society of Film Critics.

*Parable*

The film narrative begins with a parable-like prologue spoken in Yiddish depicting an uncanny occurrence in an Eastern European *shtetl* in the late nineteenth century. On a cold winter night a married couple, Velvel and Dora, encounter a traveler who is strangely familiar. Velvel has invited the traveler into their home, where he is recognised as Reb Groshkover, a man who had supposedly died three years before. Velvel offers Groshkover hospitality, but Dora, who has certain knowledge of this man's death, rudely declares him a *dybbuk* or evil spirit, uttering 'God has cursed us.' Groshkover graciously jokes to Velvel, 'What a wife you have!' But it takes only a few moments for Dora to decide on a plan of action. Calmly and deliberately, she plunges the ice pick she had been holding into Groshkover's chest, whereupon the mortally wounded man excuses himself, saying, 'I don't feel at all well,' and departs with the ice pick still lodged in his chest. Velvel cries out: 'Dear wife. We are ruined. Tomorrow they will discover the body. All is lost!' Dora replies: 'Nonsense, Velvel. Blessed is the Lord. Good riddance to evil.' A parable, perhaps, but one without resolution, for as it ends, we are left with an unanswerable question: Was Reb Groshkover a *dybbuk* or was he not? The only certainty this parabolic prologue suggests is that uncertainty will play a major role in the narrative that is about to unfold.

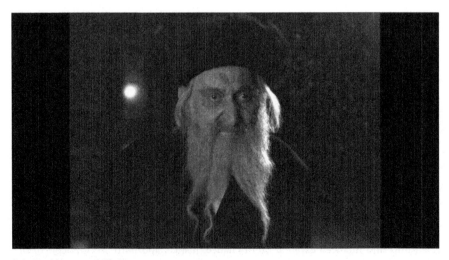

Reb Groshkover – a dybbuk?

In Jewish folklore the *dybbuk* is a malicious spirit believed to be the displaced soul of a dead person, which may have escaped from *gehenna* (hell) or could have been stolen by Satan on its way to *olam ha-ba* (the World to Come). The term *dybbuk* derives from the Hebrew word meaning 'attachment'. The *dybbuk* attaches itself to a living person, inhabiting the living body like a demon or ghost. The Coens have dismissed the notion that the *dybbuk* story has any meaningful connection to Larry Gopnick's tale of woe, describing it with self-deprecating irony as just an odd amusement, 'like the cartoons they used to show in movie theaters, before the main feature' (DVD Extra). Understood as a surrealist retelling of Jewish folklore, however, the darkly comic visitation by Reb Groschkover has notable affinities with the parabolic writings of Franz Kafka, the Jewish-Czech writer whose name has become synonymous with all things absurd and paradoxical. Over the years, Kafka and the 'Kafkaesque' have often been associated with Coen brothers movies and for good reasons. Not only here in *A Serious Man* but in their previous films, especially *Barton Fink* and *The Man Who Wasn't There*, the Coens have created a kind of cinematic equivalent to that strange blend of nightmare absurdity and theatrical farce that goes by the name of Kafkaesque. The Kafka connection is not purely speculative; the Coens often refer to scenes in their movies as Kafkaesque, citing the surrealist dream sequence titled 'Gutterballs' in *The Big Lebowski* as a 'Kafka break' (DVD Interview). 'Usually,' says Joel, 'if we haven't done it by page 70 [of a screenplay in progress], we arbitrarily throw in a "Kafka break".' In *The Big Lebowski* the Kafka break interrupts the narrative flow with a dream interlude featuring the Dude in a Busby Berkeley-style dance number, set to the music of the 1960s pop hit, 'Just Dropped In'. Without warning, this break detours from the plot and shifts the viewer from 1990 LA to a dream space filled with the Dude's subconscious fantasies and fears. Such sudden shifts from the real to the unreal are common occurrences in Kafka's stories, where waking and dreaming are often indistinguishable and interchangeable. In *A Serious Man* the Coens make frequent use of Kafka's technique to blur the distinction between fantasy and reality. It is particularly evident in the movie's three dream sequences, introduced in the narrative without cinematic cues signaling the transition from reality to dream. The viewer's assumption of reality is thus contradicted when the scene is abruptly revealed as a dream. This process of presupposition and reversal is characteristic of Kafka's writings, especially *The Trial* (1914), where the reader's assumptions are constantly subverted and the narrative frequently interrupted by the intrusion of uncanny, dreamlike digressions.

Written as a parable, the *dybbuk* story also adopts a narrative form preferred by Kafka, well known for his parabolic anecdotes. One of these parables, entitled 'Little Fabel' ('Kleine Fabel'), tells the story of a little mouse whose world grows ever more confining. 'At first it was so wide it scared me,' laments the mouse. 'I ran on and was happy to see walls in the distance to my right and left, but now these long walls approach each other with such speed that I am already in the last room, and there in the corner sits a trap, into which I am running. – "You only have to change your direction," said the cat, as it ate the mouse' (Kafka 1976: 368; my translation). No children's tale this. If read as allegory, its philosophical implications are dire. Kafka seems to be saying that freedom is an ideal state all humans strive to achieve. But too much freedom is frightening; we need boundaries and limits. More quickly than we realise, these boundaries become a prison ('the last room' with its trap), to which there is only one alternative: being eaten by the cat, which as a symbol can be construed many ways, but in the terms of the story, must at the very least signify death.

What does this little fable teach us? That all our striving for freedom is fatally doomed? That in truth we cannot abide the very freedom we idealise? Whatever meaning we might attribute to the fable, we can at least assume that Kafka takes a dim view of humanity's fate. The parable's lesson remains uncertain. Another well-known Kafka parable, entitled 'Give It Up!' ('Gibs auf!'), poses questions much like those asked by Larry Gopnick. Like 'Little Fable', this short vignette narrates with urgent brevity man's search for guidance and direction. On his way to the train station, the anonymous first-person narrator compares his watch with a tower clock and discovers that it is much later than he thought. This discovery frightens him so that he forgets the way to the station. Fortunately, a policeman (*Schutzmann*) is nearby whom the lost narrator can ask for directions: 'I ran to him and asked him breathlessly to show me the way. He giggled and said: "You want me to tell you the way?" "Give it up!" he said, and turned away from me with a grand gesture, like people who want to be alone with their laughter' (1976: 410–411, my translation). Taken as allegory, there are several ways to interpret the parable's symbolism, especially the significance of the policeman, who might represent the Law or Justice in some abstract sense, but also the Law of the father or the patriarchal social order. The '*Schutzmann*' (literally translatable as 'protector') could be construed as God, the Holy Father, or the Judaic *Hashem*. Whatever this protector might signify, he refuses to answer and turns away from the lost man. The protector cannot show him 'the way' or the path he should follow to enlightenment or salvation.

These parables are reviewed here to illustrate the problem of meaning in Kafka's fiction, where humanity's most urgent questions are raised again and again, but always remain unanswered. Commentators speak of the terror of ambiguity in Kafka's writings, a strategy he uses relentlessly to unsettle the reader searching for determinate meaning or message in his words. Kafka's terrible ambiguity is intended to create precisely the opposite of meaning and moral. In his storyworld certainty becomes an impossibility and truth (or God) is inaccessible. Perhaps the epitome of Kafka's parabolic technique is found in the sketch entitled 'Before the Law' ('Vor dem Gesetz'), summarised here in abridged translation:

> Before the Law stands a gatekeeper. A man from the country comes to this gatekeeper and asks to be admitted. The gatekeeper tells him that it is possible to enter, but not now. The man from the country looks through the gate to the interior; the gatekeeper dares him to enter, admonishing him that there are many gatekeepers after him, each more powerful than the one before. The man from the country hesitates and waits. He waits for days and years, persistently asking for admission to the Law. After many years of waiting the man grows old, his eyes grow dim, but he sees a radiance streaming from the gateway to the Law. With his dying breath he asks: 'Everyone strives to reach the Law. How

does it happen that in all this time no one but me has requested entry?' The gatekeeper replies: 'No one else could gain admittance here because this gate was intended solely for you. And now I'm going to shut it.' (1976: 148–149, my translation).

Like the figure of the *Schutzmann* in 'Give It Up!' here the Law could convey any number of allegorical meanings: Justice, Truth, God. Like the Everyman narrator of 'Give It Up!' the man from the country is barred entry, only to discover in the end that there is no single Law for all men, only an individual law for each, which the man from the country, discouraged by the gatekeeper, fails to seek. The parable 'Before the Law' is interpolated in Kafka's novel *The Trial* and is often interpreted as an allegorical fable of the protagonist's predicament. Josef K. is a serious man. He seeks knowledge of the Court and the justification for his trial, which he pursues through the absurdly labyrinthine bureaucracy of a secret and inaccessible judicial system he tries hopelessly to understand. By the end of his story, Josef K. has achieved no understanding of the Court and its inexplicable workings. He 'dies like a dog', executed by agents of the Law for undisclosed reasons. If Kafka's parable conveys any lesson, it is the inability of the human mind to comprehend truth, which, as Kafka demonstrates, cannot be communicated in ordinary rational terms and can only be made comprehensible when illustrated in parable form.

The relevance of 'Before the Law' for *A Serious Man* resides in both authors' preoccupation with the elusiveness of truth, the meaninglessness of life, and the absurdity of the human condition in a godless world. Like Kafka's countryman, Larry Gopnick seeks transcendent knowledge. He demands answers to questions that cannot be answered. He wants to know what *Hashem* has to say. Thus, like Kafka's seeker who continuously asks the gatekeeper the same questions, Larry consults with the leaders of his religious order, three rabbis, the first of whom tells Larry a parable about the parking lot. Confused and anxious about Judith, Larry seeks the council of Rabbi Scott (Simon Helberg), a junior rabbi, who suggests that Larry has simply lost sight of *Hashem* and that he must remember how 'to see *Hashem*' in the world around him. To illustrate, the rabbi asks Larry to contemplate the parking lot outside his office window: 'Not much to see,' Rabbi Scott admits, 'but if you imagine yourself a visitor, somebody who isn't familiar with these … autos and such … somebody still with a capacity for wonder… Someone with a fresh … perspective.'

Not satisfied with Rabbi Scott's lame parable, Larry next approaches Rabbi Nachtner (George Wyner), whose Germanic name connotes a darkness obscuring the light of truth. Larry's unanswered question has now become, 'What does it all mean? What is *Hashem* trying to tell me?' In answer, Rabbi Nachtner relates the parable of Dr. Sussman and the goy's teeth (musically scored with the strident staccato of Hendrix's 'Machine Gun'). Sussman, a Jewish dentist, discovers tiny incised Hebrew lettering on a patient's teeth. Knowing some Hebrew, Sussman deciphers the lettering, which reads: 'Help me. Save me.' This has never happened to Sussman. It is a singular event, a mystery. Thinking this is a sign from God, Sussman becomes obsessed with decoding the riddle, consulting the *Zohar* and the *Cabala*. But he cannot unravel the mystery. When Sussman finally seeks out Rabbi Nachtner, asking if this is a sign from *Hashem*, the rabbi can offer little help. As he explains it to Larry: 'The teeth, we don't know. A sign from *Hashem*, don't know. Helping others, couldn't hurt.' To this, Larry can only respond: 'It sounds like you don't know anything! Why even tell me the story?' Oblivious to the triviality of his parable, Nachtner continues: 'These questions that are bothering you, Larry, maybe they're like a toothache. We feel them for a while, then they go away.' 'I don't want it to just go away!' says Larry, exasperated. 'I want an answer!' 'We all want the answer,' Nachtner replies calmly, 'but *Hashem* doesn't owe us the answer, Larry. *Hashem* doesn't owe us anything. The obligation runs the other way.' Still not satisfied, Larry finally asks, 'Why does he make us feel the questions if he's not going to give us any answers?' Nachtner replies simply: 'He hasn't told me.'

The religious elder Larry wants most to consult is the aged and reclusive Rabbi Marshak (Alan Mandel). Everybody tells Larry he should see Marshak. But the ancient sage remains inaccessible, despite Larry's attempts to gain entry to his inner sanctum, closely guarded by Marshak's secretary. Larry pleads with her, saying 'This is not a frivolous request. This is serious – I'm … I'm a serious man. I need help. I need Marshak.' She only stares back inscrutably. Finally, she goes to the door behind her, opens it, and shuffles into a dim inner office filled with arcana, Judaic and otherwise. Larry cranes to see into the room, but the weak light prevents a good view. All he can see is a man, old and bent, sitting motionless behind a bare desk. Larry waits. After murmuring with Marshak, she returns and shuts the door. 'The rabbi is busy,' she says curtly. 'He didn't look busy!' contradicts Larry. 'He's thinking,' she replies. If this scene does not already strike us as Kafkaesque, indeed, as a winking parody of the Kafka's parable 'Before the Law', the Coens plant an unmistakable clue in the published screenplay, where Marshak's secretary is described as the rabbi's 'elderly East European gatekeeper' (Coen & Coen 2009: 120).

*Paradox*

What the Coen brothers appear to present in *A Serious Man* is the illustration of a paradox. By common definition, a paradox is a thought or idea that is seemingly contradictory or opposed to common sense, and yet perhaps true. The fundamental paradox of the Coens' fable resides in its invitation to confront serious ideas without taking any of them seriously, shaping their parable-like story as an incongruous mixture of science, philosophy, religion and comedy. *A Serious Man* poses serious questions: What is the purpose of suffering? Why do the righteous suffer and the evil prosper? If God exists, why does He permit such injustices? How do we understand God's mysterious will? The immediate paradox confronting Larry Gopnick arises from his misunderstanding of what it means to be 'a serious man'. Larry has tried hard to be righteous, obeying the laws of his religious faith and trying to do right by his family and community. But despite his apparent righteousness, he is beset with troubles and seeks answers, trying to understand what God is saying to him. Larry's problem stems from his belief that life, the human experience, can be explained rationally, as in a mathematical proof, when in truth what little knowledge of the world we have is based on, as Larry's student Clive says, 'mere surmise'.

The film's introductory epigraph, 'Receive with simplicity everything that happens to you,' is a commentary on the Old Testament book of Deuteronomy attributed to the eleventh-century rabbi Rashi. The biblical passage glossed is Deuteronomy 18:13: 'You must be blameless before the Lord your God.' Interestingly, this citation follows a passage condemning interpreters of signs: 'Let no one be found among you who sacrifices his son or daughter in the fire, who practices divination or sorcery, interprets omens, engages in witchcraft, or casts spells, or who is a medium or spiritualist or who consults the dead. Anyone who does these things is detestable to the Lord' (Deuteronomy 18: 10–12). Thus, in the eyes of the Jewish God *Hashem*, Larry, who uses the mathematical signs and formulas of quantum physics to divine scientific truth, is an abomination. Even more so his brother Arthur, who is writing a '*Mentaculus*', a 'probability map of the universe' written out in complex and cryptic mathematical equations – a calculus for the workings of the universe. As such, it is an attempt to comprehend the cosmos using the signs and symbols of math and physics, an attempt to explain 'what it all means'. Arthur, a gambler, discovers a lucrative practical application for his map, which makes him, if nothing else, unbeatable at poker. That Sy Abelman is an interpreter of signs is made clear when he instructs Larry 'these are signs and tokens', after giving the cuckolded husband a token bottle of wine as a peace offering.

After his sudden death, Sy Abelman is hailed as a serious man. At his funeral Rabbi Nachtner describes Sy not only as a serious man, but possibly a holy man, a *tzadik*, perhaps even a *lamid vavnik*. According to kabbalistic teachings, at any given time in history there are thirty-six righteous people called *lamid vavniks* (*lamed* = 30, *vav* = 6) on whom the fate of world depends. According to the *Cabala*, if even one of them perishes, God would destroy the whole world. Anyone could be a *lamid vavnik*. Their identity is unknown. The holy ones themselves, known as *menschen* in Yiddish, are not aware of their divine status. We cannot be certain that anyone we meet is not a *lamid vavnik*, therefore everyone should be treated as though they are one of the thirty-six. Calling Sy Abelman a holy man turns out to be a misnomer, however, when we learn during Danny's *bar mitzvah* ceremony that Sy was most likely the person writing damning letters to Larry's tenure committee. For reasons unknown (but probably having to do with Judith), Sy wanted to undermine Larry's professional success. It is possible that Sy Abelman is a *dybbuk*, embodying the return of an ancient ancestral curse, perhaps beginning with Velvel and Dora. Rabbi Nachtner hints at such a possibility in his eulogy for Sy, where he doubts if such a 'serious man' could simply disappear and repeats three times during his speech: 'Sy Abelman returns.' If Sy is a serious man, he is serious in all the wrong ways. Perhaps Larry is the *lamed vavnik*, for he too claims to be a serious man. Or maybe not. Maybe Larry is cursed, or just a *schmuck* for trying to understand his world through the narrowing lens of science and mathematics. Maybe he should 'accept the mystery' as the Korean student's father suggests. The joke, of course, is that all these characters take life too seriously, trying by different but equally serious means to decipher the meaning of life – and they are made to suffer for it.

The most serious problem the Coens wrestle with is the question of religious faith in a world where access to truth, justice and God has become difficult or impossible. To illustrate this theological dilemma, they model their narrative on the ancient story of Job in the Hebrew Bible, which teaches that God has absolute power over His creation and that man should not question His dominion, but simply submit to His will. The parallels between Job and Larry Gopnick are clearly intended. Job is a righteous man cursed and forsaken by his God who allows Satan to test Job's faith, robbing him of his health and wealth and destroying his family in an attempt to force Job to renounce the Almighty. Great calamities are visited upon Job. His livestock is stolen and his servants put to the sword; his great herds of sheep are destroyed by the 'fire of God'; his sons and daughters are killed by a 'mighty wind' that sweeps in from the desert. Hearing the report of his children's deaths, Job strips off his clothes, falls to the ground, and worships his God saying, 'Naked I came from my mother's womb, and naked will I depart. The Lord gave, and the Lord has taken away; may the name of the Lord be praised' (Job 1:20).

Despite his great suffering, Job does not curse his God, but he does protest his plight and pleads for an explanation. To comfort him in his tribulation, three friends visit Job offering opinions about his curse. The first, Eliphaz, tells Job: 'Blessed is the man whom God corrects; so do not despise the discipline of the Almighty' (5:17). The second, Bildad, assures Job that if he is pure and upright, the Almighty will restore him to his rightful place. The third, Zophar, admonishes Job to remember that no one can fathom the mysteries of God or chart the limit of the Almighty. Job replies to all three, 'Who does not know all these things?' 'I am innocent,' insists Job, 'but God denies me justice' (34:5).

Job wants an answer to the question, Why me? And he will not be satisfied until God speaks to him directly. Finally, God speaks, commanding Job: 'Brace yourself like a man; I will question you, and you shall answer me' (40:7), then unleashing a tirade on His grandeur and dominion over all things under heaven. Nothing on earth is His equal: 'He looks down on all that are haughty and He is king over all that are proud' (31:34). Job can only say to Him: 'I am unworthy – how can I reply to you?' Job does, however, repent, saying 'Surely I spoke of things I did not understand, things too wonderful for me to know' (42:3). Satisfied with Job's contrition and as reward for his unshakable faith, God restores him to his rightful place and blesses his life. 'After this, Job lived a hundred and forty years [and] he saw his children and their children to the fourth generation. And so he died, old and full of years' (42:16–17).

The relevance of Job's torment for Larry's tale of suffering is self-evident. Both men seek answers from God for their misfortune. Both pose the same question: Why me? But the Coens borrow more than the basic premise of the scriptural story. Transposing Job to Middle America in the 1960s, *A Serious Man* references its biblical source in many particulars, often citing them for humorous effect. As Job is cursed with a skin disease that plagues him with 'loathsome sores' from head to foot, so Uncle Arthur suffers a boil on his neck, referred to in clinical terms as a 'sebaceous cyst'.

Like Job, Larry's trials are many, and all the more humorous for being mostly serious. Just as Job loses everything precious, home and family, Larry loses his wife (to a deceitful hypocrite), his home (when he meekly agrees to move with his brother to the Jolly Roger) and his wealth (when Judith empties their joint bank account). Like Job, Larry is beset with trials and tribulation. A student offers him a bribe for a better grade, then after refusing the money, the student's father threatens an absurd defamation suit. An unknown antagonist writes denigrating letters to subvert his tenure bid. His bigoted next-door neighbour, Mr. Brandt, is encroaching on his property. He is plagued by a Columbia Records Club rep trying to collect for records his son has secretly ordered in his name. Distraught over his impending divorce, Larry complains to his friend Mimi Nudell: 'It was a bolt from the blue! What does *that* mean? Everything that I thought was one way turns out to be another!' She advises Larry to see the rabbi. The three friends who visit Job are mirrored in the three rabbis from whom Larry seeks advice. Two of them offer useless parables. The third, Rabbi Marshak, is as inaccessible as the Old Testament *Hashem*. In the Book of Job God does finally speak to Job, commanding him to 'brace yourself like a man; I will question you, and you shall answer me.' This commandment is explained in simpler terms by Rabbi Nachtner when he tells Larry: 'We all want the answer. But *Hashem* doesn't owe us the answer. *Hashem* doesn't owe us anything. The obligation runs the other way.'

The Coens also sneak in some less obvious biblical references, such as Larry's voyeuristic encounter with Mrs. Samsky, his sexy next-door neighbour. Climbing onto his roof to adjust the TV antenna so that Danny can watch *F Troop*, Larry observes Mrs. Samsky sunbathing in the nude. Later, he visits her and shares her marijuana joint. A subsequent dream sequence depicts Larry enjoying sexual intercourse with her. As a seductive temptress, Mrs. Samsky could be a warning to heed the Book of Job in matters concerning infidelity: 'If my heart has been enticed by a woman, or if I have lurked at my neighbour's door, then may my wife grind another man's grain, and may other men sleep with her' (31:9). Judith's coupling with Sy Abelman may somehow be a punishment for Larry's erotic dream of Mrs. Samsky. Larry's rooftop

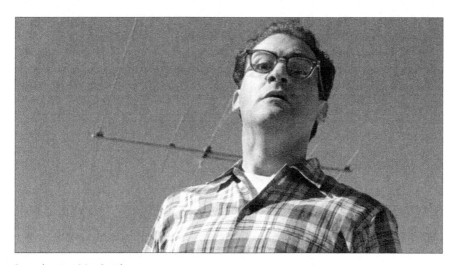

Larry discovers Mrs. Samsky.

peeping also references the biblical story told in the Second Book of Samuel (11), depicting the temptation of King David who, gazing from the roof of his palace, sees a woman bathing. She is Bathsheba. In awe of her great beauty, the king decides he must have her, even though she is married to one of his generals. To eliminate his rival, David sends the general into battle where he dies, freeing his widow to marry the king. But perhaps most important parallel between Larry and his biblical counterpart is that, like Job, Larry does not renounce his God. When Arthur breaks down and curses the Almighty, lamenting his impoverished life ('Look at everything *Hashem* has given you! And what do I get? I get fucking shit!'), Larry simply says, 'It's not fair to blame *Hashem*.' In spite of all that has happened to him, Larry does not lose his faith in God.

Not content with Job as their sole biblical source, the Coen brothers also make allusions to the story of Cain and Abel. Like the Book of Job, the story of Cain and Abel is about trying to understand and communicate with God. The story centres on the conflict that arises when both brothers make offerings to God, who then chooses to favour Abel's offering rather than Cain's, even though Cain, the older and more respectable brother, makes his offering first while Abel is simply copying his brother's genuine act of devotion. Presumably, Cain's attempt to reach the Almighty is more sincere than his brother's, but God refuses to acknowledge this. To Cain's mind, this is a clear case of divine injustice. How could God make such an irrational choice, going against what seems to Cain the most basic moral logic? The story teaches essentially the same lesson as Job. Although they may seem incomprehensible or paradoxical, the actions of the Almighty do not have to be explained or justified. In *A Serious Man* the reference to Cain and Abel is signaled by Sy's surname, *Abel*man, and by Judith's choice of Sy Abelman, a self-important fool, over Larry, her devoted husband. Like God's decision to favor Abel instead of Cain, Judith's decision seems irrational and absurdly unjust. And, as in the Bible story, where Cain kills his brother Abel, the Coens insinuate that Larry, in the role of Cain, is responsible for Sy Abelman's death in a car crash. As Larry is seen driving to work, parallel editing shows Sy on the way to his golf club. The parallel editing creates a sense of parallel existences or interconnected paths. Thus, by means of subtle editing, intercutting Sy's fatal car accident with Larry's fender bender, it is ambiguously suggested that these events are somehow connected. Although the car crashes are separated in space, temporally, they happen simultaneously, inviting us to assume, momentarily, that Larry has crashed into Sy. Unsure of the meaning or outcome of the events just witnessed, we are left in uncertainty, until later, when Larry comes home and learns from Judith that Sy is dead. Because both car crashes happen at the same moment, Larry asks his rabbi: 'Is *Hashem* trying to tell me that Sy Abelman is me? Or that we are all one, or something?'

*The Uncertainty Principle*

Early in the filmstory Larry Gopnick is shown standing in front of a college classroom busily writing out an elaborate set of equations. Larry turns to his students and explains excitedly: 'So, okay. So. So if that's that, then we can do this, right? Is that right? Isn't that right? And that's Schrödinger's paradox, right? Is the cat dead or is the cat not dead?' Larry's math may explain it all clearly, but his words, a stream of questions without answers, reveal nothing but uncertainty about the meaning of the proof. It is probable that the students also leave the classroom in uncertainty. This assumption is confirmed in the following scene in Larry's faculty office, where he meets with Clive who protests his failing grade on the mid-term exam, saying that it is 'unjust'. 'I understand the physics,' pleads the student. 'I understand the dead cat.' Larry argues that the physics cannot be understood without the math (the reason Clive failed the test). 'The math tells how it really works,' Larry insists. 'The stories I give you in class are just illustrative; they're like fables, to help give you a picture. I mean – even I don't understand the dead cat.' Apparently, Clive refuses to acknowledge the rules of scientific analysis, which in this case would require advanced knowledge of mathematical formulas and linear equations. Not satisfied, Clive pleads for a 'secret test', hoping for a better score. When Larry again refuses, Clive leaves, muttering 'very troubling, very troubling...'.

As Larry subsequently discovers, the student has planted a bribe on his desk, forcing Larry to summon Clive to his office again to tell him he thinks he has left something behind. Clive counters with disingenuous denial: 'I didn't leave anything. I'm not missing anything. I know where everything is.' Larry holds up an envelope filled with money: 'This is here, isn't it? This is not nothing, this is something. You know what it is!' Larry cautions: 'Actions have consequences. And we both know about your actions.' Clive responds: 'No sir. *I* know about my actions.' Larry presses: 'I can interpret, Clive. I know what you meant me to understand.' Clive deflects with what sounds like 'Meer sir my sir', an utterance Larry at first does not understand, forcing Clive to repeat, with careful enunciation: 'Mere surmise, sir. Very uncertain.' Even language is used against itself to defeat certainty.

The theoretical paradox Larry is teaching his students is a thought experiment devised by German physicist Erwin Schrödinger, widely considered the father of quantum mechanics. Schrödinger's cat experiment poses the theoretical question: When does a quantum system stop existing as a superposition of two states and become one or the other? To illustrate, Schrödinger proposed a hypothetical scenario in which a cat is caged in a box with a flask set to emit a lethal poison and an internal Geiger counter. If the Geiger counter detects any radiation in the box, the poison is released, killing the cat. After a certain time, the cat may or may not be killed, but until the box is opened and the cat observed, it remains uncertain whether the cat is alive or dead. Thus, the cat is presumed alive/dead, in a mixed state or 'superposition', which is the nature of all quantum systems. Although Larry can explain this to his students in mathematical terms, he admits that it proposes a paradox he doesn't fully understand in non-mathematical terms.

The real irony is that Larry doesn't see the theory's application to his own life, in which he, like the cat, finds himself in a 'mixture of states'. He has a home and family, but is simultaneously exiled to the Jolly Roger; he is married but facing divorce; he is a professor, but in limbo awaiting the tenure vote. Recently pronounced in good health by his physician, Larry suddenly faces the possibility of having a terminal illness.

When his story reaches its abrupt ending, it is suggested that he is in a very real sense suspended between life and death. Other family members are also in mixed states. His son Danny stands on the brink of adulthood, about to become a member of the faith community, but he is still a child, getting high in the school bathroom, sneaking into his Hebrew teacher's office after hours to attempt retrieval of his confiscated transistor radio. Like his father, Danny is in limbo at story's end, his fate yet to be determined by the course of a tornado's funnel cloud that looms over him. Brother Arthur is, one might say, in a permanent 'superposition', existing both in the 'normal' world of straight heterosexuals and in the closeted world of the Minnesota.

Another, related theory of quantum physics Larry teaches his students is the Uncertainty Principle. Advanced by Werner Heisenberg, another founding father of quantum physics, the Uncertainty Principle posits a fundamental indeterminacy in the measurement of sub-atomic particles caused by scientific observation, a theory Larry has written out in a convoluted mass of complex equations covering the entire chalk board. As he finishes, he turns to his students and announces: 'The Uncertainty Principle. It proves we can't ever really know what's going on. So it shouldn't bother you, not being able to figure anything out' – hardly what one would expect a physicist to conclude from an extensive mathematical proof. Part of the irony here is that Heisenberg's proof is still widely regarded as valid, despite the fact that his theory has been disproved. As later physicists have shown, the loss in precise measurement caused by observation is less than predicted by Heisenberg's theory. Nevertheless, his mathematical calculations are, paradoxically, still considered valid. There is, of course, also the comic irony of the advice Larry gives his students: 'So it shouldn't bother you, not being able to figure anything out.' But being unable to figure anything out is precisely what has been bothering Larry, whose life has been turned upside-down. As he repeatedly complains, 'Everything I thought was one way turns out to be another.' When the classroom clears, Sy Abelman has 'returned' to question Larry's explication of Heisenberg. 'If I've got it wrong,' asks Larry, 'what do I do?' Sy answers: 'So simple, Larry. See Marshak.' Larry insists he has tried to see the rabbi, but could not gain admittance, whereupon, in a Kafkaesque moment, Sy suddenly slams Larry's head violently against the chalk board, shouting 'See Marshak! I seriously fucked your wife! That's what's going on! See Marshak!'

Of course, Larry does not see Marshak, the only one who might tell him 'what it all means'. Like Kafka's 'man from the country', Larry is denied access to 'the Law'. Barred from truth and unable to obtain justice, his predicament recalls Josef K., the tormented protagonist of Kafka's *The Trial* who is arrested one morning without having committed a crime and dies without knowing his transgression. Analogously, Larry is condemned to Job-like trials for reasons that are never made clear. The miraculous reconciliation with the Almighty that ends the story of Job is not reprised in *A Serious Man* where, in the film's final scene, Larry's future well-being and that of his family are left in grave doubt. Larry decides to change the Korean student's grade, weighing his moral transgression against the practical necessity of paying his rapidly mounting debts. Apparently, *Hashem*, the vindictive God of the Hebrew Bible, disapproves of Larry's breach of ethics and, recalling the 'whirlwind' that sweeps away the lives of Job's

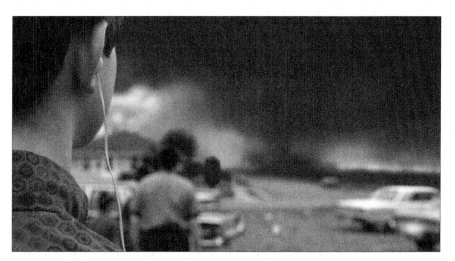

A 'whirlwind' approaches Danny's *schul.*

children, the Almighty sends a tornado toward Danny's *schul.* At the same moment, Larry receives a call from his doctor asking him to come in right away to discuss the results of his recent X-rays, inviting us to assume that Larry is afflicted with a serious illness. As ominous storm clouds gather over Danny's school, the movie ends and we are left in darkness, not knowing what terrible fate is in store for father and son. We are simply asked to 'accept the mystery'. In the end, nothing is certain and questions about the future go unanswered.

The moral of Larry's fable appears to be: What we think is true often turns out to be lies, and vice-versa. And telling an untruth, or a fable, like Schrödinger's dead/undead cat, is often the best and sometimes the only way to illustrate a paradoxical truth. These themes are articulated in the lyrics of Jefferson Airplane's 'Somebody to Love', the first song on the movie soundtrack and the last, returning at the end in the mouth of Rabbi Marshak, who reiterates them in his *bar mitzvah* confirmation interview with Danny: 'When the truth is found … to be lies,' queries the rabbi, 'then what?' Marshak's answer ('Be a good boy') could hardly be less enlightening. This is the holy man Larry hoped would give him true insight, the only man capable of answering his question: 'What does it all mean?' But the rabbi's simple question is important: When the truth is found to be lies, what then? As the screen goes blank and the end credits begin to roll, 'Need Somebody to Love' begins to play and Grace Slick answers the rabbi's question: 'You better find somebody to love.'

CONCLUSION

# The Ends of the Auteur: Drawing Conclusions About Coen Brothers Movies

One of the few legitimate generalisations that can be made about Coen brothers movies is that they always end suspended in a limbo of irresolution. The satisfaction of a conventional or meaningful conclusion where conflicts are resolved and questions answered is perpetually withheld and narrative as well as interpretive resolution is denied, abandoning characters, and the viewer, to the darkness of uncertainty. A selective review of their movies' endings serves to prove the point. The narrative of their first feature, *Blood Simple*, ends with Visser's attempt to eliminate Ray and Abby as witnesses to his crimes and thus tie up loose ends. In an ironic reversal of fortune, however, Visser becomes Abby's target and succumbs (apparently) as a result of her counterattack. Although the filmmakers have granted the viewer omniscient knowledge of what has transpired in this final scene, Abby is left guessing the identity of her assailant, thinking Visser is Marty seeking revenge. Furthermore, Visser's actual moment of death, which would bring some natural closure to the story, is withheld and any gravity or finality his dying might have brought to a noir narrative that, generically speaking, ought to have a downbeat ending, evaporates when, in reply to Abby, who says, 'I ain't afraid of you, Marty,' the wounded detective cracks wise, saying, 'Well, ma'am, if I see him, I'll sure give him the message.' The potential for dramatic pathos in Visser's death (which we never actually witness) is also short-circuited by the upbeat music ('It's the Same Old Song') that immediately follows the final image, shot from Visser's point of view, of a droplet of water falling into his eye. The unexpected humour and inappropriate music of this finale cue conflicting spectator responses, leaving the viewer disoriented and uncertain how to react.

In the final scene of the Coens' second feature, *Raising Arizona*, appended as a kind of epilogue, Hi dreams of a better future in a land, where, as he says, 'all parents are strong and wise and capable, and all children are happy and beloved'. But maybe, as

Hi must admit, his dream of a better land is just an illusion, prompting him to ask the viewer: 'And I don't know, you tell me. This whole dream, was it wishful thinking? Was I just fleein' reality, like I know I'm liable to do?' The improbable silliness of his dream is made clear in Hi's tentative conclusion: 'If not Arizona, then a land not too far away … I dunno, maybe it was Utah.'

Continuing the pattern of open endings and postponed conclusions, the final scene of *Miller's Crossing* is heavy with innuendo, but nothing is made certain. Tom's final tip of the hat to Leo is an intentionally ambiguous gesture. We are left with the sense that the story, implicitly a love story of two men, is somehow not over. *Barton Fink* concludes with one of the Coens' most confounding endings, questioning but never clarifying the distinction between reality and 'the life of the mind'. Key iconic elements (Charlie's box and the picture of the bathing beauty) are never assigned determinate meaning and left (intentionally) unexplained. By the end of *Fargo* numerous

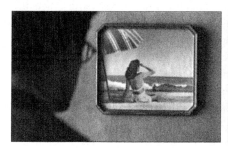 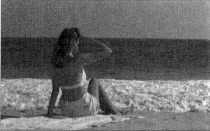

Fink's Bathing Beauty                    'Are you in pictures?'

dead bodies have piled up, including those of Jerry Lundegaard's wife and father-in-law, while Gaear has axe-murdered his partner-in-crime Carl and fed his mortal remains to the wood chipper. Brainard's chief of police has solved the murder case, bringing closure to the plot, but still cannot fathom the purpose of the criminals' horrific crimes. The final scene of Marge, a pregnant mother, and Norm, her supportive husband, safely tucked into their marriage bed, offers a picture of domestic bliss and promise for the future. But we are left with the sense that, in the darkness of the Coen universe, this unlikely ending is just another prank and only believable as a parody of the formulaic 'Hollywood' happy ending. Similarly, *The Hudsucker Proxy* appears to end happily with Norville's continuing success and the resolution of his romantic conflict with Amy. But as the story makes abundantly clear, Norville is a winner only by the grace of chance and good fortune, his story and its ending pirated from Sturges, whose happy endings are always subverted by a mischievous ironic twist. Even the heroic Ulysses figure, Everett McGill of *O Brother, Where Art Thou?*, who overcomes all obstacles to win back his wife and family, is left at story's end with one more task to perform to restore him officially as *paterfamilias* – retrieving Penny's wedding ring (the genuine article, not one of Aunt Hurlene's) from the bottom of a 9,000-hectare lake. The outcome of this final heroic labour is left entirely to the viewer's imagination.

The epilogue that ends *The Big Lebowski* is given by the film's cowboy narrator called the Stranger. Not a character in the story, the Stranger intrudes periodically into the narrative to comment on the Dude's predicament. He is brought in again in the final scene to pronounce a few benedictory words, but the patent artificiality of his entrance into the diegesis (as he looks directly into the camera addressing the audience) illustrates the screenwriters' self-conscious reluctance or inability to invent a plausible ending. As the Stranger tells it, in fact, the story doesn't really end there. He alludes to the future and another little Lebowski on the way, invoking the great chain of being: 'I guess that's the way the whole durned human comedy keeps perpetuatin' itself, down through the generations, westward the wagons across the sands of time until...' Pausing self-consciously, he breaks off his speech: 'Ah, I'm ramblin' again. Well, I hope you folks enjoyed yourselves. Catch you later on down the trail.'

Whether implied or explicit, the ending of every Coen brothers story functions as an epilogue, an afterthought delaying finality, postponing closure, promising continuation. This unwillingness to allow closure is reinforced in their films by the continual postponement of death, a recurring motif played out in numerous scenarios where the dead are denied their final repose. Sometimes, as with Julian Marty in *Blood Simple*, this entails a return from the dead prolonged by recurrence as he comes back from death not only at the moment of his burial but again in Abby's dreams. Other times, as with *The Big Lebowski*'s Donny Kerabatsos, the deceased is denied the simple dignity and finality of a proper interment, in Donny's case, when Walter clumsily releases the ashes of his cremated remains into the wind only to have them blown back into the Dude's exasperated face.

A correlated motif is seen in the disposal of dead bodies, so problematic in *No Country for Old Men*, where, in a seemingly gratuitous short scene, Sheriff Bell stops a flat-bed truck loaded with the corpses from the desert drug deal gone wrong, asking the driver, 'You look at your load lately? That's a damn outrage.' The tarp covering the body bags piled in the truck bed has come untied, exposing the dead bodies to open public view. Bell's anger is obviously driven by his respect for the dead, whose lifeless, helpless bodies, denied the common decency of burial, become the butt of a macabre joke in a scene probably intended to add a whiff of black humour. Significantly, this scene transitions via lap dissolve (an editing technique seldom seen in the Coens' films, but traditionally used to establish a symbolic connection between shots) to the image of Moss lying in a hospital bed, eyes shut and motionless, giving the momentary appearance of death – promptly dispelled when his death-like repose is disturbed by Carson Wells, holding flowers, as if visiting a grave. Interestingly, at the close of *No Country for Old Men*, a story which, told conventionally, would have to end with Chigurh's death in a violent car crash, the indestructible antagonist escapes and limps away, his improbable survival defeating any sense of justice, poetic or otherwise, that might bring closure to the narrative. Moreover, the story's narrator, Sheriff Bell, refuses to let his story come to rest, appending a dream epilogue which itself refuses to provide any conclusions about the meaning of Bell's vision in relation to his father, leaving the narrator (and his audience) in the dark and inhospitable wilderness described so vividly in his dream.

*The Man Who Wasn't There* strains to achieve closure with the execution of Ed Crane, but the finality of his physical death in the electric chair, which we witness onscreen as a glaring illumination that consumes and obliterates his image, is mitigated by his transcendent vision of a reunion with Doris in some place 'beyond earth and sky'. Furthermore, the final scenes of Ed on death row provide hints that, as the narrator of his story, Ed may not have been entirely reliable and thus, that we cannot be certain that the confessional 'true story' he is writing (for a magazine called 'True Story') is anything more than a condemned man's fantasy, a possibility strongly suggested by an unexplained visit by a flying saucer on the eve of his execution. Despite its attempts to mislead and forestall conclusions, however, the ending of *The Man Who Wasn't There* comes closer to drawing discernable conclusions than any previous Coen movie, if only to endorse the fatalistic worldview of classic noir fiction and film under the influence of existentialism. In this sense, *The Man Who Wasn't There* marks a turning point in the Coens' artistic development, signaling the filmmakers' willingness to wrestle with issues of profound human importance, always latent in their films, but seldom treated explicitly unless with dark, obfuscating irony. In R. Barton Palmer's reading of the film, the Coens' extensive allusiveness, particularly their substantial borrowings from Cain's fiction, amounts to more than a skillful imitation of the writer's style and fictional universe. Instead, the Coens rework Cain's central themes to extend and restructure the precursor-texts as, in Palmer's words, 'a new sincere version of film noir in which Cain's explorations of lust and its discontents yield a meaning that is perhaps closer to the "truth" of film noir, with its deeply ironic representation of the uncertainty of human life' (2004: 65). Compared to their inaugural film noir, *Blood Simple*, where the basic elements of Cain's fiction served as a framework for playful innovations in noir aesthetics, *The Man Who Wasn't There* emerges as a more mature work that engages seriously with Cain's unspoken philosophical preoccupations, in particular, the pulp fictionist's proto-existentialist worldview and the relationship of Cain's writings to the philosophical fiction of Albert Camus and Jean-Paul Sartre.

After their detour into light comedy between the years 2003 and 2006, during which the Coens released *Intolerable Cruelty* and *The Ladykillers*, the brothers returned to weightier themes in *No Country for Old Men* where, to preserve the philosophical integrity of McCarthy's novel just as they had honoured the existentialism of Cain's fiction, the Coens were willing to address, if not answer, troubling questions about the nature of human experience – chance versus free will and the certainty of belief versus the loss of faith – with unaccustomed sobriety.

As the endings of their stories show, the Coens do not like conclusions – not just the structural closure of narrative, but also any conclusive statements of their films' intentions or 'message'. Generally, the brothers punish characters who make assumptions and presume to draw from them meaningful conclusions. Often we have the sense that the Coens are punishing their viewers, too, for making assumptions about the meaning and purpose of their films, teasing their audiences with erudite cultural references that promise deeper significance, but only lead us in circles where we had hoped to plot a linear course terminating somewhere in the vicinity of certainty. Indeed, the rule of uncertainty, in art and in life, could be the Coens' greatest theme, the only meagre and insufficient truth they are able to voice. They explore the theme of uncertainty obsessively, in all of their works, but nowhere is it more ruthlessly travestied than in *A Serious Man*. Although the film pokes fun at 'serious men' like Larry Gopnick, whose efforts to ascertain meaning and truth by calculation amount to grand folly, behind its irony and black humour the film engages deeply with issues of religious faith and the values of family and community life. As one commentator has suggested, *A Serious Man* is perhaps the Coen brothers' 'urtext, a distillation of the themes, preoccupations, and flaws that have animated the best and the worst films of their career' (Hornaday 2009). What might constitute the flaws in their work is uncertain, but certainly *A Serious Man* anthologises the Coen brothers' central philosophical preoccupations, above all, the elusiveness of meaning, the inaccessibility of truth and the resulting uncertainty which strands us in a multitude of competing and conflicting interpretations of what constitutes knowledge. In *A Serious Man*, the 'seriousness' of science, religion and all forms of human truth-seeking is played for laughs and the viewer is commended with mock piety to 'accept the mystery' and simply bear witness to the absurd comedy of human existence, without asking 'what it all means'.

If the endings of their films are consistently inconclusive, a symptom of their refusal to assign determinate meaning or purpose to their creations, the question becomes: What, if any, are the 'ends' or aims of the Coen brothers as film auteurs? In one sense, their refusal to make conclusive statements of meaning can be understood as a function of what R. Barton Palmer has called a 'postmodern authorial absence' (2004: 51), a vacancy opened by postmodernism's deconstruction of the auteur as a unified and unique voice striving for self-expression and authenticity. This struggle was perhaps necessary in the old Hollywood studio system where the film director had to fight for creative autonomy within a repressive industrial structure. But in the postmodern/ post-studio era that struggle and the belief in the author as the originator of a uniquely personal vision has been abandoned. The auteur and his text are now to be conceived as plural. The artistic creator is no longer held responsible for the meaning of his creations. One of most essential lessons of Bakhtin's dialogism is that language, 'the word', is 'inter-individual'. Relations to others and their dialogical responses (communicated via the word) are constitutive of all individual identity. Thus, the boundaries defining self-identity become fluid, more permeable. In the work of postmodern art, individual effort yields to collaboration and the sense of authority once demanded of the artistic text gives way to the play of intertextual dialogism. Taken in this Bakhtinian sense, the name 'Coen brothers' designates something less, but, paradoxically, also something more than the term auteur is generally thought to mean. We sense in their films the presence of a guiding intelligence and sensibility, but the exact intentions of the imagination that shapes their stories and characters remain elusive, difficult to track through the multiplicities of allusion, quotation and borrowing that converge in their intricate and expansive intertexts.

One alternative to the traditional understanding of authorship, suggested by Thomas Elsaesser, is to redefine the fiction of the 'auteur' as 'the name for the *pleasure* that seems to have no substitute in the sobered-up deconstruction of the authorless voice of ideology' (1981: 11). If 'pleasure' is indeed what remains of the postmodern auteur, how do we designate the pleasure we derive from the Coen brothers? For some it might be the intellectual pleasure they discover in the richness of the Coens' densely allusive and ingeniously orchestrated intertextual constructs. Others might find a different pleasure in the visceral effects of grotesque and excessive violence or in the exuberant and innovative visual style of their films. One can take pleasure, as do the writers themselves, in the stylish wit of their dialogue or their artful rendering of regional dialects. Pleasure can be found in the sensual/intellectual enjoyment afforded by their artfully designed and executed music soundtracks, exemplified by the carefully chosen and extensive compilation of songs scoring *O Brother, Where Art Thou?*, *The Big Lebowski* and, most recently, *Inside Llewyn Davis*, where music sets the mood, dramatic or comic, in nearly every scene. Whether it be the intellectual delight of identifying the seemingly infinite varieties of literary, cinematic and cultural references embedded in their movies or the carnivalesque pleasures of low humour that hold intellect in touch with body, the pleasures of their films are innumerable and more than adequate compensation for the stubborn refusal of meaning and finality. Perhaps there is enjoyment in that as well – the delight caused by the uncertainty that unsettles meaning, but also rewards those tired of the formulas of conventional storytelling and willing to explore the pleasurable ambiguity that informs and enlivens the films of the Coen brothers.

Detractors have dismissed the Coen brothers as intellectual hedonists interested only in the cheap thrills of violence or the shallow pleasure of self-gratification the filmmakers seem to take in the meticulous craftsmanship of their films – no need for the deeper satisfactions that 'meaningful' content can supply. But perhaps there is yet another way to understand the pleasures of their films. Rather than hedonists, the Coens are perhaps more rightly considered filmic *epicureans*. As the Greek philosopher Epicurus taught, pleasure is the proper goal of a good life. But for Epicurus, pleasure is not defined as the decadence of mindless hedonism – the intoxication, gluttony and overindulgence commonly associated with epicureans. Instead, for the ancient philosopher pleasure is understood as the absence of physical discomfort and emotional distress. The good or 'blessed' life is attained by moderation and by making choices that ensure freedom from pain and anxiety and create a constant state of tranquility. Morgan Rempel has suggested that Jeffrey 'the Dude' Lebowski has adopted an epicurean lifestyle, observing that the Dude has achieved supreme contentment by renouncing the unsettling desire for the material satisfactions of wealth, power and social prestige, devoting himself instead to a life of uncomplicated pursuits – bowling, smoking weed, listening to 'the Creedence' and generally just 'takin' it easy for the rest of us sinners'. Applied to the rest of the Coens' film work, the Dude's epicurean philosophy of life prescribes a cessation of the discomfiting desire to find meaning and finality in their films. Not just in *The Big Lebowski*, but in all Coen brothers movies we are asked, in accordance with the motto of *A Serious Man*, 'to receive with simplicity' everything they have written.

The Coen brothers' epicurean aesthetic has a relevant parallel in the existentialist conception of art. As Albert Camus explains in *The Myth of Sisyphus*, authentic art must refuse to invest its world with false purpose. This refusal is the consequence of adopting an 'absurd attitude' which compels an acceptance of life's meaninglessness. The art of the absurd, insists Camus, 'must remain aware of its gratuitousness' (1991:

102). At the moment a work of art sacrifices itself to illusions and arouses hope, it ceases to be gratuitous. The absurd artist, writes Camus, 'will not yield to the temptation of adding to what is described a deeper meaning that it knows to be illegitimate' (1991: 97). In this liberation from hermeneutic necessity, both artist and audience are freed to explore the absurdity of existence, which does not of any necessity lead to nihilism and the tyranny of uncertainty, but rather to the abandonment of the struggle for meaning and purpose and a renewed and unencumbered enjoyment of the concrete aesthetic pleasures a work of art can provide. Camus calls for 'an art in which the concrete signifies nothing more than itself. It cannot be the end, the meaning, and the consolation of a life' (1991: 97). This is, essentially, what the Coen brothers have always said about their films: 'We want to talk about [our] movies, but the movies speak for themselves' (Allen 2006: 66). In other words, we should not expect the filmmakers to answer the question that plagues Larry Gopnick in *A Serious Man*, who continually asks, 'What does it all mean?' As Rabbi Nachtner explains to Larry, 'God doesn't owe us an answer. The obligation runs the other way.' This rule applies to the Coens as well. They don't owe us an answer to the meaning of their films. We are answerable to their texts. Our response is our own responsibility.

The absence of meaning postulated by existentialist philosophers compels the discovery of the absurd, but as Camus writes in *The Myth of Sisyphus*, 'One does not discover the absurd without being tempted to write a manual on happiness' (1991: 122). Even the mythic figure of Sisyphus, condemned to eternal, meaningless labour, must be imagined as happy. All that remains after the discovery of the absurd is laughter. This is the joyful wisdom that infuses the Coens' entire body of work, given expression in the aesthetic credo espoused by the movie director John L. Sullivan in Preston Sturges' *Sullivan's Travels*. After experiencing first-hand the harsh and impoverished reality facing his audiences outside the movie theatre, the fictional filmmaker is forced to conclude that his silly, lightweight comedies, the value of which he had doubted, serve the viewer something more valuable, and necessary, than the serious 'message movie' he believed he should make. His experiences have taught him that for many of his movie patrons, the laughter his comedies provide is the only comfort available in an otherwise indifferent, intractable and ultimately tragic world. Entertainment, and nothing more, is what the filmmaker owes his audience, and that, we can finally say to a certainty, is what Joel and Ethan Coen have consistently, abundantly and artfully delivered in their films.

# FILMOGRAPHY

1985 – *Blood Simple*
River Road Productions
Director: Joel Coen
Screenplay: Joel Coen and Ethan Coen
Producer: Ethan Coen
Director of Photography: Barry
    Sonnenfeld
Production Designer: Jane Musky
Original Music: Carter Burwell and Jim
    Roberge
Editors: Roderick Jaynes and Don
    Wiegmann

1987 – *Raising Arizona*
Circle Films/ 20th Century Fox
Director: Joel Coen
Screenplay: Joel Coen and Ethan Coen
Producers: Ethan Coen and Mark
    Silverman
Director of Photography: Barry
    Sonnenfeld
Editor: Michael Miller
Production Designer: Dennis Gassner
Original Music: Carter Burwell

1990 – *Miller's Crossing*
Circle Films/ 20th Century Fox
Director: Joel Coen
Screenplay: Joel Coen and Ethan Coen
Producers: Ethan Coen and Mark
    Silverman

Director of Photography: Barry
    Sonnenfeld
Editor: Michael Miller
Production Designer: Dennis Gassner
Original Music: Carter Burwell

1991 – *Barton Fink*
Circle Films/Working Title
Director: Joel Coen
Screenplay: Joel Coen and Ethan Coen
Producers: Ethan Coen and Graham
    Place
Director of Photography: Roger Deakins
Editors: Roderick Jaynes and Michael
    Barenbaum
Production Designer: Dennis Gassner
Original Music: Carter Burwell

1994 – *The Hudsucker Proxy*
Warner Bros/Working Title
Director: Joel Coen
Screenplay: Joel Coen, Ethan Coen and
    Sam Raimi
Producers: Ethan Coen and Graham
    Place
Director of Photography: Roger Deakins
Editor: Thom Noble
Production Designer: Dennis Gassner
Original Music: Carter Burwell

1996 – *Fargo*
Polygram/Working Title
Director: Joel Coen
Screenplay: Joel Coen and Ethan Coen
Producer: Ethan Coen
Director of Photography: Roger Deakins
Editors: Roderick Jaynes and Tricia
  Cook
Production Designer: Rich Heinricks
Original Music: Carter Burwell

1998 – *The Big Lebowski*
Polygram/Working Title
Director: Joel Coen
Screenplay: Joel Coen and Ethan Coen
Producers: Ethan Coen and John
  Cameron
Director of Photography: Roger Deakins
Editors: Roderick Jaynes and Tricia
  Cook
Production Designer: Rick Heinrichs
Original Music: Carter Burwell

2000 – *O Brother, Where Art Thou?*
Touchstone/Studio Canal/Working Title
Director: Joel Coen
Screenplay: Joel Coen and Ethan Coen
Producer: Ethan Coen
Director of Photography: Roger Deakins
Editors: Roderick Jaynes and Tricia Cook
Production Designer: Dennis Gassner
Music: Carter Burwell and T Bone
  Burnett

2001 *The Man Who Wasn't There*
Good Machine/Gramercy/Working
  Title/Mike Zoss Productions
Director: Joel Coen
Screenplay: Joel Coen and Ethan Coen
Producer: Ethan Coen
Director of Photography: Roger Deakins
Editor: Tricia Cook
Production Designer: Dennis Gassner
Music: Carter Burwell

2003 – *Intolerable Cruelty*
Universal Pictures/Imagine
  Entertainment/Mike Zoss Productions
Director: Joel Coen
Screenplay: Robert Ramsey, Matthew
  Stone, Ethan Coen and Joel Coen
Producers: Ethan Coen and Brian Grazer
Director of Photography: Roger Deakins
Editor: Roderick Jaynes
Production Designer: Leslie McDonald
Music: Carter Burwell

2004 – *The Ladykillers*
Touchstone Pictures/Mike Zoss
  Productions
Directors: Joel Coen and Ethan Coen
Screenplay: Joel Coen and Ethan Coen
Producers: Ethan Coen, Joel Coen, Tom
  Jacobson and Barry Sonnenfeld
Director of Photography: Roger Deakins
Editor: Roderick Jaynes
Production Designer: Dennis Gassner
Original Music: Carter Burwell

2006 – *Tuileries* (segment of *Paris, je
  t'aime*)
La Fabrique de Films
Director: Joel Coen and Ethan Coen
Screenplay: Joel Coen and Ethan Coen
Producers: Emanuel Benbihy, Claudie
  Ossard

2007 – *No Country for Old Men*
Paramount Vantage/Miramax Films/
  Scott Rudin Productions/Mike Zoss
  Productions
Director: Joel Coen and Ethan Coen
Screenplay: Joel Coen and Ethan Coen
Producers: Ethan Coen, Joel Coen and
  Scott Rudin
Director of Photography: Roger Deakins
Editor: Roderick Jaynes
Production Designer: Jess Gonchor
Music: Carter Burwell

2008 – *Burn After Reading*
Focus Features/Studio Canal/Relativity
  Media/Working Title/Mike Zoss
  Productions
Director: Joel Coen and Ethan Coen
Screenplay: Joel Coen and Ethan Coen
Producers: Joel Coen and Ethan Coen
Director of Photography: Emmanuel
  Lubezki
Editor: Roderick Jaynes
Production Designer: Jess Gonchor
Music: Carter Burwell

2009 – *A Serious Man*
Focus Features/Studio Canal/Relativity
  Media/Working Title/Mike Zoss
  Productions
Director: Joel Coen and Ethan Coen
Screenplay: Joel Coen and Ethan Coen
Producers: Joel Coen and Ethan Coen
Director of Photography: Roger Deakins
Editor: Roderick Jaynes
Production Designer: Jess Gonchor
Music: Carter Burwell

2010 – *True Grit*
Paramount Pictures/Skydance
  Productions/Scott Rudin Productions/
  Mike Zoss Productions
Director: Joel Coen and Ethan Coen
Screenplay: Joel Coen and Ethan Coen
Producers: Joel Coen, Ethan Coen and
  Scott Rudin
Director of Photography: Roger Deakins
Editor: Roderick Jaynes
Production Designer: Jess Gonchor
Music: Carter Burwell

2014 – *Inside Llewyn Davis*
Studio Canal/Anton Capital
  Entertainment
Director: Joel Coen
Screenplay: Joel Coen and Ethan Coen
Producers: Joel Coen, Ethan Coen and
  Scott Rudin
Director of Photography: Bruno
  Delbonnel
Editor: Roderick Jaynes
Production Designer: Jess Gonchor
Music: T Bone Burnett

# BIBLIOGRAPHY

*Published Screenplays by Joel and Ethan Coen*

*Blood Simple. An Original Screenplay by Joel Coen and Ethan Coen.* New York: St. Martin's Press, 1988.
*The Hudsucker Proxy.* London and New York: Faber & Faber, 1994.
*Fargo.* London and New York: Faber & Faber, 1996.
*The Big Lebowski.* London and New York: Faber & Faber, 1998.
*O Brother, Where Art Thou?* London and New York: Faber & Faber, 2000.
*The Man Who Wasn't There.* London and New York: Faber & Faber, 2001.
*Collected Screenplays. Volume 1. Blood Simple, Raising Arizona, Miller's Crossing, Barton Fink.* London and New York: Faber & Faber, 2002.
*The Ladykillers.* London and New York: Faber & Faber, 2004.
*Burn After Reading.* London and New York: Faber & Faber, 2008.
*A Serious Man.* London and New York: Faber & Faber, 2009.
*Inside Llewyn Davis.* New York: Opus, 2014.

*Books and Articles*

Abrams, Jerold J. "'A Homespun Murder Story": Film Noir and Problem of Modernity in *Fargo*.' In: *The Philosophy of the Coen Brothers.* Mark T. Conard (ed.). Lexington, KY: Kentucky University Press, 2009, 211–223.
Allen, William Rodney (ed.). *The Coen Brothers. Interviews.* Jackson, MS: University of Mississippi Press, 2006.
Anderson, John. 'Screen's Mercurial Girl Is at It Again.' *Los Angeles Times.* March 11, 1994.
Andrew, Geoff. Review of *Miller's Crossing. Time Out.* February 13, 1991.
_____. Review of *Barton Fink. Time Out.* February 12, 1992.
_____. Review of *The Big Lebowski. Time Out.* April 22, 1998.
_____. Review of *The Man Who Wasn't There. Time Out.* October 24, 2001.
_____. Review of *No Country for Old Men. Time Out.* January 15, 2008.

Bakhtin, M.M. *The Dialogic Imagination.* Michael Holquist (ed.). Caryl Emerson and Michael Holquist (trans.). Austin: University of Texas Press, 1981.

____. *Rabelais and his World.* Helene Iswolsky (trans.). Bloomington, IN: Indiana University Press, 1984a.

____. *Problems of Dostoevsky's Poetics.* Caryl Emerson (trans.). Minneapolis: University of Minnesota Press, 1984b.

____. 'The Problem of Speech Genres.' In: *M.M. Bakhtin. Speech Genres and Other Late Essays.* Caryl Emerson and Michael Holquist (eds). Austin, TX: University of Texas Press, 1986.

Baudrillard, Jean. *The Consumer Society: Myths and Structures.* London: Sage, 1998.

Benjamin, Oliver. 'What Is Dudeism?' www.dudeism.com

Benson, Sheila. 'Calendar.' *Los Angeles Times.* March, 1987.

____. Review of *Miller's Crossing. Los Angeles Times.* October 5, 1990.

Bergen, Ronald. *The Coen Brothers.* New York: Thunder's Mouth, 2000.

Biskind, Peter. 'Joel and Ethan Coen.' In: *Joel and Ethan Coen: Blood Siblings.* Ed. Paul A. Woods. London: Plexus, 2000, 144–148.

Bloom, Harold. *The Anxiety of Influence.* Oxford: Oxford University Press, 1973.

Bould, Mark. *Film Noir. From Berlin to Sin City.* London: Wallflower Press, 2005.

Bradshaw, Peter. Review of *The Man Who Wasn't There. The Guardian.* October 26, 2001.

____. Review of *A Serious Man. The Guardian.* November 19, 2009.

Brecht, Bertolt. *Brecht on Theater: The Development of an Aesthetic.* John Willett (ed. and trans.). New York: Hill & Wang, 1964.

Bridges, Jeff & Bernie Glassman. *The Dude and the Zen Master.* Blue Rider Press, 2013.

Brooker, Peter. 'Postmodern adaptation: pastiche, intertextuality and re-functioning.' In: *The Cambridge Companion to Literature on Screen.* Deborah Cartmell and Imelda Whelehan (eds). Cambridge: Cambridge University Press, 2007, 107–120.

Brown, Geoff. Review of *Miller's Crossing. The Times.* February 14, 1991.

____. Review of *The Hudsucker Proxy. The Times.* September 1, 1994.

____. Review of *Fargo. The Times.* May 30, 1996.

Buchsbaum, J. 'Tame Wolves and Phoney Claims: Paranoia and Film Noir.' In: *The Movie Book of Film Noir.* Ian Cameron (ed.). London: Studio Vista, 1992, 88–97.

Cain, James M. *Four Complete Novels.* New York: Knopf/Avenel, 1982.

Camus, Albert. *The Myth of Sisyphus.* Justin O'Brien (trans.). New York: Vintage Books, 1991.

____. *The Stranger.* Stuart Gilbert (trans.). Vintage Books. 1954.

Canby, Vincent. Review of *Raising Arizona. New York Times.* March 11, 1987.

____. Review of *Barton Fink. New York Times.* August 18, 1991.

Caro, Jason. Review of *The Man Who Wasn't There. Film Review.* October, 2001.

Chandler, Raymond. *Stories and Early Novels.* New York: Library of America, 1995a.

____. *Later Novels and Other Writings.* New York: Library of America, 1995b.

Coen, Ethan. *The Gates of Eden.* New York: Delta, 1998.

____. *The Drunken Driver Has the Right of Way.* New York: Three Rivers Press, 2001.

____. *The Day the World Ends.* New York: Broadway Paperbacks, 2012.

Cohen, Ted. *Jokes: Philosophical Thoughts on Joking Matters.* Chicago: University of Chicago Press, 1999.

Collins, Jim. 'Genericity in the Nineties: Eclectic Irony and the New Sincerity.' In: *Film Theory Goes to the Movies.* Jim Collins, Hillary Radner, and Ava Preacher Collins (eds). New York: Routledge, 1993.

Comentale, Edward & Aaron Jaffe (eds). *The Year's Work in Lebowski Studies.* Bloomington: Indiana UP, 2009.

Corliss, Richard. 'It's the Same Old Song.' *Time* January 28, 1985.

____. 'Rootless People.' *Time.* March 23, 1987.

____. Review of *No Country for Old Men. Time.* November 1, 2007.

Corrigan, Timothy. *A Cinema Without Walls: Movies and Culture After Vietnam.* New Brunswick, NJ: Rutgers University Press, 1991, 101–136.

Coughlin, Paul. 'The Past is Now: History and *The Hudsucker Proxy.*' In: *The Philosophy of the Coen Brothers.* Mark T. Conard (ed.). Lexington, KY: University Press of Kentucky, 2009, 41–53.

Deakins, Roger. Interview for *American Cinematographer.* March, 1996.

Denby, David. 'Bringing Up Baby.' *New York.* March 16, 1987.

____. Review of *No Country for Old Men. The New Yorker.* February 25, 2008.

____. Review of *A Serious Man. The New Yorker.* October 5, 2009.

____. Review of *Burn After Reading. The New Yorker.* Sept. 15, 2008.

Dickos, Andrew. *Intrepid Laughter. Preston Sturges and the Movies.* Lanham, MD: Scarecrow Press, 1985.

Dyer, Richard. 'Resistance Through Charisma: Rita Hayworth and *Gilda,*' In: Ann E. Kaplan (ed.). *Women in Film Noir (revised ed.).* London: British Film Institute, 1998, 115–122.

Fuller, Graham. Interview with the Coens in *Interview.* March, 1996.

Ebert, Roger. Review of *Raising Arizona. The Chicago Sun-Times.* March 20, 1987.

____. Review of *Miller's Crossing. The Chicago Sun Times.* October 5, 1990.

____. Review of *Barton Fink. The Chicago Sun-Times.* August 23, 1991.

____. Review of *The Hudsucker Proxy. The Chicago Sun-Times.* May 25, 1994.

____. Review of *Fargo. The Chicago Sun-Times.* March 8, 1996.

____. Review of *The Big Lebowski. The Chicago Sun-Times,* March 6, 1998.

____. Review of *O Brother, Where Art Thou? The Chicago Sun-Times.* December 29, 2000.

____. Review of *No Country for Old Men. The Chicago Sun-Times.* November 8, 2007.

____. Review of *True Grit.* RogerEbert.com. Dec. 21, 2010.

Eco, Umberto. '*Casa Blanca*: Cult Movies and Intertextual Collage.' *Substance* 14.2 (1985): 3–12.

Edelstein, David. 'Invasion of the Baby Snatchers.' In: *The Coen Brothers: Interviews.* William Rodney Allen (ed.). Jackson, MS: University Press of Mississippi, 2006, 17–24.

Elsaesser, Thomas. Preface to 'Vincente Minnelli'. *Genre: The Musical. A Reader.* Rick Altman (ed.). London: Routledge and Kegan Paul, 1981.

Eutsey, Wayne. *The Take It Easy Manifesto.* www.Dudeism.com

Falsani, Cathleen. *The Dude Abides.* Grand Rapids, MI: Zondervan, 2009.

Freud, Sigmund. *Jokes and Their Relation to the Unconscious.* James Strachey (ed.). Harmondsworth: Penguin, 1976.

____. 'The Uncanny.' *Standard Edition of the Complete Psychological Works of Sigmund Freud.* Vol. 17. James Strachey (ed.). London: Hogarth, 1955, 217–256.

Friedrich, Otto. *City of Nets. A Portrait of Hollywood in the 1940's.* New York: Harper and Row, 1986.

Fuller, Graham. Interview with the Coens. *Interview.* March, 1996.

Garner, Dwight. 'Dissertations on His Dudeness.' *New York Times,* December 29, 2009.

Giddins, Gary. Review of *Miller's Crossing. Village Voice.* September 25, 1990.

Gilbey, Ryan. Review of *The Big Lebowski. The Independent,* April 23, 1998.

Gilmore, Richard. '*Raising Arizona* as an American Comedy.' In: *The Philosophy of the Coen Brothers.* Mark T. Conard (ed.). Lexington: University Press of Kentucky, 2009, 7–25.

Gleiberman, Owen. Review of *A Serious Man. Entertainment Weekly.* October 14, 2009.

Green, Bill, Ben Peskoe, Will Russell and Scott Shuffitt (eds). *I'm a Lebowski, You're a Lebowski: Life, The Big Lebowski, and What Have You.* New York: Bloomsbury USA, 2007.

Greene, Andy. 'Decade of the Dude.' *Rolling Stone.* August 15, 2008.

Hall, Jacob. ScreenCrush.com. Dec. 4, 2013.

Hammett, Dashiell. *Complete Novels.* New York: Library of America, 1999.

Hibbs, Thomas S. 'The Human Comedy Perpetuates Itself: Nihilism and Comedy in Coen Neo-Noir.' In: *The Philosophy of Neo-Noir,* Mark T. Conard (ed.). Lexington: University Press of Kentucky, 2007, 137–149.

Hinson, Hal. 'Bloodlines.' In: Allen, *The Coen Brothers. Interviews.* Jackson, MS: University Press of Mississippi, 2006, 3–16.

Hirschberg, Lynn. 'Coen Brothers' Country.' *New York Times Magazine.* November 11, 2007.

Hoberman, J. Review of *Blood Simple. Village Voice.* January 22, 1985.

_____. *Vulgar Modernism: Writing on Movies and Other Media.* Philadelphia: Temple University Press, 1991.

_____. Review of *The Man Who Wasn't There. Village Voice.* November 6, 2001.

_____. Review of *True Grit. Village Voice.* Dec. 22, 2010.

Hornaday, Ann. Review of *A Serious Man. Washington Post.* October 9, 2009.

Howell, Peter. 'I Love *The Big Lebowski*: Even though the Wikipedia Says I Don't.' *Toronto Star.* July 7, 2011.

Hunter, Stephen. Review of *No Country for Old Men. Washington Post.* November 9, 2007.

Hutcheon, Linda. *A Theory of Parody. The Teachings of Twentieth-Century Art Forms.* New York & London: Methuen, 1985.

_____. *The Politics of Postmodernism.* New York: Routledge, 1989.

_____. 'Postmodern Film?' In: *Postmodern After-Images: A Reader in Film, Television, and Video.* Peter Brooker and Will Brooker (eds). London: Arnold, 1997.

Jameson, Fredric. *The Cultural Turn: Selected Writing on the Postmodern, 1983–1998.* London and New York: Verso, 1998.

Jenkins, Steve. Review of *Miller's Crossing. Monthly Film Bulletin.* February, 1991.

Johnston, Sheila. Interview with the Coens. *The Independent.* May 22, 1991.

Kael, Pauline. Review of *Raising Arizona. The New Yorker.* April 20, 1987.

_____. 'The Current Cinema.' *The New Yorker.* February 24, 1985.

Kafka, Franz. *Sämtliche Erzählungen.* Paul Raabe (ed.). Frankfurt: S. Fischer, 1976.

Kant, Immanuel. *Critique of Judgment.* J. H. Bernard (trans.). London: Macmillan, 1892.

Kaufmann, Stanley. Review of *Barton Fink. New Republic.* September 3, 1991.

Kempley, Rita. Review of *Raising Arizona. The Washington Post.* March 20, 1987.

_____. Review of *Barton Fink. The Washington Post.* August 21, 1991.

Klady, Leonard. Review of *Fargo. Variety.* February 12, 1996.

Krutnik, Frank. 'Desire, Transgression, and James M. Cain,' *Screen* 23 (1982): 31–44.

_____. *In a Lonely Street: Film Noir, Genre, Masculinity.* London: Routledge, 1991.

Landrum, Jason. 'Cold-Blooded Coen Brothers: The Death Drive and *No Country for Old Men.*' In: *From Novel to Film. No Country for Old Men.* Lynnea Chapman King, Rick Wallace and Jim Welsh (eds). Lanham, MD: Scarecrow Press, 2009, 199–218.

Leitch, Thomas. 'Twice-Told Tales. Disavowal and the Rhetoric of the Remake.' In: *Dead Ringers: the Remake in Theory and Practice.* Jennifer Forrest and L. R. Koos (eds). Albany: SUNY Press, 2002, 37–62.

Levine, Josh. *The Coen Brothers: The Story of Two American Filmmakers.* Toronto: ECW Press, 2000.

Levy, Emanuel. *A Cinema of Outsiders.* New York: New York University Press, 1999.

Lewis, Jon. 'The Coen Brothers.' In: *Fifty Contemporary Filmmakers.* Yvonne Tasker (ed.). London and New York: Routledge, 2002, 108–118.

MacIntyre, Alasdair. *After Virtue: A Study in Moral Theory.* Notre Dame: Notre Dame University Press, 1981.

Marling, William. *The American Roman Noir. Hammett, Cain, and Chandler.* Athens: University of Georgia Press, 1995.

Martin, Jay. *Nathanael West: The Art of His Life.* New York: Farrar, Straus, Giroux, 1970.

Maslin, Janet. '*Blood Simple*: A Black-Comic Romp.' *The New York Times.* October 12, 1984.

McCarthy, Cormac. *No Country for Old Men*. New York: Alfred A. Knopf, 2005.

____. *The Road*. New York: Alfred A. Knopf, 2006.

McCarthy, Todd. Review of *The Big Lebowski*. *Variety*. January 20, 1998.

____. Review of *A Serious Man*. *Variety*. October 1, 2009.

____. Review of *The Hudsucker Proxy*. *Variety*. January 31, 1994.

McFarland, Douglas. 'The Philosophies of Comedy in *O Brother, Where Art Thou?* In: *The Philosophy of the Coen Brothers*. Mark T. Conard (ed.). Lexington, KY: University Press of Kentucky, 2009, 41–53.

Miller, Arthur. Review of *Barton Fink*. *US Premiere*. October 1991.

Mitchell, Elvis. Interview with the Coens for the Independent Film Channel. 2000.

Moore, Roger. Review of *A Serious Man*. *The Orlando Sentinel*. October 23, 2009.

Mottram, James. *The Coen Brothers: The Life of the Mind*. Dulles, VA: Brassey's Inc., 2000.

Nagel, Thomas. 'The Absurd.' In: *The Meaning of Life: Questions, Answers, and Analysis*. Steven Saunders and David R. Cheney (eds). Englewood Cliffs, NJ: Prentice-Hall, 1980.

Naremore, James. *More than Night: Film Noir in its Contexts*. Berkeley: California University Press, 1998.

Nathan, Ian. *Ethan and Joel Coen*. Paris: Cahiers du cinema, 2012.

____. Review of *The Big Lebowski*. *Empire*. May, 1998.

*New International Bible*. International Bible Society, 1984.

Nieland, Justus. 'Dudespeak: or How to Bowl Like a Porn Star.' In: *The Year's Work in Lebowski Studies*. Edward Comentale and Aaron Jaffe (eds). Bloomington: Indiana University Press, 2009, 74–97.

Nietzsche, Friedrich. *Joyful Wisdom*. Thomas Common (trans.). New York: Frederick Ungar, 1973.

O'Brien, Geoffrey. 'Gone Tomorrow: The Echoing Spaces of Joel and Ethan Coen' *No Country for Old Men.' Film Comment* 43, 2007.

Odets, Clifford. *The Time is Ripe: The 1940 Journal*. New York: Grove Press, 1988.

Palmer, R. Barton. *Joel and Ethan Coen*. Urbana, IL: University of Illinois Press, 2004.

Peachment, Chris. Interview with the Coens. The *Sunday Telegraph*. May 26, 1996.

Peebles, Stacy. 'Hold Still: Models of Masculinity in the Coens' *No Country for Old Men.' In: From Novel to Film. No Country for Old Men*. Lynnea Chapman King, Rick Wallace and Jim Welsh (eds). Lanham, MD: Scarecrow Press, 2009, 124–138.

Podhoretz, Norman. 'Nathanael West: A Particular Kind of Joking.' In: *Nathanael West: A Collection of Critical Essays*. Jay Martin (ed). Englewood Cliffs, NJ: Prentice-Hall, 1971, 154–160.

Porfirio, Robert. 'No Way Out: Existentialist Motifs in the *Film Noir.' In: Film Noir Reader*. Alain Silver and James Ursini (eds). New York: Limelight, 1996.

Probst, Chris. Interview with Roger Deakins. *American Cinematographer*. March, 1996.

Pulver, Andrew. 'Pictures That Do the Talking.' In: Allen. *Interviews*. Jackson, MS: University of Mississippi Press, 2006, 149–159.

Raczkowski, Christopher. 'Metonymic Hats and Metaphoric Tumbleweeds: Noir Literary Aesthetics in *Miller's Crossing* and *The Big Lebowski.' In: The Year's Work in Lebowski Studies*. Edward Comentale and Aaron Jaffe (eds). Bloomington: Indiana University Press, 2009, 98–123.

Rafferty, Terrence. 'In Brief.' *The New Yorker*. October 15, 1990.

____. Review of *Barton Fink*. *The New Yorker*. August 21, 1991.

Rainer, Peter. Review of *No Country for Old Men*. *The Christian Science Monitor*. November 9, 2007.

____. Review of *A Serious Man*. *Christian Science Monitor*. October 2, 2009.

Rempel, Morgan. 'Epicurus and "Contented Poverty". *The Big Lebowski* as Epicurean Parable.' In: *The Big Lebowski and Philosophy. Keeping Your Mind Limber with Abiding Wisdom*. Peter S. Fosl (ed). Hoboken, NJ: John Wiley and Sons, 2012, 67–78.

Rich, Katey. 'NYFF: *No Country for Old Men*.' Cinema Blend.com. October 8, 2007.

Robertson, William Preston. *The Big Lebowski: The Making of a Coen Brothers Film*. New York: W. W. Norton, 1998.

Robson, Eddie. *The Coen Brothers*. London: Virgin Books, 2007.

Romney, Jonathan. Interview with the Coens. *The Guardian*. August 25, 1994.

Rowell, Erica. *The Brothers Grim: The Films of Ethan and Joel Coen*. Lanham, MD: Scarecrow Press, 2007.

Rutsky, R. L. "Metropolis." *Film Analysis. A Norton Reader*. Ed. Jeffrey Geiger and R. L. Rutsky. New York: W. W. Norton, 2005, 178–195.

Sarris, Andrew. Review of *No Country for Old Men*. *The New York Observer*. October 23, 2007.

Sartre, Jean-Paul. *Being and Nothingness: An Essay on Phenomenological Ontology*. Hazel Barnes (trans.). New York: Washington Square, 1966.

_____. *Nausea*. New York: New Directions, 2013.

_____. *Literary Essays*. New York: Wisdom Library, 1957.

Sarris, Andrew. Review of *No Country for Old Men*. *The New York Observer*. Oct. 23, 2007.

Schwarzbaum, Lisa. Review of *No Country for Old Men*. Entertainment Weekly. November 7, 2007.

Schrader, Paul. 'Notes on Film Noir.' *Schrader on Schrader*. Kevin Jackson (ed.). London: Faber & Faber, 1990, 80–94.

Scott, A. O. Review of *No Country for Old Men*. New York Times. November 9, 2007.

_____. Review of *A Serious Man*. New York Times. October 2, 2009.

Shannon, Jeff. Review of *The Hudsucker Proxy*. Seattle Times. March 11, 1994.

Sharrett, Christopher. '*Fargo*, or the Blank Frontier.' In: *The Coen Brothers' Fargo*. William G. Luhr (ed.). Cambridge: Cambridge University Press, 2004, 55–76.

Shoard, Catherine. Review of *Inside Llewyn Davis*. *The Guardian*. Jan. 16, 2014.

Shone, Tom. Review of *Fargo*. *The Sunday Times*. June 2, 1996.

Skenazy, Paul. *James M. Cain*. New York: Continuum, 1989.

Sonnenfeld, Barry. Interview. *Miller's Crossing* DVD extra.

Spicer, Andrew. *Film Noir*. Colchester: Pearson Education, 2002.

Stam, Robert. *Subversive Pleasures. Bakhtin, Cultural Criticism, and Film*. Baltimore: Johns Hopkins University Press, 1989, 54–76.

_____. 'Beyond Fidelity: The Dialogics of Adaptation.' In: *Film Adaptation*. James Naremore (ed.). New Brunswick, NJ: Rutgers University Press, 2000.

Stein, Elliott. Review of *Blood Simple*. *Film Comment*. 20. November-December 1984.

Stevens, Dana. Review of *A Serious Man*. *Slate Magazine*. October 1, 2009.

Thomas, Kevin. '*Blood Simple* is Dark Comedy.' *Los Angeles Times*. February 28, 1985.

Thompson, George J. *Hammett's Moral Vision*. San Franciso: Vince Emery Productions, 2007.

Tooky, Christopher. Review of *The Hudsucker Proxy*. *Daily Mail*. Sept. 2, 1994.

_____. Review of *Fargo*. *Daily Mail*. May 31, 1996.

Travers, Peter. Review of *No Country for Old Men*. *Rolling Stone*. November 1, 2007.

Tyree, J. M. and Ben Walters. *The Big Lebowski*. London: British Film Institute, 2007.

Usher, Shaun. Review of *Barton Fink*. *Daily Mail*. February 14, 1992.

Veitch, Jonathan. *American Superrealism. Nathanael West and the Politics of Representation in the 1930s*. Madison: University of Wisconsin Press, 1997.

Walker, Alexander. Review of *O Brother, Where Art Thou? Evening Standard*. September 14, 2000.

Walters, Ben. Review of *A Serious Man*. *Time Out*. November 17, 2009.

West, Nathaniel. *Novels and Other Writings*. New York: Library of America, 1997.

Woods, Paul A. *Joel and Ethan Coen: Blood Siblings*. London: Plexus, 2000.

# INDEX

CPSIA information can be obtained
at www.ICGtesting.com
Printed in the USA
LVOW04s1049010316

477281LV00012B/40/P